AA004321

# CLOUD COMPUTING 2017

The Eighth International Conference on Cloud Computing, GRIDs, and Virtualization

February 19 - 23, 2017

Athens, Greece

**CLOUD COMPUTING 2017 Editors**


Carlos Becker Westphall, Federal University of Santa Catarina, Brazil

Yong Woo Lee, University of Seoul, Korea

Bob Duncan, University of Aberdeen, UK

Aspen Olmsted, College of Charleston, USA

Michael Vassilakopoulos, University of Thessaly, Greece

Costas Lambrinoudakis, University of Piraeus, Greece

Sokratis K. Katsikas, Center for Cyber & Information Security, Norwegian University of Science & Technology (NTNU) - Gjøvik, Norway

Raimund Ege, Northern Illinois University, USA

**Printed from e-media with permission by:**

Curran Associates, Inc.
57 Morehouse Lane
Red Hook, NY 12571



Printed by Curran Associates, Inc. (2017)

International Academy, Research, and Industry Association (IARIA)
412 Derby Way
Wilmington, DE 19810

Phone: (408) 893-6407
Fax: (408) 527-6351

petre@iaria.org

**Additional copies of this publication are available from:**

Curran Associates, Inc.
57 Morehouse Lane
Red Hook, NY 12571 USA
Phone: 845-758-0400
Fax: 845-758-2633
Email: curran@proceedings.com
Web: www.proceedings.com

## Table of Contents

# CLOUD COMPUTING 2017

## Forward

The Eighth International Conference on Cloud Computing, GRIDs, and Virtualization (CLOUD COMPUTING 2017), held between February 19-23, 2017 in Athens, Greece, continued a series of events meant to prospect the applications supported by the cloud computing paradigm and validate the techniques and the mechanisms. A complementary target was to identify the open issues and the challenges to fix them, especially on security, privacy, and inter- and intra-clouds protocols.

Cloud computing is a normal evolution of distributed computing combined with Service-oriented architecture, leveraging most of the GRID features and Virtualization merits. The technology foundations for cloud computing led to a new approach of reusing what was achieved in GRID computing with support from virtualization.

The conference had the following tracks:

- Virtualization
- Big Spatial Data Management
- Cloud Cyber Security
- Cloud Computing
- Platforms, infrastructures and applications
- Security and Privacy in Cloud Computing
- Challenges

We take here the opportunity to warmly thank all the members of the CLOUD COMPUTING 2017 technical program committee, as well as all the reviewers. The creation of such a high quality conference program would not have been possible without their involvement. We also kindly thank all the authors that dedicated much of their time and effort to contribute to CLOUD COMPUTING 2017. We truly believe that, thanks to all these efforts, the final conference program consisted of top quality contributions.

Also, this event could not have been a reality without the support of many individuals, organizations and sponsors. We also gratefully thank the members of the CLOUD COMPUTING 2017 organizing committee for their help in handling the logistics and for their work that made this professional meeting a success.

We hope that CLOUD COMPUTING 2017 was a successful international forum for the exchange of ideas and results between academia and industry and to promote further progress in the field of cloud computing, GRIDs and virtualization. We also hope that Athens, Greece provided a pleasant environment during the conference and everyone saved some time to enjoy the charm of the city.

## CLOUD COMPUTING 2017 Committee

### CLOUD COMPUTING 2017 Steering Committee

Carlos Becker Westphall, Federal University of Santa Catarina, Brazil
Yong Woo Lee, University of Seoul, Korea
Christoph Reich, Furtwangen University, Germany
Hong Zhu, Oxford Brookes University, UK
Bob Duncan, University of Aberdeen, UK
Aspen Olmsted, College of Charleston, USA
Alex Sim, Lawrence Berkeley National Laboratory, USA

### CLOUD COMPUTING 2017 Industry/Research Advisory Committee

Antonin Chazalet, Orange, France
Sören Frey, Daimler TSS GmbH, Germany
Mohamed Mohamed, IBM, Almaden Research Center, USA
Raul Valin Ferreiro, Fujitsu Laboratories of Europe, Spain
Uwe Hohenstein, Siemens AG, Germany
Bill Karakostas, VLTN gcv, Antwerp, Belgium
Matthias Olzmann, noventum consulting GmbH - Münster, Germany
Ze Yu, Google Inc, USA
Matthias Olzmann, noventum consulting GmbH - Münster, Germany

## CLOUD COMPUTING 2017

## Committee

**CLOUD COMPUTING Steering Committee**
Carlos Becker Westphall, Federal University of Santa Catarina, Brazil
Yong Woo Lee, University of Seoul, Korea
Christoph Reich, Furtwangen University, Germany
Hong Zhu, Oxford Brookes University, UK
Bob Duncan, University of Aberdeen, UK
Aspen Olmsted, College of Charleston, USA
Alex Sim, Lawrence Berkeley National Laboratory, USA

**CLOUD COMPUTING 2017 Industry/Research Advisory Committee**
Antonin Chazalet, Orange, France
Sören Frey, Daimler TSS GmbH, Germany
Mohamed Mohamed, IBM, Almaden Research Center, USA
Raul Valin Ferreiro, Fujitsu Laboratories of Europe, Spain
Uwe Hohenstein, Siemens AG, Germany
Bill Karakostas, VLTN gcv, Antwerp, Belgium
Matthias Olzmann, noventum consulting GmbH - Münster, Germany
Ze Yu, Google Inc, USA
Matthias Olzmann, noventum consulting GmbH - Münster, Germany

**CLOUD COMPUTING 2017 Technical Program Committee**

Saeid Abolfazli, YTL Communications and Xchanging, Malaysia
Maruf Ahmed, The University of Sydney, Australia
Onur Alparslan, Osaka University, Japan
Abdulelah Alwabel, PSA University, KSA
Sergio Antonio Andrade de Freitas, University of Brasilia, Brazil
Irina Astrova, Tallinn University of Technology, Estonia
José Aznar, i2CAT Foundation, Spain
Jorge Barbosa, Universidade do Porto, Portugal
Ali Kashif Bashir, Osaka University, Japan
Luis Eduardo Bautista Villalpando, Autonomous University of Aguascalientes, Mexico
Carlos Becker Westphall, Federal University of Santa Catarina, Brazil
Ali Beklen, HotelRunner, Turkey
Andreas Berl, Technische Hochschule Deggendorf, Germany
Simona Bernardi, Centro Universitario de la Defensa - Academia General Militar, Spain
Peter Bloodsworth, National University of Sciences and Technology (NUST), Pakistan
Simone Braun, CAS Software AG, Karlsruhe, Germany

Giovanna Petrone, Universita' di Torino, Italy
Dimitrios Pezaros, University of Glasgow, UK
Ilia Pietri, University of Athens, Greece
Agostino Poggi, DII - University of Parma, Italy
Thomas E. Potok, Oak Ridge National Laboratory, USA
Abena Primo, Huston-Tillotson University, USA
Francesco Quaglia, Sapienza Universita' di Roma, Italy
Danda B. Rawat, Howard University, USA
Daniel A. Reed, University of Iowa, USA
Damir Regvart, Croatian Academic and Research Network - CARNet, Croatia
Christoph Reich, Furtwangen University, Germany
Sebastian Rieger, Fulda University of Applied Sciences, Germany
Sashko Ristov, University of Innsbruck, Austria
Takfarinas Saber, University College Dublin, Ireland
Elena Sánchez-Nielsen, Universidad de La Laguna, Spain
Wael Sellami, Higher Institute of Computer Sciences of Mahdia, Tunisia
Alireza Shameli-Sendi, Ericsson security research, Montreal, Canada
Mohammad Shojafar, Sapienza University of Rome, Italy
Suzanne Shontz, University of Kansas, USA
Altino Manuel Silva Sampaio, Escola Superior de Tecnologia e Gestão | Instituto Politécnico do Porto, Portugal
Alex Sim, Lawrence Berkeley National Laboratory, USA
George Spanoudakis, University of London, UK
Cristian Stanciu, University Politehnica of Bucharest, Romania
Vlado Stankovski, University of Ljubljana, Slovenia
Yuqiong Sun, Pennsylvania State University, USA
Kwa-Sur Tam, Virginia Tech, USA
Joe Tekli, Lebanese American University, Lebanon
Michele Tomaiuolo, DII - University of Parma, Italy
Orazio Tomarchio, Universita' di Catania, Italy
Raul Valin Ferreiro, Fujitsu Laboratories of Europe, Spain
Carlo Vallati, University of Pisa, Italy
Luis M. Vaquero, Hewlett Packard Enterprise, UK
Michael Vassilakopoulos, University of Thessaly, Greece
Jose Luis Vazquez-Poletti, Universidad Complutense de Madrid, Spain
Simeon Veloudis, SEERC - South East European Research Centre, Thessaloniki, Greece
Vladimir Vlassov, KTH Royal Institute of Technology, Stockholm, Sweden
Mandy Weißbach, Martin-Luther-University Halle-Wittenberg, Germany
Feng Yan, University of Nevada, Reno, USA
Hongji Yang, Bath Spa University, UK
Ustun Yildiz, University of California, USA
Ze Yu, Google Inc, USA
Vadim Zaliva, Carnegie Mellon University, USA
José Luis Zechinelli Martini, Universidad de las Américas, Puebla (UDLAP), Mexico

Ahmed Zekri, Beirut Arab University, Lebanon
Hong Zhu, Oxford Brookes University, UK
Wolf Zimmermann, Martin Luther University Halle-Wittenberg, Germany

**Copyright Information**

For your reference, this is the text governing the copyright release for material published by IARIA.

The copyright release is a transfer of publication rights, which allows IARIA and its partners to drive the dissemination of the published material. This allows IARIA to give articles increased visibility via distribution, inclusion in libraries, and arrangements for submission to indexes.

I, the undersigned, declare that the article is original, and that I represent the authors of this article in the copyright release matters. If this work has been done as work-for-hire, I have obtained all necessary clearances to execute a copyright release. I hereby irrevocably transfer exclusive copyright for this material to IARIA. I give IARIA permission or reproduce the work in any media format such as, but not limited to, print, digital, or electronic. I give IARIA permission to distribute the materials without restriction to any institutions or individuals. I give IARIA permission to submit the work for inclusion in article repositories as IARIA sees fit.

I, the undersigned, declare that to the best of my knowledge, the article is does not contain libelous or otherwise unlawful contents or invading the right of privacy or infringing on a proprietary right.

Following the copyright release, any circulated version of the article must bear the copyright notice and any header and footer information that IARIA applies to the published article.

IARIA grants royalty-free permission to the authors to disseminate the work, under the above provisions, for any academic, commercial, or industrial use. IARIA grants royalty-free permission to any individuals or institutions to make the article available electronically, online, or in print.

IARIA acknowledges that rights to any algorithm, process, procedure, apparatus, or articles of manufacture remain with the authors and their employers.

I, the undersigned, understand that IARIA will not be liable, in contract, tort (including, without limitation, negligence), pre-contract or other representations (other than fraudulent misrepresentations) or otherwise in connection with the publication of my work.

Exception to the above is made for work-for-hire performed while employed by the government. In that case, copyright to the material remains with the said government. The rightful owners (authors and government entity) grant unlimited and unrestricted permission to IARIA, IARIA's contractors, and IARIA's partners to further distribute the work.

# Memory Interface Simplifies Storage Virtualization

Shuichi Oikawa, Gaku Nakagawa
Department of Computer Science
University of Tsukuba
Tsukuba, Ibaraki, Japan
e-mail: {shui,gnakagaw}@cs.tsukuba.ac.jp

*Abstract*—**Using a simple library operating system (OS) as a guest OS of a virtualized environment is one of the current trends of cloud computing in order to reduce the overheads incurred by virtualization. Its persistent storage access, however, remains the same as that for the existing guest OSes; thus, it poses a problem of the long execution and data paths. This paper proposes virtualized memory storage that provides the memory interface for a library OS of a virtualized environment, and also discusses the two key benefits of virtualized memory storage, journaling acceleration by synchronous access and a modern implementation of single-level store. The proposed memory interface to virtualized memory storage can simplify both the execution and data paths, and it accelerates the access to persistent storage.**

***Keywords-operating systems; virtualization; file systems; storage***

## I. Introduction

There is a trend of using a simple library operating system (OS) as a guest OS of a virtualized environment. A library OS typically satisfies a specific need to execute a target application; thus, its simple and light-weight implementation enables higher efficiency of application execution than the traditional OS, such as the Linux and the BSD (Berkeley Software Distribution) UNIX. While a library OS lacks the protection support between an application and the kernel, it is protected from another library OS by a virtualized environment. There are several library OSes that target such a virtualized environment. Exokernel [1], [2] is one of early work that realized the kernel functions as libraries, and its success stimulated the following work. Mirage unikernel [3] is a library OS, of which applications are executed on the OCaml language runtime. OSv [4] is another library OS, applications of which are executed on the Java language runtime.

While library OSes emphasize their high performance, library OSes employ the existing block interface to persistent storage. The block interface for a virtualized environment, however, poses a significant problem to achieve high storage access performance. Fig. 1 depicts the architecture of the common storage virtualization method. It provides the block interface for a guest OS kernel; thus, a guest OS kernel requires a block device driver to interact with the block interface. Because of asynchronous nature and a long latency of the block interface, it requires the page cache to accommodate the recently accessed data. A file system is placed upon the page cache and a block device driver and interacts with them.

The problem to provide the block interface for a library OS is that the mechanisms for the block interface, a file system, the page cache, and a block device driver, are duplicated in a library OS, and they exist both in the host OS and a library OS. Because of such duplication, both the data and execution path become very long. They have to go though the layer of a file system, the page cache, and a block device driver both in a library OS and the host OS. The execution overhead of going through the file access layer twice is huge, and also data needs to be transferred several times. While a library OS kernel simplifies its mechanisms by specializing them for target applications, there is no simplicity achieved in the block interface for a virtualized environment.

This paper proposes the use of memory interface to persistent storage for a library OS of a virtualized environment. We call it *virtualized memory storage*. This architecture provides the memory storage for a library OS, and a file system is constructed upon the memory storage. Since processors can directly access memory, there is no need to interpose a device driver between a file system and storage. Virtualized memory storage makes the layer of a file system, the page cache, and a block device driver for a library OS of a virtualized environment as simple as that of the existing OS kernel, and thus it significantly simplifies and also accelerates the access for a library OS to persistent storage, since it enables the direct access for a library OS to the page cache of the host OS kernel. While this paper is based on the past work [5], [6], its focus on a library OS is different from them.

The rest of this paper is organized as follows. Section II describes the virtual memory storage and its key benefits. Section III concludes the paper and describes the future work.

## II. Virtualized Memory Storage

*Virtualized memory storage* provides the memory interface for a guest OS of a virtualized environment. Fig. 2 depicts its architecture. Virtualized memory storage constructs a single hierarchy of a file system, the page cache mechanism, and a block device driver, which is the same as the monolithic kernel, while only a file system resides in a guest OS. Virtualized memory storage consists of a memory image provided by a virtual machine monitor, and is backed by the page cache of the host OS. While such a memory image is the same as that for a main memory of a guest OS, the memory image of virtualized memory storage is backed by a persistent storage device or a file on it. Therefore, the written data on virtualized memory storage persists across the process of shutting down a guest OS and rebooting it. Virtualized memory storage is analogous to a memory image created for a user process by the mmap system call. The mmap system call maps a file

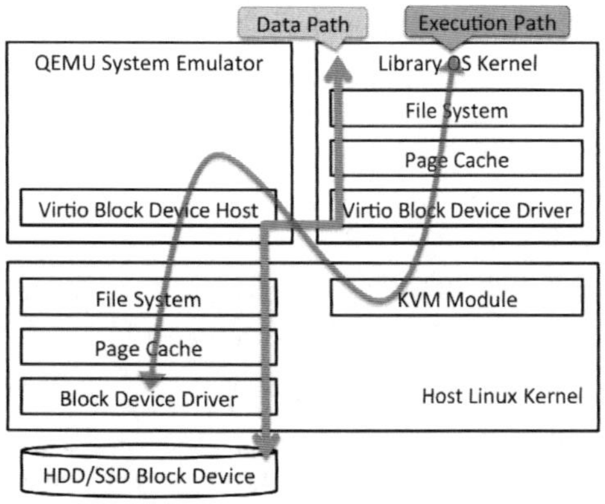


Figure 1. The common storage virtualization method that provides the block interface for a guest OS kernel.

on a virtual address space of a user process, and the user process can access a file through the mapped region of its virtual address space. In case of virtualized memory storage, the virtualization software maps a persistent storage device or a file on it on a physical address space of a guest OS, and the guest OS kernel can access the storage through the memory interface. There are several file systems that were designed to be constructed directly on memory storage. The persistent random access memory file system (PRAMFS) [7] and the storage class memory file system (SCMFS) [8] are such examples. They can be used on virtual memory storage in order to enable file access on it.

Virtualized memory storage best fits simple library OSes since it significantly simplifies the storage access architecture and also accelerates the access to persistent storage. The following are the benefits brought by virtualized memory storage: 1) No block device driver in library OSes and no device host in the host OS: A block device driver is a complicated software framework since it deals with the block and asynchronous interface of devices and also enables efficient access to them by utilizing the page cache mechanism. A block device driver in a guest OS requires a counterpart in the host OS, a device host, that emulates a block device. Virtualized memory storage gets rid of them; thus, it significantly simplifies the storage interface. 2) Simplified file system implementation: The implementation of a file system on a block device cannot be separated from the block interface even with the page cache mechanism that provides the memory interface because it needs to deal with block access natures and and to include their management. A file system on virtualized memory storage is greatly simplified since it does not include such block management and the page cache mechanism. 3) Zero copy data access: This is a great advantage of the integration of library OSes and virtualized memory storage. When an application accesses data on virtualized memory storage through a file system, the application obtains the address of the data on the virtualized memory storage. There is no need to copy from storage to buffer cache. 4) Efficient virtual machine migration: Virtualized memory storage is simply a memory image, and it can be treated in the same way as the main memory of a virtual machine. When a virtual machine is migrated from a host to another over the network, the main memory is copied between them. The same mechanism can be employed to transfer virtualized memory storage; thus, there is no specific shared storage necessary for virtualized memory storage to enable virtual machine migration.

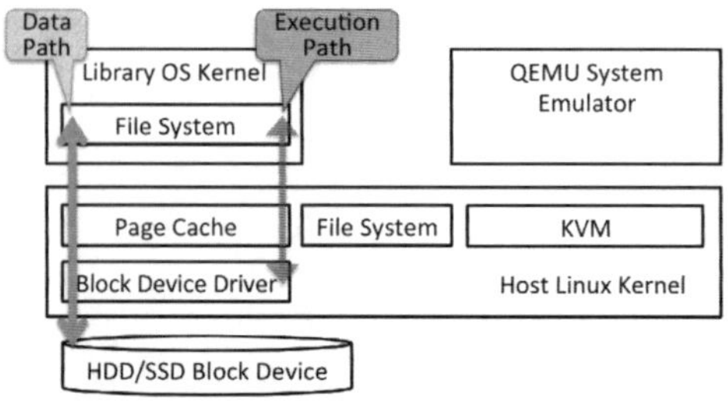


Figure 2. Virtualized memory storage that provides the memory interface for a library OS kernel.

Virtualized memory storage is secured by a virtual machine monitor since it is made independent form each other. The memory image of virtualized memory storage is created for each instance of a library OS, and its data is not shared by default. An instance of a library OS can only access its memory image but not the other images of the other instances since they are separated by the virtual memory mechanism that the virtual machine monitor sets up. Obviously, it is possible to create a shared memory image of virtualized memory storage. In this case, a whole memory image is shared; thus, all the files of the shared image are shared.

Virtualized memory storage simplifies the execution path to access storage; thus, such simplicity makes a system with it more reliable. While it removes the page cache and block device driver layers from a guest OS, it keeps the mechanisms in the host OS the same. An only difference is that it exposes the page cache of the host OS to a guest OS for data access. Only a part of the page cache is, however, exposed to a guest OS, and a guest OS does not have unlimited access to the page cache of the host OS. Thus, the introduction of virtualized memory storage does not increase security risks.

We discuss the two key benefits of virtualized memory storage below.

### A. *Journaling Acceleration by Synchronous Access*

The journaling is a mechanism to guarantee the consistency of written data. It is known as write ahead logging (WAL) for database management systems. The journaling writes data twice, first in the journal and second in the destination place. The significant cost of the journaling is brought by a latency to complete writing. Logging must be completed and it must ensure the log becomes persistent before writing in the destination place. In other words, writing in the destination place must wait for the completion of logging. Each log tends to be small data, and writing small data in block storage is a typical inefficient operation; thus, it causes a long latency to complete writing.

Virtualized memory storage employs synchronous access to storage; thus, logging does not suffer from a long latency caused by the block interface. Because the region for logging is typically preallocated and fixed, its page frames can be pinned down in the page cache of the host OS. Even without pinning them down, logging is frequently performed, and the region for logging is very likely on the page cache.

### *B. Modern Implementation of Single-Level Store*

Virtualized memory storage can be considered as an implementation of the single-level store [9]. The single-level store is the model of storage where applications access data storage objects directly through the memory interface; thus, there is only a single storage level [10]. From the point of view of the single-level store, memory and disk storage are distinct parts of computer systems since memory is byte addressable while disk storage is block addressable; thus, processors cannot access disk storage directly, and data on disk storage must be brought to memory in order for the processors to access it. Files are the abstraction of disk storage, and file systems manage disk storage to provide storage spaces with users as files. Data in files is accessed through the file application program interface (API), which is designed to deal with block addressable disk storage.

Virtualized memory storage takes the memory management one step further towards the single-level store by involving the memory interface in the hierarchy of memory and storage. Library OSes can access data on memory storage directly since memory storage is byte addressable and a file system serves name and protection services.

## III. CONCLUSTION AND FUTURE WORK

This paper proposed virtualized memory storage that provides the memory interface for a library OS of a virtualized environment in order to simplify and to accelerate the access to persistent storage. Because of a trend of using a simple library OS as a guest OS of a virtualized environment for higher performance, the proposed virtualized memory storage best fits the use cases of a library OS.

Our future work includes the implementation and evaluation of the proposed architecture. While we realized the basic mechanism of the virtualized memory storage [5], we are currently working on the implementation of a library OS on top of it.

## REFERENCES


[1] D. R. Engler, M. F. Kaashoek, and J. O'Toole, Jr., "Exokernel: An operating system architecture for application-level resource management," in Proceedings of the Fifteenth ACM Symposium on Operating Systems Principles, ser. SOSP '95. New York, NY, USA: ACM, pp. 251–266, 1995.

[2] M. F. Kaashoek, et al., "Application performance and flexibility on exokernel systems," in Proceedings of the Sixteenth ACM Symposium on Operating Systems Principles, ser. SOSP '97. New York, NY, USA: ACM, pp. 52–65, 1997.

[3] A. Madhavapeddy, et al., "Unikernels: Library operating systems for the cloud," in Proceedings of the Eighteenth International Conference on Architectural Support for Programming Languages and Operating Systems, ser. ASPLOS '13. New York, NY, USA: ACM, pp. 461–472, 2013.

[4] Cloudius-Systems, "Osv: the operating system designed for the cloud," http://osv.io [retrieved: February, 2017].

[5] S. Oikawa, "Virtualizing storage as memory for high performance storage access," in Proceedings of the 12th IEEE International Symposium on Parallel and Distributed Processing with Applications (ISPA-14), pp. 18–25, 2014.

[6] S. Oikawa, "Adapting byte addressable memory storage to user-level file system services," in Proceedings of ACM Conference on Research in Adaptive and Convergent Systems, ser. RACS 2014. ACM, pp. 338–343, 2014.

[7] "Pramfs: Protected and persistent ram filesystem," http://pramfs.sourceforge.net/ [retrieved: February, 2017].

[8] X. Wu and A. L. N. Reddy, "Scmfs: a file system for storage class memory," in Proceedings of 2011 International Conference for High Performance Computing, Networking, Storage and Analysis, ser. SC '11. New York, NY, USA: ACM, pp. 39:1–39:11, 2011.

[9] B. E. Clark and M. J. Corrigan, "Application system/400 performance characteristics," IBM Systems Journal, vol. 28, no. 3, pp. 407–423, 1989.

[10] J. S. Shapiro and J. Adams, "Design evolution of the eros single-level store," in Proceedings of the General Track of the Annual Conference on USENIX Annual Technical Conference, ser. ATEC '02. Berkeley, CA, USA: USENIX Association, pp. 59–72, 2002.

# A Performance Evaluation of Lightweight Approaches to Virtualization

Max Plauth, Lena Feinbube and Andreas Polze
Operating Systems and Middleware Group
Hasso Plattner Institute for Software Systems Engineering,
University of Potsdam
Potsdam, Germany
e-mail: {firstname.lastname}@hpi.uni-potsdam.de

*Abstract*—**The growing prevalence of the microservice paradigm has initiated a shift away from operating single image appliances that host many services, towards encapsulating each service within individual, smaller images. As a result thereof, the demand for low-overhead virtualization techniques is increasing. While containerization approaches already enjoy great popularity, unikernels are emerging as alternative approaches. With both approaches undergoing rapid improvements, the current landscape of lightweight approaches to virtualization presents a confusing scenery, impeding the task of picking an adequate technology for an intended purpose. While previous work has mostly dealt with comparing the performance of either approach with whole-system virtualization, this work provides an overarching performance evaluation covering containers, unikernels, whole-system virtualization, native hardware, and combinations thereof. Representing common workloads in cloud-based applications, we evaluate application performance by the example of HTTP servers and a key-value store.**

***Keywords–Lightweight Virtualization; Performance; Unikernel; Container***

## I. INTRODUCTION

With the increasing pervasiveness of the cloud computing paradigm for all sorts of applications, low-overhead virtualization techniques are becoming indispensable. In particular, the microservice architectural paradigm, where small encapsulated services are developed, operated and maintained by separate teams, require easy-to-use and disposable machine images. Ideally, such infrastructure should allow for fast provisioning and efficient operation.

Approaches to lightweight virtualization roughly fall into the categories of *container virtualization* and *unikernels*. Both have been gaining notable momentum recently (see Figure 1). As more and more virtualization techniques are being introduced and discussed, making a choice between them is getting harder. Published performance measurements thus far either have a strong focus on throughput and execution time or focus on highlighting the strengths of one particular approach without comparing it to a broad range of alternative unikernels and container technologies.

We close this gap by presenting the results of an extensive performance analysis of lightweight virtualization strategies, which takes into account a broad spectrum both of investigated technologies and measured metrics. Our evaluation includes containers (*Docker*, *LXD*), unikernels (*Rumprun* and *OSv*), whole-system virtualization, native hardware, and certain combinations thereof. Our goal is to evaluate metrics that are applicable to cloud applications. For this purpose, we measure application throughput performance using HTTP servers and a key-value store.

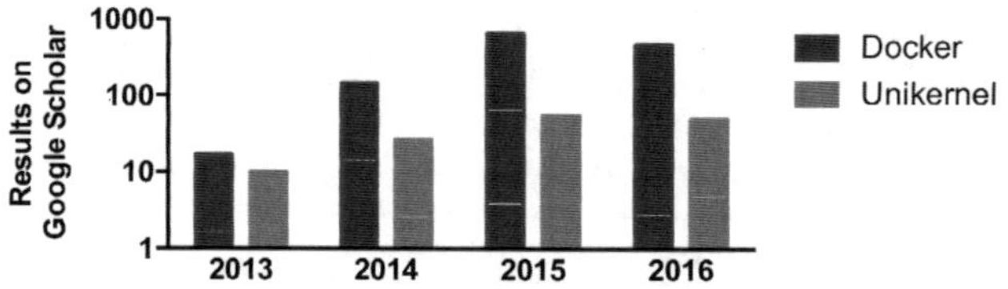


Figure 1. The increasing relevance of *Docker* and Unikernel in the research community is indicated by the number of search results on Google Scholar (as of October 19, 2016).

The remainder of the paper is organized as follows: Section II provides some background about the employed virtualization approaches. Section III reviews related work that deals with quantifying the performance impact of lightweight virtualization approaches. Afterwards, Section IV refines the scope of this work. Section V then documents the benchmark procedure yielding the results presented in Section VI. Finally, Section VII concludes this work with final remarks.

## II. BACKGROUND

"Traditional", whole-system virtualization comes with performance and memory penalties, incurred by the hypervisor or *virtual machine manager* (VMM). This problem has been addressed by introducing *paravirtualization* (PV) and *hardware-assisted virtualization* (HVM). Still, the additional layer of indirection necessitates further context switches, which hurt I/O performance. [1] A further drawback of whole-system virtualization is the comparatively large memory footprint. Even though techniques such as *kernel samepage merging* (KSM) [2] have managed to reduce memory demands, they do not provide an ultimate remedy as they dilute the level of isolation among virtual machines [3].

This work focuses on lightweight virtualization approaches, which, addressing both issues, have gained notable momentum both in the research community and in industry (see Figure 1). Figure 2 illustrates how these approaches aim at supporting the deployment of applications or operating system images while eluding the overhead incurred by running a full-blown operating system on top of a hypervisor. With *containers* and *unikernels* constituting the two major families of lightweight virtualization approaches, the main characteristics and two representatives of each family are introduced hereafter.

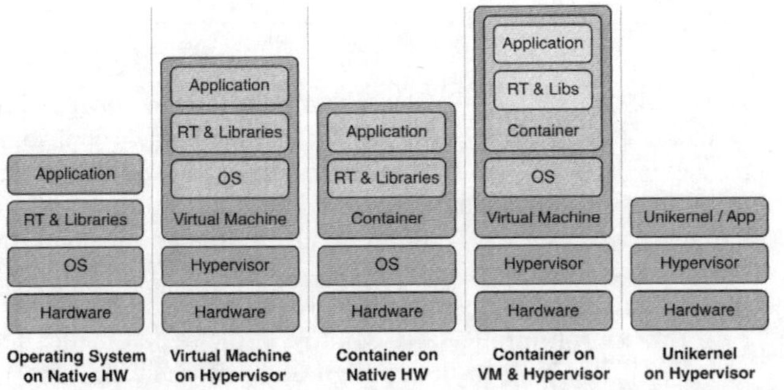


Figure 2. Illustrated comparison of the software stack complexity of various deployment strategies, including native setups, virtual machines, containers, containers within virtual machines and unikernels.

### A. Container (OS-Level Virtualization)

Containers were introduced as an oppositional approach to whole-system virtualization. They were based on the observation that the entire kernel induces overly much resource overhead for merely isolating and packaging small applications. Two classes of container virtualization approaches exist: application- and OS-oriented containers. For application-oriented containers, single applications constitute the units of deployment. For OS-oriented containers, the entire user space of the operating system is reproduced. This approach was particularly popular with *virtual private server* (VPS) solutions, where resource savings were essential. Currently, with *LXD*, this approach is becoming more prominent again, because it allows for the creation of *virtual machine* (VM)-like behavior without the overhead of a hypervisor.

In the following paragraphs, we discuss some common containerization technologies available. We do not consider orchestration-oriented tools such as Kubernetes [4], its predecessor Borg, or CloudFoundry's PaaS solution Warden [5] here.

*1) Docker:* Among the application-oriented containers, the open source project *Docker*[6] is currently the most popular approach. It relies on Linux kernel features, such as namespaces and control groups, to isolate independent containers running on the same instance of the operating system. A *Docker* container encapsulates an application as well as its software dependencies; it can be run on different Linux machines with the *Docker engine*.

Apart from providing basic isolation and closer-to-native performance than whole-system virtualization, *Docker* containerization has the advantages that pre-built *Docker* containers can be shared easily, and that the technology can be integrated into various popular *Infrastructure as a Service* (IaaS) solutions such as *Amazon web services* (AWS).

*2) LXD:* The Linux-based container solution *LXD* [7] builds up upon the *LXC* (Linux container) [8] interface to Linux containerization features. *LXD* uses the *LXC* library for providing low-overhead operating system containers. In addition to advanced container creation and management features, *LXD* offers integration into the OpenStack Nova compute component [9].

*3) lmctfy: lmctfy* (Let Me Contain That For You) [10] is an open source Google project which provides Linux application containers. It internally relies on Linux cgroups, and provides further user-mode monitoring and management features. Intended as an alternative to *LXD*, the status of *lmctfy* has been declared as stalled [11] on May 28, 2015, which is why we do not include *lmctfy* in our evaluation.

### B. Unikernel (Hypervisor Virtualization)

*Unikernels* are a reappearance of the library operating system concept, which only provides a thin layer of protection and multiplexing facilities for hardware resources whereas hardware support is left to employed libraries and the application itself. While library operating systems (e.g., Exokernel [12]) had to struggle with having to support real hardware, unikernels avoid this burden by supporting only virtual hardware interfaces provided by *hypervisors* or VMMs. [13] With the absence of many abstraction mechanisms present in traditional operating systems, the unikernel community claims to achieve a higher degree of whole-system optimization while reducing startup times and the VM footprint [14], [15].

*1) Rumprun:* The *Rumprun* unikernel is based on the *rump kernel* project, which is a strongly modularized version of the *NetBSD* kernel that was built to demonstrate the *anykernel* concept [16]. With the goal of simplified driver development in mind, the *anykernel* concept boils down to enabling a combination of monolithic kernels, where drivers are executed in the kernel, and microkernel-oriented user space drivers that can be executed on top of a rump kernel. One of the major features of the *Rumprun* unikernel is that it supports running existing and unmodified POSIX software[17], as long as it does not require calls to `fork()` or `exec()`.

*2) OSv:* The *OSv* unikernel has been designed specifically to replace general-purpose operating systems such as Linux in cloud-based VMs. Similarly to *Rumprun*, *OSv* supports running existing and unmodified POSIX software, as long as certain limitations are considered [18]. However, *OSv* provides additional APIs for exploiting capabilities of the underlying hypervisor, such as a zero copy API intended to replace the socket API to provide more efficient means of communication among *OSv*-based VMs.

## III. Related Work

Previous research has measured selected performance properties of lightweight virtualization techniques, mostly in comparison with a traditional whole-system virtualization approach.

TABLE I. OVERVIEW OF RELATED WORK ON PERFORMANCE MEASUREMENTS OF LIGHTWEIGHT VIRTUALIZATION APPROACHES.

| | **Docker?** | **LXC?** | **OSv?** | **OpenVZ?** | **Virtualization** |
|---|---|---|---|---|---|
| [20] | ✓ | ✓ | | ✓ | N/A |
| [18] | | | ✓ | | KVM |
| [1] | ✓ | | | | KVM |
| [15] | ✓ | | | | KVM |
| [21] | | | ✓ | | Xen, KVM |
| [22] | ✓ | | | | AWS |

Felter et al.[1] have presented a comprehensive performance comparison between *Docker* containers and the *KVM* hypervisor [19]. Their results from various compute-intensive as well as I/O-intensive programs indicate that "*Docker* equals or exceeds *KVM* performance in every case tested". For I/O-intensive workloads, both technologies introduce significant overhead, while the CPU and memory performance is hardly affected.

Kivity et al.[18] focus on the performance of *OSv* in comparison to whole-system virtualization with *KVM*. Both micro- and macro-benchmarks indicate that *OSv* offers better throughput, especially for memory-intensive workloads.

Table I further summarizes the most recent publications of performance measurements of lightweight virtualization techniques.

## IV. Scope of this Work

Here, we present an extensive performance evaluation of containers (*Docker*, *LXD*), unikernels (*Rumprun* and *OSv*), and whole-system virtualization. Related work has focused on subsets of the approaches we consider, but we are not aware of any comprehensive analysis of up-to-date container versus unikernel technologies. Our goal is to present data which is applicable to cloud-based applications.

Our research questions are the following:

- How fast are containers, unikernels, and whole-system virtualization when running different workloads? Do the results from related work hold in our test case?
- What is the most suitable virtualization technology for on demand provisioning scenarios?

## V. Benchmark Procedure

This section provides a description of the benchmark methodologies applied within this work. All tests were performed on the test system specified in Table II. Where applicable, all approaches were evaluated using *KVM* and native hardware. For container-based approaches, we also distinguish between native and virtualized hosts, where the latter represents the common practice for deploying containers on top of IaaS-based virtual machines.

Representing common workloads of cloud-hosted applications, we picked HTTP servers and key-value stores as exemplary applications for application performance measurements.

TABLE II. SPECIFICATIONS OF THE TEST SYSTEMS.

| | |
|---|---|
| Server model | HPE ProLiant m710p Server Cartridge |
| Processor | Intel Xeon E3-1284L v4 (Broadwell) |
| Memory | 4 × 8GB PC3L-12800 (SODIMM) |
| Disk | 120GB HP 765479-B21 SSD (M.2 2280) |
| NIC | Mellanox Connect-X3 Pro (Dual 10GbE) |
| Operating system | Ubuntu Linux 16.04.1 LTS |

As these I/O-intensive use cases involve a large number of both concurrent clients and requests, the network stack contributes to the overall application performance considerably. Hence, in order to eliminate an unfavorable default configuration of the network stack as a confounding variable, we modified the configuration on Linux, *Rumprun* and *OSv*. Since many best practices guides cover the subject of tuning network performance on Linux, we employed the recommendations from [23], resulting in the configuration denoted in Table III.

TABLE III. OPTIMIZED SETTINGS FOR THE *Linux* NETWORK STACK.

| **Path** | **Parameter** | **Value** |
|---|---|---|
| /etc/sysctl.conf | fs.file-max | 20000 |
| /etc/sysctl.conf | net.core.somaxconn | 1024 |
| /etc/sysctl.conf | net.ipv4.ip_local_port_range | 1024 65535 |
| /etc/sysctl.conf | net.ipv4.tcp_tw_reuse | 1 |
| /etc/sysctl.conf | net.ipv4.tcp_keepalive_time | 60 |
| /etc/sysctl.conf | net.ipv4.tcp_keepalive_intvl | 60 |
| /etc/security/limits.conf | nofile (soft/hard) | 20000 |

Based on this model, we modified the configuration parameters of both *Rumprun* and *OSv* to correspond to the Linux-based settings [24]. Currently, there is no mechanism in *Rumprun* to permanently modify the values of the *ulimit* parameter. As a workaround, the *Rumprun* sysproxy facility has be activated by passing the parameter `-e RUMPRUN_SYSPROXY=tcp://0:12345` to the `rumprun` command-line utility upon start. Using the `rumpctrl` utility, the configuration values of the *ulimit* parameter have to be changed remotely, as exemplified in Listing 1.

```
export RUMP_SERVER=tcp://[IP]:12345
. rumpctrl.sh
sysctl -w proc.0.rlimit.descriptors.soft=200000
sysctl -w proc.0.rlimit.descriptors.hard=200000
sysctl -w proc.1.rlimit.descriptors.soft=200000
sysctl -w proc.1.rlimit.descriptors.hard=200000
sysctl -w proc.2.rlimit.descriptors.hard=200000
sysctl -w proc.2.rlimit.descriptors.soft=200000
rumpctrl_unload
```

Listing 1. The *ulimit* values of *Rumprun* have to be changed remotely using the *sysproxy* facility and the associated `rumpctrl` utility.

### A. Static HTTP Server

We use the *Nginx* HTTP server (version 1.8.0) to evaluate the HTTP performance for static content, as it is available on all tested platforms. Regarding *OSv* however, we refrain from running HTTP benchmarks due to the lacking availability of an adequate HTTP server implementation.

To be able to deal with a high number of concurrent requests, we apply optimized configuration files for *Nginx*. Our measurement procedure employs the benchmarking tool *weighttp* [25] and the *abc* wrapper utility [26] for automated benchmark runs and varying connection count parameters. The *abc* utility has been slightly modified to report standard deviation values in addition to average throughput values for repeated measurements. The benchmark utility is executed on a dedicated host to avoid unsolicited interactions between the HTTP server and the benchmark utility. While HTTP server benchmark guidelines usually recommend executing both HTTP server and benchmark utility on the same machine [23], we intentionally included the traversal of an actual network in the setup to represent real-world conditions more accurately. As static content, we use our institute website's *favicon* [27]. We measured the HTTP performance ranging from 0 to 1000 concurrent connections, with range steps of 100 and *TCP keepalive* being enabled throughout all measurements.

### B. Key-Value Store

In our second application benchmark discipline, we use *Redis* (version 3.0.1) as a key-value store, which is available on all tested platforms. In order to rule out disk performance as a potential bottleneck, we disabled any persistence mechanisms in the configuration files and operate *Redis* in a cache-only mode of operation. For executing performance benchmarks, we use the *redis-benchmark* utility, which is included in the *Redis* distribution. The benchmark utility is executed on a separate host to represent real-world client-server conditions more accurately and to avoid unsolicited interactions between the benchmark utility and the *Redis* server. We measured the performance of GET and SET operations ranging from 0 to 1000 concurrent connections, with range steps of 100 and both *TCP keepalive* and pipelining being enabled throughout all measurements. The CSV-formatted output of *redis-benchmark* was aggregated to yield average values and standard deviation using a simple python script.

## VI. Results & Discussion

Here, we provide and discuss the results obtained from the benchmark procedure elaborated in Section V in an analogous structure. In order to retrieve a sufficiently meaningful dataset, each condition was benchmarked 30 times [28]. Furthermore, each benchmark was preceded by a warm-up procedure. For a statistically meaningful evaluation of the collected data, an ANOVA test and a post-hoc comparison using the Tukey method were applied. All values are expressed as mean $\pm$ SD (n = 30).

### A. Static HTTP Server

Container-based approaches are generally expected to introduce little overhead compared to the native operating system performance. While this appears to be true for disk I/O, memory bandwidth, and compute performance [1], networking introduces a significant amount of overhead ($p < 0.0001$) as illustrated in Figure 3a. A likely cause for this overhead is that all traffic has to go through a NAT in common configurations for both container-based approaches. Comparing containers with whole-system virtualization, it does not come as a surprise to see significant performance advantages on the side of containers for 200 concurrent clients and above ($p < 0.0001$).

We also considered the condition where containers are executed on top of whole-system virtualization images. This setup reflects the common practice in IaaS scenarios where containers are usually deployed on top of a virtual machine instead of a native operating system instance. When deployed above a hypervisor, containers evince a similar behavior as in the native use case: Containers add significant overhead on top of a virtualized Linux instance ($p < 0.0001$).

Proceeding with the evaluation of unikernel performance, it is surprising to see a similar performance of *Rumprun* compared to containers. Even though *Rumprun* can achieve slim performance enhancements over containers, significant improvements start to join in merely for 600 concurrent clients and more ($p < 0.0001$). At first sight, these results may appear disappointing given the fact that unikernels should offer better performance in I/O intensive workloads due to the absence of context switches. However, we suspect that the mediocre performance originates from comparing apples with oranges, as HTTP-servers heavily rely on the performance of the operating systems network stack, where the Linux networking stack has undergone massive optimization efforts that the *NetBSD* network stack can hardly compete with. To verify this hypothesis, we performed a brief evaluation where we executed the same benchmark setup using *NetBSD* 7.0.1 instead of *Ubuntu 16.04*. For that purpose, we used a *KVM*-based virtual machine and the same network configuration parameters as in the other setups. Here, we obtained performance measurements much slower than *Rumprun* (data not shown), which demonstrates the potential of the unikernel concept with *Rumprun* outperforming a virtualized instance of its full-grown relative *NetBSD*. With further optimizations of the network stack, *Rumprun* might achieve similar or even better performance than a regular Linux-based virtual machine.

Regarding the memory footprint, unikernels manage to undercut the demands of a full-blown Linux instance (see Figure 4a). However, containers still can get by with the least amount of memory. The major advantage of containers remains that memory can be allocated dynamically, whereas virtual machines are restricted to predefining the amount of allocated memory at the time of instantiation.

### B. Key-Value Store

As illustrated in Figure 5, the key-value store exhibits similar results regarding container-based approaches and whole-system virtualization: Regardless of native or virtualized deployments, containers come with a significant amount of overhead ($p < 0.0001$). In contrast, *Rumprun* and *OSv* offer slight but nevertheless significant performance improvements compared to Linux under many conditions. With *Redis* being less sensitive to the performance of the network stack, this use case demonstrates the potential of unikernels. Regarding memory consumption (see 4b), containers still offer the highest degree of flexibility. While *Rumprun* still undercuts the memory footprint of Linux, *OSv* required distinctly more memory in order to withstand the benchmark. However, this increased memory demand appears to be caused by a memory leak or a similar bug in the *OSv*-port of *Redis*.

## VII. Conclusion

With both containers and unikernels undergoing rapid improvements, the current landscape of lightweight approaches to virtualization presents a confusing scenery. Comparative publications thus far have mostly highlighted the strengths of

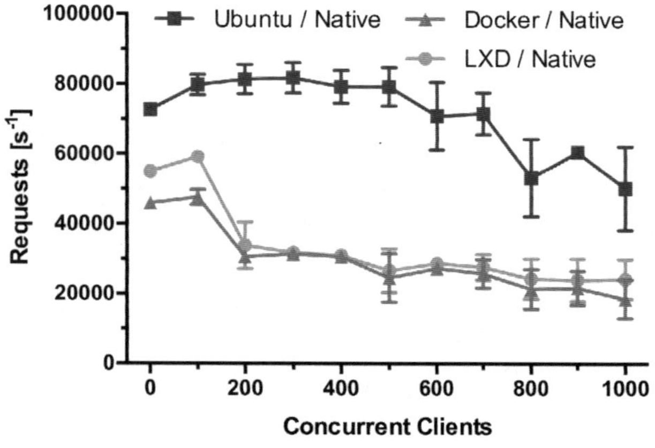


(a)

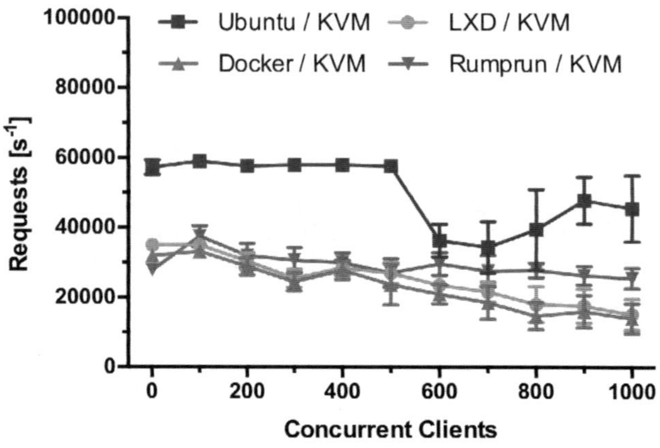


(b)

Figure 3. Throughput performance of *Nginx* (version 1.8.0) was evaluated on native hardware (a) and in virtualized environments (b). Throughput was measured using the weighttp benchmark and the modified abc wrapper utility.

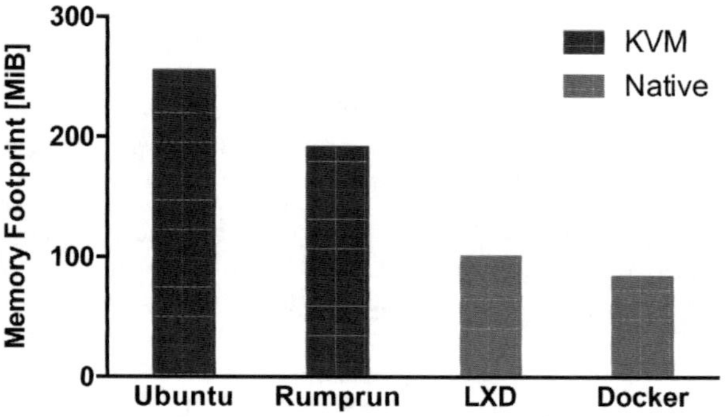


(a)

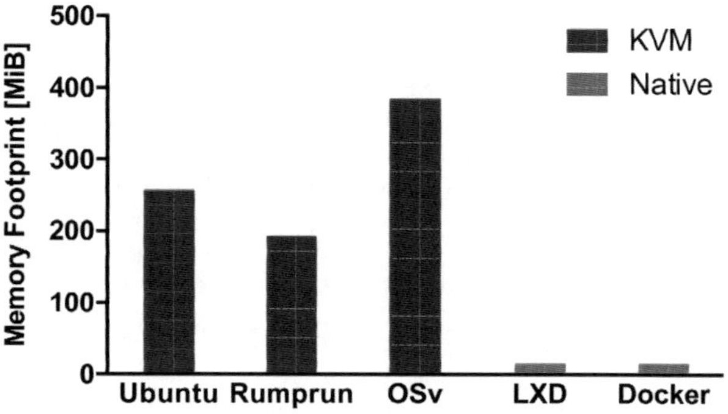


(b)

Figure 4. The memory footprints of the static HTTP server scenario (a) and the Key-Value Store scenario (b) were measured for each each virtualization technique. Due to the variety among the tested approaches, different tools were used to obtain memory consumption readings.

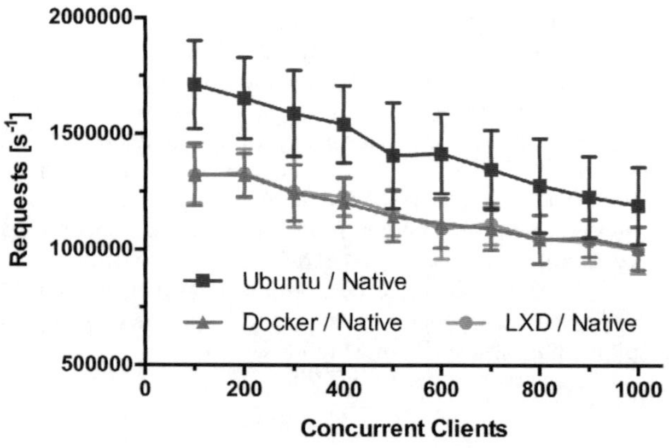


(a)

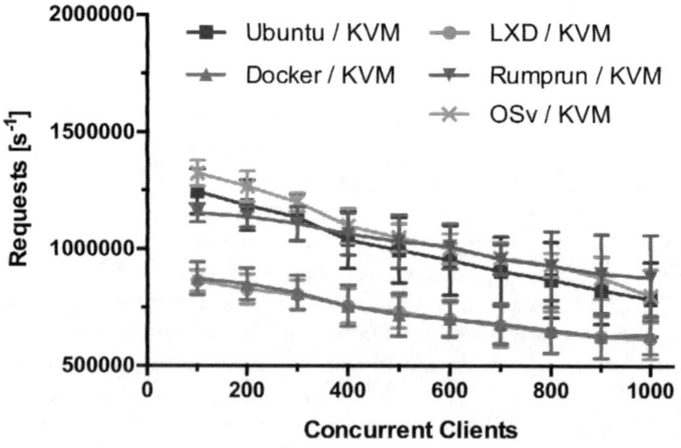


(b)

Figure 5. Throughput performance of *Redis* (version 3.0.1) was evaluated on native hardware (a) and in virtualized environments (b). The plotted values show the throughput for GET requests as retrieved through the *redis-benchmark* utility.

one particular approach without comparing it to a broad range of alternative technologies. To take remedial action, we present an extensive performance evaluation of containers, unikernels, and whole-system virtualization.

Regarding application throughput, most unikernels performed at least equally well or even better than containers. We also demonstrated that containers are not spared from overhead regarding network performance, which is why virtual machines or unikernels may be preferable in cases where raw throughput matters. These are just some aspects demonstrating that while containers have already reached a sound level of maturity, unikernels are on the verge of becoming a viable alternative. Even though we did not see unikernels outperforming a virtualized Linux instance, our brief comparison between *NetBSD* and *Rumprun* also suggested that unikernels have the potential of outperforming their full-grown operating system relatives.

## ACKNOWLEDGMENT

We would like to thank Vincent Schwarzer for engaging our interest in *unikernels* in the course of his master's thesis [24]. Furthermore, we thank the HPI Future SOC Lab for granting us access to the hardware resources used in this paper.

This paper has received funding from the European Union's Horizon 2020 research and innovation program 2014-2018 under grant agreement No. 644866.

## DISCLAIMER

This paper reflects only the authors' views and the European Commission is not responsible for any use that may be made of the information it contains.

## REFERENCES

[1] W. Felter, A. Ferreira, R. Rajamony, and J. Rubio, "An updated performance comparison of virtual machines and Linux containers," in 2015 IEEE International Symposium on Performance Analysis of Systems and Software (ISPASS), Mar. 2015, pp. 171–172.

[2] A. Arcangeli, I. Eidus, and C. Wright, "Increasing memory density by using KSM," in Proceedings of the Linux Symposium. Citeseer, 2009, pp. 19–28.

[3] G. Irazoqui, M. S. Inci, T. Eisenbarth, and B. Sunar, "Wait a minute! A fast, Cross-VM attack on AES," in International Workshop on Recent Advances in Intrusion Detection. Springer, 2014, pp. 299–319.

[4] T. K. Authors, "Kubernetes," visited on 2017-02-13. [Online]. Available: http://kubernetes.io/

[5] CloudFoundry, "Warden," visited on 2017-02-13. [Online]. Available: https://github.com/cloudfoundry/warden

[6] Docker Inc., "Docker," visited on 2017-02-13. [Online]. Available: https://www.docker.com/

[7] Canonical Ltd., "LXD," visited on 2017-02-13. [Online]. Available: https://linuxcontainers.org/lxd/introduction/

[8] ——, "LXC," visited on 2017-02-13. [Online]. Available: https://linuxcontainers.org/lxc/introduction/

[9] The OpenStack project, "Nova," visited on 2017-02-13. [Online]. Available: https://github.com/openstack/nova

[10] Google, "lmctfy," visited on 2017-02-13. [Online]. Available: https://github.com/google/lmctfy

[11] R. Jnagal, "Commit: update project status," visited on 2017-02-13. [Online]. Available: https://github.com/google/lmctfy/commit/0b317d7

[12] D. R. Engler, M. F. Kaashoek, and J. O'Toole, Jr., "Exokernel: An Operating System Architecture for Application-level Resource Management," in Proceedings of the Fifteenth ACM Symposium on Operating Systems Principles, ser. SOSP '95. New York, NY, USA: ACM, 1995, pp. 251–266.

[13] A. Madhavapeddy, R. Mortier, C. Rotsos, D. Scott, B. Singh, T. Gazagnaire, S. Smith, S. Hand, and J. Crowcroft, "Unikernels: Library operating systems for the cloud," in Proceedings of the Eighteenth International Conference on Architectural Support for Programming Languages and Operating Systems, ser. ASPLOS '13. New York, NY, USA: ACM, 2013, pp. 461–472.

[14] A. Madhavapeddy and D. J. Scott, "Unikernels: The Rise of the Virtual Library Operating System," Communications of the ACM, vol. 57, no. 1, 2014, pp. 61–69.

[15] A. Madhavapeddy, T. Leonard, M. Skjegstad, T. Gazagnaire, D. Sheets, D. Scott, R. Mortier, A. Chaudhry, B. Singh, J. Ludlam et al., "Jitsu: Just-in-time summoning of unikernels," in 12th USENIX Symposium on Networked Systems Design and Implementation (NSDI 15), 2015, pp. 559–573.

[16] A. Kantee, "Flexible Operating System Internals: The Design and Implementation of the Anykernel and Rump Kernels," Ph.D. dissertation, Aalto University, Finland, 2012.

[17] ——, "The Rise and Fall of the Operating System," ;login:, the USENIX magazine, 2015, pp. 6–9.

[18] A. Kivity, D. Laor, G. Costa, P. Enberg, N. HarEl, D. Marti, and V. Zolotarov, "OSv—Optimizing the Operating System for Virtual Machines," in 2014 USENIX Annual Technical Conference (USENIX ATC '14), 2014, pp. 61–72.

[19] KVM project, "KVM," visited on 2017-02-13. [Online]. Available: http://www.linux-kvm.org/page/Main

[20] R. Dua, A. R. Raja, and D. Kakadia, "Virtualization vs containerization to support paas," in Cloud Engineering (IC2E), 2014 IEEE International Conference on, Mar. 2014, pp. 610–614.

[21] I. Briggs, M. Day, Y. Guo, P. Marheine, and E. Eide, "A performance evaluation of unikernels," 2015.

[22] J. Nickoloff, "Evaluating Container Platforms at Scale," Mar. 2016. [Online]. Available: https://medium.com/on-docker/evaluating-container-platforms-at-scale-5e7b44d93f2c

[23] B. Veal and A. Foong, "Performance Scalability of a Multi-Core Web Server," in Proceedings of the 3rd ACM/IEEE Symposium on Architecture for networking and communications systems. ACM, 2007, pp. 57–66.

[24] V. Schwarzer, "Evaluierung von Unikernel-Betriebssystemen für Cloud-Computing," Masters Thesis (in German), Hasso Plattner Institute for Software Systems Engineering, University of Potsdam, Jun. 2016.

[25] lighty labs, "weighttp," visited on 2017-02-13. [Online]. Available: https://redmine.lighttpd.net/projects/weighttp/

[26] G-WAN ApacheBench, "abc," visited on 2017-02-13. [Online]. Available: http://gwan.com/source/ab.c

[27] Hasso Plattner Institute, "HPI Favicon," visited on 2017-02-13. [Online]. Available: http://hpi.de/favicon.ico

[28] A. Georges, D. Buytaert, and L. Eeckhout, "Statistically Rigorous Java Performance Evaluation," vol. 42, no. 10. New York, New York, USA: ACM Press, oct 2007, p. 57.

# Making the Case for Highly Efficient Multicore Enabled Unikernels With IncludeOS

Maghsoud Morshedi, Hårek Haugerud, Kyrre Begnum

Dept. of Computer Science
Oslo and Akershus University College of Applied Sciences
Oslo, Norway
Email: { maghsoud.morshedi | haugerud | kyrre.begnum } @hioa.no

***Abstract*—Today's data centers utilized for cloud services represent a significant energy consumption and costs. Standard operating systems used for cloud instances are still designed largely to run on actual or emulated hardware, making them wasteful when being idle. Ideally, the cloud should be populated with leaner and more efficient operating systems. Unikernel operating systems are a good example of such, but most Unikernels are still not ready to be used in a cloud as they are built on specialized emulators. Furthermore, they are designed for single core operation and it is impractical to run hundreds or thousands of virtual machines for large workloads without straining the underlying cloud platform. The idea presented in this paper is to have all benefits of a lean Unikernel operating system while equipping it with multicore capabilities in order to represent an energy efficient and cloud-optimized operating system that can handle larger computations. IncludeOS has shown to be an extremely efficient Unikernel operating system, utilizing a much simpler event handler and foregoing the timer interrupt altogether. In our case, the experiments demonstrated increased performance for a multi-threaded processor intensive task compared to a classic operating system, thus showcasing a real-life solution for energy efficient computation in cloud environments.**

***Keywords–Cloud computing; energy efficiency; green computing; Unikernel; multicore computing.***

## I. INTRODUCTION

Cloud computing has been focused on offering cost reduction for the consumer, business and scientific domains. However, significant energy consumption of data centers has started to constrain scaling and further cost reduction because of electricity bills and carbon dioxide footprints.

Numerous dedicated approaches for energy efficiency in cloud environments have been proposed. One traditional approach in optimising energy efficiency in such environments, is through operating system (OS) virtualization, which allows for multiple virtual machine (VM) to run on a shared cluster of physical machines. In this context, a VM represents a complete computer system with a standard OS and typically a host of a single application. The VMs can be consolidated and relocated in order to reduce energy waste. In this line of thinking, however, little attention has been paid to the role of the operating system.

By design, standard operating systems are multipurpose and are intended to run on hardware with a variety of device drivers. This allows them to support a diversity of services on physical and emulated hardware with little modification, but makes them wasteful in times when they are idle. One clear example is the timer interrupt, which triggers the kernel of an operating system to wake up at a regular pace to look for device activity. In a virtual machine, where there are very few "hardware" devices, the kernel still emulates that behavior, resulting in scores of VMs waking up and spending CPU cycles thousands of times every second. As a result, todays general purpose operating systems, though convenient, constitute a continuous energy leak for todays data centers and cloud environments.

In addition, there are also challenges which arise due to processor design. Processor architecture has evolved from featuring a single high-frequency processor, to having multiple low-frequency processor cores. This development was partly driven by frequency increment constraint on a single processor - better known as the frequency wall[1].

In contrast to a standard operating system, a Unikernel operating system is designed for a single purpose - where a single service is bundled with only the essential libraries [2], and is not designed to run on hardware. Unikernel operating systems are capable of delivering optimal performance as well as low resource consumption. However, cloud systems have not been adapted to support Unikernel operating systems due to the specialized nature of the required emulators.

Multicore processors have become the dominant processor type, and have experienced a continuous growth in the number of cores on a single processor, over time. The design of currently available Unikernels does not take advantage of the presence of multiple cores, as their operations are bound for execution on a single core. This contributes to a diminishing performance as the number of Unikernel virtual machines is gradually increased on a single host. The deployment of a large federation of single-core Unikernel VMs is impractical for a sizable workload as it strains the underlying cloud layer.

On-going Unikernel development projects are at different stages of maturity. Prominent among them is IncludeOS, which is under development at the Oslo and Akershus University College of Applied Sciences. It is being developed primarily in C++, to run on the quick emulator (QEMU)/kernel-based virtual machine (KVM) hypervisor, but with the potential of being ported to other platforms with slight modification to its binary. IncludeOS is an efficient Unikernel operating system, which utilizes a simple event handler with little memory overhead: when running a domain name system (DNS) service it imposes a total memory footprint of 158KB [3]. IncludeOS uses no regular timer interrupt, meaning that at idle, the virtual machine will use no central processing unit (CPU) cycles. Although it is efficient, IncludeOS has been a single-core operating system and not been able to utilize multiple cores for scientific and CPU-bound workloads.

This paper presents our approach to equip the IncludeOS Unikernel with multicore capabilities so that it can handle large workloads efficiently. By using multicore computing, a Unikernel operating system can handle a large processor intensive computation concurrently so that it enhances performance. The rest of the paper is organized as follows:

- The existing IncludeOS architecture and limitation along with typical challenges of multicore computing appear in Section II. In addition, this section proposes possible applications for multicore Unikernels.
- The design principles that form the multicore Unikernel architecture appear in Section III. We identify race conditions and utilize an efficient technique in Section III-A in order to minimize energy waste. Handling and distributing tasks in a multicore system appears in Section III-B. Section III-C presents our inter-communication scheme among the logical processors.
- The developed multicore capability for IncludeOS Unikernel operating system is evaluated compared to multiple single-core IncludeOS, Ubuntu VM and bare metal Ubuntu. Hence, Section IV presents the results of our experiments while Section V evaluates them.
- Section VI presents related projects in the scope of multicore Unikernel development followed by conclusion and future work in Section VII

## II. Common Challenges

A standard operating system was initially designed for a single-core processor. The transition to multicore hardware technology is a slow process due to the incredible complexity of today's established operating system kernels. For example, many of the algorithms used in a standard operating system cannot take advantage of complete multicore capabilities while cores are in full power state. Hence, multicore computing can not guarantee a sufficient performance to energy ratio improvement despite an increase in clock speed.

The adoption of multicore computing poses critical challenges in software development, which influence energy efficiency. An operating system with full parallelism will utilize all of the available computing power of a multicore processor. On the other hand, an operating system with little or no parallelism will consume more energy in comparison to their output in a multicore system. Therefore, operating system must manage cores so that each core can execute independent instruction streams concurrently in order to maximize energy efficiency for a large workload.

Multicore processors require a new generation of operating systems that capitalize form the available computing power with low energy consumption. Hence, Unikernels as a new generation of operating systems must address the fundamental challenges presented by multicore computing.

### A. Multicore Unikernel Applications

There are many compute-intensive applications in science, research and engineering that demand parallelism. With a minimal footprint and multicore computing, Unikernels could enable scientist, researchers and engineers to deploy their solutions in an efficient way. Researchers in the field of bioinformatics analyse new sequences of DNA or protein in order to predict their biological function. There are couple of packages that utilize profile-hidden Markov models (HMM) in order to search for and align sequences. These packages are very processor-intensive and utilize more than 99 percent of a single-core processor while they generally have the capacity of being parallel[4].

The telecommunication industry is recognising the possibility of cloud software defined radio (SDR) as an evolving technology. The SDR perquisites of processor-intensive digital signal processing, real-time throughput and minimum latency, show the potential of multicore Unikernel as a SDR node.

Unikernels can be leveraged as simple caching and in-memory storage solutions. In todays data-driven infrastructures, efficient, distributed databases can be built using Unikernel operating systems.

### B. IncludeOS design

The IncludeOS Unikernel operating system was designed with a modular architecture in mind such that it enables developers to attach their C++ service code to the operating system kernel during compile time, which eliminates the overhead of system calls. This provides IncludeOS the capability of attaching just what a service actually needs and minimizes the memory footprint by excluding unused features.

Application developers will write their service applications as a normal C++, standard library application. However, when including the IncludeOS library in their code with the simple addition of `#include <os>`, and subsequently compiling the code using the IncludeOS toolchain, the end result is not just a binary of the application, but a standalone, bootable virtual machine image where the operating system components that are needed by the application are statically linked into the file. This image can then be booted using QEMU/KVM and is compatible with popular cloud environments like OpenStack.

The IncludeOS comprises a modular network stack connected to the only VirtioNet device driver so that it reduces the overhead of other protocols for a service which does not use them. For example, if the application only uses TCP sockets, no UDP support will be added during compile time. Beside the modular network stack, IncludeOS' asynchronous I/O setup uses a counter based approach in order to eliminate context switching during the interrupt handling. The IncludeOS memory footprint is quite small, which enables IncludeOS to boot up quickly in about 0.3 seconds. All of the design considerations enable IncludeOS to be a lean single-threaded operating system, which can handle one task at a time.[3]. Likewise, Bratterud et al.(2015) presented detailed architecture of IncludeOS.

## III. Design Principles

The following part presents our design principles in order to adapt IncludeOS to support multicore computing. In a nutshell, multicore IncludeOS will utilize a design of a master processor managing multiple application processors. The developer writing an IncludeOS based application will organize the parallel workloads as tasks in the code. Once the VM is running, the initial bootstrap processor will become the master and distribute the tasks among the available application processors. The master will also execute task workloads in order to optimize the efficiency.

### A. Energy Efficient Memory Access

In a multicore system, parts of a program may be executed concurrently by more than one core so that it requires mutual exclusion of access over a critical memory section [5]. Any multicore operating system should employ mutual exclusion access over critical sections in order to guarantee serialized access.

In multicore IncludeOS, a bootstrap processor is responsible for booting the operating system, which then will wake up application processors in order to take advantage of them. Since application processors have been awakened through a broadcasted inter-processor interrupt (IPI) call, they can run self-configuration code concurrently following the principle of single program, multiple data [6].

The application processors will encounter a critical section problem in the early stage of the initialization procedure. The challenge begins while application processors run the self-configuration code concurrently and will manipulate a common memory location. A common option to handle this situation is to use a semaphore lock in order to serialize concurrent access to a specific memory location. Semaphore locks also introduce a new problem in virtual machines as they cost extra processor cycles to function.

The multicore IncludeOS employed instead a bus locking mechanism while manipulating a critical section in memory in order to prevent electricity waste by using semaphores. The LOCK instruction causes the bus to be locked so that the underlying hardware will manage the race condition and make an instruction atomic. Logical processors connected to the system bus generally use a low priority mechanism in order to deal with race conditions during bus acquisition. In addition, locking the bus simplifies the development of multicore support in an operating system.

### B. Multicore Task Management

In a multicore system, the operating system must manage tasks properly in order to maximize performance. There are two main task scheduling mechanisms: preemptive and non-preemptive. Standard operating systems use preemptive task scheduling in order to share limited resources between multiple tasks. Likewise, hypervisors utilize preemptive scheduling while they oversubscribe limited resources to virtual machines. Oversubscription forces hypervisors to do context switching among the available physical resources.

Multicore IncludeOS has followed the idea to keep the preemptive scheduling only at the hypervisor level. Hence, it employs a non-preemptive task management such that it adopts many virtual processors in order to handle a large workload efficiently. Indeed, the hypervisor allocates as many virtual processors as the multicore IncludeOS requires in order to handle large workloads. Fig. 1 illustrates the multicore IncludeOS operating system task management approach in which each task is handled by one core in the multicore IncludeOS.

In addition, the non-preemptive task management provides energy efficiency by reducing memory consumption and avoid context switching. The preemptive scheduling requires a bigger stack size in order to store the state of switched tasks in memory. Hence, an operating system requires more memory for a program stack whenever the number of cores increases. On the other hand, by employing non-preemptive task management

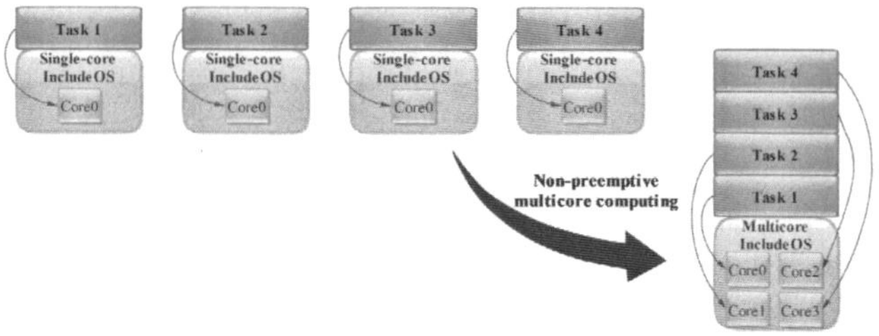


Figure 1. Multicore IncludeOS non-preemptive task management approach.

and avoiding context switching inside the operating system, the operating system can achieve fairness through multicore computing.

Distributing tasks among the virtual processors is another aspect of task management, which affects energy efficiency. The fact is that execution of a task on a logical processor when its sibling is idle is faster than when its sibling is executing a task too. This is due to how hyper-threading technology shares execution resources of each core in order to execute two or more separate threads concurrently[7]. In a processor that supports hyper threading technology, running one task per core enhances performance but at the same time the processor consumes extra electricity. In order to save power, multicore IncludeOS utilized sibling logical processors in one core and wakes the logical processors up whenever they are needed. This enables the hypervisor to change the power state of idle cores to an energy efficient state.

### C. Multicore Synchronization

A processor may require communicating with other processors in a system. A bootstrap processor in a multicore system should be able to feed in outputs of logical processors. Shared memory and message passing are the two main techniques for inter-processor communication.

Multicore IncludeOS employs shared memory in order to avoid the complexity and extra overhead of message passing between logical processors. Our design utilized the advanced programmable interrupt controller (APIC) ID in order to build an indexed array of shared memory such that logical processors access their own address space. Since multicore IncludeOS implements a master-slave architecture in order to manage application processors, each application processor plays a producer role and stores its execution result to a particular memory location identified by the APIC ID. The bootstrap processor acts as a consumer and checks the particular location for new data. Indeed, the bootstrap processor may employ busy waiting in order to check whether producers have written data in the agreed memory location. Although busy waiting for a memory location is not an efficient method, multicore IncludeOS utilized the bootstrap processor to execute tasks, as well in order to avoid wasting the processor cycles for busy waiting. In addition, the monitor/mwait mechanism eliminates busy waiting and causes the processor entering a power optimized state while waiting for a change in memory[8]. One should note that hypervisors need to support monitor/mwait before operating systems can utilize it.

## IV. Results

In order to assess the performance and efficiency of multicore IncludeOS, we compared the workload performance

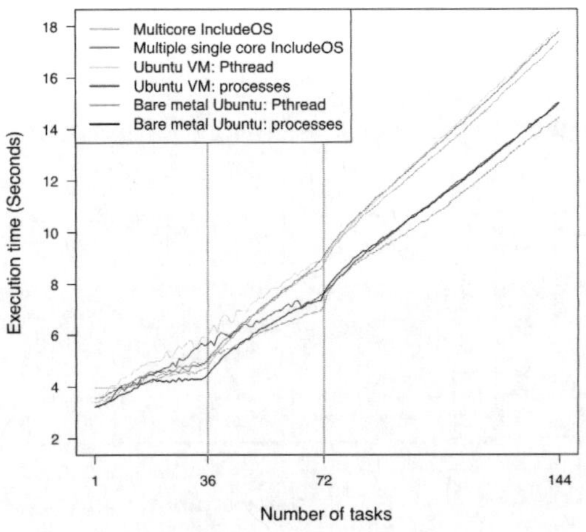


(a)

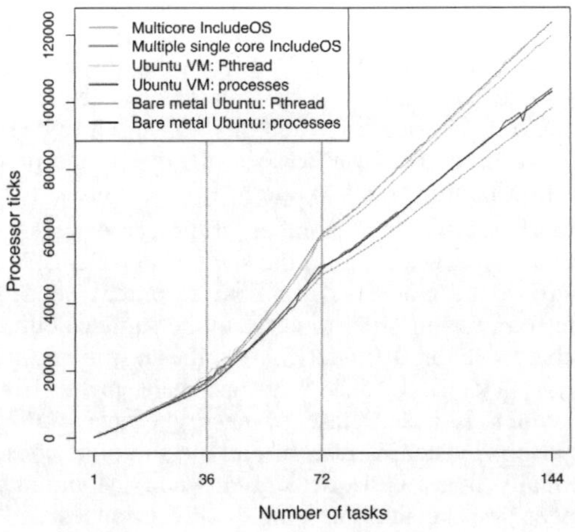


(b)

Figure 2. Execution time of prime number computation in multicore IncludeOS, multiple single-core IncludeOS, Ubuntu VM and bare metal Ubuntu with a different number of tasks in the Intel server with 36 cores supporting hyper-threading technology. Fig. (a) illustrates the execution time of workloads in seconds. Fig. (b) illustrates hypervisor processor ticks for each solution.

against a standard Ubuntu virtual machine, multiple single-core IncludeOS instances, as well as a bare metal Ubuntu installation. A series of experiments were conducted with the same processor-intensive binary being executed on all multi-threaded solutions. On the Ubuntu operating systems, parallelism was achieved both through the POSIX thread (Pthread) model and through standard processes scheduled by the kernel. In the case of multicore IncludeOS, executing multiple tasks simultaneously was achieved by making the master processor distribute the tasks to each application processor. For single-core IncludeOS, the parallelism was achieved by running one Unikernel instance for each of the tasks.

Execution time and processor ticks of the virtual machines were measured from the host in order to evaluate efficiency. The task used in the experiments was to calculate the number of prime numbers below a given large number, which is a CPU-bound task. The tasks were distributed by sending the given large number through UDP to the server for calculation. Then the server calculated the largest prime $N$ times using $N$ independent tasks. The sum of theses $N$ numbers was returned through UDP and the time for the whole process recorded. In the special case of single-core IncludeOS, the large number was sent through UDP to $N$ single-core instances, each instance returned a result through UDP and the sum was then calculated.

The experiments were performed on two machines, each with a different processor architecture. Table I shows the specification of both servers. One of the machines was equipped with Intel CPUs, which support hyper-threading technology while the second machine was equipped with AMD CPUs. Our experiments were conducted with an increasing number of task threads/application processors from 1 to twice the amount of available physical CPUs. In the case of the Ubuntu VM, the number of threads or processes was varied while with multiple single-core IncludeOS instances, the number of IncludeOS virtual machines was varied. Each experiment was repeated 30 times.

TABLE I. SERVERS SPECIFICATION.

| *Platform segment* | *Dell server* | *Dell server* |
|---|---|---|
| Processors | Intel(R) Xeon(R) CPU E5-2699 v3 | AMD Opteron 6234 |
| Processor's frequency | 2.3 GHz | 2.4 GHz |
| Memory | 128 GB | 128 GB |
| Number of processor sockets | 2 | 4 |
| Number of cores | 36 | 48 |
| Number of logical processors | 72 | 48 |

Fig. 2a shows the execution time of the prime number calculation workload for six different multi-threading solutions on the Intel server. One might expect the execution time to be roughly independent of number of tasks when there are less tasks than physical cores. The number of cores is here 36, as is indicated by the gray vertical line. However, this is not the case for the Ubuntu VM, the execution time increases by roughly 50% when increasing the number of tasks from 1 to 36. For the other systems, the increase in time is not as profound, but on the other hand it is not flat as would be expected if the system utilized the parallelism of the physical cores perfectly. The experiments below 36 cores are the most important ones as they do not involve overprovisioning of the cores. Except for the case of very few cores, multicore IncludeOS performs better than the Ubuntu VM and equally well as bare metal Ubuntu, which is included as a reference. It also performs better than the single core IncludeOS solution.

When the number of tasks increases from 36 to 72, some of the jobs needs to share an arithmetic logic unit (ALU) as there are only 36 hyper-threading cores, and the execution time is almost doubled. The slope is even steeper from 72 to 144 tasks and a bit larger than 2, which makes sense since then time-sharing is unavoidable. In these regions, the multicore

IncludeOS solution is even more efficient than its Ubuntu counterparts.

It was assumed that using Pthreads would be the most efficient way to run parallel tasks using a Linux OS and that would give the most fair comparison. As Pthreads are known to induce some overhead in certain cases, we also ran the tasks forking ordinary processes and this turned out to be more efficient in our case. This can be seen in Fig. 2a, the process results for the Ubuntu variants outperforms the Pthread results.

Fig. 2b shows the total number of processor ticks performed by the hypervisor during the same experiments, which is a measure of the grand total of CPU resources needed by each of the solutions in order to perform the same calculation. It depicts that multicore IncludeOS consumes a similar amount of processor ticks as Ubuntu VM and bare metal Ubuntu processes which is a showcase of energy efficiency. When there is no overprovisioning of cores, all the solutions consume roughly equally many CPU ticks. But when the number of tasks exceeds 36, the multiple single-core instances and the Phtread based solutions seems to introduce an overhead in terms of the need for more CPU ticks in order to consume the given workload.

In order to find out how multicore IncludeOS performs on another common processor architecture, we repeated the experiments on an AMD server. Fig. 3 illustrates the execution time of the same binary. The number of cores is 48 and there is roughly just a 10% increase in execution time when going from 1 to 48 tasks. There is no hyper-threading and hence the doubling of execution time between 48 and 96 tasks is as expected. For 30 cores and less, the Ubuntu VM performs somewhat better than multicore IncludeOS, but from then on the latter performs better. The single core IncludeOS is doing slightly better than multicore IncludeOS and the reference results of the bare metal solution is generally performing better on this platform.

As can be seen from Fig. 3, the results of the Ubuntu operating systems are quite similar when running parallel tasks as processes as when using Pthreads. For the Intel architecture, processes were most efficient.

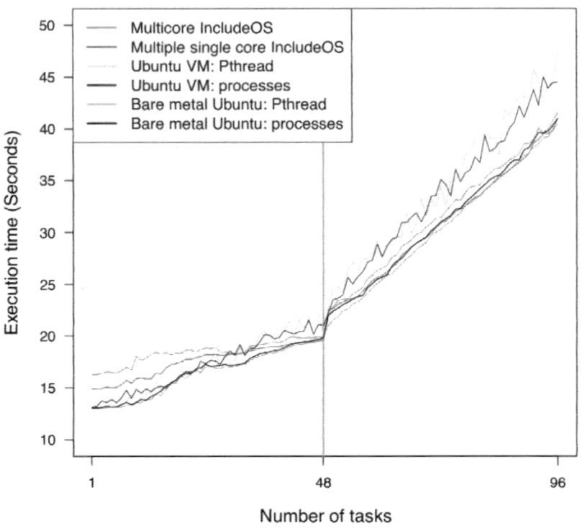


Figure 3. Execution time of prime number computation with different number of tasks in the AMD server with 48 cores.

## V. Discussion

The results from the Intel and AMD servers demonstrate that multicore IncludeOS is an energy efficient operating system, which can handle large workloads efficiently compared to standard operating systems. When comparing our multicore IncludeOS solution to systems running a full-blown operating system like Ubuntu, it must be noted that the latter is much more complex and allows the programmer to utilize multicore computing in numerous ways. However, the results show the potential efficiency when developing a fully functional multicore IncludeOS kernel.

Multicore IncludeOS did, predictably, not perform as well as other solutions for small workloads that do not require many processor cores. This is due to the multicore IncludeOS design in that it boots up with only one core and as soon as it receives requests the bootstrap processor will wake up the application processors. Finally, after the cores have no workload left, they change their state to halted mode in order to save energy. With this approach, multicore IncludeOS does not use processors while there is no workload for them. The approach, however, requires a constant time for waking up cores, which means that execution time increases and this is noticeable for few and short tasks.

Apart for the case of few tasks, multicore IncludeOS performed better than the Ubuntu VM operating system on both Intel and AMD. For experiments where the number of tasks exceeded the number of physical cores, multicore IncludeOS even performed slightly better than the reference experiments running Ubuntu on a physical server on Intel. A possible reason for this behaviour could be a distinction between the multi-threading mechanisms of the KVM kernel modules and the plain Linux kernel.

For the Intel server, the multicore IncludeOS solution performed better than single core IncludeOS for most of the experiments and just as good for the rest. An additional benefit of the multicore solution is that there is no need for the management of and communication between a potentially large number of separate virtual machines.

## VI. Related Work

There are today different approaches for Unikernel operating systems where some of them target specific use cases. Recent research on achieving a minimal operating system footprint have led to development of ClickOS[9], [10], Graphene[11], HermitCore[12], Drawbridge[13], HaLVM[14], OSV[15] and MirageOS[16], which are in varying levels of maturity. ClickOS aims to construct network appliances such as firewalls and loadbalancers and it does not support multiple processes. Graphene is a Linux compatible library OS, which implements a multi-process environment by creating multiple libOS instances that collaborate with each other in order to create POSIX abstraction. The HermitCore as a Unikernel operating system targets high-performance computing (HPC) and it uses multi-kernel approach for providing parallelism. Drawbridge represents Microsoft Windows library OS in which a fixed set of abstractions connect the library OS to the host kernel in order to achieve minimal footprint. HaLVM is utilizing the Glasgow Haskell Compiler toolsuite to enable creating a lightweight virtual machine for the Xen hypervisor. The Haskell compiler is capable of equipping the virtual machines with multicore capabilities.

The OSV project also implemented multicore computing for its Unikernel operating system. The OSV operating system is spinlock free operating system, but it is not clear how spinlock was avoided by OSV. Multicore IncludeOS dealed with race conditions through using the atomic operations and locking bus over critical sections.

In addition, the MirageOS project wants to provide an efficient runtime for single core computing with a common immutable data store so that a large cluster of cloud-based virtual machines operate over data. In this solution, virtual machines will share data instead of logical processors. Mirage project aims to run clusters of MirageOS through multiscale compiler support in order to adopt a communication model with hardware platforms constraints [16].

As illustrated in Fig. 2a, building multiple operating system instances in a cluster requires extra time to handle workloads due to increased overhead for communication between virtual machines as well as resource consumption. Sharing the data between the virtual machines will introduce new challenges in the aspect of implementation and security. As demonstrated, a multicore operating system can efficiently achieve the same level of parallelism but with lower resource consumption. It is notable that this approach increases performance for distributed systems.

## VII. Conclusion

Unikernels are designed to improve efficiency and performance but they need to utilize multicore capabilities in order to maximize performance and energy efficiency. This paper demonstrated how a multicore Unikernel approach leads to a greener cloud by adapting multicore computing to virtual environments.

The experiments demonstrated that multicore IncludeOS represents an energy efficient and cloud-optimized operating system for large workloads. Hence, it presents a real life solution as a lean and energy efficient cloud operating system with an extremely small footprint. The design principles of multicore IncludeOS improved the performance of the virtual machine as well as energy efficiency in comparison with standard operating systems and multi-kernel solutions.

### A. Future Work

The multicore capability demonstrated in this paper was developed as a modular service for IncludeOS, which enable IncludeOS to easily detach it if it is not needed by the developer. Although the master/slave based structure brings flexibility to IncludeOS, it also has disadvantages such as adding extra time for waking up application processors. In a follow-up project, multicore IncludeOS will be embedded into the IncludeOS kernel by which a significant wake up time for small to medium workloads is eliminated. In addition, multicore capability can take advantage of the x2APIC standard in order to address more than 255 cores in a virtual machine, which would enable IncludeOS to utilize many-core processors in the near future. Security study of Unikernels also requires further research in order to improve reliability of Unikernel operating systems.

## References


[1] M. J. Flynn and P. Hung, "Microprocessor design issues: Thoughts on the road ahead," IEEE Micro, vol. 25, no. 3, pp. 16–31, 2005. [Online]. Available: http://dx.doi.org/10.1109/MM.2005.56

[2] Xenproject. Unikernels. [Online]. Available: http://wiki.xenproject.org/wiki/Unikernels [retrieved: Jan, 2017]

[3] A. Bratterud, A. A. Walla, H. Haugerud, P. E. Engelstad, and K. Begnum, "Includeos: A minimal, resource efficient unikernel for cloud services," in 2015 IEEE 7th International Conference on Cloud Computing Technology and Science (CloudCom), pp. 250–257, Nov 2015.

[4] H. Stockinger, M. Pagni, L. Cerutti, and L. Falquet, "Grid approach to embarrassingly parallel cpu-intensive bioinformatics problems," in 2006 Second IEEE International Conference on e-Science and Grid Computing (e-Science'06), pp. 58–58, Dec 2006.

[5] M. Raynal, Concurrent Programming: Algorithms, Principles, and Foundations. Springer Publishing Company, Incorporated, 2012.

[6] A. A. Kamil, "Single program, multiple data programming for hierarchical computations," Ph.D. dissertation, EECS Department, University of California, Berkeley, Aug 2012, [retrieved: Jan, 2017]. [Online]. Available: http://www2.eecs.berkeley.edu/Pubs/TechRpts/2012/EECS-2012-186.html

[7] Intel 64 and IA-32 Architectures Software Developers Manual:Basic Architecture, Intel Corporation, Sep. 2016, [retrieved: Jan, 2017]. [Online]. Available: http://www.intel.com/content/dam/www/public/us/en/documents/manuals/64-ia-32-architectures-software-developer-vol-1-manual.pdf

[8] Intel 64 and IA-32 Architectures Software Developers Manual: System Programming Guide, Part 1, Intel Corporation, Sep. 2016, [retrieved: Jan, 2017]. [Online]. Available: http://www.intel.com/content/www/us/en/architecture-and-technology/64-ia-32-architectures-software-developer-vol-3a-part-1-manual.html

[9] J. Martins, M. Ahmed, C. Raiciu, and F. Huici, "Enabling fast, dynamic network processing with clickos," in Proceedings of the Second ACM SIGCOMM Workshop on Hot Topics in Software Defined Networking, ser. HotSDN '13, pp. 67–72. New York, NY, USA: ACM, 2013. [Online]. Available: http://doi.acm.org/10.1145/2491185.2491195

[10] J. Martins and et al., "Clickos and the art of network function virtualization," in 11th USENIX Symposium on Networked Systems Design and Implementation (NSDI 14), pp. 459–473. Seattle, WA: USENIX Association, Apr. 2014. [Online]. Available: https://www.usenix.org/conference/nsdi14/technical-sessions/presentation/martins

[11] C. Tsai and et al., "Cooperation and security isolation of library oses for multi-process applications," in Proceedings of the Ninth European Conference on Computer Systems, ser. EuroSys '14, pp. 9:1–9:14. New York, NY, USA: ACM, 2014. [Online]. Available: http://doi.acm.org/10.1145/2592798.2592812

[12] S. Lankes, S. Pickartz, and J. Breitbart, "Hermitcore: A unikernel for extreme scale computing," in Proceedings of the 6th International Workshop on Runtime and Operating Systems for Supercomputers, ser. ROSS '16, pp. 4:1–4:8. New York, NY, USA: ACM, 2016. [Online]. Available: http://doi.acm.org/10.1145/2931088.2931093

[13] D. E. Porter, G. Hunt, J. Howell, R. Olinsky, and S. Boyd-Wickizer, "Rethinking the library os from the top down," in Proceedings of the 16th International Conference on Architectural Support for Programming Languages and Operating Systems (ASPLOS). Association for Computing Machinery, Inc., March 2011. [Online]. Available: https://www.microsoft.com/en-us/research/publication/rethinking-the-library-os-from-the-top-down/

[14] Galois-Inc. Halvm. [Online]. Available: https://galois.com/project/halvm/ [retrieved: Jan, 2017]

[15] A. Kivity and et al., "Osv—optimizing the operating system for virtual machines," in 2014 USENIX Annual Technical Conference (USENIX ATC 14), pp. 61–72. Philadelphia, PA: USENIX Association, Jun. 2014. [Online]. Available: https://www.usenix.org/conference/atc14/technical-sessions/presentation/kivity

[16] A. Madhavapeddy, R. Mortier, J. Crowcroft, and S. Hand, "Multiscale not multicore: Efficient heterogeneous cloud computing," in Proceedings of the 2010 ACM-BCS Visions of Computer Science Conference, ser. ACM-BCS '10, pp. 6:1–6:12. Swinton, UK, UK: British Computer Society, 2010. [Online]. Available: http://dl.acm.org/citation.cfm?id=1811182.1811191

# An Automated Lightweight Framework for Scheduling and Profiling Parallel Workflows Simultaneously on Multiple Hypervisors

Maruf Ahmed, Albert Y. Zomaya
School of Information Technologies, The University of Sydney, Australia
Email: mahm1846@uni.sydney.edu.au, albert.zomaya@sydney.edu.au

***Abstract*—This work presents a lightweight framework for performing automated experiments with the execution time and performance variations of parallel workflows. The execution time variation of tasks due to consolidation is a barrier to efficiently scheduling them on *Virtual Machines* (VMs). In data centers, VMs are usually consolidated to increase resource utilization. However, this causes resource contention and performance degradation among the VMs. To address this issue, it is necessary to perform experiments with large numbers of tasks and schedules. There exists no framework particularly designed for this type of experiment. The proposed framework makes it easy to conduct experiments with large numbers of task execution patterns. Moreover, it is capable of profiling the execution time variation of each task of a workflow. The design principles, implementation issues and trade-offs of the framework are discussed in detail here. The effectiveness of the framework is demonstrated with a data-intensive scientific workflow, which processes the *Galactic Arecibo L-band Feed Array HI* (GALFA-HI) survey data with the *Montage* toolkit. With this framework, experiments have been simultaneously run on three different hypervisors and the execution time variation of each task retrieved. The three hypervisors are the *VMware ESXi* 5.5, *XenServer* 6.5 and *Xen* 4.6. This framework will enable researchers to perform large scale experiments with the execution time variations of parallel tasks on multiple hypervisors and the Cloud.**

***Keywords*–Cloud; virtualization; consolidation; performance; scheduling framework.***

## I. Introduction

Virtualization plays an important part for both the data centers and Cloud. Among other advantages, it allows consolidation of *Virtual Machines* (VMs) in data centers. To put it simply, consolidated means running multiple VMs simultaneously on the same server through virtualization. It is a common technique to increase resource utilization, reducing operational cost and energy consumption of data centers. However, the main drawback of consolidation is performance variation, due to resource contention and interferences among the VMs.

More and more applications and workflows are being deployed on the Cloud. However, scheduling of scientific applications and workflows on the Cloud is still problematic because of the task execution time variation. On consolidated servers, the task execution finish time may very unexpectedly, thus it is difficult to determine which applications are suitable to be consolidated for better performance. Recently, many works have focused on this issue [1]–[5].

These works rely on experimental results with consolidated applications, to estimate how they would react to resource contention in general. Thus, they require the running of a large number of experiments, involving scheduling various applications and workflows on VMs. However, there exists no standard framework to manage and run such large scale experiments. This work proposes a framework to easily manage and run large numbers of experiments with complex schedules and resource usage patterns on the Cloud

There are many large scale Cloud management and maintenance software stacks available for modern data centers [6]–[17]. Although they are well-equipped for performing complex maintenance, fault tolerance, and data backup services, they are not adequate for performing experiments with task scheduling and resource usages patterns of VMs for several reasons:

i) These software stacks are mainly designed for providing the Cloud services, not for performing sophisticated experiments with workloads. For example, they have special features for providing fault tolerance, VM replication, migration and high availability of VMs to a data center. The software stacks do not offer any built-in features for performing complex experiments with application scheduling patterns on the Cloud;

ii) They have many modules, and they require a lot of time and effort to master. System administrators require a lot of experience to manage these systems efficiently. On the other hand, most researchers are concerned with a quick and easy setup of experiments. It takes a lot of time to modify a large piece of software even though they do not provide friendly interfaces to conduct scientific experiments easily;

iii) Experiments with scheduling of parallel workflow on VMs often require modification the software stack of the maintenance software. Making such changes to a massive software stack with many modules is a cumbersome process. The proposed framework is designed to bypass the interaction with management software and run complex task scheduling experiments easily on the Cloud.

Recently, the understanding interactions among the VMs and improving the performance of tasks has received a significant amount of attention [1]–[5][18][19]. A simple construct of a framework, which can execute the parallel workflow on VMs residing on multiple servers can make such experimental processes much easier. Some features of the framework and contribution of this paper are briefly stated below:

i) A lightweight framework for profiling execution time variations of parallel workflow on the Cloud has been introduced. It provides a simple interface for conducting complex experiments on VMs and scheduling parallel applications across on multiple hypervisors. The primary objective is to provide an accessible platform to carry out complex experiments on the Cloud.

It can be used independent of any data center management software, thus making the general experimental process easier. There are many open source management software options. However, they have too many components and modules.

ii) They are difficult to setup for complex experiments. This framework is lightweight and easy to handle, making it easier to perform experiments with complex workload patterns.

iii) The framework allows researchers to specify an exact sequence of execution of workload pattern on VMs. A human readable *workload descriptor* file stores all the task patterns. The exact sequence of tasks that is to be executed on VMs is defined in this file. Cloud management software has many layers and hides many complexities from the users. It can be convenient for system administrators, who are only concerned with the outcome. On the other hand, during experiments measuring the impact of execution of each task may be necessary. Extensive experiments will help to understand the VM's behavior under consolidation and identify any anomaly of the schedule more quickly;

iv) Another feature of the framework is the *command descriptor* file. Parallel applications usually consist of several smaller tasks, and various command sets are required to run them. The command descriptor file contains the actual commands, and one mnemonic is issued against each set of commands. Thus, the workload descriptor file remains small and workload patterns are easy to create or modify. The command descriptor file also allows for running complex applications like web servers or database servers. The framework scans the workload file twice. During the first scan, all mnemonics are replaced, and in the second scan actual commands are executed. Thus, adding or modifying real command sets is much easier as they are stored only in one place, in the command descriptor file;

v) The framework can run experimental schedules and resource usage patterns on multiple hypervisors simultaneously. It uses the *Secure Shell* (SSH) to connect to virtualized servers, instead of the API set. The use of SSH ensures flexibility, and any hypervisors can be connected. On the other hand, using multiple API for various hypervisors is a cumbersome process. The SSH gives the ability to connect to any Cloud;

vi) The framework is implemented entirely in Java and can be run on any *operating system* (OS). It can be used as a stand-alone application or plugged-in with any other Java task scheduling program. It is lightweight, completely portable and requires no installation on the system.

To the best of our knowledge, there is no other lightweight framework written in any language, specifically to do experiments with execution time variation of parallel workflows on VMs. This framework is independent of and complementary to Cloud management software. While the management software can be used for providing Cloud services, this framework can be used to run experiments with workload patterns on the Cloud.

The effectiveness of the framework is demonstrated with a real data-intensive workflow, which processes the *Galactic Arecibo L-band Feed Array HI* (GALFA-HI) [20] survey data with the Montage toolkit [21]. The *Incremental Consolidation Benchmarking Method* (ICBM) [22] has been used to analyze the tasks of the workflow. Originally, the ICBM was introduced to analyze the execution time variations of individual tasks on VMs. In this work, it is extended to analyze the tasks of scientific workflow which has not been done previously.

The rest of the paper is organized as follows. Section II describes the problem with an example. Design goals are discussed in Section III, followed by the framework design in Section IV. Section V discusses the workflow and benchmarks used, along with experimental setup. Section VI gives the results of experiments with task execution patterns on three hypervisors. Section VII provides a brief overview and shortcomings of complementary works. A discussion about future work and conclusion are in Section VIII.

## II. PROBLEM DESCRIPTION

The task execution time variation due to VM consolidation is one of the major problems for the Cloud. It can be even more problematic for parallel applications and scientific workflows, because of having task dependencies. Fig. 1 shows an example of workflow, which processes the *GALFA-HI survey* data [20] using the *Montage* toolkit [21]. It is a data-intensive workflow that creates a mosaic image of a part of the Milky Way galaxy from some data cubes. The data cubes are released at regular intervals, as a part of an ongoing survey. Therefore, this is a widely used workflow in the field of astronomy. It has 16 tasks ($t_1$ to $t_16$) on 8 levels ($l_1$ to $l_8$). Fig. 2 shows one possible schedule of these tasks on a set of co-located VMs.

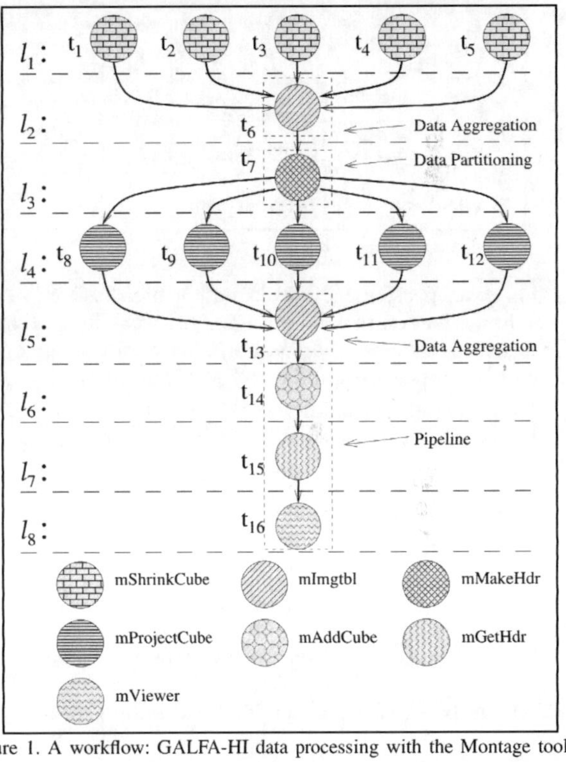


Figure 1. A workflow: GALFA-HI data processing with the Montage toolkit.

In Fig. 2, the tasks of the GALFA-HI workflow (Fig. 1) are scheduled on the VMs of a single server. Here, the server has eight simultaneously running VMs. As the tasks of the workflow have internal dependencies, they need to be scheduled hierarchically. The tasks that can be run simultaneously are grouped together in one level. The tasks of the level below are dependent on tasks of the immediate upper level.

Fig. 2 depicts that the tasks are being executed level by level on the VMs of a single server. There are VMs of three colors on the server. Light blue VMs are where the tasks of GALFA-HI are being executed. In a consolidated server, tasks from other applications are also being executed they are shown in red. Finally, white VMs represent empty VMs, where no tasks are being run at present. The tasks on additional VMs (shown in red) are responsible for resource contention and performance degradation of tasks of GALFA-HI workflow.

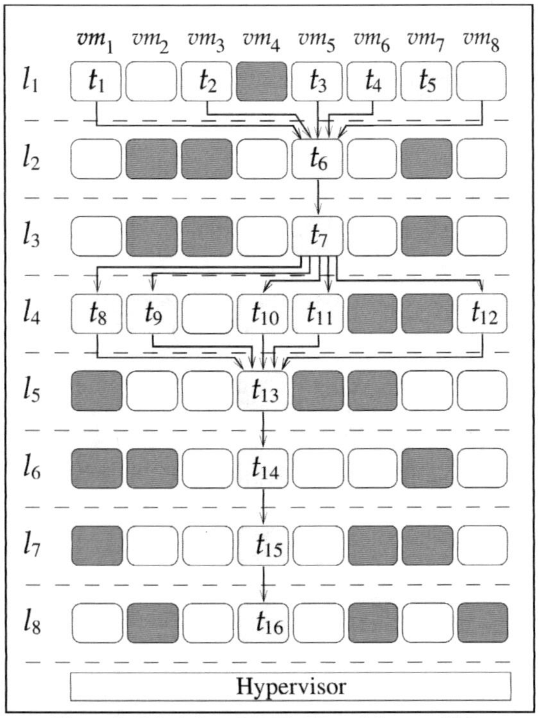

Figure 2. Scheduling GALFA-HI workflow on VMs.

In this case, performance deterioration of a task can have a cascading effect on the other tasks of the workflow, because of the task dependencies. Furthermore, the performance of tasks of the critical path would directly affect the makespan.

To efficiently schedule workflows on the Cloud it is necessary to take the execution time variations into account. Presently, there is no theoretical solution for this issue. Therefore, most recent works rely on various heuristics [1]–[5]. To design such heuristic solutions, a significant amount of experimental data may be required. This framework makes it easier to carry out large-scale experiments with VM schedules and retrieves data. The obtained data can help to design better heuristics algorithms for the system. One method to obtain such critical task execution time variation data is presented in [22], called the ICBM. This work further shows that the ICBM can be extended to scientific workflows on the Cloud.

### A. ICBM for workflow

Originally, the ICBM was introduced to retrieve the execution time variations of VMs on consolidated servers [22]. However, the ICBM has not been used with workflows before. This work shows that the concept of ICBM can be applied to parallel workflows, too. The concept of ICBM involves increasing resource usage of a virtualized server, To systematically cause execution time variations on VMs. This means that for a parallel application the same resource usage pattern has to be applied to each task. It is described next.

Fig. 3 shows the steps of ICBM for applying a CPU-intensive resource usages pattern on the GALFA-HI workflow. Initially, only tasks of the workflow are being run on the server. It is shown on Fig. 3a, at this stage tasks from no other application are run on the server. Thus, the execution finish times of tasks of the workflow are obtained, without interferences from VMs belonging to other tasks. Afterward, the workflow is run

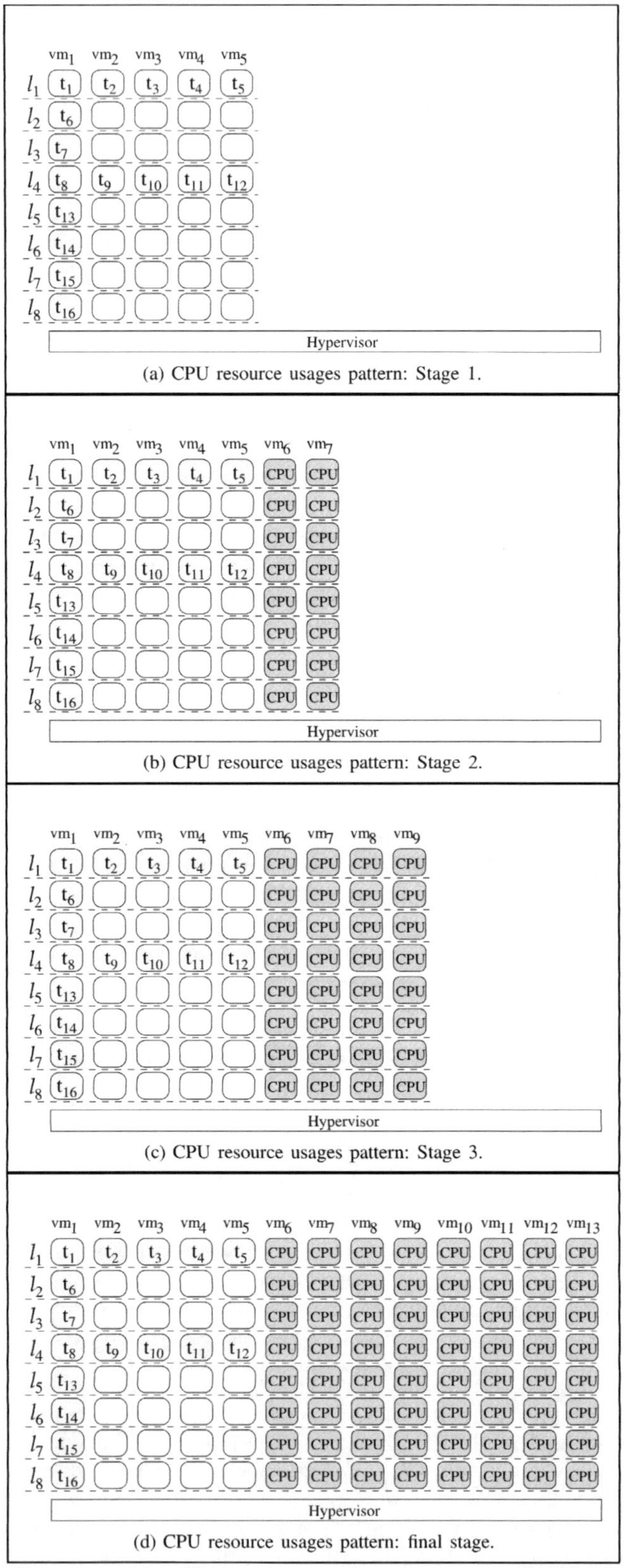

(a) CPU resource usages pattern: Stage 1.

(b) CPU resource usages pattern: Stage 2.

(c) CPU resource usages pattern: Stage 3.

(d) CPU resource usages pattern: final stage.

Figure 3. Applying CPU-intensive resource usages pattern on GALFA-HI workflow.

again. However, in this stage, two additional CPU-intensive

tasks are executed at each level of execution. This is referred to as stage 2 and shown in Fig. 3b.

At stage 3, four additional CPU-intensive VMs are being run along with the workflow (Fig. 3c). Thus, the workflow is repeatedly run and CPU-intensive VMs are increased systematically. This process is repeated until all VMs of the server are utilized, and that is the final stage of the experiment. Fig. 3d shows the final stage for this particular server configuration. This server can accommodate a maximum of 13 VMs, and all of them have been used. Tasks of the workflow are occupying five VMs, while the remaining eight are CPU-intensive VMs.

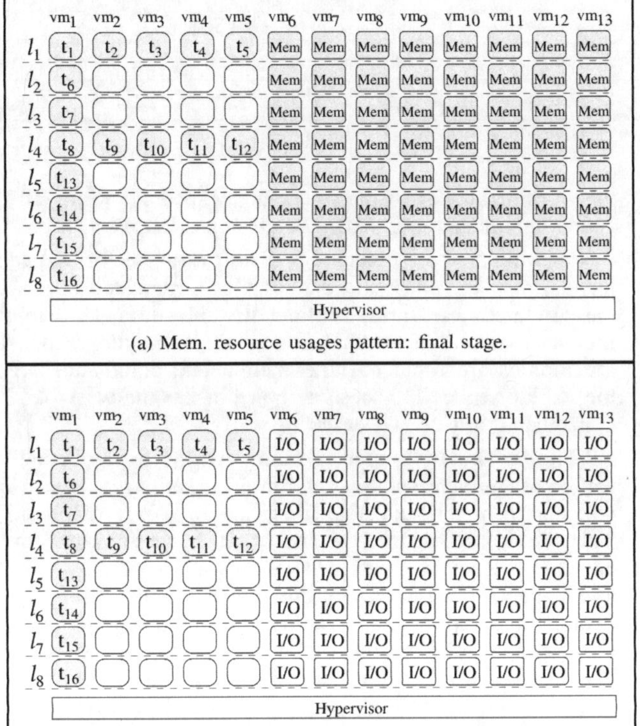

(a) Mem. resource usages pattern: final stage.

(b) I/O resource usages pattern: final stage.

(c) CPU-Mem. resource usages pattern: final stage.

Figure 4. Various resource usages pattern applied on GALFA-HI workflow.

The ICBM divides experiments into stages so that the tasks of a workflow suffer the least amount of interference at stage 1 (Fig. 3a) while they face the most CPU-intensive resource usage contention at the final stage (Fig. 3d). Then, the entire procedure is repeated for another resource intensive VMs, like memory (Fig. 4a) and I/O (Fig. 4b). Afterward, the steps are repeated for combinations of resources, too. One example of combination of resources is shown in Fig. 4c, it is for CPU-Memory. Here, the process is repeated as described above. However, one CPU-intensive and one memory-intensive VM have been added at each stage, instead of two CPU-intensive ones. Other combinational resource contentions, like CPU-I/O and Memory-I/O, are created in the same process.

From the above discussion, it is clear that experimental procedures like the ICBM require handling large numbers of task schedules. Furthermore, the exact sequence of task executions on VMs and their mutual performance inferences due to consolidation, have to be known precisely. Although, many tasks and resource scheduling software exist, none of them are designed to do experiments with task execution time variations on VMs. They use high-level interfaces and hide almost all scheduling complexities from the user. That may be convenient for average Cloud users, however it is not too beneficial for researchers conducting experiments with resource contention and consolidation. The primary objective of this work is to present a low-level, lightweight framework for experimenting with complex workload patterns automatically. This framework needs to act as both a scheduler and profiler of task execution times and be able to connect to any Cloud. In this work, the design goals, implantation issues and experimental results of the framework are discussed in detail.

## III. MOTIVATION AND DESIGN GOALS

This section discusses the primary goals and trade-offs considered while designing and implementing the framework.

**Easy to perform experiments with workflow:** The first priority is to provide an easy interface to perform complex experiments with the workflows on virtualized servers. There exist many complex Cloud management systems and programming paradigms. However, they are not designed for carrying out experiments with VM consolidation. The new framework should be able to perform complex experiments on the Cloud, independent of any management software. This work aims to provide an easy interface to design and carry out experiments with workflows on virtualized servers so that, the performance variation of each task can be profiled independently. The main application of the framework would be to discover the relationship among the execution time variations of consolidated VMs and resource utilization of the server.

**Resource usages patterns:** Experiments with consolidation are sensitive to VM placements on the server. To capture the effect of consolidation on VMs, it is necessary to create complex workload patterns and execute the tasks accordingly on VMs. Therefore, the proposed framework should provide an easy way to run the tasks according to resource usages patterns, described previously. A human readable file should contain all the workload patterns so that they are easy to create and modify. Researchers would create those files, exactly the way they want the tasks to be executed on the system. Thus, the reaction of the system to resource contentions and consolidation can be examined carefully.

**Easy to check the workload patterns:** Executing a task of the workflow usually requires several command sets. Managing a lot of commands in one workload pattern file is often problematic. There should be an easy way to rectify any potential error in the workload pattern. One way to achieve

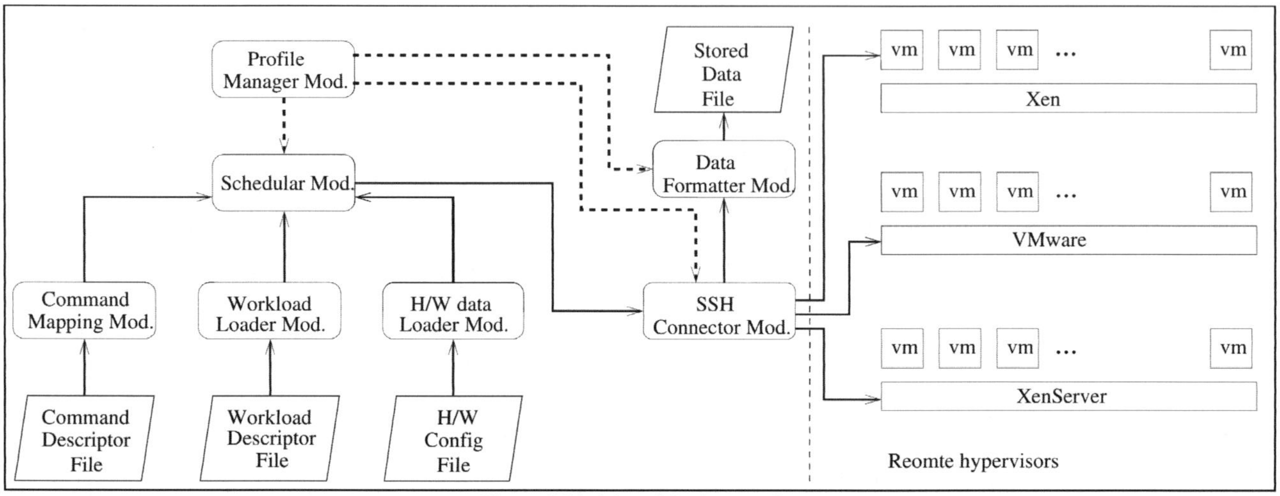

Figure 5. Modules of the framework.

this is not to inscribe full commands in the workload file, rather they are stored in a particular file, separately. Then, the workload file is created only with a short set of mnemonics During runtime, the mnemonics are mapped to actual larger command sets. The process is described in more detail in the implementation section (Section IV).

**Connection to any Cloud technology:** Modern data centers have a countless number of servers, and various hypervisors are deployed on them. It is necessary for the framework to be able to connect to a large number of VMs running on multiple hypervisors. Therefore, the framework needs a method with small connection overhead, and the ability to run tasks on any Cloud. The implementation section describes how this is achieved.

**Easy to deploy:** The framework should be easily deployable on a wide variety of systems. There are many operating systems today; therefore the framework should be as universal as possible. It should not be dependent on any Cloud management system or OS, thus, making it possible to initiate experiments from any machine, regardless of the underlying OS. Use of a common framework to perform experiments would give researchers the opportunity to share and collaborate with experimental results more widely.

In this section, motivations and design goals of the framework are described. The next section describes, how those goals are achieved during implementation.

## IV. Implementation of the Framework

This section describes the implementation process of the framework to achieve the design goals of the previous section. The framework is divided into seven modules, and each module performs a particular job. All modules are shown in Fig. 5 and described below. Solid lines represent data transfer paths, while dashed lines represent command transfer paths.

**The command mapping module:** A workflow consists of many tasks, and each task requires a set of commands to execute properly. Inscribing all commands to a workload file is counter-productive for several reasons. It makes the workload file large, and it becomes difficult to inspect the workload patterns. Furthermore, if an error is found in one of the commands, it has to be corrected in all occurrences of the workload file. This pitfall can be avoided by storing all the actual commands in a separate *command descriptor* file.

This file stores a mnemonic against a full set of real commands, then the workload pattern files are created only with these mnemonics. During runtime, first the command mapping module loads all the actual commands to memory, then all mnemonics are replaced with their actual command sets in the workload file. This design choice makes the workload file manageable in size and easier to verify.

**The workload loader module:** All the experimental resource usage patterns are stored in a *workload descriptor* file, which is a human readable file containing only mnemonics. This file describes, line by line, the dependencies and exact execution sequence of the tasks. Tasks that would be running simultaneously are stored in one line while, the tasks dependent on them are written in the line below. The workload loader module scans the tasks line by line so that they can be executed on the VMs exactly in the order intended on the workload file. This makes it easier to identify how a virtualized system reacts to a particular pattern of resource usages.

**The hardware configuration loader module:** To execute the sequence of workload patterns correctly, some basic hardware information is required. The necessary hardware configuration of all the VMs and physical host are stored in the *hardware configuration* file. The arrangements of VMs on physical hosts along with their MAC addresses are stored in this file. The *hardware configuration loader* module fetches this data from the file, so that the framework can utilize it to connect and execute workloads on the VMs.

**The scheduler module:** The *scheduler module* collects information from the above three data loading modules, and allows the tasks to be executed on VMs. At first, memory mapped commands and hardware configuration file are used, to check the consistency of the workload descriptor file. In the case of any inconsistency, the process has to be terminated. After consistency checking, the scheduler issues the necessary commands to VMs through the connecting module, which is described next. It is designed as a separate module, so that it can be modified to implement any custom task scheduling algorithm for VMs if it is required.

**The connecting module:** Another design goal is to make

the framework as universally usable as possible. The framework makes all connections through an SSH implementation in Java, called the JSch [23]. Thus, the entire framework is written in Java and can be run on any OS. It is completely portable and requires no installation. The SSH is chosen over API, to keep the framework lightweight. It allows the framework to connect to multiple hypervisors simultaneously, without having to write codes for multiple API. Furthermore, support for any new hypervisor can be easily added, without code modification.

**The data formatting module:** Raw data is sent back through the SSH channels; these data need to be formatted to use them with other applications. This module formats and stores the experimental results in output files. The data is analyzed later to discover the relation among resource usages patterns and task execution time variations.

**The profile manager module:** This is responsible for coordination among all the modules so that they can work seamlessly. The profiler is modular in design so that a module can be customized easily if required. Also, adding new modules for future functionality is much easier in this way.

The next section describes the algorithm for the framework, to demonstrate how those modules work together.

### A. *Algorithm for the framework*

Fig. 6 shows the algorithm for the framework. First, all commands are loaded on the *COMM-LIST* from the command descriptor file. The command loader module does this, by mapping all commands to their corresponding mnemonics in memory (lines 1-2). Then, the workload loader module parse the workload descriptor file, and loads workload pattern on the *WL-LIST* (lines 3-4). The WL-LIST contains a detailed execution plan, for both the parallel application and resource contention patterns. Examples of such patterns are shown in Figs. 3 and 4. Afterward, the hardware configuration data is loaded from the file to *VM-LIST* (lines 5-6). The VM-LIST contains all the data required for connecting to VMs during experiments.

Next, a *for* loop (lines 7-21) processes the WL-LIST, line by line. Recall that the tasks that are to be run simultaneously are written in a single line. Then, an inner *for* loop (lines 8-17) removes one task at a time from the line and checks for consistency against hardware data and commands. The consistent tasks are then stored in a linked list, called the *RUN-LIST*. On the other hand, if a task is not compatible then the application exits. Once all the tasks of a line are processed, the inner *for* loop exits. Then, all the mnemonics of RUN-LIST are replaced with the actual command set, with the help of COMM-LIST (line 15). Once this is done, commands are simultaneously sent to execute all tasks of the RUN-LIST (line 16). The framework then waits for the tasks to finish, and collect the execution time data (line 17). Afterward, the same process is repeated for the next line of WL-LIST, on next iteration of the outer *for* loop. The outer *for* loop exit when all the lines of WL-LIST (entire pattern) have been processed. To experiment with another resource usage pattern, the procedure needs to be restarted from the beginning.

1: Load all commands and mnemonics, from the Command Descriptor file to $COMM - LIST$.
2: Load workloads from the Workload Descriptor file to $WL - LIST$.
3: Load the VMs configuration from file to $VM - LIST$.
4: **for** Each line $\mathcal{L}_i \in WL - LIST$ **do**
5:     **for** Each task, $t_j \in \mathcal{L}_i$ **do**
6:         Let, $comm_j \in COMM - LIST$ be the command for $t_j$.
7:         Let, $vm_j \in VM - LIST$ be the VM, where to run $t_j$ .
8:         Check the consistency of $t_j$ against $comm_j$ on $vm_j$.
9:         **if** $t_j$ is consistent **then**
10:             Put $t_j$, $comm_j$ and $vm_j$ on $RUN - LIST$.
11:         **else**
12:             Exit.
13:         **end if**
14:     **end for**
15:     Replace all mnemonics of $RUN - LIST$ with actual commands.
16:     Simultaneously send commands to all $vm_j$ of $RUN - LIST$.
17:     Wait for their execution to finish and collect execution time data.
18: **end for**

Figure 6. Algorithm for the framework.

## V. WORKLOADS USED

Two types of workload have been used in the experiments. The first type is a data-intensive scientific workflow, which is used to observe the execution time variations of tasks under consolidation. The second type is a set of benchmarks suites, used to create resource contention patterns on servers.

### A. *Scientific workflow: GALFA-HI*

The GALFA-HI survey continuously scans the sky for naturally occurring hydrogen atoms [20], and several data cubes have been released so far. Five of those cubes have been processed with the Montage toolkit [21], to create a mosaic image of a part of the Milky Way galaxy. The workflow is shown in Fig. 1 it has 16 tasks and eight levels. It is a data-intensive workflow, which processes about 2 GB of raw data cubes. Experiments measure the execution time variation of tasks in this workflow due to consolidation.

### B. *Set of benchmark suites*

Three sets of benchmark suites have been used to create resource contention patterns on the tasks of the above workflow. They are the sets of CPU, memory and I/O-intensive benchmark suites. Each benchmark suite, in turn, consists of several similar types of tests. Due to space limitation, it is not possible to describe each benchmark suite separately. Next, each set is described in brief.

**CPU-intensive benchmarks:** Three CPU-intensive benchmarks have been used, they are the *Sysbench CPU* test, *Nbench* and *Unixbench*. The Sysbench CPU test has been widely used with multi-core server [24] and VM workload consolidation experiments [25]. The Nbench is a CPU-intensive benchmark suite, having ten different CPU-intensive tests [26]. The Unixbench is another CPU-intensive benchmark suite, which is used for experiments on Amazon EC2 [27].

**Memory-intensive benchmarks:** Three memory-intensive benchmarks have been used for creating resource contention patterns. The first is the *Cachebench*, which consists of eight different memory tests [28]. The second is the *Stream*, a syntactic benchmark program for measuring sustainable memory bandwidth [29]. The final one is the *Sysbench memory* test.

**I/O-intensive benchmarks:** Five I/O-intensive tests have been used to create resource contention patterns. The *Filebench* is an important I/O benchmark suite [30], which can be configured to perform various I/O-intensive tests. Five of them are used, they are the *file-server*, *web-server*, *web-proxy*, *video-server* and *online transaction processing* (OLTP) test.

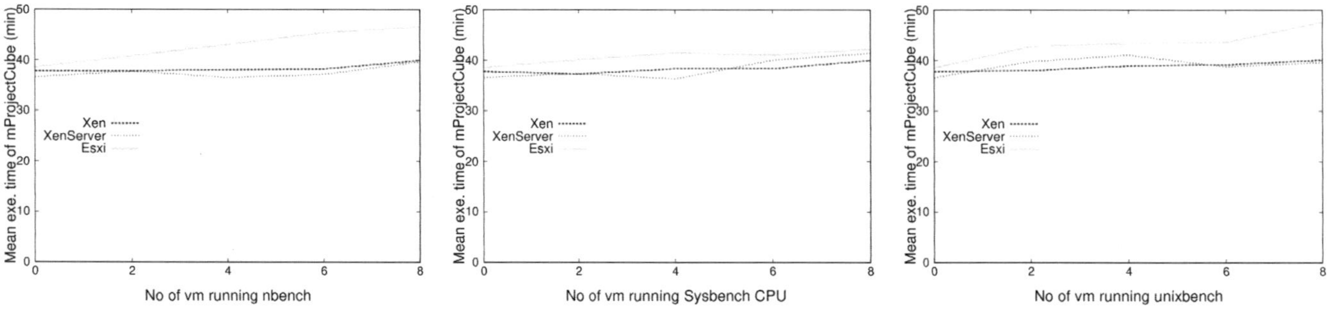


(a) TETV of mProjectCube due to the Nbench. (b) TETV of mProjectCube due to the Nbench. (c) TETV of mProjectCube due to the Unixbench.

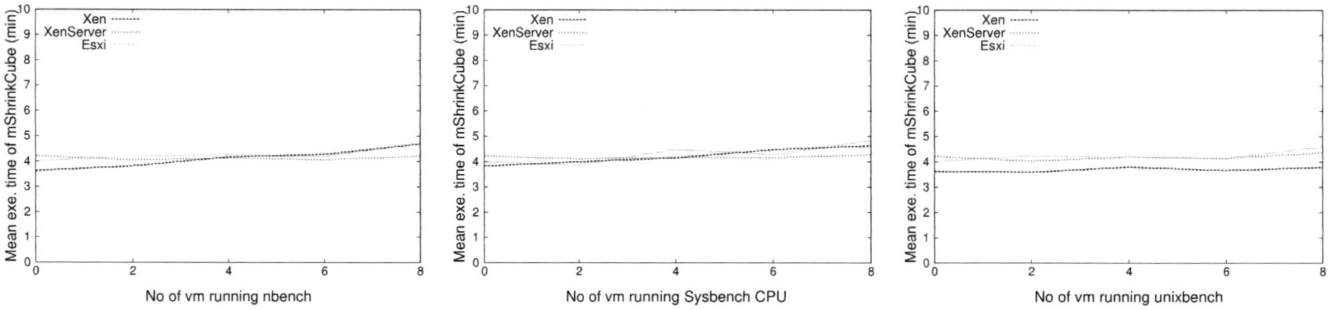


(d) TETV of mShrinkCube due to the Unixbench. (e) TETV of mShrinkCube due to the Sysbench CPU. (f) TETV of mShrinkCube due to the Sysbench CPU.

Figure 7. Task execution time variation (TETV) of the mProjectCube and mShrinkCube functions due to the CPU-intensive workload patterns on VMs.

### C. *Experimental setup*

Three Dell XPS-8500 servers of identical hardware configuration had been set up for the experiments. Each server has one Intel i7-3770 processor and 32 GB memory. The i7-3770 has four cores and eight hardware threads, each is clocked at 3.4 GHz. Three different hypervisors are installed on three servers; they are, *VMware ESXi* 5.5, *Citrix XenServer* 6.5 and *Xen* 4.6 on *Centos* 7.

Each hypervisor has 14 VMs of identical configuration. Each VM has one processor, 2 GB of Ram and 50 GB virtual disk. During experiments, the framework connects to all 42 (14×3) VMs on three hypervisors and execute workload patterns simultaneously. The framework itself runs on a remote Dell OptiPlex 9010 machine and connects to hypervisors through the LAN. The results of experiments are given next.

## VI. RESULTS

Recall that the GALFA-HI workflow (Fig. 1) has 16 tasks, comprised of seven functions. Average execution times of those seven functions without interferences are shown in Table I. In this case, the tasks are scheduled exactly like that of Fig. 3a. Due to space constraints, it is not possible to discuss execution time variations of all seven functions. Results are shown for only two functions, the *mProjectCube* and *mShrinkCube*. The rest of the functions also show variations similar that of these functions. The results are grouped according to the resources loads for convenience of discussion, for all three hypervisors.

**Variations due to CPU-intensive workload:** The graphs in Fig. 7 show execution time variations of both the mProjectCube and mShrinkCube functions for CPU-intensive workloads, on three hypervisors. In each graph, the Y-axis represents the execution time variation. The X-axis represents

TABLE I. MEAN EXECUTION TIMES OF TASKS OF GALFA-HI WORKFLOW ON VMS WITHOUT INTERFERENCES (AS SHOWN IN FIG. 3a).

| Level | Task | Time (m) |
|---|---|---|
| 1 | mShrinkCube | 3.878 |
| 2 & 5 | mImgtbl | 0.02 |
| 3 | mMakeHdr | 0.02 |
| 4 | mProjectCube | 39.774 |
| 6 | mAddCube | 12.32 |
| 7 | mGetHdr | 0.02 |
| 8 | mViewer | 0.04 |

how many CPU-intensive VMs were running on the server, besides the workflow. The first point of the X-axis is zero, meaning no other VMs were running when the execution time of the function was measured. This execution schedule is shown in Fig. 3a. The next point on X-axis is 2; here two additional CPU-intensive VMs were running at every step of the workflow execution (schedule shown in Fig. 3b). In this way, the workflow is repeatedly executed with increasing number of CPU-intensive VMs. The final point is 8, indicating eight additional CPU-intensive VMs were used, at each step of workflow execution as shown in Fig. 3d.

In Fig. 7, from left to right on the X-axis the interference from the number of CPU-intensive VMs increases. The leftmost point is the execution time of a task without any interference from other VMs. The rightmost point is the execution time of the same task with maximum interference. Fig. 7 shows that both the mProjectCube and mShrinkCube tasks show relatively less execution time variation because of CPU-intensive VMs. It applies to all three hypervisors. On ESXi hypervisor, the execution time of mProjectCube function goes from 38.52 minute (the leftmost point on the graph) to 48.13 minute (rightmost point) due to the addition of 8 VMs, each running a Unixbench benchmark suite (Fig. 7c).

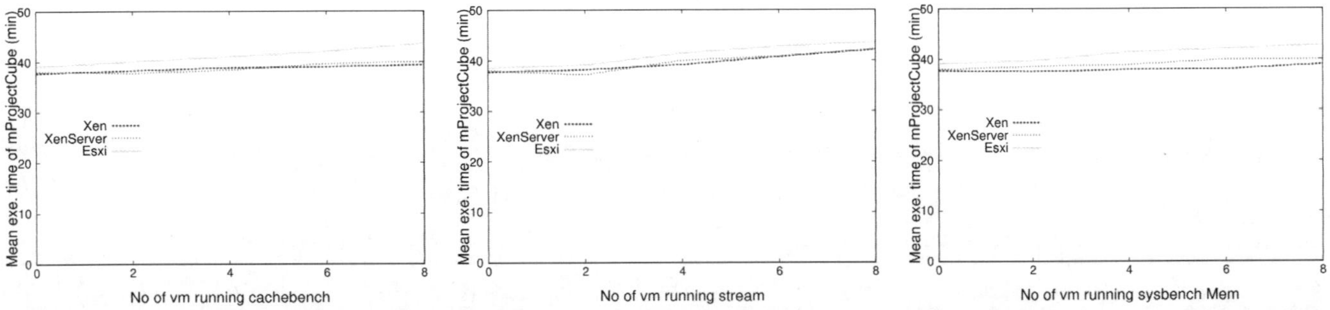


(a) TETV of mProjectCube due to the Cachebench. (b) TETV of mProjectCube due to the Cachebench. (c) TETV of mProjectCube due to the Sysbench Mem.

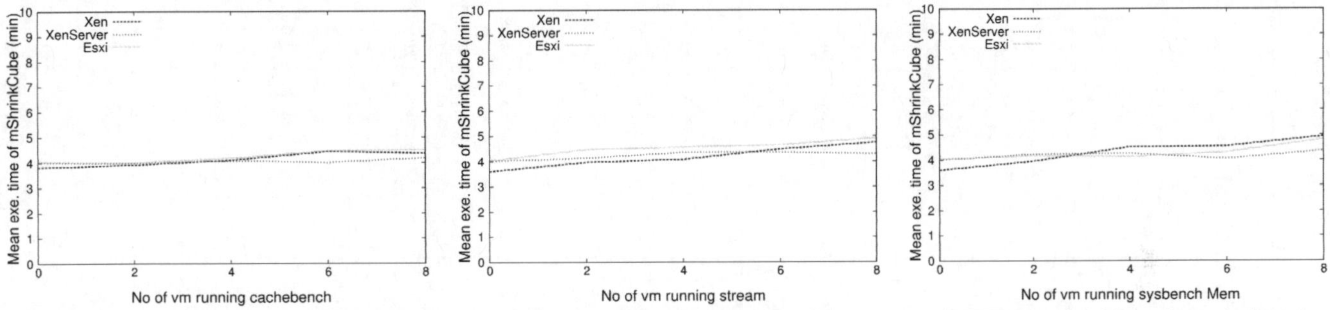


(d) TETV of mShrinkCube due to the Sysbench Mem. (e) TETV of mShrinkCube due to the Stream. (f) TETV of mShrinkCube due to the Stream.

Figure 8. Task execution time variation (TETV) of the mProjectCube and mShrinkCube functions due to the Memory-intensive workload patterns on VMs.

Therefore, consolidation with eight additional CPU-intensive VMs (in this case the Unixbench) causes 24.94% increase in execution time of the mProjectCube function. It is the highest among three hypervisors. For other hypervisors, the effect of CPU-intensive VMs is minimal. For XenServer, the maximum execution time variation among the tasks is suffered by the mProjectCube function again. It is 13.49% and caused when consolidated with eight VMs running Sysbench CPU tests (Fig. 7b). For Xen, the mProjectCube function also shows the maximum variation among the tasks; it is 6.15%. In this case, eight VMs with Unixbench were consolidated with the function (Fig. 7c).

**Variations due to memory-intensive workload:** Fig. 8 shows the execution time variations of two previous functions, due to the memory-intensive workload on VMs. For all three hypervisors, the maximum execution time variations are shown by the mProjectCube function. In all three cases, it is consolidated with VMs running the Stream benchmark (Fig. 8b). The execution time increase of ESXi, XenServer, and Xen hypervisors are 24.24%, 11.02%, and 11.56%, respectively.

**Variations due to I/O-intensive workload:** During VM consolidation experiments, the I/O-intensive tasks tend to show a greater degree of resource contention. That is why more I/O-intensive benchmarks have been used in the experiments, compared to other types. Fig. 9 shows the execution time variations of the mProjectCube and mShrinkCube functions, due to consolidation with five different I/O-intensive benchmarks.

The VMs with video servers cause huge execution time variation for both functions, on all three hypervisors (Fig. 9b). Consolidation with eight VMs with video servers, increases the execution times of mProjectCube function for ESXi, XenServer, and Xen by 683.30%, 705.83%, and 588.96%, respectively. The video servers also have similar effects on the mShrinkCube function, on all three hypervisors (Fig. 9e). The execution time increase of the mShrinkCube function for ESXi, XenServer, and Xen are 901.92%, 774.10%, and 595.34%, respectively. For other I/O-intensive benchmarks, similar results can be obtained, too. For example, Fig. 9a shows the execution time variation of the mProjectCube function due to file-servers on all three hypervisors. Here, execution time increases for ESXi, XenServer, and Xen are 154.39%, 114.78%, and 92.95%, respectively. The file-servers similarly cause execution time variation for the mShrinkCube function, too. Execution time increases for ESXi, XenServer, and Xen are 411.13%, 347.96%, and 343.15%, respectively.

From the presented execution time variation data, it is clear that combination of benchmarks can be used to create resource contention patterns for tasks on VMs. The significance of the above findings is discussed next.

**Discussion:** The experimental results show that resources like CPU, memory, and I/O, all have dissimilar effects on the task execution time. It is observed for all three hypervisors. From the results, it is clear that execution time variation directly depends on the cumulative resource requirement of the VM of a server. It has been shown previously that, by profiling the execution times of co-located VMs, it is possible to predict the task execution time variations [22]. The resource requirement of the VMs, play a huge part on execution time variations. For example, both the mProjectCube and mShrinkCube functions are I/O-intensive tasks, and they have the maximum variation for I/O-intensive benchmarks. The objective of experiments is to show that the proposed framework can profile the tasks of a scientific workflow for any workload and hypervisor. Thus, it can help to design and carry out experiments, with VM placement and consolidation for scientific workflows.

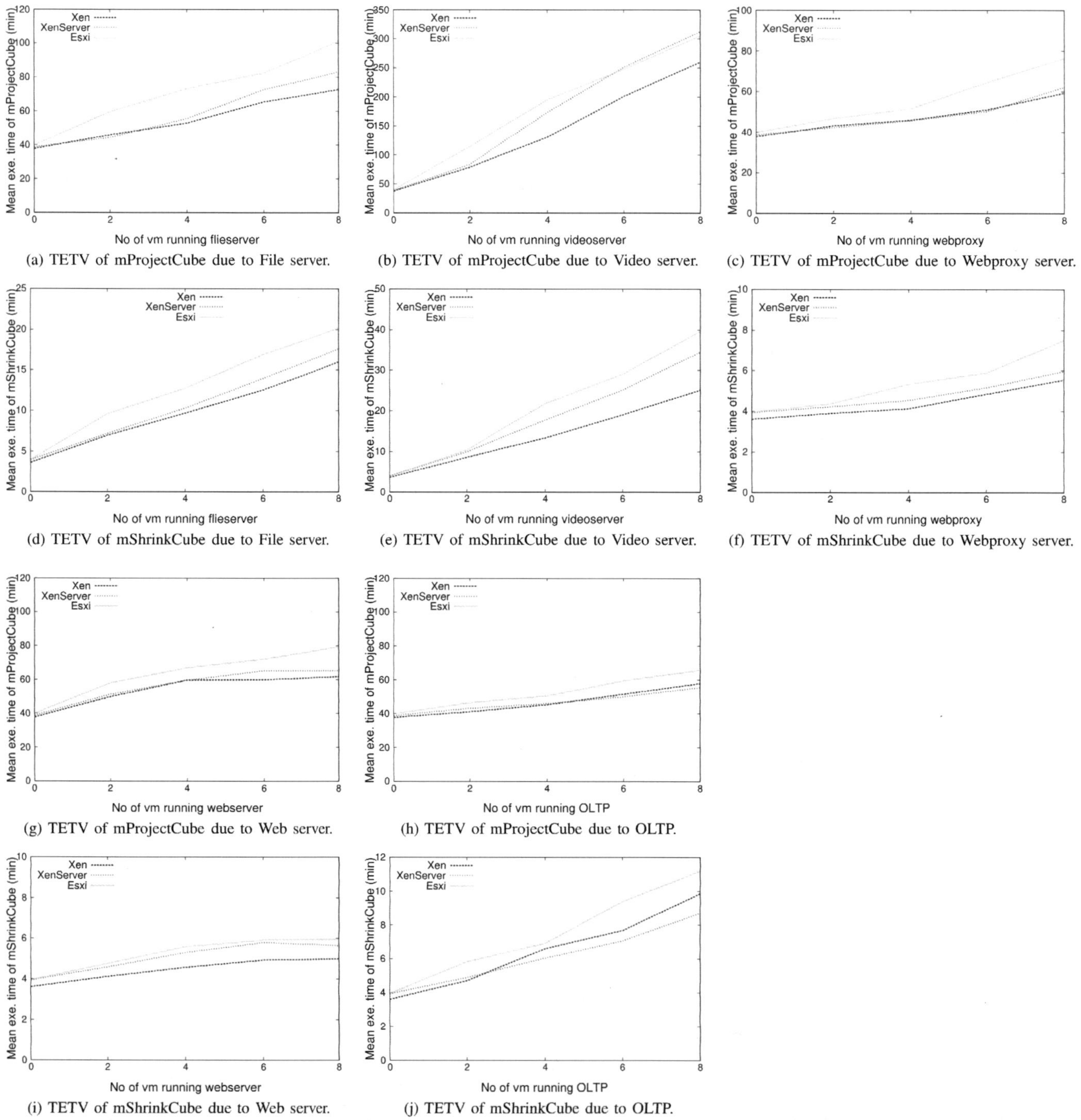


(a) TETV of mProjectCube due to File server.
(b) TETV of mProjectCube due to Video server.
(c) TETV of mProjectCube due to Webproxy server.
(d) TETV of mShrinkCube due to File server.
(e) TETV of mShrinkCube due to Video server.
(f) TETV of mShrinkCube due to Webproxy server.
(g) TETV of mProjectCube due to Web server.
(h) TETV of mProjectCube due to OLTP.
(i) TETV of mShrinkCube due to Web server.
(j) TETV of mShrinkCube due to OLTP.

Figure 9. Task execution time variation (TETV) of the mProjectCube and mShrinkCube functions due to the I/O-intensive workload patterns on VMs.

## VII. RELATED WORK

Related works can be divided into two broad categories. The first category of works deals with application performance efficiency on the Cloud and VM consolidation [1]–[5]. However, the works do not provide any general framework to do experiments with tasks of parallel applications. In contrast, this work provides a simple and effective framework that can be used for such purposes on the Cloud.

The second category of works are the Cloud management, maintenance and scheduling software [6]–[17]. They can provide many high-level functionalities for the Cloud, like running selected jobs periodically. Many complex operations can be performed with a few commands. However, they hide a lot of operational complexity from the users, and do not allow low-level control over the task execution process. On the other hand, this framework offers an easy interface for executing tasks according to the requirement of the experiment.

Although the works outlined above provide some high-level support for running tasks on the Cloud, none of them combines all the low-level functionality to carry out experiments with VM consolidation. To the best knowledge of the authors, no other previous work has proposed any such framework to perform experiments with workloads on the Cloud.

## VIII. Future work and Conclusion

There are a lot of issues related to the Cloud that depend on consolidation, like application performance, energy efficiency, and resource utilization. There are no theoretical solutions available for these problems. Further experiments are required to obtain practical solutions. In future, the framework would be used to setup larger scale of experiments with various scientific workflows and diverse sets of resource usage patterns.

This work presents the design and implementation of a framework for performing experiments with execution time variation of scientific workflows on the Cloud. Profiling of task execution time is required for better understanding of VM consolidation. The framework can apply any resource usage patterns to the tasks of a workflow. It does not compile the input files, rather it behaves like an interpreter. There is no well-accepted theocratical model for task execution variation due to consolidation. Therefore such a framework would help to set up large-scale experiments for achieving a practical solution.

To show the capability of the framework to perform experiments a real life data-intensive workflow and three hypervisors have been used. Resource contention patterns for VMs have been created by combining various types of benchmarks. The framework is lightweight and implemented in Java. It can be run on any OS and can connect to any hypervisor or the Cloud. An extensive set of experiments has been done on three well-known hypervisors, and results are successfully retried, demonstrating that the framework is capable of executing any workflow schedule and resource usage pattern on multiple hypervisors. This framework can be a powerful tool for experimenting with VM consolidation and task execution time variation of workflows.

## References


[1] T. Zhu, D. S. Berger, and M. Harchol-Balter, "SNC-Meister: Admitting More Tenants with Tail Latency SLOs," in *SoCC '16*, (New York, NY, USA), pp. 374–387, ACM, 2016.

[2] R. Taft, W. Lang, J. Duggan, A. J. Elmore, M. Stonebraker, and D. DeWitt, "STeP: Scalable Tenant Placement for Managing Database-as-a-Service Deployments," in *SoCC '16*, (New York, NY, USA), pp. 388–400, ACM, 2016.

[3] R. R. Sambasivan, I. Shafer, J. Mace, B. H. Sigelman, R. Fonseca, and G. R. Ganger, "Principled Workflow-centric Tracing of Distributed Systems," in *SoCC '16*, (New York, NY, USA), pp. 401–414, ACM, 2016.

[4] K. Rajan, D. Kakadia, C. Curino, and S. Krishnan, "PerfOrator: Eloquent Performance Models for Resource Optimization," in *SoCC '16*, (New York, NY, USA), pp. 415–427, ACM, 2016.

[5] C.-C. Hung, L. Golubchik, and M. Yu, "Scheduling Jobs Across Geo-distributed Datacenters," in *SoCC '15*, (New York, NY, USA), pp. 111–124, ACM, 2015.

[6] F. Guthrie, S. Lowe, and K. Coleman, *VMware vSphere Design*. Alameda, CA, USA: SYBEX Inc., 2nd ed., 2013.

[7] M. Liebowitz, C. Kusek, and R. Spies, *VMware vSphere Performance: Designing CPU, Memory, Storage, and Networking for Performance-Intensive Workloads*. Alameda, CA, USA: SYBEX Inc., 1st ed., 2014.

[8] D. E. Williams, *Virtualization with Xen(Tm): Including XenEnterprise, XenServer, and XenExpress: Including XenEnterprise, XenServer, and XenExpress*. Syngress Publishing, 2007.

[9] G. Ahmed, *Implementing Citrix XenServer Quickstarter*. Packt Publishing, 2013.

[10] N. Sabharwal and R. Shankar, *Apache CloudStack cloud computing: leverage the power of CloudStack and learn to extend the CloudStack environment*. Community experience distilled, Birmingham: Packt Publ., 2013.

[11] K. Jackson, *OpenStack Cloud Computing Cookbook*. Packt Publishing, 2012.

[12] A. Paradowski, L. Liu, and B. Yuan, "Benchmarking the Performance of OpenStack and CloudStack," in *ISORC '14*, (Washington, DC, USA), pp. 405–412, IEEE CS, 2014.

[13] S. A. Baset, "Open Source Cloud Technologies," in *SoCC '12*, (New York, NY, USA), pp. 28:1–28:2, ACM, 2012.

[14] P. Sempolinski and D. Thain, "A Comparison and Critique of Eucalyptus, OpenNebula and Nimbus," in *CLOUDCOM '10*, (Washington, DC, USA), pp. 417–426, IEEE Computer Society, 2010.

[15] D. Nurmi, R. Wolski, C. Grzegorczyk, G. Obertelli, S. Soman, L. Youseff, and D. Zagorodnov, "The Eucalyptus Open-Source Cloud-Computing System," in *CCGRID '09*, (Washington, DC, USA), pp. 124–131, IEEE Computer Society, 2009.

[16] S. Pousty and K. Miller, *Getting Started with OpenShift*. O'Reilly Media, Inc., 1st ed., 2014.

[17] D. Bernstein, "Cloud Foundry Aims to Become the OpenStack of PaaS," *IEEE Cloud Computing*, vol. 1, no. 2, pp. 57–60, 2014.

[18] M. Silva, M. R. Hines, D. Gallo, Q. Liu, K. D. Ryu, and D. d. Silva, "CloudBench: Experiment Automation for Cloud Environments," in *IC2E '13*, (Washington, DC, USA), pp. 302–311, IEEE CS, 2013.

[19] C. Delimitrou, D. Sanchez, and C. Kozyrakis, "Tarcil: Reconciling Scheduling Speed and Quality in Large Shared Clusters," in *SoCC '15*, (New York, NY, USA), pp. 97–110, ACM, 2015.

[20] J. E. G. Peek, C. Heiles, K. A. Douglas, M.-Y. Lee, J. Grcevich, S. Stanimirovi, M. E. Putman, E. J. Korpela, S. J. Gibson, A. Begum, D. Saul, T. Robishaw, and M. Kro, "The GALFA-HI Survey: Data Release 1," *The Astrophysical J. Supplement Series*, vol. 194, no. 2, p. 20, 2011.

[21] G. B. Berriman, J. Good, B. Rusholme, and T. Robitaille, "The Next Generation of the Montage Image Mopsaic Engine," in *American Astronomical Society Meeting Abstracts*, vol. 227 of *American Astronomical Society Meeting Abstracts*, p. 348.13, Jan. 2016.

[22] M. Ahmed and A. Y. Zomaya, "Profiling and Predicting Task Execution Time Variation of Consolidated Virtual Machines," in *CLOUD COMPUTING '16*, pp. 103–112, IARIA, 2016.

[23] JCraft, Inc., "JSch - Java Secure Channel." URL: `http://www.jcraft.com/jsch/`. Retrieved: May, 2016.

[24] H. Park, S. Baek, J. Choi, D. Lee, and S. H. Noh, "Regularities Considered Harmful: Forcing Randomness to Memory Accesses to Reduce Row Buffer Conflicts for Multi-core, Multi-bank Systems," *SIGPLAN Not.*, vol. 48, pp. 181–192, Mar. 2013.

[25] J. Ouyang, J. R. Lange, and H. Zheng, "Shoot4U: Using VMM Assists to Optimize TLB Operations on Preempted vCPUs," in *VEE '16*, (New York, NY, USA), pp. 17–23, ACM, 2016.

[26] C. C. Eglantine, *NBench*. TypPRESS, 2012. ISBN: 9786136257211.

[27] Z. Ou, H. Zhuang, J. K. Nurminen, A. Ylä-Jääski, and P. Hui, "Exploiting Hardware Heterogeneity Within the Same Instance Type of Amazon EC2," in *HotCloud '12*, (Berkeley, CA, USA), pp. 4–4, USENIX Association, 2012.

[28] P. J. Mucci, K. London, and P. J. Mucci, "The CacheBench Report." URL: `www.earth.lsa.umich.edu/ keken/benchmarks/cachebench.pdf`. Retrieved: February, 2016.

[29] J. D. McCalpin, "Memory Bandwidth and Machine Balance in Current High Performance Computers," *IEEE CS TCCA Newsletter*, pp. 19–25, Dec. 1995.

[30] OpenSolaris Project, "Filebench." URL: `http://filebench.sourceforge.net/wiki/index.php/Main_Page`. Retrieved: February, 2016.

# Closest-Pairs Query Processing in Apache Spark

George Mavrommatis, Panagiotis Moutafis, and Michael Vassilakopoulos
Data Structuring & Engineering Lab
Dept. of Electrical & Computer Eng.
University of Thessaly
Volos, Greece
e-mail: {gmav, pmoutafis, mvasilako}@uth.gr

***Abstract*— Processing of spatial queries when the datasets involved are big can be accomplished efficiently in a parallel and distributed environment. The (K) Closest-Pair(s) Query, KCPQ, is a common query in many real-life applications involving geographical, or, in general, spatial data. It consists in finding the (K) closest pair(s) of objects between two spatial datasets. Although, processing of this query has been studied extensively for centralized environments, few solutions have appeared for parallel and distributed frameworks. Apache Spark is such a framework that has several advantages compared to other popular ones, like Hadoop MapReduce. In this work, we present an algorithm for processing the KCPQ in Apache Spark and experimentally study its efficiency and scalability, using big real-world datasets.**

***Keywords-Closest-Pairs Query; Spatial Query Processing; Apache Spark.***

## I. INTRODUCTION

Geographic information systems (GIS) [1] have been around for several decades. They provide the means for storing, querying, analyzing and sharing geographic information and have proven valuable in many modern application domains (e.g., disaster management, mapping, urban planning, transportation planning, environmental impact analysis, etc.).

The term *Big Data* refers to unprecedented volumes of data. Such data appear in numerous modern applications, like applications based on sensor networks, commercial transactions, social media, web searches, etc.

Spatial databases [2] are specialized databases that support storage and querying of multidimensional data (usually, points, line-segments, regions, polygons, volumes). They are core elements of GIS. Processing of spatial queries can become very demanding if the volume of data on which such a query is applied is big, or if the volume of the combinations of data objects that need to be examined for answering such a query are big.

Some typical spatial queries are: the point query, range query, spatial join, and nearest neighbor query [3]. Spatial Join queries find all pairs of spatial objects from two spatial data sets that satisfy a spatial predicate, like intersects, contains, is enclosed by, etc. Nearest neighbor queries locate the spatial object(s) that is (are) nearest to a query object. The (K) Closest-Pair(s) Query, KCPQ, discovers the (K) closest pair(s) of object(s) (usually ordered by distance), between two spatial datasets. It combines join and nearest neighbor queries: like a join query, all pairs (combinations) of objects from the two datasets are candidates for the result, and like a nearest neighbor query, the (K) smallest distance(s) is (are) the basis for inclusion in the result (and the final ordering) [4][5]. The KCPQ can be very demanding if the datasets involved are big, since all the combinations of pairs of objects from the two datasets are candidates for the result.

For example, we can use two spatial datasets that represent the archaeological sites and popular beaches of Greece. A KCPQ (K=10) can discover the 10 closest pairs of archaeological sites and beaches (in increasing order of their distances). The result of this query can be used for planning tourist trips in Greece that combine traveler's interest for history / civilization and leisure / enjoyment.

Parallel and distributed computing using shared-nothing clusters on big data has been very popular during last years. Hadoop MapReduce [6] is an open-source software framework for storing data and running applications on such clusters. MapReduce is file-intensive and computing nodes intercommunicate only through sorts and shuffles. Therefore, MapReduce is suitable mostly for non-iterative batch processing jobs.

Apache Spark [7] is another, more recent, open-source cluster-computing framework with an application programming interface based on Resilient Distributed Datasets (RDDs), read-only multisets of data items distributed over the cluster of machines [8]. It was developed to overcome limitations of the MapReduce paradigm. Through RDDs a form of distributed shared memory is provided and the implementation of iterative algorithms is facilitated.

Recently, the utilization of main memory in processing KCPQs on big datasets in centralized systems has been explored [9][10]. In this paper, considering ideas and methods presented in [9][10] we present a Spark based algorithm for computing KCPQs. Moreover, we present an experimental analysis of the performance of this algorithm, based on big real-world datasets.

More specifically, in Section II, we review related frameworks and work; in Section III, we present Spark basics, we define the query that we study and present our algorithm; in Section IV, we present experimentation settings and the results of experiments we performed for studying the efficiency of the proposed method. Finally in the last section, we present our conclusions and our plans for future work.

## II. RELATED WORK

Extensions of Hadoop MapReduce supporting large-scale spatial data processing include Parallel-Secondo [11], Hadoop-GIS [12] and SpatialHadoop [13]. In [14], a general plane-sweep approach for processing KCPQs in SpatialHadoop and a more sophisticated version that first computes an upper bound of the distance of the K-th closest pair from sampled data points have been presented.

Extensions of Apache Spark supporting large-scale spatial data processing include

- SpatialSpark [15], that has been used for spatial join algorithms based on point-in-polygon test and on point-to-polyline distance,
- GeoSpark [16], that supports spatial range, join query and K nearest neighbors queries,
- LocationSpark [17], that offers several spatial query operators, including range search, K nearest neighbors, spatio-textual operations, spatial join and K nearest- neighbors join, and
- Spatial In-Memory Big data Analytics (SIMBA) [18] that supports box and circle range queries, K nearest neighbors, distance joins and K nearest-neighbors joins.

The KCPQ has been actively studied in centralized environments, when both [19][20][21][22][23], one [24], or none [9][10] of the two spatial datasets are indexed. Two improvements of the classic plane-sweep algorithm and a new plane-sweep algorithm, called Reverse Run Plane Sweep, were proposed in [9] for processing KCPQs when the two datasets are not indexed and reside in main-memory. In [10], it is assumed that the (big) spatial datasets reside on secondary storage and are progressively transferred in main memory, by dividing them in strips, for processing utilizing the methods of [9].

To the best of our knowledge, the only work about KCPQs in a parallel and distributed framework is [14]. In this paper, we utilize ideas presented in [9][10] to develop an algorithm for processing KCPQs in Spark, by separating data in strips and utilizing a plane-sweep approach within each strip.

## III. CLOSEST-PAIR QUERIES IN SPARK

Hadoop MapReduce processing is based on pairs of Map and Reduce phases. It is an excellent solution for one-step computations on massive datasets, but it not very efficient for problems that require multi-step computations. The output of each step is stored in the distributed file system, so that it can be used as input for the next, or one of the following steps. Replication and disk storage contribute to slowing down the overall computation. Apache Spark (or more simply, Spark) is an alternative to Hadoop MapReduce. It's not intended to replace Hadoop MapReduce, but to extend it and allow the development of solutions for different big data problems and requirements.

Spark was written in the Scala Programming Language. Programmers usually write Spark applications in Java, Scala, or Python, with Scala being the most popular choice. In addition to Map and Reduce operations, it supports SQL queries, streaming data, machine learning and graph data processing. These capabilities can be combined in a data pipeline. With Apache Spark, programmers can combine data pipelines in a directed acyclic graph (DAG). The DAG execution model can be seen as a generalization of the MapReduce model. Moreover, Apache Spark supports in-memory data sharing across DAGs. Spark can run on top of an existing Hadoop Distributed File System (HDFS) infrastructure. Spark also supports lazy evaluation and holds intermediate results in memory. When data cannot fit in memory, disk storage is utilized. In fact, part of a data set can reside in memory and another part on secondary storage. The RDD is the fundamental data structure of Spark. An RDD can be resembled to a database table. It is a read-only collection of objects, partitioned in the cluster of machines.

In the following, we present our algorithm for KCPQ processing in Spark. Let two datasets P and Q of spatial objects, a positive natural number K and a distance function between pairs of data objects formed from P and Q (members of the Cartesian Product of P and Q). The KCPQ discovers K pairs of data objects formed from P and Q that have the K smallest distances between them among all pairs of data objects that can be formed from P and Q.

Since distances between objects may not be unique, note that if multiple pairs of objects have the same K-th distance value between them, more than one sets of K different pairs of objects can form the result of this query. The presented algorithm can be easily tailored to report all such sets of pairs.

Our algorithm, for 2-dimensional space (for the ease of exposition), consists of the following steps:

- Samples $P' \subset P$ and $Q' \subset Q$ are taken from both datasets P and Q. Spark function sample() was used for sampling the two datasets. sample() takes a parameter, *fraction*, denoting the expected size of the sample as a fraction of the dataset in question.
- Proper keys are set, a join between P' and Q' is performed and the K closest pairs (CP) among all joined pairs are computed. Function join() is also provided by the Spark API.
- Let *Bound* be the K-th smaller distance as computed previously. This is our pruning factor.
- Both datasets are divided into n strips [25] corresponding to ascending intervals along one of the dimensions (x axis dimension is assumed in the following, w.l.o.g) (Fig. 1). Partitioning of each of the two datasets into strips of unequal width was done by sampling, calculating the border points from samples and applying the partition to the whole dataset.

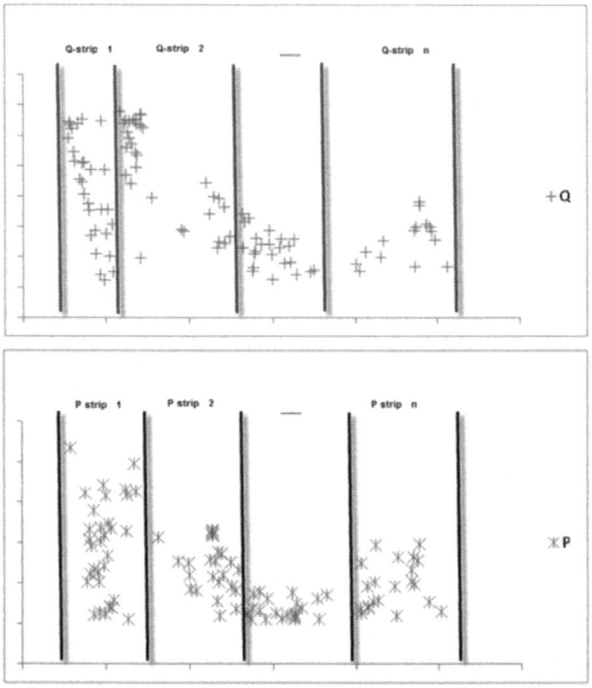


Figure 1. Strips partitioning.

- Using the distance of the K-th CP (*Bound*), combinations of strips are examined. If two strips reside in a distance smaller than the distance of the K-th CP, the pairs between data objects of these two strips are examined as candidates for the result. To achieve this, all (vertical) pairs of strips from P and Q are being evaluated with respect to their x-axis distance combined to the *Bound*.
- Pairs of strips are classified into two categories, namely eligible and not eligible for further processing. The first category consists of two major subcategories: overlapping pairs, and pairs that do not overlap but have their x-distance smaller than *Bound*. For example, (Fig. 2) strip Ps1 from P overlaps with strips Qs1 and Qs2 from Q. Furthermore, the x-distance between Ps1 and Qs3 is d1 < *Bound*, while the x-distance between Ps1 and Qs4 is d2 > *Bound* (this holds for every consecutive Q-strip). Therefore, the eligible pairs that we derive for Ps1 are (Ps1,Qs1), (Ps1,Qs2) and (Ps1,Qs3). These pairs, and all other pairs identified by this procedure, are the pairs that will be subject to computation by the cluster. Note, that in the case of pairs like (Ps1, Qs3), not all points from both strips need to be considered. For example, since we know a bound for the K CPs, we can use it as a pruning condition with the filter() function of Spark to reduce Qs3 to these points that their x-axis distance from Ps1 is smaller than *Bound*.

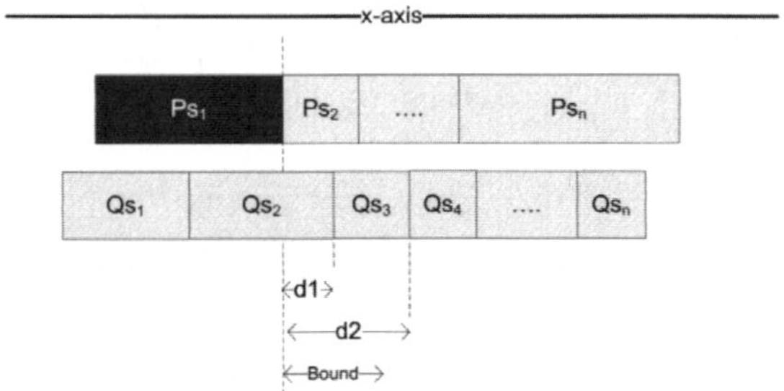


Figure 2. Eligible pairs of strips.

- Within each eligible pair of strips from P and Q Plane-sweep is applied for calculating K CPs storing the result in a maximum binary heap (maxHeap) [9][10]. A separate maxHeap is utilized for each partition. *Bound* is sent -we used Spark's broadcast() function- to all workers and they use it as stop condition for the plane sweep algorithm.
- All binary heaps are used to form a RDD consisting of tuples (*distance*, *Ppoint*, *Qpoint*). Since all eligible pairs of strips contain all pairs of points from P and Q that may contribute to the final solution and there are no duplicate pairs, taking the first (sorted on distance) K tuples with the smaller distances, yields the final (and exact) solution.

## IV. EXPERIMENTAL EVALUATION

To evaluate the performance of our algorithm, we used the following three big real 2d datasets from OpenStreetMap [13]: WATER resources consisting of 5,836,360 line segments, PARKS (or green areas) consisting of 11,504,035 polygons and BUILDINGS of the world consisting of 114,736,611 polygons. To create sets of points, we used the centers of the Minimum Bounding Rectangles (MBRs) of the line-segments from WATER and the centroids of polygons from PARK and BUILDINGS.

All experiments were conducted on a cluster of 5 nodes. Each node has 4 vCPUs running at 2.1GHz, with a total of 16GB of main memory per node, running Ubuntu Linux 16.04 operating system. Spark 2.0.2 running on Hadoop 2.7.2 Distributed File System (HDFS) was used as our parallel computing system. The block size of HDFS was 128 MB. Of the 5 computing nodes, one was running the NameNodes for Hadoop and Master for Spark, while the remaining four (4 nodes x 4 vCPUs = 16 vCPUs) were used as HDFS DataNodes and Spark Worker nodes. Java openjdk ver. 1.8.0 and Scala code runner ver. 2.11 were used.

All datasets are text files stored in HDFS. Each line contains an index and a pair of coordinates. We used the textFile() function of Spark to import the data, and set the numPartitions parameter to 4. Typically, Spark creates one partition for each block. We can increase the number of partitions by passing a larger value but it is not possible to have fewer partitions than the blocks of each file.

We measured total execution time (i.e., response time) in seconds (sec) that expresses the overall CPU, I/O and communication time needed for the execution of each query.

We varied sample fraction (values used: 0.01, 0.001, 0.0001), the number of closest pairs K (values used: 1, 10, 100, 1000, 10000) and the number of strips per dataset (values used: 16, 32, 64, 80). We tested all possible combinations between the three datasets (PARKSxWATER, BUILDINGSxWATER, BUILDINGSxPARKS). In the following, we present a representative portion of the results.

In Fig. 3, we present the results for the PARKSxWATER combination, for K=10, using different combinations of n (number of strips) and f (sample fraction). As one can see, there is a tradeoff between total execution time and the time taken in order to sample the datasets and compute the value of *Bound*. If we take a small fraction of the datasets as sample, the bound we compute is not tight enough, therefore leading to increased KCPQ computation time. The larger the fraction of dataset we sample, the better (lower) is the upper bound we obtain. But if we surpass a certain fraction, then the computation of Bound in the sample dominates the total computation time.

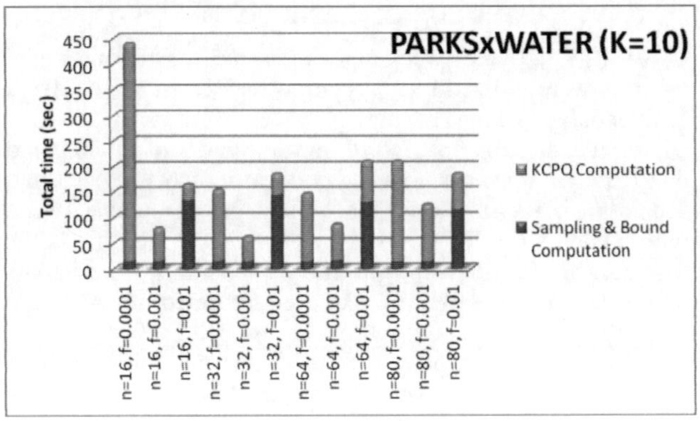


Figure 3. Effect of sample fraction.

Studying the results of the above experiment leads us to the observation that a fraction of 0.001 is a good selection for the rest of our experiments.

In Fig. 4, we present the results for the PARKSxWATER combination, for all K values, using 16, 32, 64 and 80 strips per each dataset. Initially, we ran each experiment independently from the others. We faced a problem, though. Phase two (the KCPQ computation) relies on the value of *Bound* that is computed in phase one. Since phase one uses a randomly selected sample, *Bound* is likely to be different in each experiment. In order to be able to extract better and comparable results, we used the following procedure for our second experiment: having taken into consideration that phase one is independent from phase two, we conducted the first phase of the experiment (K=1, n=16, fraction=0.001) and saved the calculated value of *Bound*. In all consecutive phases of the experiment, the bound was computed as usual, but we used the value we found in the first phase of the experiment instead.

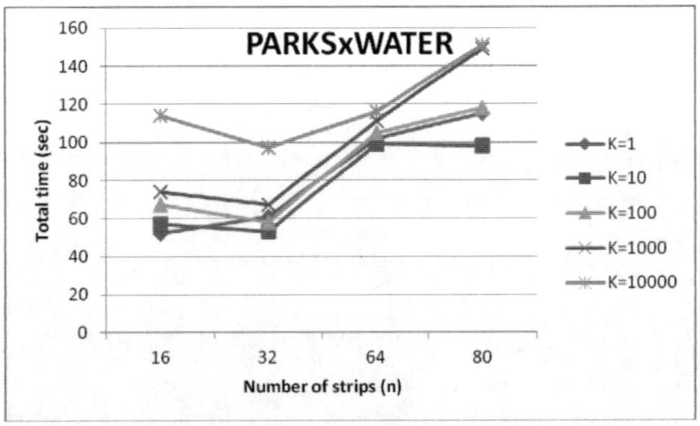


Figure 4. KCPQ (PARKS x WATER).

As we observe, n = 32 strips seems to be the optimal partitioning size for PARKS and WATER datasets, although n = 16 gives similar results. As K increases from 1 to 10,000, execution time is hardly affected, in some cases showing a tendency to increase slightly, as expected.

We conducted our third experiment in order to see to what extent the value of *Bound* affects the running time of the algorithm. We used a value for *Bound* with an order of magnitude 10 times greater than the one previously used. Time for sampling and bound computation was taken into account when counting total running time. Fig. 5 presents the running times compared to the ones that were measured in the previous experiment.

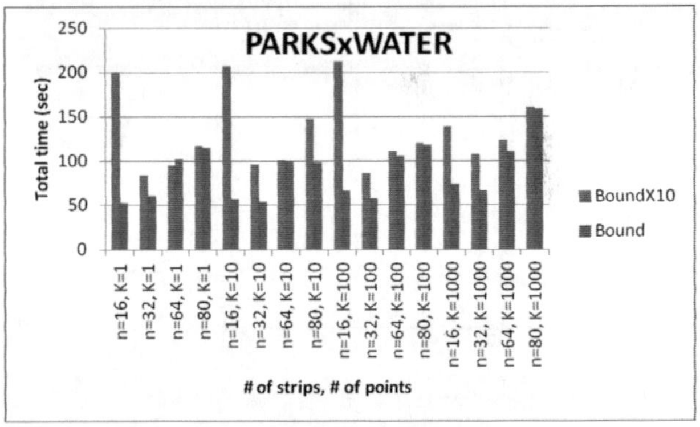


Figure 5. Effect of lower Bound

From the above comparison, we conclude that the value of *Bound* is more significant than the number of strips and the number of partitions provided to Spark as well.

In Fig. 6, we present the results for the BUILDINGSxWATER combination, for several K values using 8, 16, 32 and 64 strips per each dataset (once again *Bound* was set to a constant value for all cases, to an order of e-05). We observe than in the case of BULDINGS the algorithm gives better results for a lower number of strips than in the case of PARKS.

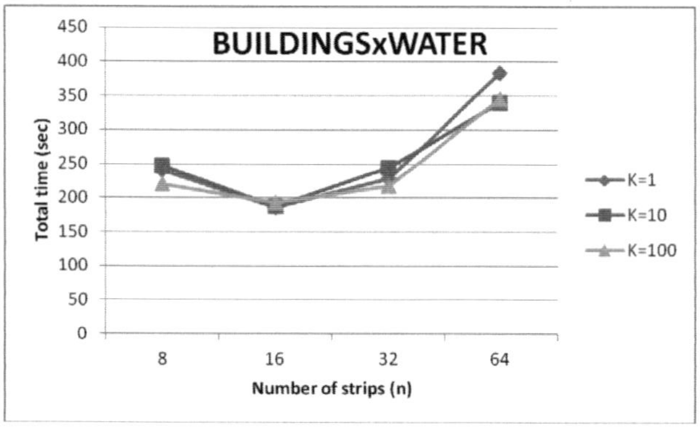


Figure 6. KCPQ (BUILDINGS x WATER).

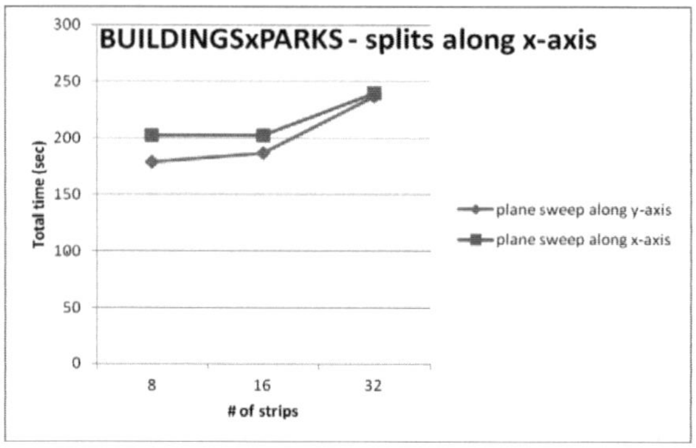


Figure 8. Split axis vs plane sweep axis.

We believe that this has to do with a combination of the characteristics of the multi-parametric system we study (hardware, HDFS, Spark, our algorithm). The combination of available cores, starting partitions, Spark partitioning procedures, number of strips that lead to a number of eligible pairs, results to an increased number of partitions that in the cases of larger n (strips) overwhelms the computing cluster.

In all previously described experiments, both datasets are being sliced into strips along x-axis (y-axis can also be used). Then, within each partition created by the eligible pairs of points from P and Q, plane sweep is applied along the other axis, in our case the y-axis. It is possible to slice the strips and sweep along the same axis (Fig. 7).

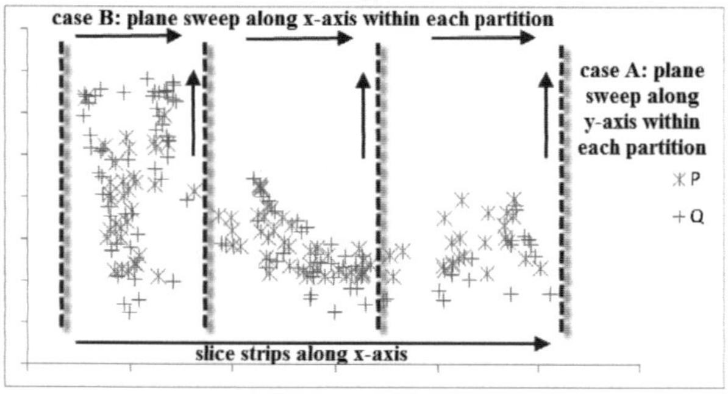


Figure 7. Strips Slice & Plane Sweep cases.

In order to check which choice is better (slicing and sweeping along the same or different axes), we conducted our next experiment. We used the BUILDINGSxPARKS combination with n = 8, 16, 32, K =10 and fraction f = 0.001.

We ran each combination three times, used the average time and the results are being presented in Fig. 8.

The results seem to lead us to the conclusion that "crossing" the axes for slicing and sweeping is more efficient than working on the same axis. This observation is clearer in the cases of smaller strips number, when the algorithm gives the best results.

Although this is consistent with other observations we have made during our experiments, we believe that it needs further investigation, an action we plan to take in the near future.

## V. CONCLUSIONS AND FUTURE PLANS

In [9][10], plane-sweep algorithms and separation of data in strips were utilized for computing KCPQs in a centralized environment, taking advantage of main memory. In this paper, we present an algorithm for Spark, a parallel and distributed framework that supports in-memory processing, separating data in strips and processing by plane sweep within each strip. To the best of our knowledge, this is the first KCPQ algorithm in Spark. By conducting experiments on big real datasets we have explored the performance of our algorithm.

In the future, we plan to further elaborate this algorithm by exploring different ways to create strips of variable size and investigate partitioning schemes for Spark to reduce the need for examining combinations of data that reside in different strips and also reduce the network communication traffic. Another important research direction is finding a better, fast and stable technique that will yield a good upper bound for the KCPQ problem in a parallel system. We also plan to compare the performance of our algorithm against other solutions working in parallel and distributed environments. Finally, we plan to study the scalability of our algorithm.

## REFERENCES


[1] S. Shekhar and H. Xiong, Encyclopedia of GIS. Springer, 2008.

[2] P. Rigaux, M. Scholl, and A. Voisard, Spatial databases - with applications to GIS. Elsevier, 2002.

[3] A. Corral and M. Vassilakopoulos, "Query processing in spatial databases," Encyclopedia of Database Technologies and Applications, pp. 511-516, 2005.

[4] A. Corral, Y. Manolopoulos, Y. Theodoridis, and M. Vassilakopoulos, "Closest Pair Queries in Spatial Databases," SIGMOD Conference, pp. 189-200, 2000.

[5] A. Corral, Y. Manolopoulos, Y. Theodoridis, and M. Vassilakopoulos, "Algorithms for processing K-closest-pair queries in spatial databases," Data Knowl. Eng., vol. 49, no. 1, pp. 67-104, 2004.

[6] J. Dean and S. Ghemawat, "MapReduce: Simplified data processing on large clusters," OSDI 2004, pp. 137-150, 2004.

[7] M. Zaharia, M. Chowdhury, M. J. Franklin, S. Shenker, and I. Stoica, "Spark: Cluster computing with working sets," Proceedings of the 2nd USENIX Conference on Hot Topics in Cloud Computing, pp. 10–10, 2010.

[8] M. Zaharia, et al., "Resilient Distributed Datasets: A fault-tolerant abstraction for in-memory cluster computing," NSDI 2012, pp. 15-28, 2012.

[9] G. Roumelis, M. Vassilakopoulos, A. Corral, and Y. Manolopoulos, "A new plane-sweep algorithm for the K-closest-pairs query," SOFSEM 2014, pp. 478-490, 2014.

[10] G. Roumelis, A. Corral, M. Vassilakopoulos, and Y. Manolopoulos, "New plane-sweep algorithms for distance-based join queries in spatial databases," GeoInformatica, vol. 20, no. 4, pp. 571-628, 2016.

[11] J. Lu and R. H. Güting, "Parallel Secondo, Boosting Database Engines with Hadoop," ICPADS 2012, pp. 738-743, 2012.

[12] A. Aji, et al., "Hadoop-GIS: A high performance spatial data warehousing system over MapReduce," PVLDB, vol. 6, no. 11, pp. 1009-1020, 2013.

[13] A. Eldawy and M. F. Mokbel, "SpatialHadoop: A MapReduce framework for spatial data," ICDE 2015, pp. 1352-1363, 2015.

[14] F. García-García, A. Corral, L. Iribarne, M. Vassilakopoulos, and Y. Manolopoulos, "Enhancing SpatialHadoop with closest pair queries," ADBIS 2016, pp. 212-225, 2016.

[15] S. You, J. Zhang, and L. Gruenwald, "Large-scale spatial join query processing in Cloud," ICDE Workshops 2015, pp. 34-41, 2015.

[16] J. Yu, J. Wu, and M. Sarwat, "GeoSpark: a cluster computing framework for processing large-scale spatial data," 23rd ACM SIGSPATIAL/GIS, pp. 70:1-70:4, 2015.

[17] M. Tang, Y. Yu, Q. M. Malluhi, M. Ouzzani, and W. G. Aref, "LocationSpark: A distributed in-memory data management system for big spatial data," PVLDB vol. 9, no. 13, pp. 1565-1568, 2016.

[18] D. Xie, et al., "Simba: Efficient in-memory spatial analytics," SIGMOD Conference 2016, pp. 1071-1085, 2016.

[19] A. Corral, Y. Manolopoulos, Y. Theodoridis, M. Vassilakopoulos, "Algorithms for processing K-closest-pair queries in spatial databases," Data Knowl. Eng., vol. 49, no. 1, pp. 67-104, 2004.

[20] A. Corral, Y. Manolopoulos, Y. Theodoridis, and M. Vassilakopoulos, "Closest pair queries in spatial databases," SIGMOD Conference 2000, pp. 189-200, 2000.

[21] G. R. Hjaltason and H. Samet, "Incremental distance join algorithms for spatial databases," SIGMOD Conference 1998, pp. 237-248, 1998.

[22] H. Shin, B. Moon, and S. Lee, "Adaptive and incremental processing for distance join queries," IEEE Trans. Knowl. Data Eng., vol 15, no. 6, pp. 1561-1578, 2003.

[23] C. Yang and K-I. Lin, "An index structure for improving closest pairs and related join queries in spatial databases," IDEAS 2002, pp. 140-149, 2002.

[24] G. Gutierrez and P. Sáez, "The k closest pairs in spatial databases - When only one set is indexed," GeoInformatica, vol. 17, no. 4, pp. 543-565, 2013.

[25] A. Aji, H. Vo, and F. Wang, "Effective spatial data partitioning for scalable query processing," CoRR abs/1509.00910, 2015.

# A Raster SOLAP Designed for the Emergency Services of Brussels Agglomeration

Kasprzyk Jean-Paul
SEGEFA
e-mail: jp.kasprzyk@ulg.ac.be

Donnay Jean-Paul
Geomatics Unit
e-mail: jp.donnay@ulg.ac.be

University of Liege
Department of Geography
Liege, Belgium

***Abstract*— In order to quickly reach incident locations, emergency services have to fairly distribute their resources on the territory. This distribution is based on an analysis which depends on heterogeneous spatial data like past interventions (recurring risk), specific geographical places (sporadic risk), road network or socio-economic variables. On the other hand, Spatial Online Analytical Processing (SOLAP) tools are designed for the collection and the analysis of large spatial data sets. In this study, an original raster SOLAP model is implemented for emergency services of Brussels agglomeration. It allows decision-makers to freely generate risk maps (continuous fields), depending on several dimensions (time, intervention type, risk type, etc.), and to compare them with the accessibility of firefighters and ambulances. Simulations can also be performed on resources locations to see their impact on the main accessibility.**

***Keywords-GIS; Risk Analysis; Data Warehouse; Fields; Firefighting.***

## I. INTRODUCTION

In order to quickly reach incident locations, emergency services (including firefighters and medical aids) have to fairly distribute their resources on the territory. This distribution is a complex problem since it has to be adapted to a risk model which depends on heterogeneous spatial data sets: past interventions, population, buildings, road network, etc.

On the other hand, Business Intelligence [8] and Geographic Information Systems (GIS) include efficient tools for the collection and the analysis of large amounts of spatial data. Amongst them, SOLAP Spatial Online Analytical Processing (SOLAP) tools allow decision makers to freely explore spatial data warehouses through interactive maps, tables or charts [1][2]. The information from SOLAP is summarized (aggregated), thus more easily analyzed by the decision-makers. The objective of this research is the design of a SOLAP adapted to the needs of the emergency services of Brussels. Thanks to SOLAP, they should be able to easily collect the data and analyze the risk so as to adequately deploy their resources in the territory of the Brussels agglomeration.

The remainder of this paper is structured as follows. Section II is a state of the art about risk analysis for emergency services (subsection II-A) and SOLAP including explanations about SOLAP basics (subsection II-B). A raster SOLAP model adapted to risk analysis is then deducted from this review of the literature (research hypothesis in subsection II-C). Section III describes the raster SOLAP model developed to reach the research objective. Its main architecture (subsection III-A) is composed on the one hand of a vector data warehouse in charge of data collecting/archiving (subsection III-B), and on the other hand, of several raster data cubes which allows risk calculations by the SOLAP (subsection III-C). The SOLAP model is then validated in section IV by the SOLAP interface, which allows users to explore raster data cubes through interactive risk maps. Section V contains conclusions and perspectives of this paper.

## II. STATE OF THE ART

### A. *Risk Analysis*

Risk can be divided into two distinct categories (and so two distincts models): recurring risk and sporadic risks [9].

Recurring risk is the probability of incidents, which can be estimated from historical interventions. These data are mainly characterized by time, space and intervetion type. In particular, space can be modeled as a field [3][18] thanks to Kernel Density Estimation (KDE) [13]. It is very popular to identify hotspots of punctual events in a continuous space. For instance, it is offenly used by police for crime prevention [7][8]. Moreover, when points are aggregated with KDE, shapes of the hotspots suffer less from the Modifiable Areal Unit Problem (MAUP) [25] than with spatial aggregations, depending on administrative entities (communes, census tracts, etc.).

Sporadic risk does not depend on incidents frequencies, but on specific places that would require important resources from emergency services in the event of an incident: tunnels, schools, hospitals, etc. Once identified, these locations can be incorporated into a multicriteria analysis [11] to determine the sporadic risk, by weighting the human and material damages incurred in their vicinity.

In addition to the probabilistic nature of the recurring risk, it is possible to study the conditions favoring the emergence of the risk, no longer for an operational purpose, but for an urban planning objective. Population density, age of buildings and other environmental variables can be considered in a geographic regression model to explain the frequency of incidents [14].

Once the risk model has been completed, the adequacy of the response by the emergency services can be assessed by the travel times required by the various concerned resources (personnel and specific equipment) to reach the claims sites. This step requires an up-to-date and precise road graph with average speeds adapted to the emergency vehicles.

### B. SOLAP

A SOLAP server allows decision makers to query data hypercubes (also simply called "data cubes") extracted from a data warehouse. Data hypercubes are models of pre-aggregated data depending on several dimensions (for example: month, commune and incident type) [1]: combinations of dimension members define facts, and an aggregated measure is associated to every fact. For example, the combination of January 2016 (member of dimension "month"), fire incident (member of dimension "incident type") and Anderlecht (member of geographical dimension "commune") is a fact with an associated number of incidents (measure).

Users navigate into data hypercubes through interactive tables, charts or maps. Maps can represent spatial facts (defined by at least one geographical dimension like communes), and tables/charts can represent non-spatial facts (defined by non-spatial dimensions like months, incident types, etc.).

The SOLAP server is able to calculate the measure of every possible fact defined at a less detailed level of dimensions than the one stored in the data hypercube (for example, the number of incidents for the whole year 2016 instead of January 2016). This typical SOLAP operation is called "roll up" (on the time dimension in the previous example) and the reverse operation is called "drill down". Filters on dimension members (for instance, facts defined by a specific month of the time dimension) are called "slices" in the SOLAP vocabulary.

Despite the heavy calculations that a "roll up" operation can require, a SOLAP must show quick results. For this purpose, the SOLAP literature proposes different strategies [1] like the precomputing of different hypercubes at different levels of details or the use of different physical structures: hypercubes modelled by arrays (Multidimensional OLAP or MOLAP) [11], by relational tables (Relational OLAP or ROLAP) [20] or both (Hybrid OLAP or HOLAP) [13].

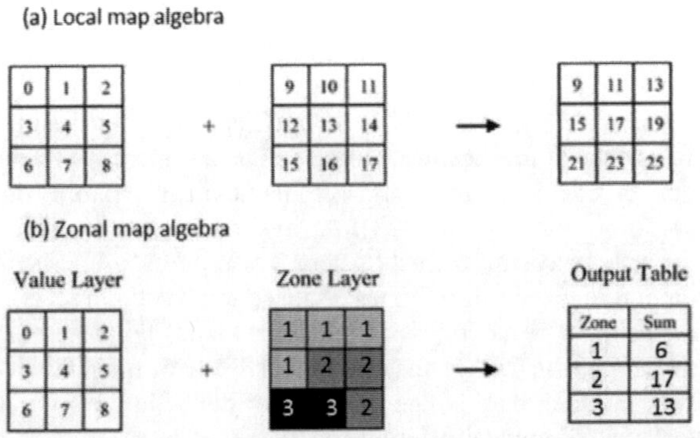


Figure 1. Examples of map algebra operators, adapted from [23]

Most of SOLAP tools are only able to use the vector model to represent spatial facts on maps [16] [29]. However, several researches showed the potential of raster SOLAP [17][18] [20][22] [24] [28]. The raster model is well adapted to the representation of data which are continuous in space (fields). Pixels of a raster can spatially define every type of geographical entities while the vector model uses three different primitives: point, line and polygon. The physical structure of raster is quite similar to MOLAP (arrays of data) and so the SOLAP aggregations can easily be computed by raster functions which are already implemented in most of spatial database management systems (DBMS). The most important functions [23] are local map algebra (Figure 1a) for aggregations on non-spatial dimensions and zonal map algebra (Figure 1b) for aggregations on geographical dimensions. Moreover, as the $X$ and $Y$ dimensions of space are defined in the multidimensional structure of raster SOLAP (a spatial member is a pixel) [17][18], any geographical dimension (for examples: the communes of Brussels) can be imported on the fly as a zone layer during the analysis.

### C. Hypothesis

This distribution of resources for emergency services is a complex problem that requires the design of a risk model. As said in subsection II-A, a risk model integrates spatial data about recurring risk (historical interventions), sporadic risk (hospitals, schools, etc.) and socio-economic characteristics. Then, the risk model has to be confronted to the accessibility of emergency service resources. As said in subsection II-B, SOLAP tools are very useful for the integration and the analysis of large amounts of spatial and heterogeneous data, as required by the risk analysis. In particular, raster SOLAP has important advantages for this study: a continuous representation of a space for recurring risk, a single spatial primitive (pixel) for every type of geographical entities, etc. Therefore, a raster SOLAP can be designed to help emergency services of Brussels to fairly distribute their resources on the territory.

## III. RASTER SOLAP MODEL

### A. *Main architecture*

The main structure of the SOLAP is a typical "Business Intelligence" architecture (Figure 2). Data are extracted from different sources and archived in a spatial data warehouse (subsection III-B). At this stage, data are still in their native vector format. Then, vector data are used to create five raster data cubes (subsection III-C): recurring risk for fires, recurring risk for medical aids, sporadic risks, accessibility of firefighters and accessibility of medical aids. Users can then manipulate these raster cubes in the SOLAP interface to compute different risk maps.

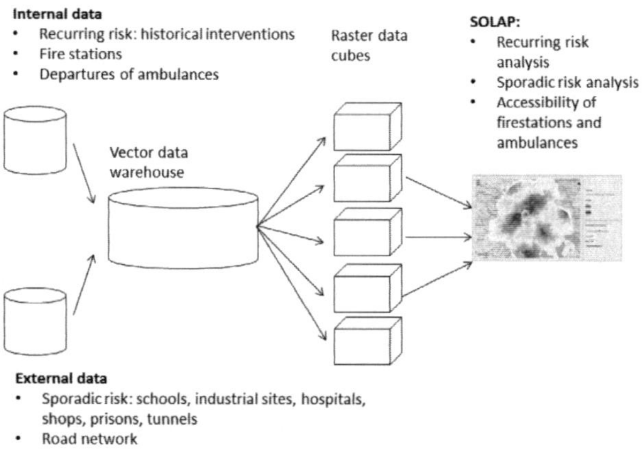


Figure 2. Main architecture of the SOLAP

As mentioned above, spatialized variables of demography, environment, buildings, etc., can also be integrated into the SOLAP for urban planning objective, but this aspect is not developed here.

### B. *Spatial data warehouse*

Some data were directly provided by emergency services of Brussels (internal data):

- fire stations and departures of ambulances georeferenced as points;
- past interventions from 2012 to 2016 georeferenced as points with time and type (the two main categories are fires and medical aids) for recurring risk (around 350 000 incidents).

Some data were obtained from the appropriate suppliers or directly downloaded (open data). A first category of these external data are the ones defined by emergency services as sources of sporadic risk:

- school buildings with more than 1000 students (around 80 points with an attribute "number of students");
- dangerous industrial sites (UE Seveso directive) with a "risk level" attribute (4 points);
- prisons (2 points);
- hospitals with a "number of beds" attribute (around 80 points);
- main shopping zones with a "type" attribute (around 100 polygons) [2];
- tunnels with a length superior to 400m (around 200 polygons).

A second category of external data is the road graph of Brussels extracted from Open Street Map (OSM) [26]. It covers a larger territory than Brussels because the quicker path between two points inside Brussels is not always entirely included in the city (which is surrounded by an important motorway). Arcs are associated to an average speed that was fixed with firefighters of Brussels for each road type of OSM. There is a speed for the two crossing directions in order to model prohibited directions (associated to a very slow speed). Note that OSM road data for Brussels are geometrically based on accurate UrbIS data which are supplied by Brussels Regional Informatics Centre (BRIC) [6].

### C. *Raster Data Cubes*

#### *1) Recurring risk*

Conceptually, the multidimensional structure of a raster data cube can be described by a star schema. Figure 3 is the star schema for recurring risks. It is characterized by three non-spatial dimensions and two spatial dimensions. The raster SOLAP model used in this study, including the management of KDE, is based on [17][18]. Note that recurring risk data cubes about fires or about medical aids are described by the same star schema. Only the members of the "incident type" dimension are different.

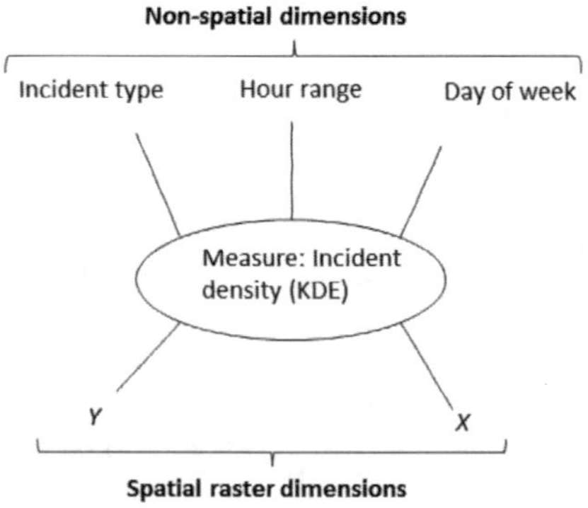


Figure 3. Star schema of a recurring risk data cube

Non-spatial dimensions are incident type, hour range (3 hours) and day of the week. Physically, these dimensions are managed as a ROLAP model [20]: a non-spatial fact is the record of a fact table and the member of each non-spatial dimension describing the fact is stored in a specific attribute (incident type, hour range and day of week). The measure of the non-spatial detailed fact is stored in a raster attribute. The theoretical number of records of the fact table is determined by the Cartesian product of the three non-spatial dimensions. For instance, the raster cube for fire recurring risk should have 224 records (detailed facts): 4 incident types * 8 hour ranges * 7 days of week. This value grows exponentially with the number of dimensions. For this reason, a raster cube cannot involve too many non-spatial dimensions to be able to quickly compute "roll up" aggregations. Note that concretely, the number of detailed facts can be inferior to the theoretical value if the density of the data cube is less than 100% (some detailed facts can have a null measure). This is an advantage of the ROLAP model, which does not have to store null facts (contrary to MOLAP or raster).

Physically, spatial dimensions (*X* and *Y*) are directly managed in the ROLAP measure (a raster attribute). At the raster level, a spatial fact is a pixel which is characterized by a raster measure (the pixel value), a member for *X* and a member for *Y*. These spatial dimensions members are determined by the position of the pixel in the raster array like for MOLAP. Therefore, the raster SOLAP model is also characterized by MOLAP advantages (fast aggregations on arrays) and disadvantages (null pixels have to be stored). Note that every raster of the fact table is characterized by the same resolution (100 m) and the same spatial coverage [16].

When a raster cube is created for recurring risks, a KDE raster is computed for the ROLAP measure of every non-spatial fact with the same parameters: resolution of 100 m, a quartic KDE function and a KDE bandwidth of 500 m (this parameter determines the smoothing of the field). It has been demonstrated [17] that aggregating KDE measures with local map algebra is equivalent to the computation of a KDE with all the points that should be involved in the SOLAP aggregation (if KDE parameters are identical for every non-spatial fact). Therefore, maps resulting from SOLAP operations on these data cubes are KDE fields of recurring risk. They are the result of a simple sum aggregation (local map algebra), then normalized to range from 0 to 100. An example is given by Figure 4. It is a map of recurring risk for indoor fires including all days of the week and all hour ranges.

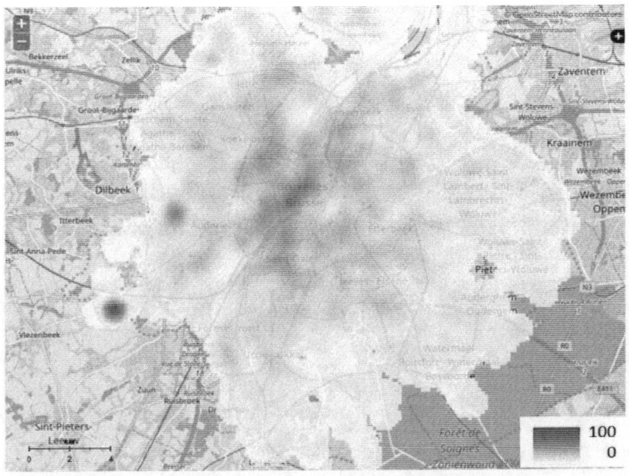


Figure 4. Recurring risk for indoor fires

The other raster data cubes are characterized by a similar star schema for the spatial dimensions (resolution of 100 m). Consequently, only the non-spatial dimensions and the raster measure (pixel value) will be discussed in the following subsections.

2) *Sporadic risks*

The star schema of the raster cube for sporadic risk is only characterized by one non-spatial dimension: the source of risk. Its dimension members are schools, hospitals, tunnels, industrial sites, commercial areas and prisons. When punctual entities (schools, hospitals, industrial sites and prisons) are rasterized, their spatial shape is a buffer of 300 m. For zonal entities (tunnels and shopping zones), the shape of the native polygons is used.

The raster measure is a weight reflecting the risk generated by the source:

- hospitals: number of beds;
- schools: number of students;
- commercial areas: 1 for secondary poles, 2 for primary poles and shopping centers, 3 for "rue Neuve" (a very populated shopping street in Brussels) [2];
- industrial sites: 1 for "low risk" industries and 2 for "high risk" industries in the Seveso description;
- prisons: 1 for all;
- tunnels: 1 for all.

After their rasterisation, these six measures are normalized to range from 0 to 100.

As it is characterized by only one non-spatial dimension (source of risk), the fact table for sporadic risk has only six non-spatial facts (records). The local map algebra operation for the SOLAP aggregation on this dimension is a weighted sum for which weights were determined with the Brussels fire department:

- hospitals: 0.2;
- schools: 0.2;

- commercial areas: 0.1;
- industrial sites: 0.15;
- prisons: 0.2;
- tunnels: 0.15.

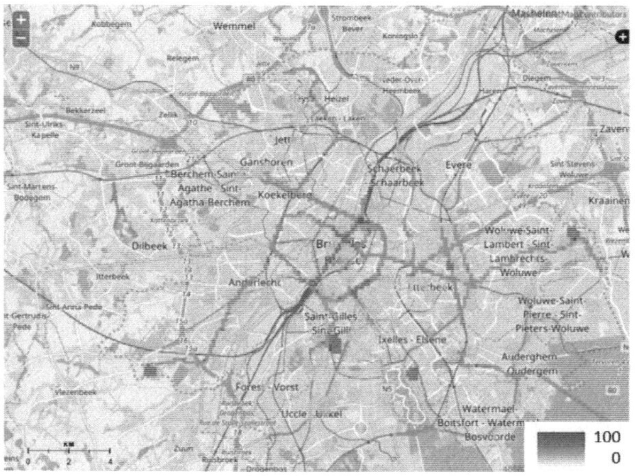


Figure 5. Sporadic risk

Figure 5 shows a map of sporadic risks including all sources (pixels values are normalized to range from 0 to 100).

*3) Resources accessibility*

The star schema of the two raster cubes for resources accessibilities are also characterized by one non-spatial dimension: fire stations for firefighters (first raster cube) and departures of ambulances for medical aids (second raster cube). The measure of a non-spatial fact is a raster modelling the accessibility of a specific resource. The measure of a spatial fact (a pixel value) is the travel time from the resource to the pixel location (in minutes). Note that in some cases, ambulances can start from fire stations too. These particular resources are present in both raster cubes (fire stations and ambulances departures).

When raster cubes are built, measures are calculated in this way. For a specific resource (a non-spatial fact), a vector routing algorithm calculates a travel time value for every node of the OSM graph through the quicker path. Then an interpolated value is associated to every pixel of a raster covering the region of interest.

As asked by emergency services, users can choose one threshold amongst three different values: 4 minutes, 7 minutes and 10 minutes. Beyond these thresholds, the accessibility of a resource is considered as null. Therefore, during the analysis, every pixel exceeding the chosen threshold is set to null. After that, remaining pixel values are transformed in order to obtain an accessibility index which grows when it gets closer to the resource and ranges from 0 to 100 (1).

$$p' = (100 - \frac{p}{\max} * 100) \tag{1}$$

In (1), $p'$ is the new pixel value, $p$ is the original pixel value (travel time in minutes) and *max* is the maximum pixel value in the raster.

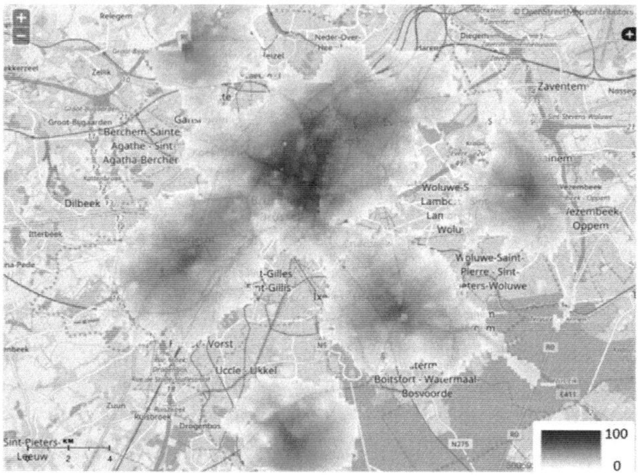


Figure 6. Accessibility of fire stations with a travel time threshold of 7 minutes

Finally, the local map algebra operation for the SOLAP aggregation on the resource dimension is a weighted sum. The weights can be set on the fly by the user in order to obtain an accessibility field adapted to previous risk maps. They reflect the amount of humans/materials present in the fire station or ambulance departure. For instance, Figure 6 shows an accessibility map of all fire stations with equal weights and with a travel time threshold of 7 minutes (pixels values are normalized to range from 0 to 100).

## IV. VALIDATION

The raster SOLAP for emergency services of Brussels is implemented with open source tools only. The spatial DBMS PostgreSQL/PostGIS manages the vector data warehouses and the raster cubes. SOLAP aggregations are implemented with map algebra functions of PostGIS [28]. MapServer [21] delivers map results through Web Map Services (WMS) which are shown in the SOLAP web interface.

The SOLAP interface allows the user to do "slice" and "roll up" operations on the five raster cubes (recurring risk for fires and medical aids, sporadic risk, accessibility of firefighters and ambulances). It is also possible to add new resources and directly see their effect on the accessibility: after setting the new location on the interactive map, PGRouting (PostGIS extension for routing algorithms) calculates all the quicker paths and then PostGIS raster builds the new measure in the accessibility raster cube. As previously said, weights of fire stations and ambulance departures can also be modified on the fly. In addition to the risk analysis, emergency services are thus able to perform simulations about the spatial distribution of their resources.

The tool is also designed to easily integrate new data for future analysis. The creation of all raster cubes is automatized, including recurring risk (a KDE function has been implemented in PL/PGSQL language).

Let's remember that SOLAP is a powerful tool to easily explore data. It gives all the keys that form the basis of a complete risk analysis: different sources of risk described through time/space dimensions and accessibility of emergency services resources. It is then up to the user to compare and interpret the different risk maps obtained with the SOLAP.

## V. CONCLUSIONS AND PERSPECTIVES

The aim of this research was the design of a SOLAP for emergency services of Brussels agglomeration, which have to fairly distribute their resources on the territory (fire stations and ambulances). After a review of the literature about risk analysis and SOLAP, a raster SOLAP model was chosen to reach the objective. Following this model, a data warehouse was created to collect and archive spatial data involved in the risk study of Brussels (historical interventions, specific places of risk, road network, etc.). Several raster data cubes were then created to model the different aspects of the analysis: recurring risk, sporadic risk, accessibility of firefighters and ambulances. Finally, the model was validated by the implementation of the SOLAP architecture and its interface. It allows users to freely explore data by applying SOLAP operations ("slices" and "roll up") on raster data cubes through interactive risk maps. Moreover, simulations can be performed on resources locations and weights (reflecting the amount of present human/materials) to see their effect on the main accessibility.

This research highlighted the interest of raster SOLAP for risk analysis. In comparison with vector SOLAP (most of current SOLAP tools), raster allows a continuous visualization of space adapted to the analysis of recurring risk through KDE maps. Moreover, all types of spatial entities can be described by a single primitive: the pixel. Raster SOLAP is quite easy to implement with spatial DBMS because raster operations (map algebra) can be directly used for data aggregations. More generally, SOLAP allows decision makers to proceed to risk analysis in a user-friendly environment which also includes the automatic integration of new data for future analyzes.

Finally, further improvements could be provided to this study. First, it was only possible to set one average speed to every arc of the road graph with the available data. This does not reflect the real situation of Brussels because the important congestion of the road network mainly depends on time dimensions: hour of the day and day of the week. With richer data, it would be easy to integrate these dimensions in raster cubes for accessibility. Secondly, for technical reasons, it was not possible to extract the durations of interventions from historical data. If it was available, the risk analysis could take it into account as a weight for each point when KDE measures are computed. Indeed, the requisition time of emergency resources is an important factor in risk analysis.


## ACKNOWLEDGMENT

The authors would like to express their thanks to SIAMU ("Service d'Incendie et d'Aide Médicale Urgente de la Région de Bruxelles-Capitale") for providing this interesting case study.


## REFERENCES


[1] Y. Bédard, "Spatial OLAP", Forum annuel sur la R-D, Géomatique VI: Un monde accessible, Montréal, November 1997.

[2] Y. Bédard, "Beyond GIS: Spatial Online Analytical Processing and Big Data", The 2014 Dangermond Lecture, Santa-Barbara, 2014.

[3] S. Bimonte, Integration of geographic information in data warehouses and online analysis: from modeling to visualization (Intégration de l'information géographique dans les entrepôts de données et l'analyse en ligne: de la modélisation à la visualisation), PhD, Institut National des Sciences Appliquées de Lyon, Lyon, 2007.

[4] S. Bimonte and M. A. Kang, "Towards a model for the multidimensional analysis of field data, in Proceedings of the Fourteenth east European conference on advances in databases and information systems", B. Catania, M. Ivanovic and B. Thalheim, Eds. Berlin : Springer-Verlag, 2010, pp. 58-72.

[5] Brussels-Capital Region. Retail Observatory 2011, available at <http://urbanisme.irisnet.be/pdf/observatoire-du-commerce-2011>, retrieved [January, 2017].

[6] BRIC, Brussels Regional Informatics Centre — CIRB-CIBG-BRIC, Available at <http://cirb.brussels/>, [retrieved : January, 2017]

[7] S. P. Chainey, L. Tompson, and S. Uhlig, "The utility of hotspot mapping for predicting spatial patterns of crime", Security Journal, vol. 21, 2008, pp. 4-28.

[8] S. P. Chainey, "Examining the influence of cell size and bandwidth size on kernel density estimation crime hotspot maps for predicting spatial patterns of crime", Bulletin of the Geographical Society of Liege, vol. 60, 2013, pp. 7-19.

[9] T. Chee et al., "Business Intelligence systems: state-of-the-art review and contemporary applications, Symposium on Progress in Information and Communication Technology", Kuala Lumpur, 2009, pp. 96-101.

[10] P. Chevalier et al, Locating fire stations: An integrated approach for Belgium, Socio-Economic Planning Sciences, Vol. 46(2), 2012, pp. 173–182.

[11] E. F. Codd, S. B Codd, and C. T. Salley, Providing OLAP (On-line Analytical Processing) to User-Analysts: An IT Mandate, E.F Codd and Associates, 1993.

[12] M. N. Demers. GIS Modeling in Raster. New York : John Wiley & Sons, 2001.

[13] M. Di Salvo, M. Gadais, and G. Roche-Woillez, The kernel density estimation : methods and tools (L'estimation de la densité par la méthode du noyau: méthodes et outils), Lyon : Certu, 2005.

[14] B. Espinasse, Data warehouses: OLAP systems: ROLAP, MOLAP and HOLAP (Entrepôt de données: Systèmes OLAP: ROLAP, MOLAP et HOLAP). Ecole Polytechnique Universitaire de Marseille, 2013.

[15] N. Guldaker and P. O. Hallin, Spatio-temporal patterns of intentional fires, social stress and socio-economic

determinants: A case study of Malmö, Sweden, Fire Safety Journal, Vol. 70, 2014, pp. 71–80.

[16] Intelli³, available at <http://www.intelli3.com>, [retrieved : january, 2017].

[17] ISO 19123. Geographic information - Schema for coverage geometry and functions, 2005.

[18] J. P. Kasprzyk, Integration of spatial continuity in the multi-dimensional structure of a data warehouse – raster SOLAP (Intégration de la continuité spatiale dans la structure multidimensionnelle d'un entrepôt de données – SOLAP raster), PhD, Université de Liège, 2015, Available at <http://hdl.handle.net/2268/182360>.

[19] J. P. Kasprzyk and J. P. Donnay, A raster SOLAP for Visualization of crime data fields. GEOProcessing 2016 : The Eighth International Conference on Advanced Geographic Information Systems, Applications, and Services, Venice, 24-28 april 2016, pp. 109-117.

[20] R. Kimball and M. Ross, The Data Warehouse Toolkit: The Definitive Guide to Dimensional Modeling, Third Edition, New York : John Wiley and Sons, 2013.

[21] J. Li, L. Meng, F. Z. Wang, W. Zhang, and W. Cai. "A Map-Reduce-enabled SOLAP cube for large-scale remotely sensed data aggregation", Computers and Geosciences, vol. 70, 2014, pp. 110-119.

[22] Mapserver 7.0.0 beta1 documentation, available at <http://mapserver.org/>, [retrieved: march, 2016].

[23] R. McHugh, Integration of the matrix structure in spatial cubes (Intégration de la structure matricielle dans les cubes spatiaux), Master thesis. Université Laval, Québec, 2008.

[24] J, Mennis, R. Viger, and C. D. Tomlin, "Cubic Map Algebra functions for spatio-temporal analysis, Cartography and Geographic Information Systems", vol. 30, no. 1, 2005, pp. 17–30.

[25] M. Miquel, Y. Bédard, and A. Brisebois, "Conception of geospatial data warehouses from heterogeneous sources: application example in forestry" (Conception d'entrepôts de données géospatiales à partir de sources hétérogènes : Exemple d'application en foresterie), Ingénierie des Systèmes d'Information, vol. 7, no. 3, 2002, pp. 89-111.

[26] S. Openshaw, The modifiable areal unit problem. Norwick (Norfolk), Geo Books, 1983.

[27] Open Street Map, Open Street Map, Available at <https://www.openstreetmap.org/>, [retrieved: January, 2017].

[28] M. Plante, Towards matrix cubes supporting on the fly spatial analysis in decision support (Vers des cubes matriciels supportant l'analyse spatiale à la volée dans un contexte décisionnel), Master thesis, Université Laval, Québec, 2014.

[29] P. Racine and S. Cumming, Store, manipulate and analyze raster data within the PostgreSQL/PostGIS spatial database. FOSS4G, Denver, September 2011.

[30] Spatialytics, Open Source GeoBI, available at <http://www.spatialytics.org/>, [retrieved: January, 2017].

# Sensor Selection for Resource-Efficient Query Execution in IoT Environments

Maria G. Koziri
Dept. of Computer Science
Univ. of Thessaly
Lamia, Greece
email: mkoziri@uth.gr

Thanasis Loukopoulos
Dept. of Computer Science and Biomedical Informatics
Univ. of Thessaly
Lamia, Greece
email: luke@dib.uth.gr

***Abstract*—In an IoT environment, the geographically dispersed sensors that are eligible for participating in a spatial query, can scale to the orders of millions or even billions. Therefore, judiciously selecting among the candidates is of paramount importance to reduce query complexity. Such selection must minimize the total resources used while maintaining the highest possible accuracy in results. In this paper, we turn our attention to the problem of assigning query filters over a subset of the available sensor nodes, assuming that queries are resident in the system, e.g., performing monitoring activities. We present a rigorous problem formulation that captures the dependencies between query accuracy, and resource consumption, focusing in particular on energy consumption. The relevant decision problem is shown to be NP-complete, thus, we propose a heuristic based on the greedy method to solve it. Simulation experiments show that compared to an algorithm that performs random assignments, significant improvement by more than 100% (resource wise) is expected.**

***Keywords-sensor networks; IoT; sensor selection; query plan; energy efficiency; resource consumption.***

## I. INTRODUCTION

As the number of smart devices has exceeded the population of earth and is still growing at a fast pace, the premise of IoT [5] is to enable (among others) the interoperability of the various devices that could act as potential sensors and/or actuators. At the same time, the advent of cyber physical systems (CPS) [8] that combine the physical sensors and actuators with the cyber world provide a novel ground for smart applications where the needs for interoperability and efficient resource allocation are of paramount importance.

Of particular interest in such huge scale systems is the problem of efficient spatial query execution. Consider for instance a system that gathers temperature information at the various city districts and sends warnings to health authorities in the case of extreme conditions. A simple strategy whereby all the available sensors are involved in the query (assuming a large number of them), will likely lead to waste of resources at the sensors and increased network load. In contrast, using only a subset of the available sensors per involved district location, might lead to results of almost equal quality, while saving resources.

In this paper, we consider a generic sensor system running monitoring spatial queries that involve (among others) sensor locations. We tackle the problem of sensor selection, with the goal of achieving sufficient query accuracy, while minimizing the total energy consumed, thus, improving the lifetime of the sensing nodes (assuming they operate on battery). Specifically, we illustrate a rigorous formulation for the problem and propose a greedy algorithm to solve query–sensor assignment.

The remaining of the paper is organized as follows. Section II discusses the related work. The problem formulation is illustrated in Section III, while a greedy heuristic approach is presented in Section IV. Experimental results are included in Section V. Finally, Section VI concludes the paper.

## II. RELATED WORK

Our work is also closely related to in-network query processing where the problem is to assign the operators comprising a query in the network nodes. In [4] and [14], operator placement was discussed in the context of WSNs with the aim of optimizing routing cost in the query tree, while in [25] a more generic approach that aims at placing general purpose application trees is proposed.

The effects of query operator placement are largely dictated by data availability in the processing node. Techniques, such as caching [10] and data replication [13] were studied in the past in order to move data closer to where they will be required. In [26], operator placement is considered together with data caching. Query caching is also the aim of [12] where the potential of caching OLAP queries at the level of Internet proxies was examined, while in [18] caching is considered at the level of a single cell in a cellular network.

Much research has been devoted in the past on developing suitable middleware and programming frameworks in the context of wireless sensor networks. Example works include the systems described in [11][19][24] to name a few. [19] provides an adaptive mechanism for efficient data fusion and filtering. Optimal resource allocation for filtering in a distributed system is discussed in [2]. The systems of [11] and [24] are broader in scope in the sense that they model an application as a set of communicating mobile agents, that can carry any type of functionality, e.g., sensing, actuating, aggregating or controlling etc. Both systems attempt to reduce network overhead using different algorithmic techniques. Another system of similar scope, i.e., mobile agent framework for WSN is [1]. Compared to [11] and [24], it tackles equivalent application scope, nevertheless, it lacks similar mechanisms for network communication reduction. In the context of IoT, agent based systems include [3] and [7]. The major challenge tackled by these systems is the interoperability of heterogeneous sensing and computing nodes. As demonstrated by the systems the agent framework provides a suitable abstraction layer for integrated applications.

Adaptive resource management in sensor networks is discussed in [6], [15] and [23]. In [23], the grouping of sensors into predefined number of clusters is discussed. [6] proposes an adaptive scheme that dynamically adjusts sampling rate in the sensor network, while [15] discusses resource/sensor allocation to cope with peaks in sampling rates. A survey on the issue of adaptive sensor network organization can be found in [21]. Of particular interest is the case where the sensor network is comprised of cameras meaning that the data to be transmitted is of high volume compared to for example monitoring temperature. In [22], methods to efficiently perform monitoring over a camera network are discussed, while [9] is rather orthogonal, studying the reduction in network consumption that is achievable in social media networks by using new video coding standards. It is worth noting that social media comprise key components of cyber physical systems and therefore any resource savings are cumulative to the ones achieved at the sensor network level.

In a previous work of ours [17], we implemented a framework that enabled for communication and coordination of various smart devices through the remote invocation of applications on them. In this paper, we envision that a voluntary participation scheme is in effect and that all the required functionality by each participant is coded as a native application. This is for instance the case with smart city environments such as [16]. A central administration entity tracks the geographic locations of participants, for instance by using some of the efficient spatial indexing schemes proposed in the literature, e.g., [20] and is responsible for selecting the nodes to participate in a system query. In the sequel, we describe the criteria and the optimization problem induced by the aforementioned selection.

## III. PROBLEM FORMULATION

Let $Q$ be the total number of queries to be executed in the system. Each query $Q_i$ has $S_i$ selection predicates. Let $S$ be the total number of predicates from all queries in the system. Clearly:

$$S = \sum_{i=1}^{Q} S_i \qquad (1)$$

Assuming a total ordering of the $S$ predicates, we denote with $F_k$ the $k^{th}$ such predicate. Let $A$ be a binary $Q\times S$ matrix encoding whether the predicate $F_k$ is used by $Q_i$ as follows: $A_{ik}=1$ iff $Q_i$ contains $F_k$, otherwise, $A_{ik}=0$. Each $F_k$ can be assigned over a number of sensing nodes (if compatible), resulting into multiple streams of data (equaling the assigned sensors) being transmitted to a base station for filtering and joining. This model reflects the scenario where sensing nodes have direct Internet connections, e.g., smart devices under cellular networks.

Let the total number of participating sensing nodes be $N$, and $N_j$ denote the $j^{th}$ such, assuming a total ordering of them. Let a binary $N\times S$ matrix $C$ encode whether a node $N_j$ is compatible with $F_k$ predicate as follows: $C_{jk}=1$ iff $N_j$ is compatible with $F_k$ and $C_{jk}=0$, otherwise. We should note that a node might be compatible with more than one predicates. To explain it, consider a query that returns the average temperature and humidity from two different location areas. The query can be viewed as containing four predicates, i.e., the combinations of the two locations and the two measured parameters. Depending on the measurement power of a sensing node it can participate in one or more predicates (max two if location areas are disjoint).

Each $N_j$ has a resource level $r(N_j)$ representing a generic metric of the node's processing power or energy levels in case nodes run on battery and energy preservation is deemed the most important factor. Similarly, each predicate $F_k$ requires a resource consumption of $r(F_k)$. We would like to mention that assuming constant resource consumption by query predicates is not far from reality. For instance, in camera networks, video feeds are usually transmitted and processed at bitrates that remain almost constant.

In order for a query $Q_i$ to execute properly, a predicate $F_k$ must be assigned to at least $R_{ik}$ nodes. Clearly $R_{ik}=0$ iff $A_{ik}=0$. Let $B$ be a $Q\times S\times N$ matrix encoding the potential query benefit, whereby $B_{iku}$ is the benefit of assigning $u$ sensors at the $F_k$ predicate for $Q_i$. We assume that: $B_{iku}=0$ for all $u<R_{ik}$ and $B_{iku}>0$ for $u\geq R_{ik}$.

Finally, let a Boolean matrix $X$ of size $N\times S$ encode the predicate to node assignment as follows: $X_{jk}=1$ iff $F_k$ is assigned to $N_j$ and 0 otherwise. We are now in position to formulate the selection problem as a two function optimization one, whereby the first function aims at maximizing query benefit and the second function aims at minimizing the maximum proportional resource reduction at a node. The following equations depict the target functions:

$$D1 = \max\{\frac{\sum_{k=1}^{S} X_{jk} r(F_k)}{r(N_j)}, \quad 1 \leq j \leq N\} \qquad (2)$$

$$D2 = \sum_{i=1}^{Q}\sum_{k=1}^{S} A_{ik} B_{iku} \mid u = \sum_{j=1}^{N} X_{jk} \qquad (3)$$

Therefore, the problem can be posed as follows: *Find X such that (2) is minimized and (3) is maximized, subject to the following constraints*:

$$\sum_{j=1}^{N} X_{jk} \geq R_{ik} \ , \forall 1 \leq i \leq Q, \forall 1 \leq k \leq S \qquad (4)$$

$$X_{jk} \leq C_{jk} \ , \forall 1 \leq j \leq N, \forall 1 \leq k \leq S \qquad (5)$$

$$\sum_{k=1}^{S} X_{jk} r(F_k) \leq r(N_j), \forall 1 \leq j \leq N \qquad (6)$$

Constraint (4) effectively dictates that a sufficient number of sensors must be allocated to each predicate. Constraint (5) captures compatibility restrictions between predicates and sensors. Notice that an incompatible node ($C_{jk}=0$) leads to $X_{jk}=0$, i.e., the predicate will not be assigned to the node. Constraint (6) captures node capacity, i.e., it forbids the assignments to a node that would require resource consumption greater than the available one.

Before closing the section we would like to mention that the two objectives *D*1 and *D*2 are conflicting with each other. It is easy to observe that *D*1 is minimized when equality holds in (4), while *D*2 is maximized when all eligible sensors participate in a predicate (assuming that $B_{iku}$ entries grow monotonically to $u$).

When optimizing two target functions one can resort to designing algorithms that produce a set of Pareto optimal solutions to choose from. Instead, we decided to convert the two function optimization problem into a single function optimization one by introducing a weighting constant $\alpha$. In particular, let $min\{B_{ik}\}$ denote the (minimum) benefit when $u=R_{ik}$ and $max\{B_{ik}\}$ the maximum such value when:

$$u = \sum_{j=1}^{N} C_{jk} \tag{7}$$

Then, $b_{ik}$ denotes the average max to min benefit ratio for a predicate $F_k$ at $Q_i$ as follows:

$$b_{ik} = max\{B_{ik}\}/min\,\{B_{ik}\} \tag{8}$$

For each predicate we calculate the benefit to resource ratio (let $r_{ik}$) as follows:

$$h_{ik} = \left(\sum_{j=1}^{N} C_{jk}\right)/R_{ik} \tag{9}$$

$$r_{ik} = b_{ik}/h_{ik} \tag{10}$$

Clearly, (8) and (9) hold if $F_k$ is used by $Q_i$, i.e., $R_{ik}\neq 0$. Then we can get an estimation of the total benefit to resource consumption ratio as follows:

$$r = \frac{\sum_{k=1}^{S}\sum_{\forall i}^{A_{ik}=1} r_{ik} r(F_k)}{\sum_{k=1}^{S} r(F_k)} \tag{11}$$

When comparing the maximum and minimum assignment policies $r$ represents the ratio of benefit gains to resource consumption increase. Thus, we can identify the constant $\alpha$ as a proportion of $r$ (depicting how much query benefits are favored over resource consumption).The following two equations summarize the problem formulation which now targets at maximizing the composite function *D*:

$$a = dr \tag{12}$$

$$D = \frac{a}{D1} + D2 \tag{13}$$

Solving the problem as formulated using (13) (but also in the formulation that uses (2) and (3)) can be shown to be NP-hard. In particular, it can be shown that it contains a 2-processor scheduling component as far as (2) is concerned. For this reason we resort to heuristics in order to compute solutions. In the sequel, we describe one such heuristic.

## IV. Greedy Algorithm

The algorithm presented in this section is based on the greedy paradigm. It works in two steps. In the first step, it covers the constraint expressed in (4), i.e., assign just enough sensors to meet the demand for each predicate. This is done with respect to constraints (5) and (6) as follows. First, all predicates are sorted according to $r(F_k)$. Then, starting with the one with the highest resource requirement, it assigns it to $R_{ik}$ different sensors in an iterative manner. At each iteration, all eligible sensors are considered and the assignment that incurs the minimum cost as per (2) is selected.

Having satisfied constraint (4) the algorithm then proceeds by optimizing (13) in an iterative manner. At each iteration all possible predicate to sensor assignments are considered and the one that maximizes most (13) is selected and implemented. The process continues until no eligible sensor-predicate assignments exist or (13) can't be further improved.

## V. Experiments

We conducted simulation experiments using the following setup. We fixed the number of queries (unless otherwise stated) to 100, each with a predicate number varying uniformly between 3 and 10. Predicates required between 20 and 100 sensing nodes (randomly chosen) to execute properly and incurred resource consumption between 1 and 10 units. We assumed a total number of sensing nodes equaling 10,000, with each of them being compatible to 1/10[th] of the total predicates (randomly selected). Sensing nodes had resource capacity of 100 load units.

We compared the performance of greedy algorithm as opposed to random selection for the case where each predicate $F_k$ must be assigned to $R_{ik}$ nodes exactly. Results depict the average of 10 runs.

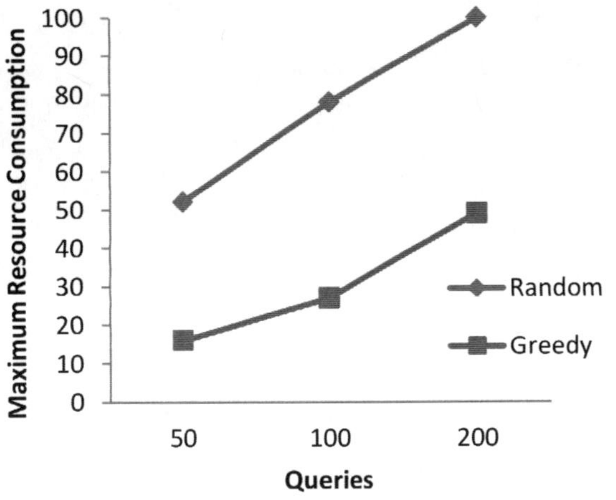


Figure 1. Maximum resource consumption for increasing number of queries (sensor nodes=10,000).

Figure 1 shows the results for the baseline scenario of 100 queries over 10,000 sensors as well as the performance when the number of queries are doubled or halved keeping the rest of the setup the same. It is evident that the performance difference between Greedy and Random is significant. In most cases, Greedy incurs a maximum resource consumption of less than half compared to Random. As expected peak resource consumption rises to the number of queries introduced in the system.

To further confirm the viability of the proposed heuristic in Figure 2 we plot the performance of Greedy and Random as the number of available sensors increases. Notice, that the maximum resource consumption with Greedy exhibits a steeper decline compared to Random when moving from the baseline scenario to the one having double the sensors.

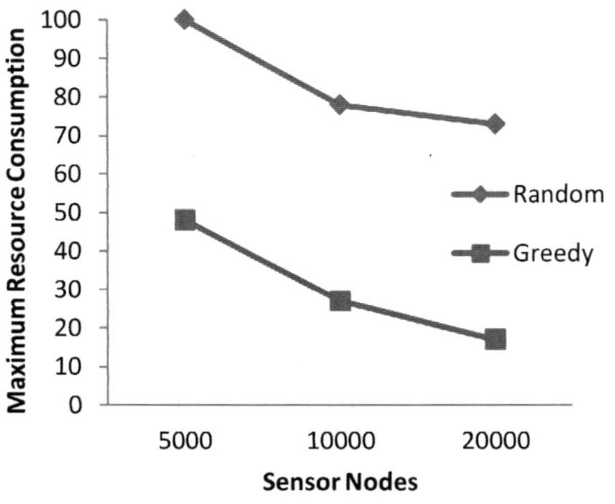


Figure 2. Maximum resource consumption for increasing number of sensor nodes (queries=100).

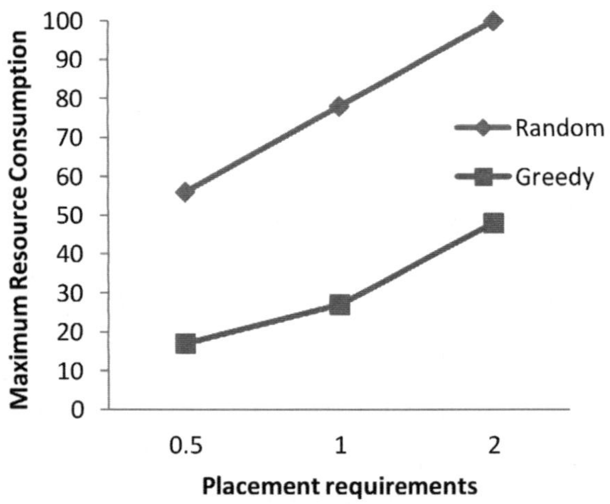


Figure 3. Maximum resource consumption for increasing placement requirement of predicates (queries=100, sensor nodes=10,000).

Last, in Figure 3 we evaluated the performance of the algorithms when each predicate exhibits half (0.5 in x-axis) and double (2 in x-axis) the requirements for sensors to be placed at, compared to the baseline scenario (1 in x-axis). Results are comparable to the ones exhibited in the Figures 1 and 2, with Random incurring between 2 and 3 times more overhead compared to Greedy.

## VI. CONCLUSIONS

In this paper, we tackled the problem of assigning query operators to sensing nodes in IoT environments, whereby a huge number of potential participants exist. We provided a rigorous problem formulation that captures typically the trade-off between increasing quality of query results and resource consumption. We proposed a heuristic based on the Greedy paradigm to tackle the problem and compared its performance against Random assignment. Preliminary experimental results indicate that Greedy incurs between half and one third of the overhead of Random.

## ACKNOWLEDGMENT

This work was partially supported by travel grant of the postgraduate program: "Informatics and Computational Biomedicine", School of Science, Univ. of Thessaly.

## REFERENCES

[1] F. Aielo, G. Fortino, R. Gravina, and A. Guerrieri, "A Java-based Agent Platform for Programming Wireless Sensor Networks," The Computer J., vol 54(3), pp. 439-454, 2010.

[2] N. Assimakis, M. Adam, M. Koziri, S. Voliotis, and K. Asimakis, "Optimal decentralized Kalman filter and Lainiotis filter," Digital Signal Processing, vol. 23(1), pp. 442-452, 2013.

[3] I. Ayala, M. Amor, and L. Fuentes, "The Sol agent platform: Enabling group communication and interoperability of self-configuring agents in the Internet of Things," JAISE, vol. 7(2), pp. 243-269, 2015.

[4] G. Chatzimilioudis, A. Cuzzocrea, D. Gunopoulos, and N. Mamoulis, "A Novel Distributed Framework for Optimizing Query Routing Trees in Wireless Sensor Networks via Optimal Operator Placement," J. of Computer and System Sciences, vol. 79(3), pp. 349-368, 2013.

[5] J. Gubbi, R Buyya, S. Marusic, and M. Palaniswami, "Internet of Things (IoT): A vision, architectural elements, and future directions," Future Generation Computer Systems, vol. 29(7), pp. 1645-1660, 2014.

[6] N. Hu, T. F. La Porta, and N. Bartolini, "Self-Adaptive Resource Allocation for Event Monitoring with Uncertainty in Sensor Networks," MASS 2015, pp. 370-378.

[7] E. Jung, I. Cho, and S. M. Kang, "iotSilo: The Agent Service Platform Supporting Dynamic Behaviour Assembly for Resolving the Heterogeneity of IoT," Int. J. of Distributed Sensor Networks, vol. 10, 2014.

[8] S. K. Khaitan and J. D. McCalley, "Design Techniques and Applications of Cyber Physical Systems: A Survey," IEEE Systems Journal, vol. 9(2), pp. 350-365, June 2015.

[9] M. G. Koziri, et al., "A framework for scheduling the encoding of multiple smart user videos," SMAP 2016, pp. 29-34.

[10] N. Laoutaris, G. Smaragdakis, A. Bestavros, I. Matta, and I. Stavrakakis, "Distributed Selfish Caching," IEEE TPDS, vol. 18(10), pp. 1361-1376, 2007.

[11] H. Liu, T. Roeder, K. Walsh, R. Barr, and E. G. Sirer, "Design and implementation of a single system image operating system for ad hoc networks," in Proc. MobiSys 2005, pp. 149-162.

[12] T. Loukopoulos and I. Ahmad, "Policies for Caching OLAP Queries in Internet Proxies," IEEE TPDS, vol. 17(10), pp. 1124-1135, 2006.

[13] T. Loukopoulos, N. Tziritas, P. Lampsas, and S. Lalis, "Implementing Replica Placements: Feasibility and Cost Minimization," IPDPS 2007, pp. 1-10.

[14] Z. Lu, Y. Wen, R. Fan, S. - L. Tan, and J. Biswas, "Toward Efficient Distributed Algorithms for In-Network Binary Operator Tree Placement in Wireless Sensor Networks," IEEE JSAC, vol 31(4), pp. 743-755, 2013.

[15] N. Nguyen and M. M. H. Khan, "A closed-loop context aware data acquisition and resource allocation framework for dynamic data driven applications systems (DDDAS) on the cloud," Journal of Systems and Software, vol. 109, pp. 88-105, 2015.

[16] F. Paganelli, S. Turchi, and D. Giuli, "A Web of Things Framework for RESTful Applications and Its Experimentation in a Smart City," IEEE Systems Journal vol. 10(4), pp. 1412-1423, 2016.

[17] P. Papadopoulos, T. Loukopoulos, I. Anagnostopoulos, N. Tziritas, and M. Vassilakopoulos, "RAC: a remote application calling framework for coordination of mobile apps," PCI 2015, pp. 394-399.

[18] K. Poularakis, G. Iosifidis, and L. Tassiulas, "Approximation algorithms for mobile data caching in small cell networks," IEEE Trans. on Communications, vol. 62(10), pp. 3665-3677, 2014.

[19] U. Ramachandran, et al., "Dynamic data fusion for future sensor networks," ACM TOSN, vol. 2(3), pp. 404-443, 2006.

[20] G. Roumelis, M. Vassilakopoulos, T. Loukopoulos, A. Corral, and Y. Manolopoulos, "The xBR^+ -tree: An Efficient Access Method for Points," DEXA (1) 2015, pp. 43-58.

[21] C. Sengul, A. C. Viana, and A. Ziviani, "A survey of adaptive services to cope with dynamics in wireless self-organizing networks," ACM Comput. Surv. 44(4), pp. 23:1-23:35, 2012.

[22] P. J. Shin, J. Park, and A. C. Kak, "A predictive duty cycle adaptation framework using augmented sensing for wireless camera networks," ACM TOSN, vol. 10(2), pp. 22:1-22:31, 2014.

[23] M. N. Tahan, M. Dehghan, and H. Pedram, "Upper and lower bounds for dynamic cluster assignment for multi-target tracking in heterogeneous WSNs," JPDC vol. 73(10), pp. 1389-1399, 2013.

[24] N. Tziritas, et al., "Middleware Mechanisms for Agent Mobility in Wireless Sensor and Actuator Networks," S-CUBE 2012, pp. 30-44.

[25] N. Tziritas, T. Loukopoulos, S. U. Khan, and C. - Z. Xu, "Distributed Algorithms for the Operator Placement Problem," IEEE TCSS, vol. 2(4), pp. 182–196, Feb. 2015.

[26] L. Ying, Z. Liu, D. Towsley, and C. H. Xia, "Distributed Operator Placement and Data Caching in Large-scale Sensor Networks," INFOCOM 2008, pp. 977-985.

# Anomaly Detection in Cloud Based Application using System Calls

Marin Aranitasi
Polytechnic University of Tirana, Faculty of Information Technology, Department of Fundamentals of Informatics
Tirana, Albania
Email : maranitasi@fti.edu.al

Mats Neovius
Åbo Akademi University, Faculty of Science and Engineering, Department of Computer Science
Turku, Finland
Email: mneovius@abo.fi

*Abstract*—**Cloud computing is a rapidly developing computing paradigm. It enables dynamic on-demand resource distribution computing in a cost-effective manner. However, it introduces compelling concerns related to privacy and security of the data. As many of these have been extensively studied and are monitored effectively, this paper proposes a novel solution relying on detecting anomalies in system calls behavior of the system. We use Dempster-Shafer theory of evidence for learning the normality and show how to parametrize this in the method presented. The method is scalable to any set of system calls. Finally, we propose further challenges on this track.**

***Keywords- Cloud computing; Security; System calls;.***

## I. INTRODUCTION

With the advances of (Inter) networking and the advent of the concept cloud computing, computing resources are provided "on-demand" from a virtualized pool. According to NIST [1] essential characteristics of cloud computing include on-demand self-service, network access, pooling, elasticity and measured service. Service models include Software as a Service (SaaS), Platform as a Service (PaaS) and Infrastructure as a Service (IaaS) with deployment models including private, community, public and hybrid clouds. Common to these are that the hardware is abstracted from the consumer who typically "pay-per-use" of resources whose availability is elastically adjusted by momentary demand [2]. As a consequence, cloud computing encompasses a new means to provide virtually unlimited resources to paying customers whenever needed. Hence, the cloud has revolutionized the way computing infrastructure is used [3] to offer adaptive utility computing.

With novel computing paradigms, concerns on their feasibility arise. In cloud computing this concern relates, among others, to security [4] and privacy. Commonly agreed security requirements include data integrity, confidentiality, access controllability and privacy preservability. These threats do not restrict themselves to point-of-sales activity, but are much more sophisticated extending to data integrity and privacy concerns including espionage, malicious insiders and curious and greedy service providers.These security threats are also the main impediments to wider deployment of cloud computing solutions especiallyin domains operating on sensitive data such as used in the accounting industry [5]. These concerns lend themselves also to emerging cloud-based applications such as the Internet of Things and Big Data [16]. In addition, legislation may add technical impediments for privacy protection such as the Regulation (EU) 2016/679 and EU-U.S. Privacy Shield [6]. The extent to which this affects the Attribute Authority (AA) and the Third Party Auditor (TPA) roles and their functionality is yet to be discovered. Because of these reasons, many solutions are still hosted "in-house"with typically higher initial investment cost, higher maintenance costs and with restrictions on availability.

On the type of attacks on enterprise clouds, Verizon's security report [7] states that roughly 80% of all breaches are of external origin and 80% have a financial motive, with roughly 20% having espionage as the motive. Moreover, Verizon report that a system is compromised in minutes or seconds and exfiltration of the data happens typically within a day. And despite all the effort by specialists to protect a system from getting compromised, these keep on happening. Research is also directed on this track with searchable and homomorphic encryption research flourishing. Both approaches do, however, rely on a policy and a shared secret lifting the importance of the AA and TPA. Possibly as of this advancements, tactics to perform social attacks granting access to internal attacks develop; with rudimentary known ones including phishing. Other well-known risks the cloud based application faces include data protection risks, system outages including (D)DoS attacks, data loss, vendor lock-in and vendor failure [8].

Common to social and DoS attacks are that no policy-based technological appliance can protect against these. As social attacks typically provide access to restricted data where the attacker would need to know what to search for or how to stir the system up, these are often well targeted with a certain purpose in mind. Alleged examples include Stuxnet, US expelling 35 Russian diplomats at the end of 2016 accused to have tried to influence US presidential elections and the noticed espionage at the Finnish foreign ministry in 2013. With respect to DoS attacks, with the IoT proposal and its envisioned spread, the zombies for botnets are ubiquitous and maintained by ordinary persons lacking maintenance skills. First recorded DDoS attacks with IoT devices are reputed to have occurred in 2015 by CCTV [9] with other larger attacks overloading Twitter, PayPal and Spotify [10] in 2016. Also, if an IoT device operates on private data, its owner's concern is to keep it uncompromised and if compromised, being promptly informed about this. This is forecast as an immense problem with the advances of automated data analysis including image recognition and profiling. Moreover, privacy may be compromised by such a device in a manner enabling identity hijacking.

With respect to these concerns, this paper does not aim to advance on the policies, encryption or similar purely technological advances, but have a main contribution in presenting a method for detecting behavioral anomalies. This method learns a pattern of normality and reacts on events outside this pattern, i.e. anomalies. As an implementation we use system calls of a cloud application, as these are needed whether searchable or homomorphic encryption each time a system accesses the kernel. In this context, we mean by cloud application any cloud based backend software communicating with a set of agents including IoT systems. Thus, compared to policy-based models, this paper takes nearly the reverse view that relies on an agent's past activity to indicate its current activity rather than on Boolean logic and cryptography.

The rest of this paper is organized as follows: Section II present the background and the motivation of the paper. Section III is divided in five subsections and presents our solution to the security issues identified. The first and the second talks about system calls and system call patterns. The other subsections talk about the mathematical method of the proposed solution. Conclusions are presented in section IV.

## II. BACKGROUND AND MOTIVATION

In the cloud, main security concerns relate to data privacy or integrity being compromised. Recent infamous ones include Sony PlayStation data breach [11], Dropbox privacy leakage [12] and the alleged major security breach in May 2016 compromising 273M passwords. Typically, the severity of these attacks is measured by the sensitivity of the data being exposed or the harm it causes. It is also speculated that many of the most severe ones do not reach the headlines because of loss of reputation. Moreover, the laws stating the consequences have often not been tested yet, imposing little scrutiny on companies. Moreover, breaches of Service Level Agreements (SLA) dictating the division of responsibilities between the customer and the Cloud Service Provider (CSP) occur frequently. These are seldom made public because of the reputation implications on both parties with an exception of black-hat hackers. Reasons for security breaches may relate to improper configuration, SW bugs, HW errors or power failures [13]. In addition, SW not being up-to-date may contain known exploits. This holds especially for the CSP, where "a single vulnerability or misconfiguration can lead to a compromise across an entire provider's cloud" [14] [17].

With the cloud and its essential characteristics including differences in national legislation, SLA may start to include paragraphs stipulating spatial distribution. This implies that the administrator passwords of the computers used for this application must not have been disclosed to areas not included in the SLA. This concern goes especially for outsourced data services where the owner's exclusive control over their data is compromised when stored on a server whose admin password is known by someone else. For example, Google's privacy policy states that Google reserves the right to review application, project and customer data for compliance with the acceptable use policy [17]. In this case, it comes down to what is "acceptable use policy". Moreover, for personal data, the cloud computing sets a stage of novel problems that need to be dealt with including those who have the right to process the data, what is the level of privacy etc. addressed in e.g. Regulation (EU) 2016/679 and EU-U.S. Privacy Shield [5]. Hence, the cloud used by an application may need to be spatially constrained opposing the principal characteristics of cloud computing.

Means to restrict access and preserve data privacy and integrity includes sophisticated policies on data backup and distribution over nodes. In cases of a cloud application, this is the responsibility of the application service provider and its SLA's with Cloud Service Provider's (CSP). These are often professionally maintained and alternative means to gain access are developed and gaining popularity, e.g. phishing or malwares opening a backdoor or as a key logger. On the CSP, as they share infrastructure, platforms and underlying virtualization software, they form a single point of failure attracting targeted and very sophisticated attacks. If vulnerability is found in any layer, it affects everyone on this cloud. For this, CSA recommend a defense-in-depth strategy. Contemporary attacks are also often more directed and if successful, pose a greater risk.Moreover, common to most attacks are that they often go unnoticed until it is too late, e.g. data exfiltration has already taken place. In such cases, restoring the data from a backup may not suffice as privacy has been compromised.

## III. HOW WE MIGHT APPROACH THESE ISSUES

In this paper we take the in-depth approach and present a method that builds the normal behavior of an agent on a cloud system. We construct the normality by analyzing system calls by its user with the aim of detecting system anomalies by monitoring specific system calls of specific applications. This normality would define the way the system works "normally", with any anomaly indicating a situation calling for further attention.

In the next section we present the system calls and we define the set of system calls to use for monitoring and explain the reason why we choose those calls. After that we are going to present the mathematical tool for analyzing and for detecting possible threats in the system.

### *A. System calls*

By definition, a system call is an atomic request in a Unix-like operating system made via a software interrupt by an active process for a service performed by the kernel [16].

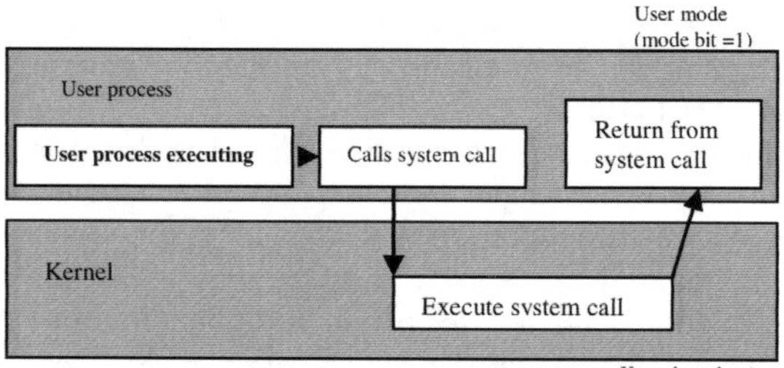


Figure 1. System calls

The system call provides an interface to the operating system's services. Application developers often do not have direct access to the system calls, but can access them through an application programming interface (API). The functions that are included in the API invoke the actual system calls. This is illustrated in Figure 1. By using the API, certain benefits can be gained:

- Portability: as long a system supports an API, any program using that API can compile and run.
- Ease of Use: using the API can be significantly easier than using the actual system call.

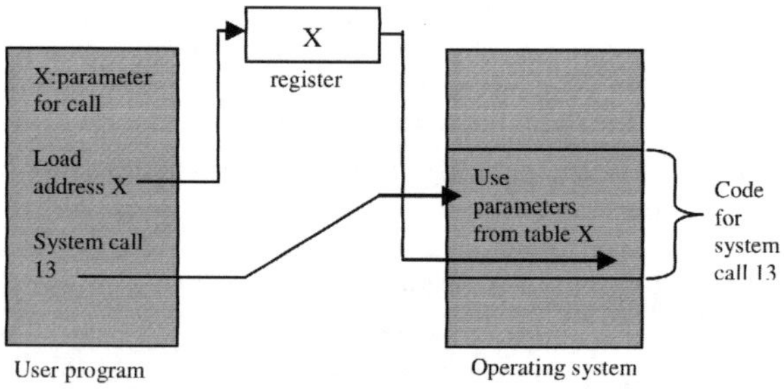


Figure 2. System call parameters

Three general methods exist for passing parameters to the OS as shown in Figure 2:

1. Parameters can be passed in registers.
2. When there are more parameters than registers, parameters can be stored in a block and the block address can be passed as a parameter to a register.
3. Parameters can also be pushed on or popped off the stack by the operating system.

The system calls are plentiful and vary between operating systems, with Linux kernel having 300+ system calls and Windows 7 having close to 700. These can be categorized to 5 different categories: a **process control** is a running program that needs to be able to stop execution either normally or abnormally. When execution is stopped abnormally typically a dump of the memory is taken to be examined by a debugger. The **file management** system calls include create (), delete (), read (), write (), reposition (), or close (). Also, there is a need to determine the file attributes – get and set file attribute. Often the OS provides an API to make these system calls. The **device management** process usually requires several resources to execute, if these resources are available, they will be granted and control returned to the user process. These resources are also thought of as devices. Some are physical, such as a video card, and others are logical, such as a file.User programs *request* the device, and when finished they *release* the device. Similar to files, we can *read*, *write*, and *reposition* the device. The **information management** system call exists purely for transferring information between the user program and the operating system. An example of this is *time*, or *date*. The OS also keeps information about all its processes and provides system calls to report this information. The **communication**system call exists in two models of interprocess communication, the message-passing model and the shared memory model.

- Message-passing uses a common mailbox to pass messages between processes.
- Shared memory use certain system calls to create and gain access to regions of memory owned by other processes. The two processes exchange information by reading and writing in the shared data.

According to the characteristics of the system calls we propose to monitor 2 categories of system calls:

1. Communication
2. File management.

For the communication category we propose to monitor accept (), socket (), connect () system calls, and for the file management category we propose to monitor read (), write (),delete () andcreate () system calls.These are the system calls that rank as the most common threats in the CSA report and are vital for any cloud based application. We think that monitoring the data sent across the network is not a good idea because there is a high overhead tracing those system calls and they do a lot variable invocation for sending and receiving data. Hence, this might not be favorable to do with the method presented below without packet inspection.

### *B. System call patterns*

We assume the system calls monitored to behave in anatomic manner and the set of them to be exclusive and exhaustive. That is, we assume the system calls not to be subject to race conditions hence assuming an atomic part to be executed from the beginning till the end and each and every one is exactly one of the possible. On such a foundation a pattern could be constructed from analyzing the system call log, i.e. by the recorded evidence. Moreover, the pattern could be augmented by contextual bindings by some machine learning method. The outcome could reasonably be a probability of a certain or a sequence of system calls happening. Applying a timed window on this analysis would provide a timed pattern for the system calls, e.g. a diurnal pattern when human behavior is analyzed.

To detect anomalies, a valid approach is to teach a model what normality is by analyzing the past. Yet, the model must consider the possibility of a change in the system or its behavior implying a change in normality. Realistically, this could mean a software update or installation of new software. Hence, the valid system call pattern calls for an adaptive method providing a level of certainty that the system indeed operating normally. In case of anomaly the system could inform the user about the task behaving anomalously prompting the user to authorize the anomaly.

### *C. Mathematical foundation of the proposed method*

On the problem and domain outlined in this paper, we propose to use Dempster-Shafer theory, aka, evidence theory. The evidence theory is a generalization of Bayesian theory of subjective probabilities on a set of exclusive and exhaustive events $X$, here the system calls. The power set $2^X$ denotes all combinations of system calls, realistically enabling comparing any category of system calls to discover new domain specific patterns. On this, the mass $m$ is the level of certainty on a set of events with $m : 2^X \rightarrow [0,1]$, $m(\emptyset) = 0$ and $\sum_{2^X} m = 1$. On this, the certainty (belief)*bel* of a set of outcomes $A \subseteq X$ is $bel(A) = \sum_{x \subseteq A} m(x)$ and plausibility *pl* is $pl(A) = \sum_{x \cap A \neq \emptyset} m(x)$ as for the possibility of this outcome. This implies that $bel < pl$ whenever $m(X) \neq 0$ and $A \subset X$. The semantics of this is that the difference between *bel* and *pl* denote the uncertainty. Moreover, the complement of a set of events $A$ denoted $\bar{A}$ is the evidence against this event, i.e. $pl(A) = 1 - bel(\bar{A})$. Consequently, the Dempster-Shafer theory

Realistically, in the context of this paper, the *bel* and *pl* would define the uncertainty, i.e. the tolerance between normal (base truth) and anomaly behaviour that initially is 1. The theory provides a foundation for a three-valued logic, whose parameters are: belief as certainty in favour of a proposition $bel$, uncertainty as for do not know $pl - bel$ and disbelief $\overline{bel}$ as for certainty against this proposition $1 - pl(A)$. They share the property of $pl(A) + \overline{bel} = 1$, i.e. they are additive. In cases when $bel(A) = pl(A)$, the uncertainty is 0 and the theory behaves as traditional probability theory.

### *D. The adaptive method*

Having the Dempster-Shafer theory as a solid foundation with a plethora of extensions that enable calculation with it, the problem of defining the values for the parameters is central. On this, inspired by Krukow's [18] and Teacy et al. [19], Neovius et al. [20, 21, 22] have in previous work presented a method for recording and mapping experiences to Dempster-Shafer theory. They consider an event an experience that in the context of this paper is a system call. Hence, let the set of system calls $S$ and the communication $C = \{accept, socket, connect\}$ and file management $F = \{read, write, delete, create\}$ categories be exclusive and exhaustive, i.e. $S = C \cup F$ and $C \cap F = \emptyset$ and similarly for the elements.

With these system calls, we model an experience as a four tuple $(\delta, \epsilon, \zeta, \eta)$ where $\delta$ is the subject system's and application's identification, $\epsilon$ the timestamp, $\zeta$ the set of system call and $\eta$ a score $\in \{0, 1\}$. This view can be reduced to that only events that actually took place are recorded, i.e. that the score is always 1. Thus, an experience $(\delta, unixtime, open, 1)$ indicates that on a device and *app* $\delta$ at a time called the *open* system call and this was triggered. For an entity, the history of the device's system calls can be modelled as a set of such four tuples, i.e. $\{(\delta, \epsilon, \zeta, \eta)\}$ . Projections on this history $Exp(\delta, \epsilon, \{read\}) = \{(\eta)\}$ in case the cardinality *card* of the result indicate the amount of connect system calls that were made at time $\epsilon$. Realistically, $\delta$ could be IMEI code augmented by an application, say FB including its version.

With the realistic assumption that recent behaviour weighs heavier, we may apply a decay function on this. Let decay be denoted by $\lambda$ where $\lambda \in [0,1]$ with semantics of the closer to 1 indicating less decay and 0 being a vacuous view. Then decay at $\epsilon_m$ denoted $d_{\epsilon_m}$ is defined: $d_{\epsilon_m}\left(Exp(\delta, \epsilon_i, s \subset S)\right) = (\lambda^{\epsilon_m - \epsilon_i} * \eta)$. A cyclic (diurnal) history is an abstracted view of this projection with $\lambda = 1$ with $\epsilon_m$ denoting the moment and $\epsilon_n \leq \epsilon_m$ the timespan, i.e. $Abs_{\epsilon_m}\left(Exp(\delta, \epsilon_n, s \subset S)\right)$is the abstract score $\sum_{d_{\epsilon_m} Exp(\delta, \epsilon_n, s \subset S)} \eta$. That is, for a comparison view over a 2 hour time span yesterday $\epsilon_m$ is set -23hours and $\epsilon_n$ to -25hours from this moment. The definition of such views are defined by some contextual predicate constructed by a domain specialist; a fundamental question omitted in this paper.

### *E. Detecting anomalies with the method*

Utilizing the history of events and building a decayed view of the cyclic behavior on each system call provides a basis for normality. For comparison and anomaly detection, the cardinality needs to be put in context. Hence, a projection on the complementary experiences within this category of system calls is motivated. Thus, having $Exp(\delta, \epsilon, \{read\})$, the category's complementary projection is $Exp(\delta, \epsilon, \{write, delete, create\})$, i.e. $Exp\left(\delta, \epsilon, \overline{\{read\}}\right)$. The cardinality of the outcomes provides the relative distribution of these system calls over $\epsilon$ on $\delta$. The tolerance is then defined as the a priori weight of uncertainty *W*. The scale of *W* is domain $\delta$ and category specific with the property small values risking anomalies with low values; and larger $W$ prolonging the cold start.

As an example, assume the projections over a time span where the system calls cardinality is 95 and the score for projection on $read$ to be 73 and for that on $\overline{read}$ to be 22. However, let the abstracted projections result in 70 and 21 respectively as of decay.Moreover, let for readability $W = 5$, making the example specific cardinality 100. Normalizing these gives the scores 0.70, 0.21 with uncertainty $u$being $0.04 + \frac{W}{cardinality\ +W} = 0.09$. Consider a reference vector $bel(\vec{r}) = (x_i)$ that in this case is $bel(\vec{r}) = (0.7, 0.21)$; much alike the belief and certainty for the two projections. The plausibility of these projections are then $pl(\vec{r}) = (0.79, 0.3)$. With these abstracted values, we propose to define an anomaly behavior as when the current *bel* and *pl* does not overlap with the reference *bel* and *pl* vectors. What actions to perform if this happens is again domain specific.

## IV. Conclusion

Cloud computing can lead to numerous business advantages to organizations. As a result of its popularity, many security issues have been exposed by company experts and academic researchers.Numerous of these researches haveproved that security should be a top priority for companies, especially low- to medium-sized enterprises ones. Moreover, the common ground is that security related solutions developed for static client server systems cannot be used in cloud based computing.

In this paper we take a novel view, assuming that a system under attack will behave anomalously. To address this assumption, we presented a soft security means to construct a cloud based solutions' behavioral normality. Knowing the normal behavior, we define the anomalous behavior to be simply anything that is not normal. We stress that the implications of detecting anomalies is domain specific.

As future work, we intend to validate this method with real life data. We will also formalize the normality vs. anomalies more formally. Once having these results, validation on a larger scale is possible.

## References


[1] US national institute of standards and technology.http://csrc.nist.gov/, 2016, accessed 15.1.2017

[2] D. Fernandes, L. Soares, J. Gomes, M. Freire, and P. Inacio, "Security issues in cloud environments: aSurvey". International Journal of Information Security, pp. 113–170, 2013

[3] F. Shahzad, "State-of-the-art Survey onCloud Computing Security Challenges, Approaches and Solutions". *Procedia Computer Science, 37*, 357–362, 2014

[4] I. Iankoulova and M. Daneva, "Cloud computing security requirements: A systematic review". In: *Research Challenges in Information Science RICS*, pp. 1–7, 2012

[5] R. Duncan, "Accounting for stewardship in the cloud" PhD Thesis, University of Aberdeen, 2016.

[6] European Comission. "Comission Implementing Decision of 12.7.2016 pursuant to Directive 95/46/EC of the European Parliament and of the Council on the adequacy of the protection provided by the EU -U.S. Privacy Shield" 2016 http://ec.europa.eu/justice/data-protection/files/privacy-shield-adequacy-decision_en.pdf accessed on 13.01.2017

[7] Verizon "Data Breach Investigations Report" 2016 http://www.verizonenterprise.com/verizon-insights-lab/dbir/2016/ accessed on 13.01.2017

[8] M. Williams, "New Tools for Business,A Quick Start Guide to Cloud Computing", Kogan Page, 2010.

[9] S. Khandelwal, "Hacking CCTV Cameras to Launch DDoS Attacks".The Hacker News, 2015, http://thehackernews.com/2015/10/cctv-camera-hacking.html, accessed on 15.1.2017.

[10] T. Reuters, "Major cyberattack knocks Twitter, Paypal, Spotify offline Friday" CBC news, 2016,http://www.cbc.ca/news/technology/dyn-ddos-attack-websites-down-1.3815417, accesed on 13.01.2017

[11] E. Petterson, "Sony to pay as much as $8 million to settle data breach case", Bloomberg Technology, 2015https://www.bloomberg.com/news/articles/2015-10-20/sony-to-pay-as-much-as-8-million-to-settle-data-breach-claimsaccesed on 13.01.2017

[12] S. Yin, "Dropbox accounts were accessible by anyone fo four hours on Sunday" PCMag UK, 2011.http://uk.pcmag.com/storage-devices-reviews/9092/news/dropbox-accounts-were-accessible-by-anyone-for-four-hours-onaccesed on 13.01.2017

[13] R. Ko and S. Lee "Cloud computing vulnerability incidents: A statisctical overview", Cloud Security Alliance, 2013.

[14] F. Rashid, "The dirty dozen: 12 cloud security threats", Infoworld magazine, 2016, http://www.infoworld.com/article/3041078/security/the-dirty-dozen-12-cloud-security-threats.html, accesed on 13.01.2017.

[15] Linux Information Project "System call definition" 2016 http://www.linfo.org/system_call.html accessed on 13.01.2017

[16] S. De Capitani, S. Foresti, and P. Samarati, "Data Security Issues in Cloud Scenarios", In Proceedings of the 11th International Conference on Information Systems Security, 2015.

[17] Cloud security alliance, "Cloud Computing top threats in 2016".https://downloads.cloudsecurityalliance.org/assets/research/top-threats/Treacherous-12_Cloud-Computing_Top-Threats.pdfaccesed on 13.01.2017

[18] K. Krukow, "Towards a theory of trust for the global ubiquitous computer," PhD thesis, University of Aarhus, Denmark., 2006.

[19] W. Teacy, J. Patel, N. Jennings, and M. Luck, "TRAVOS: Trust and Reputation in the Context of Inaccurate Information Sources," Autonomous Agents and Multi-Agent Systems, vol. 12, no. 2, pp. 183-198. , 2006.

[20] M. Neovius, "Trustworthy Context Dependency in Ubiquitous Systems," TUCS dissertations nr. 151. PhD thesis, Turku, Finland, 2012.

[21] M. Neovius, M. Stocker, M. Rönkkö, and L. Petre, "Trustworthiness Modelling on Continuous Environmental Measurement," in Proc. of the 7th Int. Conf. on Environmental Modelling and Software, 2014.

[22] M. Neovius, "Adaptive Experience-Based Composition of Continuously Changing Quality of Context," in Int. Conf. on Adaptive and Self-Adaptive Systems and Applications, 2015.

# Strategies for Intrusion Monitoring in Cloud Services

George R. S. Weir
Department of Computer and Information Sciences
University of Strathclyde
Glasgow, UK
e-mail: george.weir@strath.ac.uk

Andreas Aßmuth
University of Applied Sciences
OTH Amberg-Weiden
Germany
e-mail: a.assmuth@oth-aw.de

***Abstract*— Effective activity and event monitoring is an essential aspect of digital forensic readiness. Techniques for capturing log and other event data are familiar from conventional networked hosts and transfer directly to the Cloud context. In both contexts, a major concern is the risk that monitoring systems may be targeted and impaired by intruders seeking to conceal their illicit presence and activities. We outline an approach to intrusion monitoring that aims (i) to ensure the credibility of log data and (ii) provide a means of data sharing that supports log reconstruction in the event that one or more logging systems is maliciously impaired.**

***Keywords-Cloud security; intrusion monitoring; message authentication codes; secret sharing.***

## I. INTRODUCTION

A news report from a recent computer electronics trade show featured a light bulb with an in-built spy camera. Although the application of this device is the realm of physical security rather than the world of computer, Clouds and networks, we can derive two general lessons from this example technology. Firstly, the purpose of the device is surveillance. Secondly, the device aims for covert operation. These joint concepts of covert surveillance are important in the context of security, whether in the home, on a network or in the Cloud. The primary role for this spying light bulb is surveillance, i.e., in the event of a security incident, to record data that may later have evidential value. Capturing such data in a covert manner aims to reduce the likelihood that the recording facility will be detected and thereby, minimise the prospect that the data collection will be deliberately impaired and the telling data subverted.

While covert surveillance affords no immediate defence against security breaches, it does illustrate the desirability of establishing auditable data in order that light may later be shed on unauthorised or anomalous events that have initially gone undetected by relevant human agency. With varying degrees of transparency, the logging features in computer operating systems, individual computer applications, network operations and Cloud environments go some way toward addressing this requirement by recording data that may subsequently be consulted, in a process of digital forensics, as evidence of past events. Thereby, 'a forensic investigation of digital evidence is commonly employed as a post-event response to a serious information security incident.' … 'Forensic readiness is defined as the ability of an organisation to maximise its potential to use digital evidence whilst minimising the costs of an investigation' [1, p.1].

Although considerable efforts are directed in computer security toward protection and prevention of illicit access and system misuse, digital forensic readiness is increasingly recognised as a necessary measure toward recovery, understanding vulnerabilities and pursuit of those responsible for cyber-misdeeds (e.g., [2]).

In the following, Section 2 reviews the characteristics of Cloud services and the facilities available to the customer. Section 3 characterises the attack context, with reference to recognised phases and the likely associated intruder behaviour. In Section 4, we elaborate upon the role of monitoring as a basis for forensic readiness in Cloud Services, with specific attention to the variety of strategies that may be employed, both overt and covert, as well as their likely effectiveness as mechanisms for event reconstruction and on-going resilience. Section 5 presents an example monitoring approach that contains specific aspects toward a solution to the forensic readiness problem in the Cloud context. As summarised in Section 6, our proposed approach would generate auditable information that can be used subsequently for digital forensics analysis in a post-hack scenario, within a setting of Cloud Services.

## II. CLOUD SERVICES

In this section, we briefly review the characteristics of Cloud Services, in order to highlight the security concerns associated with different use contexts.

The US National Institute of Standards and Technology (NIST), has provided a detailed account of Cloud Services [3]. This includes a description of typical service models:

- Software as a Service (SaaS);
- Platform as a Service (PaaS); and
- Infrastructure as a Service (IaaS).

In the first case, the customer is given access to applications running on the service provider's Cloud infrastructure, usually through a variety of client devices and software interfaces. Aside from specific application configuration options, in this arrangement the customer is given no control over the underlying Cloud infrastructure (op. cit., p.2). This level of service extends from simple file storage, through hosted Web sites and database management to specific Web services, including RESTful applications [4], and use of 'containers' [5].

In the second case, the customer is permitted to deploy their own applications on to the service provider's Cloud infrastructure. Customer control extends to configuration and management of these Cloud-hosted applications but, as before, the customer has no facility to control any other aspects of the underlying Cloud infrastructure [3, p.2].

In the third case, the customer has greater scope for software deployment on to the Cloud infrastructure, extending to 'arbitrary software, which can include operating systems and applications' (op. cit.). Still, in this arrangement, the customer's control is limited to the deployed software applications, including operating systems (e.g., virtual machines) and associated networking features (such as software firewalls) [3, p3].

These service models characterise typical Cloud Service Provider (CSP) offerings and the increasing levels of access and software capability, is reflected in increasing levels of cost to the consumer. Notably, in each of these contexts, management and control of the Cloud infrastructure resides with the CSP, who must be relied upon to manage most security aspects that may impinge upon the purchased services.

The range of applications and software facilities afforded by Cloud services is extensive, and indications are that many mission-critical services are moving to Cloud implementations as a means of limiting security concerns and assuring greater resilience. The virtual nature of Cloud services also means that system recovery or replacement can be quick, reliable and cost-effective [cf. 6]. Such outsourcing of local software applications is recognised as commercially attractive for factors, such as:

- Cost (reduction in local expertise and local infrastructure);
- Reliability (service-level agreements can assure availability);
- Resilience (speedy recovery in the event of data or service loss);
- Technical extensibility (support for multiple instances of applications with increasing availability of service to meet growing demand).

To simplify the categories of Cloud uses, we may broadly differentiate two end-user contexts. In the first, the customer employs the Cloud service as a data storage facility. (This is a specific instance of the Software as a Service.) Here, security for the customer is limited to concerns of authorised access, continuity of service and data maintenance. In the second context, the end-user employs the Cloud service as a means of computation. (This broadly covers all other Cloud interaction.) Here, security for the customer extends to all traditional aspects, including data protection, access authentication, service misappropriation and service availability. While some of these issues may lie within the control of the consumer, the CSP has ultimate management of the infrastructure that affords all of the higher-level service provision. The extent to which the CSP can reliably manage the security and associated integrity of provided services, depends ultimately upon the availability of techniques for detecting and recording the details of any illicit operations that take place within the Cloud service context. Without recourse to such facilities, the CSP cannot be counted upon to maintain consumer services in a satisfactory fashion since there is lack of assurance that such services have not been infiltrated, impaired or subverted. In addition, ability for the CSP to restore services to pre-compromise level depends largely upon the CSP's facility to identify any delta between pre- and post-intrusion services. Inevitably, this leads back to the issue of digital forensic readiness as applied to the Cloud context.

## III. The Attack Context

In general, there are three phases to a successful cyber-attack:

1. reconnaissance and information gathering;
2. infiltration and escalation and, finally;
3. exfiltration, assault and obfuscation.

In phase 1, the adversary gathers any information needed to gain access to the system, e.g., open ports, versions of operating systems and software services, security measures (such as firewalls, IDS, etc.) [6]. Using this information, the adversary gains access to the system in phase 2 [8].

The process of gaining access might consist of several steps, for example, if the adversary has to comprise another system first, in order to get into the actual target. In this process, the adversary also tries to escalate available privileges in order to gain super-user access to the system.

In phase 3, the adversary extracts any information from the system that might prove to be useful [9]. If the goal of the attack is stealing confidential data, such as user accounts, passwords or credit card information, this data is extracted by the adversary and possibly sold to third parties. If the cyber-attack has another goal, e.g., sabotage, the adversary extracts the data needed to launch the actual assault, often triggered by a certain date or specific event. In any case, the adversary can be expected to perform whatever action is required to cover their tracks. Among other actions, they may install a rootkit that exchanges current files and services within the system with modified versions of these particular files and services. Such system modifications may extend to altering process information, e.g., a program to list all running processes on the system may be modified to list all running processes except for the processes run by the adversary. Additionally, the adversary may target existing log files that might contain traces of the intrusion.

Such strategies are reflected in many network-based intrusions since, in many instances, network vulnerability is predicated upon known weaknesses in networked hosts.

## IV. Monitoring Strategies

As previously noted, digital forensic readiness requires the monitoring and recording of events and activity that may impinge upon the integrity of the host system. Much of this capability is provided natively by the local system, using standardly available operating system logging, perhaps with additional active security monitoring, such as dynamic log analysis [10] or key file signature monitoring [11].

The situation for Cloud-based services reflects in many respects the context of a networked host. Where a customer employs Cloud purely as a storage medium, minimum security requirements will seek to ensure authenticated access and secure data backup. In turn, the monitoring requirements associated with this service must capture details of user logins (including source IP, username and success or failure of login attempts). Additionally, any file operations that change the status of data stored under the account of that customer must also be recorded. In the event of unauthorised access (e.g., stolen user credentials), such default monitoring may offer little protection, aside from identifying the identity of the stolen credentials and recourse to subsequent backup data recovery. Such monitoring is essentially Operating System-based, albeit that in the Cloud setting, this OS may be virtual.

This context of Cloud usage faces the same challenges in monitoring and security that confront any networked host, with the added complication that a Cloud-based virtual host may face added vulnerability via its hosting virtualiser [12]. Furthermore, Cloud services are often configured to provide new virtual OS instances automatically to satisfy demand, and in turn, shut these down when demand falls. A side-effect of such service cycling is that system logs are lost to the customer, and subsequent digital forensic analysis may be unavailable.

In the 'traditional' network setting, numerous techniques have been devised to afford post-event insight on system failures and unwelcome exploits. In all major operating system contexts, whether virtualised, Cloud-based or native, system logging affords the baseline for generating auditable records of system, network and user activity. Such system level monitoring is well understood and in the event of intrusion is likely to be a primary target in order to compromise the record and eliminate traces of illicit activity.

For networked hosts and, by extension, as a monitoring strategy for local area networks, a wide-variety of Intrusion Detection Systems (IDS) have been developed and deployed with a view to rapid determination of malicious activity. These techniques may be rule-based [e.g., 13]. In most cases, the IDS monitors and cross-correlates system-generated logs in order to identify anomalous event sequences. Many approaches to anomaly-based intrusion detection have been reported [14]-[19]. Inevitably, such systems may themselves become targets in order to inhibit their detection capability and maintain a 'zero-footprint' on the part of the intruder [20].

In a Cloud context, each node is using its own logging daemon or agent to log important events. But in comparison to a single computer, the log information might be essential and therefore relevant for the whole cloud infrastructure. For that reason, cloud infrastructures use a centralised log server that receives the log information of all attached nodes. The task of this log server is not only the recording of log files of all nodes but also to monitor the cloud infrastructure. In case of a cyber-attack, the log server ideally detects the attack (maybe assisted by an intrusion detection system) and starts countermeasures. This exposed role of the log server makes it a very attractive target for cyber-attacks itself, or, as described above, means that an adversary has to deal with the log server in phase 2. Since the hardware of such a log server might also break down even without any cyber-attack, in practice more than one log server is used at the same time to provide redundancy.

A practical solution might consist of two log servers in "active-active-mode" which means that both are operating at the same time, but in case of one system failure, the other takes over for the whole cloud infrastructure. The operation of these two log servers might be supervised by a third server which in case of failure or attack sends an alarm to the administrator. Unfortunately, the problem stays more or less the same: this third monitoring server is a single point of failure and is therefore attractive as a target for any adversary attacking the cloud infrastructure. If an adversary manages to take out the monitoring server and to tamper with the log information on at least one of the two log servers, the Cloud provider might not be capable of determining which log files are correct and which are manipulated.

Any logging service which is introduced in addition to the traditional daemons or agents has to meet at least the following constraints:

1. the new logging service must not cause too much additional load, either on the nodes (concerning computation) or on the network (concerning network traffic), and;
2. the computation of additional security measures in order to provide authenticity and integrity must be efficiently feasible.

## V. EXAMPLE MONITORING APPROACH

Message Authentication Codes (MACs) as described in almost any textbook about cryptography can readily be used to address this monitoring dilemma. MACs can be constructed using cryptographic hash functions or using block ciphers, for instance. Either construction ensures efficient computation of the MACs under a secret key. MACs are used to provide authenticity and integrity; therefore, they meet both conditions.

A solution that we propose starts with a secure boot process for each node of the Cloud infrastructure. During boot, the common log daemon or agent is started and it starts recording events in various log files. We suggest to compute a MAC for each event and to store these additional bits with the plaintext message of the event in the log file. We assume that the plaintext message also contains a time stamp. For the next event to be recorded in a log file, the plaintext of the event is concatenated with the previous MAC before computing the MAC for this event. This leads to a MAC chain which can be checked for each step using the plaintext and MAC of the previous event - but only if the secret key is known. Since the adversary does not know the secret key, he is not capable of computing valid MACs and therefore not capable of tampering with the MAC chain in order to hide his tracks.

The use of Message Authentication Codes is only the first step towards a solution to the problem. An adversary could simply delete or deliberately falsify all log files (including the MACs). This would probably make it impossible to reconstruct the steps of the cyber-attack in a post-hack analysis.

In order to deal with this issue and to make use of the benefits of a Cloud infrastructure, we propose the additional step of using secret sharing techniques - or so called threshold schemes - as published by Adi Shamir in 1979 [21].

The idea is to divide some data D into n pieces $D_1, \ldots, D_n$ in such a way that:

(a) $D$ can be reconstructed easily of any $k < n$ pieces $D_i$

(b) the knowledge of only $k-1$ or even fewer pieces $D_i$ leaves the data completely undetermined.

Shamir named such a scheme a "$(k, n)$ threshold scheme". He points out that by using such a $(k,n)$ threshold scheme with $n = 2k-1$, it is necessary to have at least $k = \left\lceil \frac{n+1}{2} \right\rceil$ parts $D_i$ to reconstruct $D$. A lesser number of $\left\lfloor \frac{n}{2} \right\rfloor = k-1$ parts makes the reconstruction impossible.

Shamir introduced a $(k,n)$ threshold scheme based upon polynomial interpolation. The data $D$ can be interpreted as a natural number and $p$ is a prime number with $D < p$. All of the following computations are made in the prime field $GF(p)$. Given $k$ points in the 2-dimensional plane, $(x_1, y_1), \ldots, (x_k, y_k)$ with distinct coordinates $x_i$, there is one and only one polynomial $q$ of degree $k-1$ such that $q(x_i) = y_i$ for all $i = 1, \ldots, k$. At first, the coefficients $a_1, \ldots, a_{k-1}$ are chosen at random and $a_0 = D$, which leads to the polynomial

$$q(x) = a_0 + a_1 x + a_2 x^2 + \cdots + a_{k-1} x^{k-1}.$$

The n different pieces of D are computed as $D_1 = q(1)$, $D_i = q(i), \ldots, D_n = q(n)$. Provided that their identifying indices are known, any subset of k elements $D_i$ can be used to compute the coefficients $a_i$ of the polynomial q which allow the computation of the data $D = q(0)$. From any subset of less or equal $k-1$ pieces $D_i$, neither the coefficients $a_i$ nor the data D can be calculated. (For further details, we direct the reader to the original paper [21].)

In our proposed solution to the problem of providing additional forensic information for post-hack analysis, $D$ is the data to be written in a log file: the plaintext message of the event, n randomly chosen nodes of the cloud infrastructure and the corresponding MAC, computed from the concatenation of the event message, the previous MAC and the addresses of these n nodes. The n pieces $D_i$ that are derived from D as stated before, and D is sent to the traditional centralised log server. The n pieces $D_i$ are additionally sent to the n nodes which store this information. For the next event, we repeat this procedure but choose n (possibly) different nodes.

In case of a cyber-attack and if a post-hack analysis is necessary, at first all pieces of logging information are gathered from all nodes. Using the time stamps and the MAC chains, the order of the logged events can be reconstructed. The decentralised stored pieces of logging information are put together to reconstruct D from any k of the n parts. This means, even if an adversary succeeds in manipulating some of the nodes and the centralised logging system, the events can be reconstructed. Finally, the integrity and authenticity of these events can be checked using the MAC chain.

The proposed approach may identify and retain information on an intruder's actions that result in stolen, modified or deleted data. This is a feature with growing importance, as legislative demands on data protection increase. For instance, the EU General Data Protection Regulation that is due to come into force in May 2018, will require companies to notify all breaches within 72 hours of occurrence, with a potential penalty of up to 4% of global turnover based on the previous year's accounts.

Note that this solution is not proposed as a general basis for monitoring the Cloud infrastructure. Rather, its purpose is to provide secure logging information for a post-hack analysis by distributing their parts randomly over all nodes. Thereby, reliable system monitoring can be established by means of multiple log servers, with the added assurance of Message Authentication Codes.

## VI. CONCLUSIONS

Recognising the importance of securing log data as a basis for digital forensic reconstruction in the event of system intrusion, a multiple server solution combined with Message Authentication Codes affords a mechanism that allows for safe deposit and reconstruction of monitor data. This can operate in a Cloud setting in which each logging node is a virtual server.

An important benefit from this distrusted solution is that digital forensic reconstructions are possible for virtual machines that are 'cycled', since their native OS logs can be maintained in a recoverable and verifiable form beyond the OS of those machines. This provides the safeguard of digital forensic readiness for Cloud customers in the event that an intruder accesses private data on the Cloud service and causes that system to cycle as an attempt to delete all traces of illicit data access.

The possibility, however slight, that an intruder may gain access to and potentially compromise all peers in this configuration, can be mitigated by also allowing log data to transfer 'upwards' to one or more 'superior' systems (e.g., the parent operating systems in which the peer log servers are virtualised).

Evidently, Cloud service provision has a requirement for robust monitoring that is sufficient to withstand direct assault from an intruder within the host context. Conventional OS monitoring goes some way toward providing the equivalent of a light bulb with an in-built spy camera, but needs to be enhanced with a reliable mechanism for validating and reconstituting log data, such as we have outlined in this paper.

## REFERENCES

[1] R. Rowlingson, "A ten step process for forensic readiness", International Journal of Digital Evidence, vol. 2, no. 3, pp. 1-28, 2004.

[2] K. Reddy, H. S. Venter, and M. S. Olivier, "Using time-driven activity-based costing to manage digital forensic readiness in large organisations", Information Systems Frontiers, vol. 14, no. 5, pp. 1061-1077, 2012.

[3] P. Mell and T. Grance, "The NIST definition of cloud computing", NIST, 2011. Available from http://faculty.winthrop.edu/domanm/csci411/Handouts/NIST.pdf, [retrieved: February, 2017].

[4] S. A. Shaikh, H. Chivers, P. Nobles, J. A. Clark and H. Chen, "Network reconnaissance", Network Security, vol. 11, pp. 12-16, 2008.

[5] L. Richardson and S. Ruby, RESTful web services. O'Reilly Media, Inc., 2008.

[6] B. Benatallah, Q. Z. Sheng and M. Dumas, "The self-serv environment for web services composition", IEEE Internet Computing, vol. 7, no. 1, pp. 40-48, 2003.

[7] B. P. Rimal, E. Choi and I. Lumb, "A taxonomy and survey of cloud computing systems", INC, IMS and IDC, pp. 44-51, 2009.

[8] B. F. Murphy, Network Penetration Testing and Research, NASA, 2013. Available from https://ntrs.nasa.gov/archive/nasa/casi.ntrs.nasa.gov/20140002617.pdf, [retrieved: February, 2017].

[9] J. Andress and S. Winterfeld, Cyber warfare: techniques, tactics and tools for security practitioners. Elsevier, 2013.

[10] A. Oliner, A. Ganapathi and W. Xu, "Advances and challenges in log analysis", Communications of the ACM, vol. 55, no. 2, pp. 55-61, 2012.

[11] G. H. Kim and E. H. Spafford, "The design and implementation of tripwire: A file system integrity checker", Proceedings of the 2nd ACM Conference on Computer and Communications Security, ACM, pp. 18-29, 1994.

[12] J. S. Reuben, A survey on virtual machine security. Helsinki University of Technology, vol. 2, no. 36, 2007.

[13] K. Ilgun, R. A. Kemmerer and P. A. Porras, "State transition analysis: A rule-based intrusion detection approach", IEEE transactions on software engineering, vol. 21, no. 3, pp. 181-199, 1995.

[14] P. Garcia-Teodoro, J. Diaz-Verdejo, G. Maciá-Fernández and E. Vázquez, "Anomaly-based network intrusion detection: Techniques, systems and challenges", Computers and Security, vol. 28, no. 1, pp. 18-28, 2009.

[15] C. Chapman, S. Knight and T. Dean, USBcat-Towards an Intrusion Surveillance Toolset, arXiv preprint arXiv:1410.4304, 2014.

[16] X. Wang, D. S. Reeves, S. F. Wu and J. Yuill, "Sleepy watermark tracing: An active network-based intrusion response framework", Trusted Information, Springer US, pp. 369-384, 2002.

[17] C. V. Zhou, C. Leckie and S. Karunasekera, "A survey of coordinated attacks and collaborative intrusion detection", Computers and Security, vol. 29, no. 1, pp. 124-140, 2010.

[18] A. Patcha and J. M. Park, "An overview of anomaly detection techniques: Existing solutions and latest technological trends", Computer networks, vol. 51, no. 12, pp. 3448-3470, 2007.

[19] H. Sukhwani, V. Sharma and S. Sharma, "A Survey of Anomaly Detection Techniques and Hidden Markov Model", International Journal of Computer Applications, vol. 93, no. 18, pp. 26-31, 2014.

[20] G. Tedesco and U. Aickelin, Strategic alert throttling for intrusion detection systems, arXiv preprint, arXiv:0801.4119, 2008.

[21] A. Shamir, "How to share a secret", Communications of the ACM, vol. 22, no. 11, pp. 612-613, 1979.

# Creating an Immutable Database for Secure Cloud Audit Trail and System Logging

Bob Duncan
Computing Science
University of Aberdeen
Aberdeen, UK
Email: bobduncan@abdn.ac.uk

Mark Whittington
Business School
University of Aberdeen
Aberdeen, UK
Email: mark.whittington@abdn.ac.uk

***Abstract*—Conventional web based systems present a multiplicity of attack vectors. One of the main components, the database, is frequently configured incorrectly, often using default settings, which leave the system wide open to attack. Once a system has been attacked, valuable audit trail and system log data is usually deleted to cover the trail of the perpetrator. Given the average industry time between breach and discovery, there is often little forensic trail left to follow. Of equal importance is that in cloud settings, where new instances are automatically spooled and shut down to follow the demand curve, any data stored on the running instance before shut down is lost. We demonstrate how the configuration of a simple immutable database, running on a separate private system can go a long way to resolving this problem.**

***Index Terms*—Cloud security and privacy; immutable database; forensic trail.**

## I. INTRODUCTION

Achieving information security is not a trivial process, and in the context of cloud computing, it becomes increasingly more difficult. Because cloud technology is enabled by the Internet, one of the key weaknesses comes from web services, which invariably are structured with a database back-end. There are a host of well understood vulnerabilities surrounding the use of modern databases, and while there are a number of mitigating strategies that can be deployed, often they are not, as evidenced by their continual recurrence on annual security breach reports.

Duncan and Whittington [1] have written about the difficulties surrounding proper audit of cloud based systems. They have talked about the need for enterprises to maintain a proper audit trail in their systems, and about the weaknesses arising as a result of poor configuration of database systems, particularly in the context of cloud systems [2]. They have proposed addressing this problem through the use of an immutable database for the purpose of secure audit trail and system logging for cloud applications [3].

Some five years ago in 2012, Trustwave [4], were reporting an average time taken by enterprises of 6 months between breach and discovery. Discovery was often made by third parties external to the enterprise, rather than by the enterprise themselves. This time lag between breach and discovery has been significantly reduced, but nevertheless is a great concern, particularly in the light of forthcoming legislation, such as the ED General Data Protection Regulation (GDPR). Looking at the latest security breach reports, it is clear that many enterprises will be unable to comply with the requirement to report any breach within 72 hours. This would suggest that many firms are not monitoring their systems properly, do not maintain proper audit trails, thus leading to inadequacy in retaining a proper forensic trail to understand exactly what information has been accessed, modified or deleted.

In this paper, we outline how we might approach developing a solution to satisfy these issues and concerns. In Section II, we provide some background and discuss the motivation for this work, and in Section III, we discuss what an immutable database needs to be. In Section IV, where we outline how we can create and configure an immutable database using existing software, in this case we have chosen MySQL for illustrative purposes. In Section V, we discuss typical attack vectors against database systems. In Section VI, we discuss our conclusions.

## II. BACKGROUND AND MOTIVATION

In this paper, we use the MySQL database language to illustrate what is currently possible. While not all databases are exactly similar, most exhibit the same weaknesses, often arising through improper configuration. Equally, the software environment chosen to integrate with the database is often subject to the same poor configuration, thus leading to the ongoing success of attackers. These weaknesses in configuration are frequently exploited by attackers, and there is often a poor understanding of how proper use of the audit trail can help to improve security significantly. Thus, we shall first discuss the purpose of audit and the significance of the audit trail.

### *A. Audit and the Audit Trail*

There are many areas of business activity that merit diligent checking and verification by an objective person or organization from outside the organization itself. Some of these may be undertaken voluntarily by the firm, others such as the audit of financial systems and results are mandated. Clearly cloud computing audit is a new, immature field and it would be surprising if there were not lessons to learn from the experiences — and failures — of audit processes and practices that have been honed over decades if not centuries [5].

Whenever a new technical area emerges it will be difficult to find people with the appropriate skillset — a technical knowledge of the area and competency in carrying out an audit. As commercial organisations, audit companies may seek to extend their audit competence into new technical areas, not just cloud audit, but perhaps environmental audit as another example. Over a century of experience in the development of audit tools and practices then needs to be applied to a new technical domain. Alternatively, computing specialists might pick up an audit skillset. A logical outcome would be for audit firms to recruit computer cloud experts and seek to harmonise their skills with those of audit already embedded in the firm. The culture clash between accountants and cloud experts would be a potential side effect from such a strategy.

One tool the accountants have used for decades is the audit trail and this is a phrase already in the cloud computing literature by the National Institute of Standards and Technology (NIST) [6], for example. However, the same phrase may not carry the same meaning in both settings. Quoting from the Oxford English Dictionary (OED) [7]: "(a) Accounting: a means of verifying the detailed transactions underlying any item in an accounting record; (b) Computing: a record of the computing processes that have been applied to a particular set of source data, showing each stage of processing and allowing the original data to be reconstituted; a record of the transactions to which a database or a file has been subjected". So, disparity of definition is recognized by the OED.

Accountants are members of professional bodies (some national, some global) that limit membership to those who have passed exams and achieved sufficient breadth and length of experience that they are deemed worthy to represent the profession. Audit is a key feature of these exam syllabi and the tracing back to the source each accounting activity (the trail) is a foundational aspect of audit.

Whilst NIST [6], gave a clear explanation of an audit trail in a computing security setting and in keeping with the OED definition (b), the use of the term in research in cloud audit seems less precise and consistent. For example, Bernstein [8], sees the trail including: events, logs, and the analysis of these, whilst Chaula [9], gives a longer, more detailed list: raw data, analysis notes, preliminary development and analysis information, processes notes, and so on. Indeed, Pearson and Benameuer [10] accept that the attaining of consistent, meaningful audit trails in the cloud is a goal rather than reality. More worryingly Ko et al. [11], point out that it is quite possible for an audit trail to be deleted along with a cloud instance, meaning no record then remains to trace back, understand and hold users to account for their actions and Ko [12], then details the requirements for accountability. Indeed, the EU Article 29 Working Party [13], highlights poor audit trail processes as one of the security issues inadequately covered by existing principles.

Whilst the audit trail might seem a long and tedious list of activities and interventions, it can be of enormous value in chasing down the root of a cyber-attack, in much the same way as an accountant might use it to trace the steps and individuals involved in enabling an inappropriately authorised payment. At root, the concept should be implemented in a way that it ought even enable the reconstruction of a system were it to have been completely deleted, not just trace an errant one transaction. The audit trail may be duplication, but it is necessary given the risk of manipulation, compromise or loss. Our discussions with IT professionals, who have asserted their confident reliance on data backups, show a level of unmerited trust as an inappropriate intervention will be repeated in every backup until it is discovered. Backups of a corrupted system will not achieve a rebuild to an uncorrupted one the audit trail gives this opportunity. Referring back to Ko et al. [11], establishing an excellent audit trail is worthless if it is only to be deleted along with a cloud instance. The establishment of an adequate audit trail often needs to be explicit as software can allow audit trails to be switched off in its settings.

Once an audit trail has been established, it contents need to be protected from any adjustment. As Anderson [14], points out, even system administrators must not have the power to modify it. Not only is this good practice even with well trained and ethical individuals, but it is always possible that a hacker might be able to attain administrator status. Therefore, the audit trail needs the establishment of an immutable database (i.e., one that only records new activities but never allows adjustment of previous ones). This is the primary goal of this first test for the successful development of a system to preserve both the audit trail and system logs. In the next section, we discuss the motivation for this work.

### B. Motivation

Given how easily many enterprises unwittingly make life much easier for attackers, we are motivated to do something about it that should neither be expensive to implement, nor technically challenging. It is obvious from analysis of past successful attacks, that one of the key goals of the attacker is to attack both the audit trail and the system logs, in order to obfuscate, or delete all trace of their visit, and everything that they have done whilst inside the compromised system.

The lack of proper monitoring by enterprises, and the ease with which attackers can carry out this, important for them, exercise also makes it much harder for the enterprise to even know they have been breached, let alone understand what exactly has been read, modified, deleted, or ex-filtrated from their systems. Since this will form a cornerstone of forthcoming legislation, this requirement must be addressed.

We strongly believe that enterprises must make provision to ensure the maintenance of both a proper audit trail, and the preservation of as much forensic evidence as possible. For the reasons already discussed above, they must also take particular note of the need to preserve both audit trail data and systems log data when using the cloud. Thus we now take a look at one of the weakest links in this chain, the database.

The cloud paradigm is essentially web based technology, facilitated by a database back end. There are many well known web based vulnerabilities, yet it is clear from analysis of security breach reports, that many enterprises are continually failing to implement even the simplest of preventative measures to mitigate these weaknesses. In addition, it is also clear that many enterprises are failing to monitor their systems properly to detect breaches, given the disparity in time between breach and discovery. As far back as 2012, Verizon [15] highlighted the fact that discovery of security breaches often took weeks, months or even years before discovery, with most discovery being advised by external bodies, such as customers, financial institutions or fraud agencies. While improvements have been made in the intervening years, the situation is far from perfect.

Thus it is appropriate to consider the work done by the Open Web Application Security Project (OWASP) carry out a survey every 3 years in which they collate the number of vulnerabilities which have the greatest impact on enterprises. In TABLE I, we can see the top ten list from 2013, 2010 and 2007:

TABLE I. OWASP TOP TEN WEB VULNERABILITIES — 2013 - 2007 [16]

| 2013 | 2010 | 2007 | Threat |
|---|---|---|---|
| 1 | 1 | 2 | Injection Attacks |
| 2 | 3 | 7 | Broken Authentication and Session Management |
| 3 | 2 | 1 | Cross Site Scripting (XSS) |
| 4 | 4 | 4 | Insecure Direct Object References |
| 5 | 6 | - | Security Misconfiguration |
| 6 | - | - | Sensitive Data Exposure |
| 7 | - | - | Missing Function Level Access Control |
| 8 | 5 | 5 | Cross Site Request Forgery (CSRF) |
| 9 | - | - | Using Components with Known Vulnerabilities |
| 10 | - | - | Unvalidated Redirects and Forwards |

Sitting at the top of the table for 2013, again for 2010, and in second place in 2007, we have injection attacks. It is very clear that enterprises are consistently failing to configure their database systems properly. Injection attacks rely on misconfigured databases used in dynamic web service applications, which allow SQL, OS, or LDAP injection to occur when untrusted data is sent to an interpreter as part of a command or query. The attacker's hostile data can trick the interpreter into executing unintended commands or accessing data without proper authorization. This can lead to compromise, or deletion of data held in enterprise databases.

But injection attacks are not the only attacks which involve databases, numbers 3 and 8 also are directly related to either missing input validation or output sanitation. Equally, databases might also be use in most of the other top ten vulnerabilities, which means database mis-configuration, or failure to configure systems which use database systems properly account one way or another for most of the successful attacks.

Attackers continue to use methods which continue to work, which is clear to see from the continued success of the same attacks, year after year. Thus, we consider this area to be of vital importance for ensuring that any enterprise may achieve a high level of security. And given the importance of the audit trail and system log data, we believe the best approach would be to use an immutable database to record this data properly, which we shall discuss in the next Section.

## III. What is an Immutable Database?

We can describe an immutable database as a secure database implementation capable of meeting the criteria for a proper audit trail, namely, that it should only be capable of being read by a restricted number of authorised users. It must not permit the editing of any transactions, and must not allow any transaction to be deleted. Only new records can be added, no modifications are permitted, and no deletions may take place, thus preserving the original input for subsequent examination.

Looking at the fundamental requirements of the audit trail in Section II-A, it is clear that a conventional database structure fails to deliver on a number of these requirements. A conventional database structure allows any records to be seen, by anyone authorised, or an attacker able to gain adequate credentials to do so. Worse, there is nothing to prevent modification, or deletion of these records. Thus a conventionally set up database is totally unsuitable for an audit trail. The same argument holds for system logs, which should have the same characteristics as an audit trail.

Thus, an audit trail and system log database must have the same characteristics as the manual system, namely restricted access to view the audit trail, with NO option to add, modify or delete records [2]. Naturally, in a cloud setting, as there may be anything from a single instance up to many thousands of instances running at any given time, it would be sensible to host the logging systems on a completely different server or servers at a location remote from the cloud instances, such that all the instances will have their audit trail and system logging data stored in the remote system. This can reduce the probability that a successful attack on the cloud instance can be leveraged to attack the logging database. Ideally, the logging server or servers should be dedicated entirely to running a secure immutable database, with preferably no direct means of public access.

We accept that this means that the logging database is likely to become a prime target for attack. Thus the logging database should be protected with the highest level of security settings, and should be subject to special monitoring to provide instant warning of any attack.

We made the decision that there would be insufficient time to consider writing bespoke software for our purposes. Thus we would restrict ourselves in this work to evaluating what we could do with an existing system. In [2], we observed that short of writing new bespoke database software, or making serious modifications to existing database software, we would be left with three options we could use to meet our objective:

1) Remove all user access for all users to modifying or deleting records and the database itself;
2) Remove the Modify Record and Delete Record command from the software;
3) Use an Archive Database.

In the next section, we examine the pros and cons of each option, in order to come up with the best practical solution to this problem.

## IV. Creating an Immutable Database

Having decided that we would not consider writing some bespoke software, but instead would see how we could configure something utilising existing software, we then evaluated the three options listed in Subsection III.

1) On the positive side, this option is the simplest to configure, does not involve any software modification, and will not impact on software updates. On the negative side, should an attacker gain access to the database and be able to escalate privileges, there would be nothing to prevent them from reversing the restrictions;
2) On the positive side, this option would take away the ability of an attacker, should they get in to the database and be able to escalate privileges, to reverse the restrictions. On the negative side, this could complicate software updates;
3) On the positive side, this presents an extremely simple solution, no software needs modifying, and there is nothing for the attacker to reverse. On the negative side, the Archive Database does not support key searching. This is likely to make searches cumbersome. However. in the short term, we could resolve this issue by extracting a copy of all the data into a conventional database with full key search capabilities for rapid examination.

Thus, we took the view that for the purposes of this work, we would use option 3, using the Archive Database option, in order to create the system logging and audit trail databases. We assume the application database will run using conventional settings, although it is important to take account of the following four weaknesses in conventional systems.

First, default logging options can result in insufficient data being collected for the audit trail. Second, since there is often a lack of recognition that the audit trail data can be accessed by a malicious user gaining root privileges, we recommend the audit trail and system logs should be sent to the external immutable database, set up using the Archive Database configuration, for this purpose. Third, failure to ensure log data is properly collected and moved to permanent storage can lead to loss of audit trail data, either when an instance is shut down, or when it is compromised. Sending all audit trail and system log data to the external immutable database/s will ensure that the data will not be lost when the instance is closed down. Fourth, the recommended mitigation techniques suggested by OWASP should be implemented in the main web application software.

Now, we consider the minimum audit trail data we would wish to collect. MySQL offers the following audit trail options:

- Error log — Problems encountered starting, running, or stopping mysqld;
- General query log — Established client connections and statements received from clients;
- Binary log — Statements that change data (also used for replication);
- Relay log — Data changes received from a replication master server;
- Slow query log — Queries that took more than long_query_time seconds to execute;
- DDL log (metadata log) — Metadata operations performed by Data Definition Language (DDL) statements.

By default, no logs are enabled, except the error log on Windows. Some versions of Linux send the Error log to syslog. Thus for a straightforward implementation, we would wish to collect the Error Log, the General query log, the Binary log and the Slow query log. Where replication is in use, adding the Relay log is recommended. Where DDL statements are used, then the DDL log should also be activated.

While Oracle offer an audit plugin for Enterprise (paid) editions of MySQL, which allows a range of events to be logged, by default most are not enabled. The MariaDB company, whose author originally wrote MySQL, have their own open source audit plug-in, and offer a version suitable for MySQL. It has the following functionality:

- CONNECTION — Logs connects, disconnects and failed connects (including the error code);
- QUERY — Queries issued and their results (in plain text), including failed queries due to syntax or permission errors;
- TABLE — Which tables were affected by query execution;
- QUERY_DDL — Works as the 'QUERY' value, but filters only DDL-type queries (CREATE, ALTER, etc);
- QUERY_DML — Works as the 'QUERY' value, but filters only Data Manipulation Language (DML) DML-type queries (INSERT, UPDATE, etc.).

Where a company falls under the provisions of the new EU GDPR regulations, using the MariaDB audit trail plug-in and turning on ALL 5 logging options would be a prudent move. Admittedly this would require a considerable increase in storage requirements for the log output. However, since they would then be in a position to provide full disclosure to the regulator of all records accessed, tampered with or deleted, this would go a very long way to mitigate the amount of fine they might be subject to, which could be as high as 4% of their global turnover.

Thus, this approach will address the first problem, that of insufficient audit trail and system logging data being collected. If the data is sent to a well protected external database, an attacker who has compromised the running instance will not be able to cover their trail. The system logs could be retained on the instance to make the attacker think that they have covered their tracks. Thus, the second point is addressed. By sending a copy of all log data to the secure immutable database, we can address the third point, thus ensuring no data is lost on shut down of the instance. Finally, if the OWASP mitigation techniques are used to harden the web application, there will be less likelihood of a successful breach taking place. Plus the immutable database on the secure external server satisfies the requirements of a proper audit trail [14].

There is also no doubt that adding an Intrusion Detection system (IDS) is also a useful additional precaution to take, and again, this should be run on an independent secure server under the control of the cloud user.

Equally, where the MySQL instance forms part of a LAMP server, then it would also be prudent to make some elementary security changes to the setup of the Linux operating system, the Apache web server, and to harden the PHP installation.

There is one additional task that would be very worthwhile. That is to set up an additional control instance to monitor every new instance added to the application, which regularly checks whether the instance is still functioning as expected. This would allow this system to warn of instances unexpectedly being closed down, which might be a sign of an attack. In addition, the log files in the immutable database could be monitored for specific patterns, which might indicate the possibility of an attack.

One of the biggest issues is the fact that there is such a lag between breach and discovery, and this approach could provide much earlier warning of such an event. However, of greater interest, is the fact that a full forensic trail would be instantly available for immediate investigation. And it would be possible to disclose the extent of the breach well within the required disclosure time of 72 hours from the time of breach to disclosure.

As we see from [17], see Figure 1, that in 2015, 75% of breaches happened within days, yet only 25% of discoveries are actually made within the same time-frame. This still leaves a large gap where compromised systems may still be under the control of malicious users. Our proposed approach would go some way to reducing this problem.

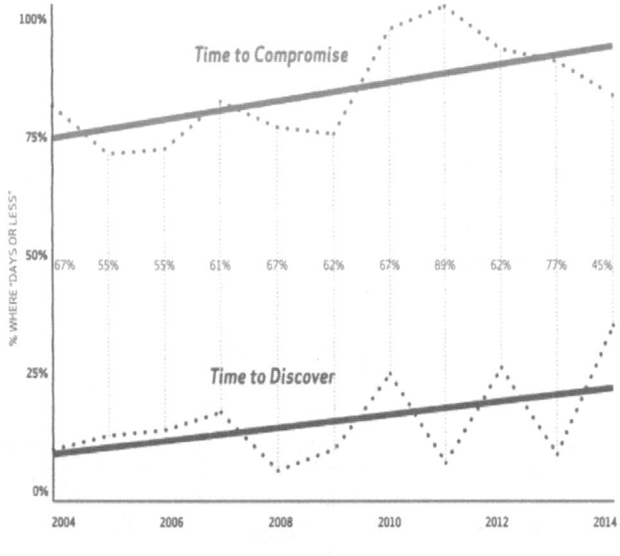


Fig. 1. The Lag Between Breach and Discovery © 2015 Verizon

This presents a clear indication that very few firms are actually scrutinising their server logs. We take a quick look at some typical database attacks and possible mitigation for these attacks in the next Section.

## V. Typical Database Attack Methodologies

SQL injection attacks are relatively straightforward to defend against. OWASP provide an SQL injection prevention cheat sheet [18], in which they suggest a number of defences:

- Use of Prepared Statements (Parameterized Queries);
- Use of Stored Procedures;
- Escaping all User Supplied Input;

They also suggest that companies should enforce least privilege and perform white list input validation as useful additional precautions to take.

For operating system injection flaws, they also have a cheat sheet [19], which suggests that LDAP injection attacks are common due to two factors, namely the lack of safer, parameterized LDAP query interfaces, and the widespread use of LDAP to authenticate users to systems. Their recommendations for suitable defences are:

- Rule 1 Perform proper input validation;
- Rule 2 Use a safe API;
- Rule 3 Contextually escape user data.

And for LDAP system injection flaws, their cheat sheet [20], recommends the following injection prevention rules:

- Defence Option 1: Escape all variables using the right LDAP encoding function;
- Defence Option 2: Use Frameworks that Automatically Protect from LDAP Injection.

None of these preventative measures suggested by OWASP are particularly difficult to implement, yet judging by the recurring success of these simple attacks, companies are clearly failing to take even simple actions to protect against them.

Thus, in addition to making the simple suggestions we propose above, cloud users should also make sure they actually review the audit trail logs. It is vital to be able to understand when a security breach has occurred, and exactly which records have been accessed, compromised or stolen. While recognising that this is not a foolproof method of achieving cloud security, it is likely to present a far higher level of affordable, achievable security than many companies currently achieve.

Implementing these suggestions will not guarantee security, but will make life so much more difficult for the attacker that they are more likely to move on to easier 'low hanging fruit' elsewhere. There is currently an abundance of other options for them to choose from.

However, the company must remain vigilant at all times. It would be prudent to subscribe to security feeds, and follow leaders in the field to ensure they remain aware of all the latest security vulnerabilities and exploits. Of course, companies must realise that the threat environment is not restricted to outside parties alone. A greater concern is the threat posed by malicious internal actors, which can be even more serious where they act in concert with outside parties. This presents one of the most serious weaknesses to the security of a company. Equally, laziness on the part of staff or lack of knowledge, particularly where they have not been regularly trained to provide them with full awareness of all the latest threats, including social engineering attacks, and the consequence of falling victim to them, can also pose an extremely serious risk to company security.

In the event of a security breach, not if, but rather when it happens, it may be necessary to conduct a forensic examination to establish how the company defences were breached. With traditional distributed systems, there is usually something for the forensic computer scientists to find, somewhere in the system. They are completely accustomed to dealing with being able to find only partial traces of events, from which they can build a forensic picture of the breach. This becomes more problematic the longer the time between breach and discovery.

However, once a company adopts cloud use, this becomes far more problematic. While forensic computer scientists can work wonders with a range of partial discoveries, deleted or otherwise, once a cloud instance is shut down, there is virtually zero chance of regaining access to the shut down system. The disk space used by that system could be re-used, literally within seconds, and where the time interval between breach and discovery is considerably longer, as is generally the norm, then this opportunity becomes a physical impossibility. Thus, for forensic purposes, companies need to pay far more attention to what is actually going on in the cloud.

The suggestions we make can go a long way to providing a greater level of security, and perhaps more importantly, can ensure there is actually a forensic trail to follow in the event of a breach.

## VI. CONCLUSION

We have considered a wide range of security issues in cloud based systems, with a view to highlighting that the attack surface of any cloud based system extends well beyond technical issues. We have identified that databases present a considerable weakness in cloud based systems, in addition to the unintended potential loss of forensic data caused by the manner in which scalability is handled in large cloud systems.

We have suggested a simple approach that could be easily implemented, with minimal technical knowledge, which would offer a considerable improvement on cloud security, with the additional benefit of maintaining a vastly improved forensic trail to explore in the event of a breach. Equally, our proposal also offers the benefit of being able to discover precisely which records have been viewed, compromised, or deleted. This presents a significant mitigation in the event that any regulator proposes a significant fine, since the company will be in a position to comply fully with the reporting requirements.

We plan to test this proposal to identify any loss in performance resulting from not being able to use key searching in the immutable databases, and to identify how it will stand up to attack. In the longer term, it would be useful to develop a software solution that might add the key search capability to the immutable database.

## REFERENCES


[1] B. Duncan and M. Whittington, "Enhancing cloud security and privacy: The cloud audit problem," in *Cloud Comput. 2016 Seventh Int. Conf. Cloud Comput. GRIDs, Virtualization*. Rome: IEEE, 2016, pp. 119–124.

[2] B. Duncan and M. Whittington, "Enhancing cloud security and privacy: The Power and the weakness of the audit trail," in *Cloud Comput. 2016 Seventh Int. Conf. Cloud Comput. GRIDs, Virtualization*. Rome: IEEE, 2016, pp. 125–130.

[3] B. Duncan and M. Whittington, "Cloud cyber-security: Empowering the audit trail," *Forthcom. Int. J. Adv. Secur.*, vol. v9, no. 3&4, p. 15, 2016.

[4] Trustwave, "2012 Global Security Report," Tech. Rep., 2012.

[5] B. Duncan and M. Whittington, "Compliance with standards, assurance and audit: Does this equal security?" in *Proc. 7th Int. Conf. Secur. Inf. Networks*. Glasgow: ACM, 2014, pp. 77–84.

[6] B. Guttman and E. A. Roback, "NIST special publication 800-12. An introduction to computer security: The NIST Handbook," NIST, Tech. Rep. 800, 2011. [Online]. Available: csrc.nist.gov/publications/nistpubs/800-12/handbook.pdf Last Accessed: Jan 2017

[7] OED, "Oxford English Dictionary," 1989. [Online]. Available: www.oed.com

[8] D. Bernstein, E. Ludvigson, K. Sankar, S. Diamond, and M. Morrow, "Blueprint for the intercloud - Protocols and formats for cloud computing interoperability," in *Proc. 2009 4th Int. Conf. Internet Web Appl. Serv. ICIW 2009*, 2009, pp. 328–336.

[9] J. A. Chaula, "A socio-technical analysis of information systems security assurance: A case study for effective assurance," Ph.D. dissertation, 2006. [Online]. Available: http://scholar.google.com/scholar?hl=en{\&}btnG=Search{\&}q=intitle:A+Socio-Technical+Analysis+of+Information+Systems+Security+Assurance+A+Case+Study+for+Effective+Assurance{\#}1 Last Accessed: Jan 2017

[10] S. Pearson and A. Benameur, "Privacy, security and trust issues arising from cloud computing," in *2010 IEEE Second Int. Conf. Cloud Comput. Technol. Sci.*, no. December. Ieee, nov 2010, pp. 693–702.

[11] R. K. L. Ko et al., "TrustCloud: A framework for accountability and trust in cloud computing," *Proc. - 2011 IEEE World Congr. Serv. Serv. 2011*, pp. 584–588, 2011.

[12] L. F. B. Soares, D. a. B. Fernandes, J. V. Gomes, M. M. Freire, and P. R. M. Inácio, "Security, privacy and trust in cloud systems," in *Secur. Priv. Trust Cloud Syst.* Springer, 2014, ch. Data Accou, pp. 3–44.

[13] EU, "Unleashing the potential of cloud computing in europe," 2012. [Online]. Available: http://eur-lex.europa.eu/LexUriServ/LexUriServ.do?uri=SWD:2012:0271:FIN:EN:PDF Last Accessed: Jan 2017

[14] R. J. Anderson, *Security engineering: A guide to building dependable distributed systems*, C. A. Long, Ed. Wiley, 2008, vol. 50, no. 5.

[15] Verizon, N. High, T. Crime, I. Reporting, and I. S. Service, "2012 data breach investigations report," Verizon, Tech. Rep., 2012.

[16] OWASP, "OWASP top ten vulnerabilities 2013," 2013. [Online]. Available: https://www.owasp.org/index.php/Category:OWASP_Top_Ten_Project Last Accessed: Jan 2017

[17] Verizon, "Verizon 2015 data breach investigation report," Tech. Rep., 2015.

[18] OWASP, "OWASP SQL injection cheat sheet," 2016. [Online]. Available: https://www.owasp.org/index.php/SQL_Injection_Prevention_Cheat_Sheet Last Accessed: Jan 2017

[19] OWASP, "OWASP injection prevention cheat sheet," 2016. [Online]. Available: https://www.owasp.org/index.php/Injection_Prevention_Cheat_Sheet Last Accessed: Jan 2017

[20] OWASP, "OWASP LDAP injection prevention cheat sheet," 2016. [Online]. Available: https://www.owasp.org/index.php/LDAP_Injection_Prevention_Cheat_Sheet Last Accessed: Jan 2017

# Platform As A Service Effort Reduction

Aspen Olmsted, Kaitlyn Fulford
College of Charleston
Department of Computer Science, Charleston, SC 29401
e-mail: olmsteda@cofc.edu, fulfordke@g.cofc.edu

***Abstract*— In this paper, we investigate the problem of development costs in Platform as-a Service (PAAS) cloud-based systems. We develop a set of tools to analyze the size of code executed to support features in the PAAS. In this research, we specifically focus on stable open source platforms to ensure as much of an equivalent offering from each platform. A distinction is made between PAAS and Platform Infrastructure as-a Service (PIAAS). The focus of the paper is on the features provided to the developer that are not provided by traditional network operating systems. Our study demonstrates a cost savings of nearly thirteen million dollars to develop the application services provided by a typical PAAS.**

***Keywords-PAAS; cloud computing; CRM***

## I. INTRODUCTION

In this work, we investigate the problem of estimating the cost of developer services provided by a platform as a service (PAAS) cloud-based system. In traditional client-server architectures, developers spend a great deal of their effort developing functionality that is not specific to the business domain where the application will operate in.

Cloud computing has traditionally been made up of three broad categories of offerings:

- Software-As-A-Service (SAAS) – This category includes applications that run in a Web browser and do not require any local software and hardware besides the Web browser and Internet connection. Examples of software in this category are Google Docs [1] and Microsoft Office 365 [2].
- Infrastructure-As-A-Service (IAAS) – This category includes virtualization software that allows an operating system to be run in the cloud. Typically, the user will pick a hardware configuration and install an operating system into the virtual hardware configuration. IAAS was designed to free the user from the purchase of hardware and allow for hardware upgrades easily. Examples of IAAS offerings are Amazon EC2 [3] and Rackspace [4].
- Platform-As-A-Service (PAAS) – This category includes pre-build components that a developer can use when developing a cloud application. The goal of PAAS is to allow the developer to focus on the development of a solution for the business functions and not software functions that span many application domains. A good example of PAAS is force.com where the developer is provided many of the essential parts of an application out of the box.

Over the years, software development has matured to allow the developer to spend a larger percentage of their development time on the business problem instead of the infrastructure for the application. In the early days of programming, each instruction the programmer wrote matched an instruction in the hardware. The late 1980s and 90s were dominated by 3rd generation languages such as C, PASCAL or ADA where each instruction written by the developer was compiled to many machine instructions. The 21st century has been dominated by byte code compiled languages that have runtime engines that execute the code on different hardware platforms. The Java Runtime Engine (JRE) and the Microsoft .NET Runtime Engine (.NET) are the most dominate examples of the byte code engines that free the developer from thinking about the underlying hardware. PAAS is the next evolution in freeing up the developer times, so they can focus on the problem they are trying to solve instead of the technical plumbing required for the solution.

The organization of the paper is as follows. Section 2 describes the related work and the limitations of current methods. In Section III, we document typical services provided. Section IV analyzes different PAAS providers and the services they provide. Section V explores the alternative costs to develop the individual services. We conclude and discuss future work in Section VI.

## II. RELATED WORK

The NIST Definition of Cloud Computing defines PAAS as "the capability provided to the consumer [...] to deploy onto the cloud infrastructure consumer-created or acquired applications created using programming languages, libraries, services, and tools supported by the provider. The consumer does not manage or control the underlying cloud infrastructure including network, servers, operating systems, or storage, but has control over the deployed applications and possibly configuration settings for the application-hosting environment" [1]. In the same document, they define SAAS and IAAS similarly to our definitions in the introduction.

Kolb and Wirtz [2] investigate ways to construct applications for the cloud that are portable across different PAAS providers. Their work assumes lower level services in the offerings than our work. We are less interested in maintenance costs to move platforms as we are in startup costs for Greenfield Engineering. In software engineering,

Greenfield Engineering occurs when you are starting from scratch, or you are re-engineering your product on a different architectural paradigm where you cannot port your current code base.

Baliyan and Kumar [3] explore how services provided by a PAAS provider effect the Software Development Lifecycle (SDLC). Again, in their work they consider just a few services. In our work, we think about many more services. The larger perspective on service would have an even greater impact on their work.

In our model of services, end-users can create new objects, new forms for data entry, new reports to display the data in detail and aggregate form and new dash boards. Ng [4] looks at PAAS as a model for deploying end-user programming through a model of Tasks. The programming model provided by the platforms in our study has demonstrated success in allowing end-users to extend the application.

Boehm, Clark, Horowitz, Westland, Madachy and Selby [5] developed an algorithm to estimate effort for a software engineering project. The algorithm uses variables that represent programmer and programming experience required in the project. For this study, we used the "nominal" value for each variable to get an average cost. Madachy [6] provides an online tool to calculate the effort including maintenance over the life of the software.

## III. PAAS SERVICES

With PAAS, the developer does not need to be concerned with the operating system on which the specified platform runs. For example, the platform will provide a service to save a file and the developer does not need to worry what operating system the platform is running on. We group the service offerings into two distinct categories:

### A. *Infrastructure Services*

- Node Configuration – This service allows the end user to modify configuration settings to allow the system to scale to handle larger or smaller workloads by adding or removing nodes, storage or Central Processing Units (CPUs). This service allows the implementation to start with minimal hardware to save costs during start-up. Additional resources can then be added as the application user base grows without the need to re-engineer the application.
- Load Balancing – This service allows the end user to setup multiple systems to ensure uptime when loads are higher, or network partitions occur. Each system is an exact replica and the load will be distributed across the replicas. The application will need to be designed properly for replication. The system must not store resources in a specific replica. Each request could be sent to a different replica. Both persisted data and session state should be stored in the database service.
- Logging – The logging service allows an audit log to be enabled to help diagnosis application and platform issues. The service should allow the log to be toggled on and off so that space is not wasted when an audit is not needed. Ideally, there will be different granularity of audits available, such as errors, warnings, and information.
- Database – The database service allows the application to persist data across executions of the application. Traditionally, this has been a relational database such as Oracle [11] or MySQL [12] but may be a NoSQL [13] database that is better at distribution. The database service should provide Create, Read, Update and Delete (CRUD) services and potentially transaction support.
- Scheduled Jobs – This service allows bulk operations to be scheduled at specific and recurring timeframes. Example jobs include sending out bulk emails, updating de-normalized database fields, and communicating with external systems. Often, this service is delivered through a cronjob interface where jobs can be schedule down to the specific second of each hour.

### B. *Application Services*

- Authentication – The authentication service provides a way to define users and allow authentication in the application being developed. Ideally, this would provide both the administrative tool for creating users and groups along with the user interface the end users interact with to authenticate themselves. The authentication should provide multifactor authentication where something the end user knows along with someplace they are or something they have.
- Authorization – The authorization service provides a way to define which users can see different data, forms, and reports in the application. The authorization service should provide an administrative tool to assign access permission to both users and groups to objects created in the system. The objects should be both standard objects and custom objects defined by the developer and end users.
- Rule Engine – A rule engine allows for customization of correctness rules at implementation time. Business rules control organization policies that may change often and should not be coded in the software solution.

- Workflow – This service provides for several discrete application steps to be sequenced together. Often, a human interaction (Approval) is part of the workflow.
- Bulk Email – Bulk email allows for email marketing with proper adherence to Email SPAM rules [14]. Bulk email may be used for attracting or recruiting new customers or confirming transactions with current customers.
- Importing – An importing feature allows the end user to import new instances of objects into the platform. Ideally, this would allow data from several different data formats including Comma Separated Values (CSV) and Microsoft Excel format. The tool should provide a validation step so that imported data does not corrupt the current database.
- Exporting – An exporting feature allows the end user to dump instances of the objects into an external file such as a Comma Separated Values (CSV) or Microsoft Excel formatted file. The tool should allow a Query by Example (QBE) where novice users can visually build export queries and see the results in the application.
- Activity tracking – Activity tracking allows for linking of phone calls, emails, meetings, and notes to objects persisted by the application. Activities may be originated in an external system with an interface to the new system that is being built. An example could be a Web browser extension that allows emails in a Web email application to be linked to a related activity to an object in the new system.
- Object Customization – Object custom allows end users to add additional data to be collected in the application without changing the source code. Most enterprise systems require some form of customization either through integration to external systems or enhancements to specific features in the current system. Object customization allows the end user to make the changes without needing the software to be modified at each individual enterprise.
- New Object Creation – New object creation services allow end users to define new objects to store data that is collected in the application. Like with object customization, new object creation can be used to customize the software without changing the source code. Often, the new objects need to relate to a current object in the system. These related objects should seamlessly be displayed in the user interface.
- Detail View – The detail view renders the object details based on the configured layout. The detail view also renders one-to-many related data. The related data is often rendered in tabs.
- Edit View – The edit view renders an editable object screen based on the configured layout. The edit view is used to modify one specific object and potentially related objects.
- Data Update – The data update service provides a CRUD interface to a backend data store. The data update service abstracts the vendor specifics of the back-end data store services and allows business rule hooks to fire on the CRUD operations.

TABLE 1. APPLICATION SERVICES BY PLATFORM

| Service | Salesforce | Zoho | SugarCRM | SuiteCRM | vTiger | Heroku |
|---|---|---|---|---|---|---|
| Authentication | ✓ | ✓ | ✓ | ✓ | ✓ | ✓ |
| Authorization | ✓ | ✓ | ✓ | ✓ | ✓ | |
| Rule Engine | ✓ | | ✓ | | | |
| Workflow | ✓ | ✓ | ✓ | ✓ | ✓ | |
| Bulk Email | ✓ | ✓ | ✓ | ✓ | ✓ | |
| Activity tracking | ✓ | ✓ | ✓ | ✓ | ✓ | |
| Object Audit | ✓ | | ✓ | ✓ | ✓ | |
| Importing | ✓ | ✓ | ✓ | ✓ | ✓ | |
| Exporting | ✓ | ✓ | ✓ | ✓ | ✓ | |
| Object Customization | ✓ | ✓ | ✓ | ✓ | ✓ | |
| New Object Creation | ✓ | ✓ | ✓ | ✓ | ✓ | |
| User Interface Customization | ✓ | ✓ | ✓ | ✓ | ✓ | |
| Multi-Select Fields | ✓ | ✓ | ✓ | ✓ | ✓ | |
| Report Display | ✓ | ✓ | ✓ | ✓ | ✓ | |
| Report Creation | ✓ | ✓ | ✓ | ✓ | ✓ | |
| Dashboard Display | ✓ | ✓ | ✓ | ✓ | ✓ | |
| Dashboard Creation | ✓ | ✓ | ✓ | ✓ | ✓ | |
| Web-services | ✓ | ✓ | ✓ | ✓ | ✓ | |
| Mobile Application | ✓ | ✓ | ✓ | | ✓ | |
| Partner Portal | ✓ | | | | | |
| Customer Portal | ✓ | | ✓ | ✓ | ✓ | |
| Anonymous Sites | ✓ | | | | | ✓ |
| Price per user/month | $25 | $35 | $65 | N/A | N/A | N/A |

- User Interface Customization – The user interface customization service allows for forms in the application to be modified by the end users without changing the source code. This is often required to allow implementations to vary slightly by collecting custom data.
- Multi-Select Fields – Multi-select fields are a way to simplify end user customizations. A multi-select field represents an easy way to store a one-to-many relationship of data without the need of adding new objects. Multi-select fields also save on the number of tuples stored in the system. Often, cloud providers charge for data storage based on the number of tuples. [7]
- Report Display – The report display service allows execution of pre-defined reporting queries. The report display should prompt the user with replaceable run-time parameters. The report should be exportable to pdf and spreadsheet formats. Ideally, there would be a scheduling service where the report parameters would be based on the run date. For example, a start date parameter should be replaced based on an offset from the date the report is run.
- Report Creation – The report writer service allows both the developer and the end users to define management information system (MIS) reports that can be run and customized by the changing of run-time parameters. Typically, this includes both tabular reports that group rows of records with aggregate calculations and cross-tab reports that aggregate values based on the intersection of the row and column.
- Dashboard Display – The dashboard display service renders dashboard charts and allows them to be refreshed automatically. The dashboard is a graphical display of a metric the organization wants to measure.
- Dashboard Creation – Dashboards allow both the developer and the end users to define graphical dashboards that allow visualization of data stored in the application. Dashboards typically are bar or pie charts and are updated several times an hour.
- Mobile Application – A mobile application allows end users to perform create, read, update, and delete (CRUD) operations on objects stored in the application without the need of creating custom mobile applications. Similar to the detail and edit view services above, any object in the system should be visible and editable.
- Partner Portal – A partner portal is a service to provide pages, forms, reports and dashboards to authenticated users with a lower training level. Typically, these are users that use the application infrequently compared to an employee.
- Customer Portal – A customer portal is a service to provide custom pages and forms to authenticated users with no training required. The service is intended for customer self-service sites where the customer can identify themselves and perform transactions.
- Anonymous Sites – The anonymous site service allows development of pages and forms to unauthenticated users. This is typically the part of an organizations website where customers do not need to identify themselves.

## IV. PLATFORM ANALYSIS

In this study, we analyze several PAAS providers including Salesforce [8], Zoho CRM [9], SugarCRM [10], SuiteCRM [11], vTiger [12] and Heroku [13]. We chose the first five platforms because they each provide many of the services we discussed in detail. The last platform was added to show the difference between PAAS and PIAAS offerings. Each of the first five PAAS offerings was developed as Customer Relationship Management (CRM) system. The CRM vertical market software space requires integration with Enterprise Resource Planning (ERP) systems. The integration requirement led the CRM vendors to develop their products as platforms instead of just the vertical market products. TABLE 2 shows the distributed services offered by each platform. The Load Balancing service is marked for the three PHP [18] platforms because the state of the session is stored in the database. Having the session state stored in the database allows additional business tier servers to be added to the configuration in the cloud. Though only Heroku has a graphical user interface (GUI) to manage node configuration, the PHP solutions can be hosted by an IAAS provider that provides the feature. TABLE 1 shows the

TABLE 2. DISTRIBUTED SERVICES BY PLATFORM

| Service | Salesforce | Zoho | SugarCRM | SuiteCRM | vTiger | Heroku |
|---|---|---|---|---|---|---|
| Node Configuration | | | | | | ✓ |
| Load Balancing | | | ✓ | ✓ | ✓ | |
| Logging | ✓ | | ✓ | ✓ | ✓ | ✓ |
| Database | ✓ | ✓ | ✓ | ✓ | ✓ | ✓ |
| Scheduled Jobs | ✓ | ✓ | ✓ | ✓ | ✓ | |

application services offered by each platform. The final row shows a cost per user if the PAAS provider is providing both the infrastructure and the application services.

## V. Effort Study

To calculate the effort savings provided by the different PAAS service providers, we calculated the source lines of code (SLOC) in a stable platform release. For this study, we choose to use the SuiteCRM [10] systems as our model. SuiteCRM is open source software, so we had access to the source code developed to provide the platform.

SuiteCRM is written in the PHP programming language using a MySQL database as its persistence layer. Using the debugger extension xDebug [13], we are able to trace all lines of code executed on the server when interacting with the application. xDebug creates a trace file with these lines of code. We developed tooling to parse the trace file and store the data in a MySQL database based on the function executed.

Because of the nature of Web application architectures, a single round trip from the Web browser to the Web server will often execute two distinct sets of functionality. For example, when a user enters their login credentials, the post to the server authenticates the user and then executes the code to display the homepage of dashboards. Our tooling allows a trace to add to the functional cost or subtracted from the functional cost. In the earlier example, we trace the combined functionality and then subtract the individual functionality of building the home screen.

For the study, we wanted the cost for local application software engineers in the Charleston, SC area. The Bureau of Labor Statics [14] estimated the average cost for an application software engineer is $96,200/year. Hadzima [15] estimates the cost of an employee's benefits and taxes at between 25% and 40% of base salary. On top of the salary cost, the employer must pay for rent for office space, equipment, recruitment, training, etc. For our study, we are estimating the hourly cast at $71.50 per hour for an application programmer's time. In TABLE 3 we show the estimated cost to pay an application programmer in the Charleston, SC area to redevelop the functionality provided by the service. We analyzed SuiteCRM and looked at the organized source lines of code (SLOC). SuiteCRM stores the service source code in module folders on the file systems. We counted the executable lines of code and compared to the executed lines of code from the trace. Each trace represented a slightly higher number of lines of code because of shared libraries. We felt it was not appropriate to count all the shared lines of code per service, but we also felt it was not appropriate to ignore them completely. We decided to take the average between the two-line counts. We plugged the average number into the Constructive Cost Model (COCOMO) II formula [26] with our local application programmer cost of $71.50 per hour. The fifth column in TABLE 3 shows the cost per service and the total cost of all services. We eliminated a few services from the study as the source code was not available. The table does not show the cost of the infrastructure services. The infrastructure services can be provided by an IAAS provider if the development is done to leverage the services.

## VI. Conclusion

In this paper, we analyzed the programming effort required to reproduce services provided by a cloud PAAS provider. Our solution utilizes two methods to estimate the number of lines of code requried for a service; SLOC and an execution trace. We utilize an average of the two methods to apply the COCOMO II costing algorithm. Our study demonstrates a cost savings of nearly thirteen million dollars. The savings comes from not needing to develop the application services provied by the PAAS providers in our study.

In this research, we focused on application services provided by a PAAS. Future work needs to study the infrastructure services costs and the application development knowledge required to leverage the provided distribution services.

TABLE 3. COST PER SERVICES

| Service | SLOC | Trace | Average | CoCoMoII |
|---|---|---|---|---|
| Authentication/ Authorization | 1156 | 1437 | 1297 | $ 590,131 |
| Workflow | 954 | 1146 | 1050 | $ 467,789 |
| Bulk Email | 702 | 1054 | 878 | $ 384,246 |
| Activity tracking | 1178 | 1302 | 1240 | $ 561,674 |
| Object Audit | 656 | 873 | 765 | $ 330,225 |
| Importing | 1654 | 1857 | 1756 | $ 823,478 |
| Exporting | 945 | 1246 | 1096 | $ 490,375 |
| Object Customization | 2164 | 2874 | 2519 | $ 1,224,557 |
| New Object Design | 1474 | 1826 | 1650 | $ 768,981 |
| Detail View | 291 | 464 | 378 | $ 152,095 |
| Edit View | 1828 | 464 | 1146 | $ 515,031 |
| Data Updates | 656 | 989 | 823 | $ 357,860 |
| User Interface Customization | 2073 | 2482 | 2278 | $ 1,096,353 |
| Multi-Select Fields | 402 | 512 | 457 | $ 187,395 |
| Report Display | 1912 | 2356 | 2134 | $ 1,020,384 |
| Report Creation | 2957 | 3345 | 3151 | $ 1,566,362 |
| Dashboard Display | 1342 | 1672 | 1507 | $ 696,016 |
| Dashboard Creation | 1874 | 2198 | 2036 | $ 968,972 |
| Web-services | 986 | 1822 | 1404 | $ 643,884 |
| Total | | | | $ 12,845,808 |

## REFERENCES


[1] Google, "About Google Docs," 2017. [Online]. Available: https://www.google.com/docs/about/. [Accessed 10 02 2017].

[2] Microsoft, "Office products," 2017. [Online]. Available: https://products.office.com/en-us/products. [Accessed 10 02 2017].

[3] Amazon Web Services, Inc, "Amazon Elastic Compute Cloud - Virtual Server Hosting," 2017. [Online]. Available: https://aws.amazon.com/ec2/. [Accessed 10 02 2017].

[4] Rackspace, "Rackspace.com - Rackspace® Managed Cloud," 2017. [Online]. Available: https://www.rackspace.com/. [Accessed 10 02 2017].

[5] P. Mell and P. Grance, "The NIST Definition of Cloud," 09 2011. [Online]. Available: http://nvlpubs.nist.gov/nistpubs/Legacy/SP/nistspecialpublication800-145.pdf. [Accessed 07 09 2016].

[6] S. Kolb and G. Wirtz, "Portability in Platform as a Service," in *2014 IEEE 8th International Symposium on Service Oriented System Engineering*, Oxford, United Kingdom, 2014.

[7] N. Baliyan and S. Kumar, "Towards Software Engineering Paradigm for," in *2014 Seventh International Conference on Contemporary Computing*, Noida, India, 2014.

[8] J. Ng, "Extending the Cloud From an App Development Platform into a Tasking Platform," in *2015 IEEE World Congress on Services*, New York, NY, 2015.

[9] B. Boehm, B. Clark, E. Horowitz, C. Westland, R. Madachy and R. Selby, "Cost models for future software life cycle processes: COCOMO 2.0," *Annals of Software Engineering,* vol. 1, no. 1, p. 57–94, 1995.

[10] M. Ray, "COCOMO II - Constructive Cost Model," 2016. [Online]. Available: http://csse.usc.edu/tools/COCOMOII.php. [Accessed 07 09 2016].

[11] Oracle, "Oracle Database," 2017. [Online]. Available: https://www.oracle.com/database/index.html. [Accessed 10 02 2017].

[12] Oracle, "MySQL Database," 2017. [Online]. Available: https://www.mysql.com/. [Accessed 10 02 2017].

[13] Wikimedia Foundation, Inc, "NoSQL," 2017. [Online]. Available: https://en.wikipedia.org/wiki/NoSQL. [Accessed 10 02 2017].

[14] Wikimedia Foundation, Inc, "Email spam," 2017. [Online]. Available: https://en.wikipedia.org/wiki/Email_spam. [Accessed 10 02 2017].

[15] A. Olmsted and G. Santhanakrishnan, "Cloud Data Denormalization of Anonymous Transactions," in *Cloud Computing*, Rome, Italy, 2016.

[16] Salesforce.com, inc, "Run your business better with Force.," 2006. [Online]. Available: http://www.salesforce.com/platform/products/force/?d=70130000000f27V&internal=true. [Accessed 03 02 2016].

[17] Zoho Corporation Pvt. Ltd, "Zoho CRM is ready," 2016. [Online]. Available: https://www.zoho.com/crm. [Accessed 07 09 2016].

[18] SugarCRM, "Discover a different kind of CRM," 2016. [Online]. Available: http://www.sugarcrm.com/. [Accessed 07 09 2016].

[19] SalesAgility, "SuiteCRM – CRM for the world," 2016. [Online]. Available: https://suitecrm.com/. [Accessed 07 09 2016].

[20] vTiger, "Grow sales, improve marketing ROI, and deliver great customer service," 2016. [Online]. Available: https://www.vtiger.com/. [Accessed 07 09 2016].

[21] Salesforce, "Cloud Application Platform," 2016. [Online]. Available: https://www.heroku.com/. [Accessed 07 09 2016].

[22] The PHP Group, "About PHP," 2017. [Online]. Available: http://php.net/. [Accessed 10 02 2017].

[23] D. Rethans, "Xdebug - Debugger and Profiler Tool for PHP," 2016. [Online]. Available: www.xdebug.org. [Accessed 07 09 2016].

[24] Bureau of Labor Statisics, "Occupational Employment Statistics," 2016. [Online]. Available: http://www.bls.gov/oes/current/oes_16700.htm. [Accessed 07 09 2016].

[25] J. Hadzima, "How Much Does An Employee Cost?," [Online]. Available: http://web.mit.edu/e-club/hadzima/how-much-does-an-employee-cost.html. [Accessed 07 09 2016].

[26] R. Madachy, "COCOMO II - Constructive Cost Model," [Online]. Available: http://csse.usc.edu/tools/COCOMOII.php. [Accessed 10 02 2017].

# On Exploiting Resource Diversity in the Public Cloud for Modeling Application Performance

Mark Meredith
Dept. of Comp. Sci. and Engg.
The Penn State University
Email: mwm126@cse.psu.edu

Bhuvan Urgaonkar
Dept. of Comp. Sci. and Engg.
The Penn State University
Email: bhuvan@cse.psu.edu

***Abstract*—Cloud computing platforms, such as Amazon EC2, Google Computing Engine, and Microsoft Azure, offer dozens of virtual machine (VM) types with a wide range of resource capacity vs. price trade-offs, requiring a customer to consider numerous resource configurations when evaluating service needs. We investigate the possibility of exploiting this diversity of VM types to predict the performance of workloads on new VM types using black box modeling. The performance model used is a multiple linear regression of the average application response time as a function of VM load (throughput in requests per second), the number of CPU cores, and main memory capacity. For three different types of data storage applications - Redis (key-value stores), Apache Cassandra (a NoSQL database) and MySQL (an ACID database) - the model accuracy improves when the training data spans more diverse VMs. E.g., for Redis, the $R^2_{predicted}$ measure of model efficacy improves from 0.4-0.5 with 2 VM types for training and 0.7 for 3 VM types to 0.8 for 4 VM types. These results suggest further interesting research challenges, such as the possibility of automating the process of calibrating performance models using diverse resource types on a public cloud leading to "performance modeling as a service."**

***Keywords*—*public cloud; tenant workload; performance modeling***

## I. Introduction

Many enterprises are migrating their information technology (IT) needs to public cloud computing platforms, a trend that is projected to continue unabated in the foreseeable future [11]. Procuring resources cost-effectively from a public cloud poses significant technical challenges. One such challenge concerns the problem of determining the set of IT resources (including their capacities) - virtual machines (VMs), the virtual network connecting these VMs, storage, etc. - that would be needed to cost-effectively meet the predicted workload of the tenant's software applications while offering satisfactory performance and availability to its users. In order to solve this problem, a tenant must first solve the problem of assessing the performance the users of its application software are likely to experience if the application were assigned a given set of IT resources to meet its predicted workload. Our interest in this paper is in this latter problem, often labeled *application performance modeling* [13] [17] [18] [21] [25] [29] [31] [34]. Of course, application performance modeling has many other uses besides cost optimal resource procurement, e.g., anomaly detection [7] [15] and capacity planning [19].

Whereas application performance modeling has been an area of extensive research for many decades across many communities, solving it for the public cloud ecosystem presents a tenant with non-trivial novel sources of complexity. In particular, most modeling solutions have traditionally been developed for settings involving privately owned and operated data centers or clusters. These solutions may not be readily adapted to a public cloud.

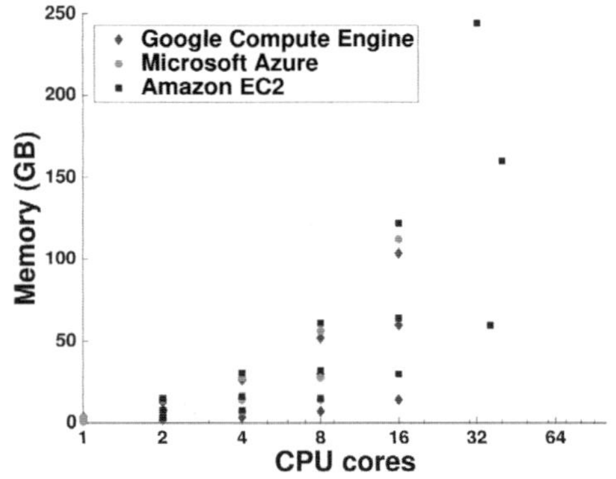


Fig. 1. An illustration of the diversity in VM capacities offered by popular public cloud providers.

One of the most important differences between these two settings (from the point of view of application performance modeling) is the immense *diversity of resources* that a typical public cloud offers. There are other important differences complementary to our focus in this paper and part of our future work. E.g., in a private setting, the user of a machine (tenant application) coincides with its owner while in a public setting the two are separated via virtualization techniques with implications for how much information about physical resource usage is available to the tenant's models. We focus on VMs in this work although our arguments likely apply to other resource types as well. To appreciate this diversity, let us consider some examples from the most prominent public cloud providers that offer many VM types since they need to cater to many different types of customers. Here, VM instance types are organized into groups based on use case. Instances within a group generally have the same CPU generation and clock speed, and vary by the number of CPUs and memory. Amazon EC2 offers over 40 VM types organized into eight different groups, varying in CPU, memory, network bandwidth, storage speed, and pricing [1]. Google Compute Engine offers 15 instance types organized into four groups:

Standard, High CPU, High Memory, and Shared Core (for lightweight applications) [12]. Finally, Microsoft Azure offers 30 instance types organized into 4 groups [33]. Fig. 1 shows 44 VM instance types from these three providers capturing the large spectrum of CPU cores and memory that their VMs pack. We show VMs with a wide range of CPU and memory capacities offered by Amazon EC2 [1], Google Compute Engine [12], and Microsoft Azure [33]. The number of cores on these VMs ranges from 1 to 32 whereas their memory capacity ranges from 0.75GB to 256GB.

A typical privately owned data center, on the other hand, is likely to possess a much smaller number of machine types. Keeping machines (and their software configurations) relatively homogeneous brings about significant benefits related to ease of system administration and cost savings (e.g., due to bulk purchase offers from IT vendors). Although factors, such as incremental procurement over time, meeting specialized needs (e.g., machines with GPUs), etc., do result in some differences among machine types even in a private data center, the overall degree of heterogeneity is significantly smaller than that seen in a public cloud.

This high diversity of resource types in a public cloud introduces an additional source of complexity into a tenant's VM autoscaling decision-making. Since the number of machine types in traditional IT environments is small and relatively fixed, performance models have conventionally been developed and calibrated using performance measurements ("profiling") on the same/similar type of machines on which the application would eventually execute. On the other hand, a tenant of a public cloud would be interested in predicting the performance its workload might experience on a wide variety of VM types that the provider offers. This is because the VM types most cost-effective for a tenant's workload might change over time due to: (i) changes in the tenant's own workload (e.g., many applications show periodic time-of-day or seasonal variations in their workload intensities) and (ii) dynamism and variety in the cloud provider's pricing schemes (e.g., Amazon EC2 offers spot pricing for most of its instance types and such spot instances are usually much cheaper than their on-demand counterparts). Additionally, existing work also shows that even during a period of stationary workload, procuring heterogeneous VMs (e.g., a combination of "small" and "large") can often offer a better cost vs. performance trade-off than procuring the same types of VMs (e.g., a larger number of only "small" or a smaller number of only "large") [35] Approaches based on calibrating a tenant's performance models separately on the dozens of resource types that public clouds offer are likely to not scale well.

We wish to explore if a tenant might actually be able to benefit from this diversity by deliberately and carefully exploiting it to ease the creation and calibration of its application performance models. The intuition underlying our premise is that choosing a small subset of the offered VMs may suffice for calibrating a tenant's performance models well if this subset were chosen carefully. In particular, this subset should capture well the overall diversity across the VMs offered by the provider.

**Our Approach and Contributions:** In this paper, we take a small first step towards exploring the above idea by evaluating the following hypothesis: *using a more diverse set of VMs for calibrating/training a performance model helps improve its accuracy*. Specifically, we devise a multiple linear regression modeling framework for predicting the performance of interactive data serving applications. We calibrate this model for three different types of real-world applications: (i) Redis [23], an open-source in-memory NoSQL key-value store, (ii) Apache Cassandra [5], a Table/key-value hybrid NoSQL database, and (iii) MySQL, a popular open-source ACID database [22]. We use "training sets" of varying sizes (i.e., numbers of VM types) for our calibration and investigate the impact of the training set size on model efficacy. Our results are promising. E.g., for Redis, we find that the $R^2_{predicted}$ measure of model efficacy improves from 0.4-0.5 with 2 VM types for training and 0.7 with 3 VM types to 0.8 for 4 VM types.

Whereas the benefits of exploiting heterogeneity have been explored in other contexts (most notably for cost/performance optimization in cloud settings [10] [16] [24] [35]), to the best of our knowledge, our paper is the first to systematically explore its role in aiding performance model calibration. Our work is complementary to traditional performance modeling research. At the same time, it opens up a promising new area for further exploration. As part of our own future work, we plan to investigate if/how public cloud providers could offer "performance modeling as a service," whereby all/many aspects of the model calibration by exploiting diversity would be offered as an automated facility to their tenants.

The rest of this paper is organized as follows. In Section II, we provide an overview of a generic cost-conscious tenant's decision-making and where application performance modeling fits within it. In Section III, we describe the performance modeling techniques that we employ. In Section IV, we present our empirical evaluation of our hypothesis using three real-world applications as our case studies. Finally, we discuss related work in Section V.

## II. Context and Overview

The tenant would employ observations of its workload intensity in the past to predict its future workload. Consider the example of a key-value store or a database application that we employ in our evaluation in Section IV. Such an application might keep track of request arrival rates (possibly for different request classes) and then use a suitable prediction mechanism for estimating future arrival rate. Whereas some tenant applications exhibit significant predictability (e.g., captured well via Markovian or autoregressive models) [3] [6] [27] [28], others are known to exhibit poor predictability and must resort to short-term ("myopic") estimates [9] [14] [32]. Regardless, having made these predictions, the tenant must then ascertain the number and type of VMs that it must procure from the cloud to meet its performance needs (or deallocate from its existing resource pool).

We show one way of thinking about this decision-making, wherein the tenant determines (using its application performance model) multiple VM allocation choices that would allow it to meet its predicted workload with the requisite performance goals. These choices are then compared in terms of their costs (or expected profits, if the tenant wishes to maximize expected profits rather than minimizing costs) via an optimization problem that incorporates idiosyncrasies of the prices offered by the public cloud. The actual realization of this overall decision-making may be different from how we describe it here. Our description is deliberately designed to highlight the role of the application performance model. Finally, the most cost-effective choice identified by the optimizer is used as the basis for actually procuring the appropriate number and type of VMs from the cloud provider.

Significant research exists both on predicting workloads and on performance modeling (see Section V) for a wide variety of application types. Recall that our interest in this paper is not on devising new techniques for workload prediction or application performance modeling. Rather, we are interested in evaluating the role VM diversity might play in calibrating a *given* performance model. Towards this, we adapt a popular modeling approach as described next.

## III. Our Modeling Methodology

This section describes the general performance modeling ideas used. In Section IV, this basic model is adapted to three application case studies on the Amazon AWS cloud. The primary interest in this paper is not in identifying the most accurate performance model but rather in exploring if diversity in the VMs used for calibrating the chosen model helps improve its efficacy. Therefore, although numerous modeling choices exist in the literature for such applications, we use a relatively simple multiple linear regression approach because: (i) it serves as a good starting point for evaluating the hypothesis, (ii) it is easy to cast, train, and evaluate, and (ii)it works well - especially under low/moderate throughputs for the normal operating regions of well-provisioned, performance-sensitive tenant workloads.

**Multiple Linear Regression:** Given a data set $\{y_i, x_{i1}, \ldots, x_{ip}\}_{i=1}^{n}$, a linear regression on multiple independent variables $x_p$ and dependent variable $y$ is a set of parameters $\beta_i$ that model a linear relationship between $y$ and $x_i$ as $y_i = \beta_1 x_{i1} + \ldots + \beta_p x_{ip} + \varepsilon_i$ [26].

The parameters $\varepsilon_i$ are the error terms, an unobserved random variable. The parameters $\beta_i$ are chosen to minimize the values of $\varepsilon_i$ for the entire data set. Specifically, the $\beta_i$ are chosen to minimize the sum of squares $\sum_{i=1}^{n} \varepsilon_i^2$.

We choose as our dependent variable the average latency $y_L$ and as our independent variables: (i) workload/application properties - throughput, degree of replication, and read/write ratio and (ii) resource capacity of the VMs being used - number of CPU cores, clock rate of each CPU, memory, network bandwidth, and type of storage (SSD vs. magnetic).

We define a training set $S = \{VM_i\}_{i=1}^{n}$ as a set of virtual machines, each characterized by $x_p$. In each of our experiments,

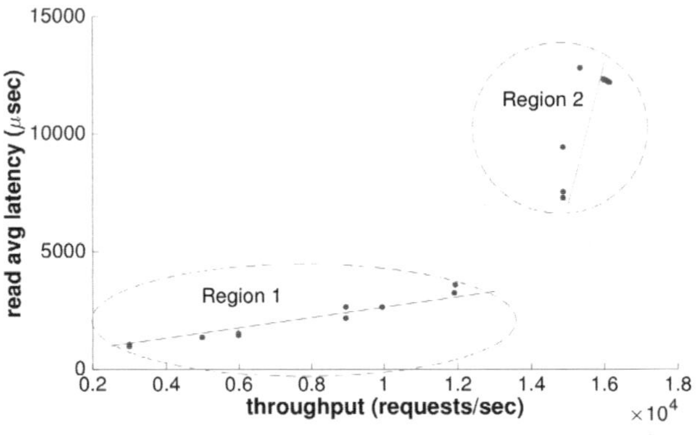


Fig. 2. Two regions of latency vs. throughput for Redis.

we run the application whose performance we wish to model on $VM_i$ for various $x_T$ and measure the latency $x_L$. We then find a multiple linear regression $M_S$ on $\{y_{iL}, x_{iT}, \ldots, x_{ip}\}_{i=1}^{n}$. (For a given instance $VM_i$, the values of $x_{ip}$ are fixed for all measurements for that instance.)

**Measure of Model Efficacy:** We use the predicted coefficient of multiple determination ($R^2_{predicted}$) as our measure of model accuracy which is defined as follows. For a test instance $VM_{test}$ with $x_{test,i}$, $R^2_{predicted} = 1 - \frac{\sum_{i=1}^{n}(y_{test,i} - \hat{y}(x_{test,i}))^2}{\sum_{i=1}^{n}(y_{test,i} - \bar{y}_{test})^2}$, where $\hat{y}(x_{test,i}) = \sum_{i=1}^{n} \beta_i x_{test,i}$, and $\bar{y}_{test}$ is the mean of $y_{test,i}$.

To see evidence supporting our hypothesis, we expect to see the following behavior: for larger training sets $S$, the model should fit better to $VM_{test}$, corresponding to an increasing $R^2_{predicted}$, assuming sufficient variability in the values of $x_p$ for $VM_j \in S$ to cover the values of $x_p$ for $VM_{test}$.

**Discussion:** Our linear regression based model is known to perform poorly when queueing delays become dominant contributors to overall latency [29]. For example, if we were to model the entire set of latency observations (for experiments done using Redis, more details in Section IV-B) using our model, we would obtain a poorer predictor than the two separate linear regression models shown in Fig. 2, one each for the "low/moderate" (Region 1) and "high" (Region 2) throughput regions. This suggests two points: (i) using domain knowledge (e.g., the distinction between low and high throughput regions), a tenant may be able to use linear regression to obtain better models, and (ii) more sophisticated models may be warranted for the needs of certain tenants. Again, since our interest is in the impact of diversity on modeling accuracy, we focus only on modeling performance in Region 1 for the rest of this paper.

It is important to keep in mind the basic assumption of linear regression about the independent variables being independent of each other (i.e., the $x_p$ for $VM_j \in S$ need to be independent). Interestingly, among the independent variables in our model, the number of cores and memory capacity are prone to be problematic on this front - typically larger VMs come both with more CPUs and more memory - see Fig. 1. To overcome this problem, we attempt to choose VM types in our experi-

TABLE I
AWS INSTANCE TYPES EMPLOYED IN OUR EVALUATION.

| Instance name | Abbr. | # cores | Memory | Network |
|---|---|---|---|---|
| m3.large | $VM_1$ | 2 | 7.5 GB | Moderate |
| m3.xlarge | $VM_2$ | 4 | 15 GB | Moderate |
| m3.2xlarge | $VM_3$ | 8 | 30 GB | High |
| r3.large | $VM_4$ | 2 | 15 GB | Moderate |
| r3.xlarge | $VM_5$ | 4 | 30.5 GB | Moderate |
| r3.2xlarge | $VM_6$ | 8 | 61 GB | High |

ments where this correlation is weak. Furthermore, the results we present in this paper are for a subset of our experimental findings wherein the entire working set fits in VM memory, rendering memory moot as a predictor of performance (we do incorporate memory in our more general experiments). Finally, the potential shortcomings of predicted $R^2$ as a measure of model accuracy should be kept in mind when interpreting our results [26].

## IV. EVALUATION

### A. Methodology and Setup

We carry out our evaluation on the EC2 public cloud offered by Amazon Web Services (AWS) [1]. We adapt our generic performance model from Section III for three different types of latency-sensitive data-serving applications: (i) Redis (an in-memory open-source NoSQL key-value store) [23], (ii) Apache Cassandra (a NoSQL key-value store that can be configured for different consistency levels), and the popular MySQL ACID database [22]. We use the open-source Yahoo! Cloud Serving Benchmark (YCSB) as our workload generator [8]. We run the YCSB client on a m4.2xlarge EC2 instance running Ubuntu Linux 14.04. We monitor the system load average on the client machine to verify that the client is not the bottleneck during our tests.

We describe a subset of our overall results wherein for each experiment we load the concerned database with 1,000,000 records, each containing ten fields of 100 bytes each (the default). This amounts to an overall working set of about 1GB. Each experiment consists of subjecting the database to a particular thoughput and recording the average latency (separately for reads and writes). YCSB defines several standard workloads that we experiment with. We experiment with different workloads offered by YCSB and present a subset of our overall results - workload "A" for MySQL and "B" for Redis and Cassandra. Workload A has 50% read and 50% write requests and employs a uniform popularity distribution. Workload B has 95% reads and 5% writes, and the popularity of requests is chosen based on a zipfian distribution. We repeat each experiment several times to achieve significantly tight confidence intervals. Amazon EC2 is hosted in multiple geographic regions around the world, and multiple zones within each region. We create our testing client and servers within the same region (us-west) and availability zone (2b) to minimize the effect of network latency. Finally, we pick all VMs having individual CPUs offering the same clock rate.

We select the VM instances listed in Table I. There are three instances from the M3 group (standard) and three from the R3 group (memory optimized). The memory/CPU ratio is the same within each group, with the R3 group having twice the memory/cpu as the M3 group. A more extensive study with more instances would allow the use of more independent variables in the model, e.g., including testing of instances in the C3 group (compute optimized), which have half as much memory/CPU as M3.

With the above choices, the measurements and modeling reported here effectively only employ a subset of all the independent variables listed in Section III: number of CPU cores, throughput, number of replicas, and read-write ratio. In particular, our working set of 1GB fits fully within any of the chosen VMs, effectively rendering memory capacity moot as a predictive variable. In our more general experiments, however, we explore a much larger set of workload choices.

### B. Case Study 1: Redis

Redis is an open-source, key/value NoSQL database. Redis is in-memory and, therefore, very fast. Redis also optionally supports persistence, so unlike memcached it can be used as a primary database or as a cache. We deploy Redis on AWS using Amazon ElastiCache, a web service that abstracts the deployment and administration of the OS and database software. Elasticache supports up to five read replicas of the primary database. We report results with a single replica here.

For a VM type on which we wish to predict Redis performance, we choose training sets of different sizes among the remaining VM types. We find that each time we add a new instance type to the training set, $R^2_{predicted}$ does improve for both read and write latency. Generally, we observe that a training set of only 3 VM types appears to offer high accuracy with further additions offering relatively low gains. This bodes well for cost-efficacy of our model calibration approach - instead of having to calibrate its performance model for dozens of VM types (with associated costs), a tenant may be able to achieve comparable model accuracy using a much smaller set. We present representative findings in Figs. 3 and 4.

### C. Case Study 2: Apache Cassandra

Apache Cassandra is a Table/Key-Value hybrid NoSQL database. It is suitable for applications that require high availability provided by replication. In terms of the CAP theorem, Cassandra prioritizes availability and performance over consistency, making it highly performant and scalable, though consistency is eventual rather than strong, for typical Cassandra applications. We do our testing on Cassandra clusters with 5 nodes. We run our testing with a replication factor of three, so every database record is stored on three of the five nodes. We record report results both when using Cassandra's weak (or eventual) and strict consistency settings.

For a sample VM type that we want to predict the performance of Cassandra, we select training sets of increasing size from the remaining VM types. We select $VM_4$ for prediction,

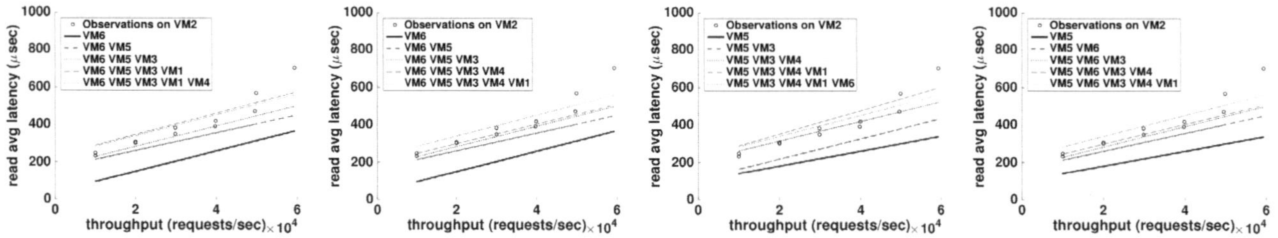


(a) (b) (c) (d)

Fig. 3. Prediction of Redis read latency on $VM_2$ compared for model calibration using a variety of training sets ranging in size from 1 to 5 VM types.

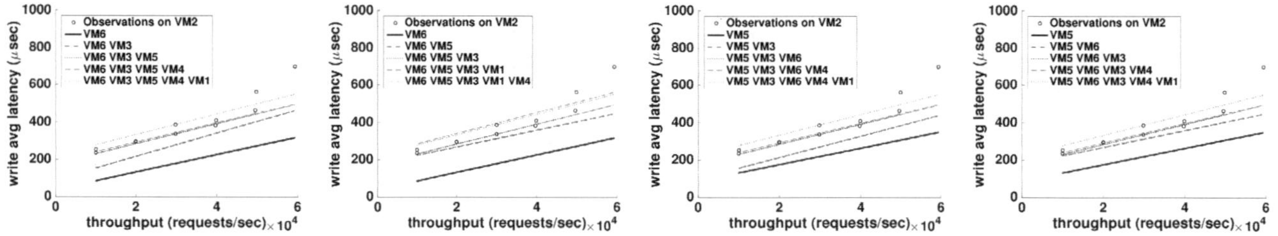


(a) (b) (c) (d)

Fig. 4. Prediction of Redis write latency on $VM_2$ compared for model calibration using a variety of training sets ranging in size from 1 to 5 VM types.

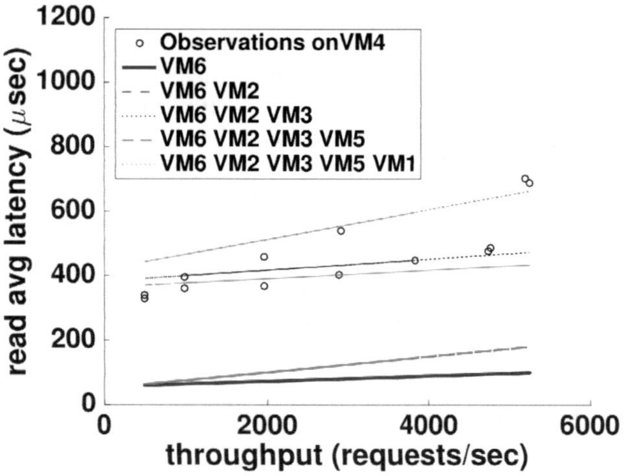


Fig. 5. Read latency/throughput plot for MySQL.

and do multiple linear regressions on the training set for sizes 1 through 5 for read latency and write latency data. Again, we observe that every time another VM type is added to the training set, the associated $R^2_{predicted}$ improves for $VM_4$ for both read and write latency (results omitted for space). We conclude that our evaluation offers supporting evidence for our second case study.

### *D. Case Study 3: MySQL*

MySQL is an extremely popular ACID SQL database server, the backbone of numerous commercial applications. For our testing we deployed MySQL using Amazon Relational Database Service (Amazon RDS) [2], which abstracts away the deployment and administration of OS and relationship database software. We benchmark MySQL on the six VM types listed in Table I.

The MySQL data shows a higher variation in latency than our other case studies, and our linear regression model does not fit it as well as it does the previous two applications. We show a sample result for MySQL in Fig. 5. We do continue to see that the model accuracy as captured by $R^2_{predicted}$ does continue to improve with the addition of more VM types to the training set, although the value of $R^2_{predicted}$ is lower than observed for Redis and Cassandra.

This may be due to the higher write latency of SQL databases, or possibly something with Amazon's RDS architecture that made our YCSB testing method unsuitable. Another possibility is that the network availability for RDS varies over time, making consistent results harder to reproduce. This requires further investigation that forms part of our future work. Despite these inadequacies in our modeling, however, the basic expectation we have regarding the role of diversity does appear to hold.

## V. RELATED WORK

Performance modeling of software applications has a long history in a variety of domains. Approaches range from explicit modeling leveraging knowledge the internal workings of system (e.g., based on queueing theory or more general Markovian models [17] [18] [25] [31]), "black box" approaches (ranging from relatively simple regression [29] similar to this paper to more sophisticated statistical learning-based [13] [20]

[21] [34]), and combinations ("gray-box" approaches) [4] [30]. As explained earlier, we choose to work with a very simple modeling approach because our main interest was not in high accuracy modeling but on evaluating the improvements that can result from exploiting diversity. All existing work on modeling is complementary to our ideas and we hope to explore the efficacy of our hypothesis with more sophisticated modeling techniques.

A substantial body of work exists on exploiting different forms of heterogeneity (not just in cloud platforms but also in other types of systems) for cost and/or performance optimization [10] [16] [24] [35]. Our goal is different from these works in that our interest is in using diversity for improving modeling accuracy.

## VI. Conclusions

The diversity of resource types offered by public clouds is much higher than in conventional privately-owned data centers. The complexity of options available makes decision on resource acquisition more complex, with the larger range of service available. Tenants may need to calibrate their application performance models for a large number of resource configurations. In a private cloud, the system on which such calibration is done is the same as the machines on which the application eventually runs. This paper investigates the possibility of exploiting this diversity to ease the tenant's performance modeling.

To explore this idea we applied a linear regression model to the relationship between latency and throughput for several popular database servers. The model expressed the average response time of a class of interactive server applications as a linear combination of the offered throughput (requests/s), the number of CPU cores and memory in the procured VM, and degree of replication employed by the application. For three different real-world applications - Redis, Apache Cassandra, and MySQL - the model accuracy increased for more diverse sets of VMs. For example, the $R^2_{predicted}$ measure of model efficacy for Redis improved from 0.4-0.5 with 2 VM types for training and 0.7 for 3 VM types to 0.8 for 4 VM types. Qualitatively similar results were observed for Apache Cassandra and MySQL. Although this modeling approach is very specific, the basic observation could be expanded to more accurately model more VM types in more detail. This would lead to more interesting research challenges, such as automating the process of calibrating performance models using diverse resource types on a public cloud allowing providers to offer "performance modeling as a service" to their tenants.

## References

[1] Amazon EC2 Pricing. http://aws.amazon.com/ec2/pricing/, [last accessed October 2016].

[2] Amazon Relational Database Service. https://aws.amazon.com/rds/, [last accessed October 2016].

[3] M. F. Arlitt and C. L. Williamson. Internet web servers: Workload characterization and performance implications. *IEEE/ACM Trans. Netw.*, 5(5), Oct. 1997.

[4] A. C. Arpaci-Dusseau and R. H. Arpaci-Dusseau. Information and control in gray-box systems. In *Proc. ACM SOSP*, 2001.

[5] The Apache Cassandra Project. http://cassandra.apache.org/, [last accessed October 2016].

[6] A. Chandra, W. Gong, and P. J. Shenoy. Dynamic resource allocation for shared data centers using online measurements. In *Proc. IWQoS*, 2003.

[7] I. Cohen, M. Goldszmidt, T. Kelly, J. Symons, and J. S. Chase. Correlating instrumentation data to system states: A building block for automated diagnosis and control. In *Proc. USENIX OSDI*, 2004.

[8] B. F. Cooper, A. Silberstein, E. Tam, R. Ramakrishnan, and R. Sears. Benchmarking cloud serving systems with ycsb. In *Proc. ACM SOCC*, 2010.

[9] M. E. Crovella and A. Bestavros. Self-similarity in world wide web traffic: Evidence and possible causes. *IEEE/ACM Trans. Netw.*, 5(6), Dec. 1997.

[10] Farley, B. et al. More for your money: Exploiting performance heterogeneity in public clouds. In *Proc. ACM SOCC*, 2012.

[11] Forbes. http://www.forbes.com/sites/louiscolumbus/2015/04/05/predicting-the-future-of-cloud-service-providers/, [last accessed October 2016].

[12] Google Compute Engine: Machine Types. https://cloud.google.com/compute/docs/machine-types, [last accessed October 2016].

[13] H. Herodotou and S. Babu. A what-if engine for cost-based mapreduce optimization. *IEEE Data Eng. Bull.*, 36(1):5–14, 2013.

[14] J. Jung, B. Krishnamurthy, and M. Rabinovich. Flash crowds and denial of service attacks: Characterization and implications for cdns and web sites. In *Proc. WWW*, 2002.

[15] T. Kelly. Detecting performance anomalies in global applications. In *Proc. 2nd Conference on Real, Large Distributed Systems*, 2005.

[16] G. Lee and R. H. Katz. Heterogeneity-aware resource allocation and scheduling in the cloud. In *Proc. USENIX HotCloud*, 2011.

[17] D. A. Menascé. Response-time analysis of composite web services. *IEEE Internet Computing*, 8(1):90–92, 2004.

[18] D. A. Menascé and S. Bardhan. Queuing network models to predict the completion time of the map phase of mapreduce jobs. In *38. International Computer Measurement Group Conference, Las Vegas, NV, USA, December 3-7, 2012*, 2012.

[19] D. A. Menasce and P. Ngo. Understanding cloud computing: Experimentation and capacity planning. In *Proc. International Computer Measurement Group Conference*, 2009.

[20] M. Mesnier, M. Wachs, B. Salmon, and G. R. Ganger. Relative fitness models for storage. *SIGMETRICS Perform. Eval. Rev.*, 33(4), Mar. 2006.

[21] N. Mi, G. Casale, L. Cherkasova, and E. Smirni. Sizing multi-tier systems with temporal dependence: benchmarks and analytic models. *J. Internet Services and Applications*, 1(2):117–134, 2010.

[22] MySQL. https://www.mysql.com/, [last accessed October 2016].

[23] Redis IO. http://redis.io/, [last accessed October 2016].

[24] C. Reiss, A. Tumanov, G. R. Ganger, R. H. Katz, and M. A. Kozuch. Heterogeneity and dynamicity of clouds at scale: Google trace analysis. In *Proc. ACM SOCC*, 2012.

[25] B. Schroeder, A. Wierman, and M. Harchol-Balter. Open versus closed: A cautionary tale. In *Proc. USENIX NSDI*, 2006.

[26] C. R. Shaliz. *Advanced Data Analysis from an Elementary Point of View*. 2015. http://www.stat.cmu.edu/~cshalizi/ADAfaEPoV/ADAfaEPoV.pdf, [last accessed October 2016].

[27] D. Shen and J. L. Hellerstein. Predictive models for proactive network management: Application to a production web server. In *Proc. NOMS*, 2000.

[28] M. S. Squillante, D. D. Yao, and L. Zhang. Web traffic modeling and web server performance analysis. *SIGMETRICS Perform. Eval. Rev.*, 27(3), Dec. 1999.

[29] C. Stewart, T. Kelly, and A. Zhang. Exploiting nonstationarity for performance prediction. In *Proc. ACM SIGOPS EuroSys*, 2007.

[30] E. Thereska and G. R. Ganger. Ironmodel: Robust performance models in the wild. In *Proc. ACM SIGMETRICS*, 2008.

[31] B. Urgaonkar, G. Pacifici, P. Shenoy, M. Spreitzer, and A. Tantawi. An analytical model for multi-tier internet services and its applications. In *Proc. ACM SIGMETRICS*, 2005.

[32] Wang, C. et al. Recouping energy costs from cloud tenants: Tenant demand response aware pricing design. In *Proc. ACM e-Energy*, 2015.

[33] Microsoft Azure: Virtual Machines Pricing. https://azure.microsoft.com/en-us/pricing/details/virtual-machines/, [last accessed October 2016].

[34] Z. Zhang, L. Cherkasova, and B. T. Loo. Parameterizable benchmarking framework for designing a mapreduce performance model. *Concurrency and Computation: Practice and Experience*, 26(12), 2014.

[35] Z. Zhang, L. Cherkasova, and B. T. Loo. Exploiting cloud heterogeneity to optimize performance and cost of mapreduce processing. *SIGMETRICS Perform. Eval. Rev.*, 42(4), June 2015.

# On the Development of a One-Time Pad Generator for Personalising Cloud Security

Paul Tobin*, Lee Tobin†, Michael McKeever‡, and Jonathan Blackledge§
* School of Electrical and Electronic Engineering
Dublin Institute of Technology, Dublin 2, Ireland
Email: paul.tobin@dit.ie
† CASL Institute Level 3, UCD Science Centre East
University College, Belfield, Dublin 4, Ireland,
Email: lee.tobin@ucdconnect.ie
‡ School of Electrical and Electronic Engineering
Dublin Institute of Technology, Dublin 2, Ireland
Email: mick.mckeever@dit.ie
§ Military Technological College
Sultanate of Oman,
Email: Jonathan.blackledge59@gmail.com

***Abstract*—Cloud computing security issues are being reported in newspapers, television, and on the Internet, on a daily basis. Furthermore, in 2013, Edward Snowden alleged backdoors were placed in a number of encryption systems by the National Security Agency causing confidence in public encryption to drop even further. Our solution allows the end-user to add a layer of unbreakable security by encrypting the data locally with a random number generator prior to uploading data to the Cloud. The prototype one-time pad generator is impervious to cryptanalysis because it generates unbreakable random binary sequences from chaos sources initiated from a natural noise. Specialised one-to-Cloud applications for this device means key distribution problems do not exist, even when used at different locations. A JavaScript application maximised the encryptor key entropy using a von Neumann algorithm and modulo-two arithmetic, where the key passed the National Institute of Standards and Technology statistical suite of tests. It is hoped that the final size of the generator should be similar to a typical Universal Serial Bus device.**

***Keywords–Cloud security, Snowden, backdoors, one-time pad, chaos, noise, entropy, von Neumann.***

## I. Introduction

To address the problems of poor security on the Cloud, a prototype random number generator was created to encode data locally before being stored on the Cloud. Traffic on the Cloud Infrastructure as a Service (IaaS) is forecast to increase by twenty percent by 2019 [1], but security issues are affecting public confidence in this service. Breaches in security are rarely discovered instantly [2] and up to six months may elapse before being reported. The elapsed time between discovering security breaches has been reduced [3], but to satisfy the European Union (EU) General Data Protection Regulations (GDPR) coming into law in March 2018, mandatory breach notification must be reported by companies within 72 hours. Heavy fines of up to 4 percent of the annual turnover of a company will be imposed if they fail to report within this time [4].

Hacking on servers is reported almost daily in newspapers, TV and online [5], a problem compounded by the alleged presence of backdoors in public encryption. Microsoft employees, Dan Shumow and Niels Ferguson gave a presentation in 2007 and hinted at the possibility of a backdoor in a random number generator: On the Possibility of a backdoor in the National Institute of Standards and Technology (NIST) SP800-90 Dual Elliptic Curve Pseudo Random Number Generators [6] [7]. Interestingly, in April 2014, NIST dropped the Dual EC PRNG from their standards [8]

The New York Times in 2013 linked this presentation to documents leaked by Edward Snowden [9], where he alleged backdoors were placed by the National Security Agency (NSA) in certain public encryption systems [10]. Hence, nobody knows for sure what weaknesses exist in public encryption but probably the Advanced Encryption Standard (AES) algorithm is secure and has no backdoors. That said, an encryption system whereby the client can encode his data locally before being stored in the Cloud, is a solution to certain Cloud security problems. Our prototype provides a layer of security using the unbreakable One-Time Pad (OTP) random binary number stream generated from two chaos generators. This is not a novel idea but how the sources are connected and initialised using a cosmic noise source, is.

### A. One-time pad history

Figure 1 shows the SIGSALY encryption system developed by A. B. Clarke and Alan Turing in Bell Labs during WWII [11]. SIGSALY weighed 55-tons and had a key distribution problem requiring a key the same length as the plaintext. Nevertheless, it produced unbreakable OTP encryption ciphers for encrypting transatlantic conversations between Churchill and Roosevelt. Similar OTP systems were used between Russian and American governments in the 60's, for securing the famous "hotline". Our prototype random number generator should be no bigger than a typical Universal Serial Bus (USB) device and with no key distribution problems because it stays with the client who may use it at different locations.

### B. Paper Organisation

Section I explains why local encryption is necessary and explains how the OTP was successfully used during WWII and again in the sixties, to give unbreakable security protecting conversations between heads of state.

Figure 1. The 55-ton SIGSALY encoding system.

Section II outlines the structure of the OTP encoder and discusses the nature of a random generator initialised using cosmic natural noise and how it may be classified as a true random binary number generator. A medical application example for protecting patient confidentiality is given in Section III. Section IV explains the prototype design and discusses how OTPs were generated from chaotic analogue oscillators. In Section V, we discuss the JavaScript application for maximising OTP entropy and show how it interfaces with the data. NIST randomness p-test results for simulation and prototype circuits are discussed in Section VI, and the conclusion stated in Section VII.

## II. THE OTP PROTOTYPE

Figure 2 outlines the system for generating OTP random bit streams for encoding data locally prior to uploading to the Cloud.

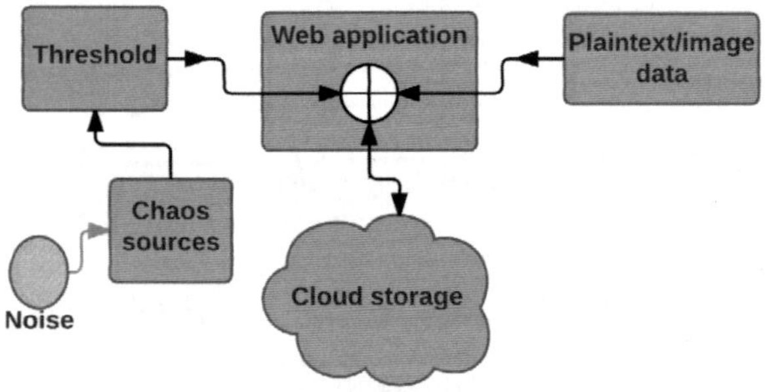


Figure 2. Prototype OTP generation.

Chaotic oscillators generated on a computer produce random binary sequences that have finite sequence lengths and hence are not truly random. This is due to the finite state of computer arithmetic [12] [13] and produce cryptographically poor ciphers. Random sequences generated from chaotic maps implemented on computers, similarly, have repeatable sequence lengths and also produce weak keys [14] [15] [16]. However, random binary sequences from analogue chaos circuits initiated from natural noise, have an infinite number of states and so produce random binary streams which have, in theory, infinite sequence lengths and generate excellent ciphers. The prototype can produce unlimited amounts of unbreakable OTP ciphers from deterministic chaos sources initialised with noise from a Frequency Modulation (FM) receiver and qualifies the prototype as a truly random source, rather than a pseudo random source [17] [18] [19]. Initial Conditions (IC) for each generator are applied to each chaos source, but for simulation only, the IC noise was provided from a random noise generator in PSpice called ***RND***. In [20], we explained how the OTP was exported from the simulator circuit and stored to a text file using PSpice ***VECTOR1*** parts and processed in the JavaScript application. However, a different technique must be used for the prototype and is considered in the following section.

### A. Storing the OTP in an Arduino Shield

The OTP stream from the prototype was stored in an Arduino memory shield attached to the main Arduino board. An exclusive OR gate connected across two monostables created a clock stream from the two gate inputs and was used for writing 'ones' to the shield. Effectively, the gate removed the random temporal element from the bit stream (but not the randomness). The complete prototype is undergoing tests at present, but initial tests show it is producing cryptographically-strong encryptors. Only one chaotic oscillator was examined in this paper; the other chaos source is a novel implementation of the Chua oscillator [21].

## III. A MEDICAL APPLICATION FOR THE PROTOTYPE

There are many potential applications for the prototype generator and here a medical application explains how patient information displayed on medical images, is protected. The following scenario is a patient who has persistent headaches and high blood pressure and is recommended by the doctor to have a Magnetic Resonance Imaging (MRI) scan at the nearest hospital. Such scans are produced using the international standard for storing, distributing and processing medical images and is referred to as the Digital Imaging and Communications in Medicine (DICOM) format [23]. However, these images show patient private information around the peripheral of the image [22] and must be protected from unwanted interception, otherwise patient confidentiality is compromised.

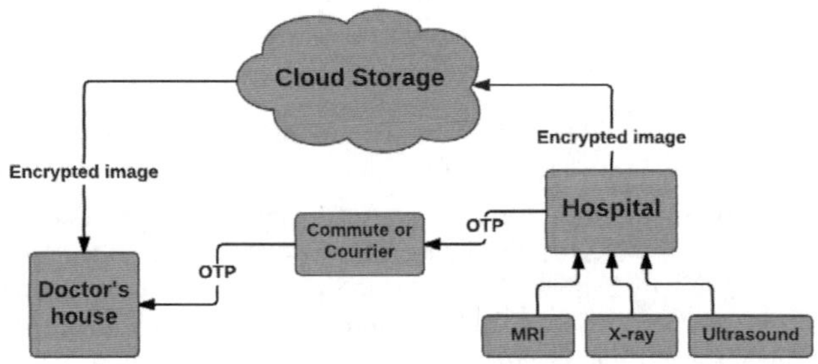


Figure 3. Encoding medical images.

At present, the procedure for sending MRI scans to the doctor's office is not secure. After scanning the patient, the hospital sends the MRI images containing patient personal information by post. Alternatively, they give them directly to the patient to bring to the doctor. Both methods have security weaknesses as the images could be lost in transit. Our solution involves hospital staff encoding the scanned images using the OTP generator and uploading the encoded images to the Cloud directory assigned to that doctor. The hospital staff then saves the encoding OTP to a memory device and gives it to the patient who then gives it to the doctor to decode the scans at his office. A similar legal application concerns the legal profession operating between office and court. Here, data is encoded locally before uploading to the Cloud and the OTP replaces all those bulky folders carried previously. There are many such applications where people operating between two locations could use the encoder system to prevent sensitive information being lost in transit.

## IV. THE LORENZ CHAOTIC ANALOGUE OSCILLATOR

Claude Shannon's 1949 paper [24] outlined presciently how digital chaotic maps could encrypt data using symmetric key encryption. Since then chaos cryptography has grown considerably, and from 2000, many chaotic maps were used in multi-algorithmic systems for encrypting data on a randomised block-by-block basis [25]. Our prototype uses Lorenz and Chua chaotic analogue chaos oscillators to create cryptographically-strong encryptors because of their ergodic properties. Edward Lorenz, a meteorologist, modelled weather patterns in the sixties and discovered chaos theory and Sensitivity to Initial Conditions (SIC), one of the hallmarks of chaos systems, when he truncated places of decimal from five down to three in his model after one run and it produced different results. The following first-order coupled equations appeared in his 1963 [26] paper (largely ignored at the time):

$$\begin{aligned} x &= -P\int_{t_0}^{t}\{x-y\}dt \\ y &= -\int_{t_0}^{t}\{-Rx+y+10xz\}dt \\ z &= -\int_{t_0}^{t}\{Bz-10xy\}dt \end{aligned} \qquad (1)$$

The equations in integral form allow for electronic integrator implementation and also include a scaling factor of ten to reduce signal amplitudes for electronic devices. The parameters Lorenz used were: $B = 2.666$, $P = 10$, $R = 28$, but these were changed to: $B = 2.8$, $P = 11$, and $R = 27.5$ to maximise the cryptographic strength or entropy, of the OTP.

### A. Thresholding the chaos signal

A random binary OTP stream was produced by thresholding the $x$ signal at two voltages corresponding to the values at the centres of the *(x-y)* attractor shown in Figure 4 (b). These centres are the Fixed Points (FP) of (1), where one centre could represent a '1' when in that region, and when the other centre is visited, a '0' is created. The FPs are determined by assuming the system is approximately linear at the origin, i.e., ($x = y = z = 0$), so the coordinates at each lobe centre are calculated as follows:

$$\frac{dx}{dt} = 10(y-x) = 0 \Rightarrow x = y \qquad (2)$$

Hence, we may write:

$$\frac{dy}{dt} = Rx - x - xz = 28x - x - xz = 0 \qquad (3)$$

Substituting $z = 27$, yields:

$$\frac{dz}{dt} = x^2 - Bz = 0 \Rightarrow = \pm\sqrt{B(R-1)} \qquad (4)$$

The FPs are the coordinates of the lobe centres $C_{1,2}$, given by:

$$C_{1,2} = \{+\sqrt{B(R-1)}, -\sqrt{B(R-1)}, (R-1)\} \qquad (5)$$

Substituting the Lorenz parameter values gives the locii of the attractor as:

$$C_{1,2} = \{+8.48V, -8.48V, 27V\} \qquad (6)$$

Magnitude scaling by 10 yields FPs equal to ± 0.8485 V at 2.7 V. Adding a bias shifting voltage to the bipolar $x$-signal makes it polar in form and gives threshold levels of 3.15 V and 4.84 V. The upper and lower threshold voltages are superimposed on the biased $x$-signal as shown in Figure 4 (a), and the out-of-phase set and reset sequences from each comparator were converted to constant widths by two 74121 monostables and superimposed on the Lorenz strange attractor as shown in Figure 4 (b).

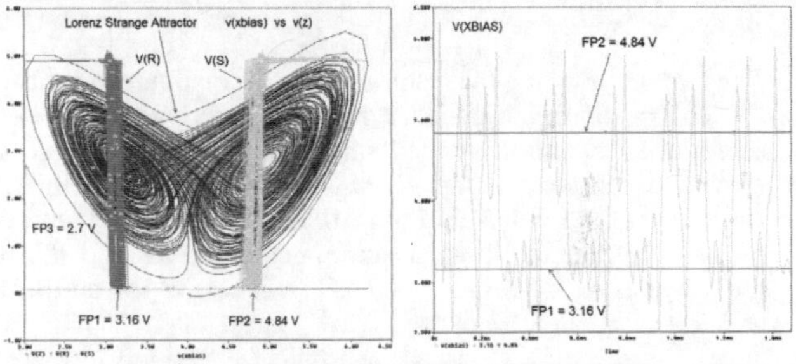


Figure 4. (a) FP thresholds (b) Butterfly attractor.

The threshold components were calculated by assuming a total potentiometer of 1 MΩ and Vref = 1.24 V:

$$Vhigh = 4.84\ V = Vref\frac{R10 + R11 + R12}{R12} \qquad (7)$$

Similarly for $R11$,

$$Vlow = 3.15\ V = Vref\frac{R10 + R11 + R12}{R11 + R12} \qquad (8)$$

Figure 5 is the Lorenz chaotic oscillator circuit to realise (1). The circuit was simulated using the latest v 17.2 Cadence® Orcad PSpice V17.2 using Analogue Behavioural Model (ABM) parts to achieve multiplication and integration but subsequently were replaced with actual model parts [27] [28]. The four-quadrant AD633 device modelled the cross-product nonlinear terms, *xy* and *xz*, terms necessary for chaos production and the TL084 quad operational amplifier integrated circuit solved the equation using a summing inverting integrator configuration.

The set and reset pulses from the monostables were connected to a 7486 exclusive OR gate (XOR) which outputs a clock stream for controlling when the OTP ones and zeroes are written to the Arduino shield attached to the main Arduino. The 'ones' are written to the shield from the monostable reset output, and the clock signal determines when the 'zeroes' are written. This is a different procedure to that used for storing the OTP during simulation [20], where the OTP was written to a text file using vector parts and processed in a JavaScript application.

Chaos oscillator initial conditions were obtained from a detuned 433 MHz FM receiver integrated circuit.

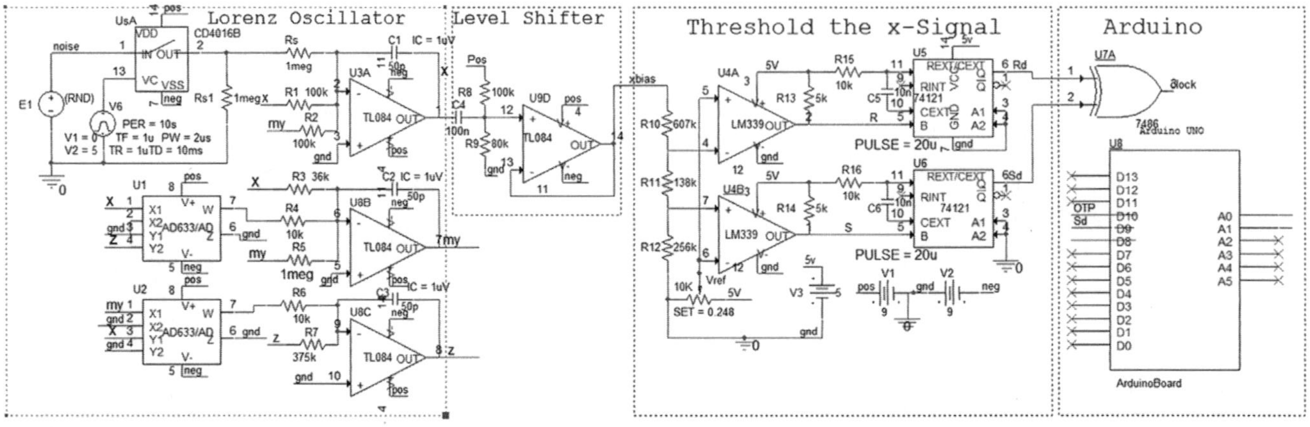


Figure 5. Generating the OTP.

The output level of the natural noise is random and ensures the chaos sources produce a random output that cannot be reproduced by an unwanted third party. The oscillator and threshold components are: $R1 = R2 = 100$ kΩ, $R3 = 36.3$ kΩ, $R4 = 10$ kΩ, $R5 = 1$ MΩ, $R6 = 10$ kΩ, $R7 = 357$ kΩ, and $C = 50$ pF. The potential divider components are: $R8$ and $R9$, bias the $x$ signal by 4 V, $R10 = 607$ kΩ, $R11 = 138$ kΩ and $R12 = 256$ kΩ.

## V. JavaScript Interface Application

The original MRI scan in Figure 6 shows where the patient information was located but removed for obvious reasons. The JavaScript application performs modulo two arithmetic between the OTP from the Arduino shield and the pixel array data from the bitmap medical image. In this example, the encoded image displays horizontal lines (see Figure 6), which would makes the encoded image susceptible to cryptanalysis because it now contains a bias and should be avoided at all costs. However, the bias was deliberately introduced by making the OTP purposely short because the application code repeated some of the random streams to make the OTP the same length as the image. In the middle pane, we observe no bias lines, even with no von Neumann correction applied. The OTP from the actual prototype should always be the same length as the plaintext, otherwise, the encryptor is weak.

The interface also applies the von Neumann (vN) algorithm to deskew, or unbias, the generated OTP bit stream. Whenever a '00' and '11' dibit pair occurs in the stream, they are rejected. Dibit '01' is converted to 0 and '10' to 1 [29]. However, the algorithm is inefficient because 75 percent of the data is lost. Another important requirement, often not applied when using this algorithm, is that the dibit streams should be from two uncorrelated chaos data streams. In the prototype, this alternate bit independence is achieved by using two independent chaotic data streams.

## VI. Testing the One-Time-Pad

To resist cryptanalysis and to ensure an encryptor is truly random for correct certification, we considered the following tests:

- The autocorrelation test should display a single Kronecker delta auto-correlation function,
- The Power Spectral Density (PSD) should be uniform,
- The OTP must have maximum entropy by operating the chaos sources in a chaotic region to produce positive Lyapunov Exponents (LE) [30] [31].

Shannon entropy measures randomness but essentially is the Kolmogorov Complexity (KC), created simultaneously by Andrey Kolmogorov and Ray Solmonoff and specifies the minimum length to which a string of binary digits may be compressed (a truly random sequence is incompressible) [32]. According to Brudno's theorem and for certain phase space conditions, the Kolmogorov-Sinai Entropy (KSE) is the Algorithmic Complexity (AC) for all trajectories [33].

However, the cryptographic strength of random number sequences was also tested using the NIST suite of tests (revised in 2010). There are other test suites such as the ENT, TestU01, CryptX, Diehard, but the NIST suite of tests is universally accepted as the most comprehensive [34]. The NIST suite contains non-parameter tests for short OTP sequences and parameter tests for several million bit sequences. Table I shows the NIST results from simulation and prototype circuits, and from true noise sequences downloaded from [35].

## VII. Conclusion

Poor Cloud security was addressed and we proposed a solution for a system which created an extra layer of security using a OTP random number generator. The generator used analogue chaos sources initialised by a natural noise source to generate unlimited amounts of unbreakable OTPs that passed the NIST statistical tests. Personalising encryption locally by the client, prior to uploading data to the Cloud, gave complete control provided a new encryptor is used each time. This makes it expensive in encryptor keys but memory is cheap and plentiful.

During testing, the JavaScript application [36] was used to investigate how parameter changes affected the OTP entropy. The application also applied a von Neumann algorithm to maximise the entropy of the OTP. The GDPR legislation in 2018, will see hefty fines being imposed on companies who fail to meet the 72-hour deadline and it could be argued that our prototype means data was never available to a third party. Refinements to this system are being investigated such as extracting the patient personal information in the DICOM's metadata and encoding it separately from the medical image.

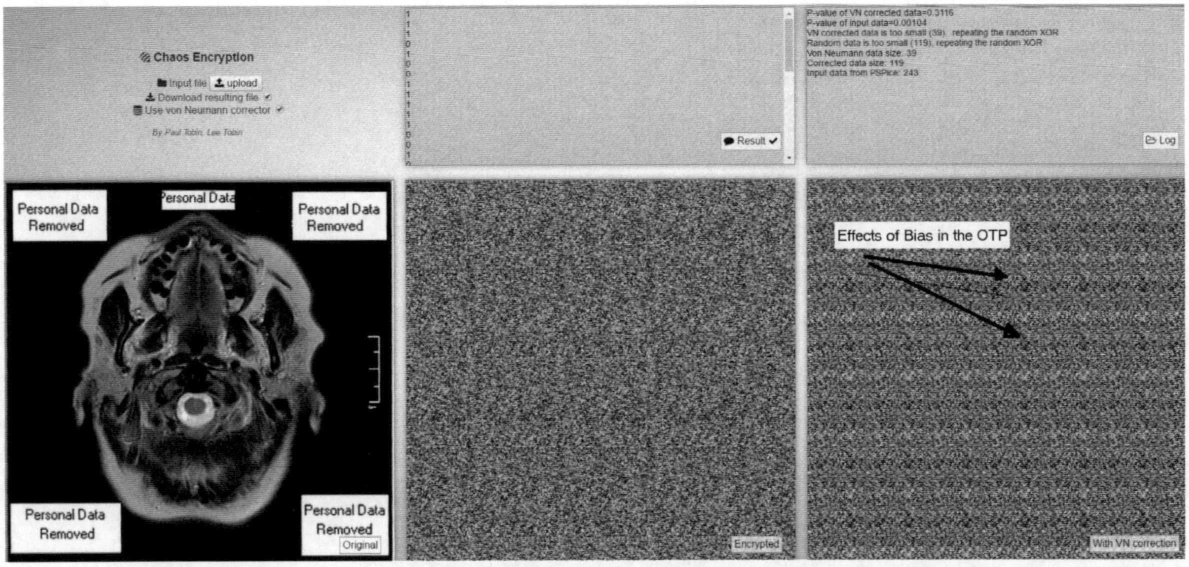


Figure 6. One-time pad JavaScript application.

TABLE I. NIST RESULTS for NOISE, SIMULATION and PROTOTYPE.

| *Statistical Test* | *P-value natural noise* | *P-value simulation OTP* | *P-value prototype OTP* | *Passed/Fail* |
|---|---|---|---|---|
| Frequency test | P = 0.4122 | P = 0.503 | P = 0.403 | Pass |
| Block frequency | P = 0.116 | P = 0.216 | P = 0.303 | Pass |
| Runs | P = 0.7846 | P = 0.508 | P = 0.683 | Pass |
| Block Longest Run Ones | P = 0.5388 | P = 0.490 | P = 0.553 | Pass |
| Binary Matrix Rank | P = 0.7138 | P = 0.333 | P = 0.430 | Pass |
| D Fourier Transform | P = 0.5206 | P = 0.216 | P = 0.420 | Pass |
| Non-overlap Tp Match | P = NA | P = Na | P = NA | NA |
| Overlapping Tp Match | P = 0.7729 | P = 0.002 | P = 0.090 | Pass |
| Universal | P = NA | P = NA | P = NA | NA |
| Linear Complexity | P = 0.9525 | P = 0.263 | P = 0.590 | Pass |
| Serial | (P1 = 0.1971, P2 = 0.544) | P1 = 0.197, P2 = 0.544 | P1 = 0.490, P2 = 0.509 | Pass |
| Approximate Entropy | P = 0.1143 | P = 0.201 | P = 0.290 | Pass |
| Cumulative Sums | P = 0.4444 | P = 0.563 | P = 0.490 | Pass |
| Random Excursions | P = NA | P = 0.216 | P = 0.230 | Pass |
| Random Excursion Variant | P = NA | P = 0.216 | P = 0.240 | Pass |

This would result in a much smaller OTP which could then be recombined with the image before uploading to the Cloud.

## ACKNOWLEDGEMENT

The authors are grateful to Professor Michael Conlon and Dr Marek Rebow, Dublin Institute of Technology, for arranging the author's collaborative research programme.

## REFERENCES

[1] [Online]. Available: http://www.cisco.com/c/en/us/solutions/collateral /service provider/global cloud index gci/Cloud Index White Paper.pdf, 2016, [retrieved: Mar 10, 2016].

[2] B. Duncan and M. Whittington,"Enhancing Cloud Security and Privacy: The Power and the Weakness of the Audit Trail", Conference on CLOUD COMPUTING, [retrieved: Sept 14, 2016], pp. 119-144.

[3] Verizon, "Verizon 2015 Data Breach Investigation Report", Tech. Rep., 2015, [retrieved: Sept 10, 2016]

[4] [Online]. Available: http://www.allenovery.com/SiteCollection Documents/Radical changes to European data protection legislation.pdf.

[5] [Online]. Available: https://en.wikipedia.org/wiki/Sony Pictures hack, [retrieved: May 10, 2016].

[6] D. Shumow and N. Ferguson, "On the possibility of a back door in the NIST SP800-90 Dual Ec Prng.", CRYPTO 2007 Rump Session, http://rump2007.cr.yp.to/15-shumow.pdf, August 2007.

[7] D. Hankerson, A.J. Menezes and S. Vanstone, "Guide to elliptic curve cryptography", Springer Science and Business Media, 2006.

[8] [Online]. Available: https://www.nist.gov/news-events/news/2014/04/ nist-removes-cryptography-algorithm-random-number-generator-recommendations.

[9] [Online]. Available: http://www.nytimes.com opinion aaron-sorkin journalists shouldn't help the Sony hackers.html, [retrieved: April 10, 2016], 2014.

[10] The New York Times, "Secret Documents Reveal N.S.A. Campaign Against Encryption", 2013.

[11] W. R. Bennett, "SIGSALY', IEEE Transactions on Communications", 31.1, 1983.

[12] P. M. Binder and R.V Jensen, "Simulating chaotic behavior with finite-state machines", Physical Review A 34(5), 1986, pp. 44604463.

[13] G. lvarez and S. Li, "Some basic cryptographic requirements for chaos-based cryptosystems", Int. J. Bifurcat. Chaos 16(8), 2006, pp. 21292151.

[14] S. Li et al, "On the security of a chaotic encryption scheme: problems with computerized chaos", Comput. Phys. Commun. 153(1), 2003, pp. 5258.

[15] E. Salih, "Security analysis of a chaos-based random number generator for applications in cryptography", 15th International Symposium on

Communications and Information Technologies (ISCIT), IEEE, 2015, pp. 319-322.

[16] S. Ergn, S. Gler and U. Asada, "IC Truly Random Number Generators Based on Regular and Chaotic Sampling of Chaotic Waveforms", Nonlinear Theory and its Applications, IEICE transactions, Vol. 2, 2011, pp. 246-261.

[17] E. K. Barker, Kelsey "Recommendation for the Entropy Sources Used for Random Bit Generation (draft)", NIST SP800-90B, August, 2016.

[18] S. Ergn, U. Gler and K. Asada, "A High Speed IC Truly Random Number Generator Based on Chaotic Sampling of Regular Waveform", IEICE Transactions on Fundamentals of Electronics, Communications and Computer Sciences, Vol. E94 A, 1, 2011, pp. 180-190.

[19] B. Schneier, "Applied Cryptography second edition", John Wiley and Sons 1996.

[20] P. Tobin, L. Tobin, M. McKeever and J. Blackledge, " Chaos-based Cryptography for Cloud Computing", 27th ISSC conference Ulster University, Londonderry, June 21-22, doi: 10.1109, 2016, pp. 1-6.

[21] P. Kennedy, "Genealogy of Chuas Circuit.", In Chaos, CNN, Memristors and Beyond: A Festschrift for Leon Chua With DVD-ROM, composed by Eleonora Bilotta, 2013, pp. 3-24.

[22] J. Blackledge, A. Al-Rawi, and P. Tobin, "Stegacryption of DICOM Metadata". In Irish Signals and Systems Conference 2014 and 2014 China-Ireland International Conference on Information and Communications Technologies (ISSC 2014/CIICT 2014). 25th IET June, pp. 304-309, 2013. Chicago.

[23] P. Jees, and T. Diya, "Medical Image Protection in Cloud System", matrix, V2, 2016, pp. 3.

[24] C.E. Shannon, "Communication Theory of Secrecy Systems", Bell Technical Journal, vol.28-4, 1949, pp. 656715.

[25] J. Blackledge, "Cryptography and Steganography": New Algorithms and Applications, Centre for Advanced Studies Text-books, Warsaw University of Technology, ISBN: 978-83-61993-05-6, 2012.

[26] E. Lorenz, "Chaos and Strange Attractors: The Lorenz Equations", 1963, pp. 532-538.

[27] P. Tobin, "PSpice for Circuit Theory and Electronic Devices", www.morganclaypool.com, ISBN:1598291564, pp. 127, 2007.

[28] P. Tobin, "PSpice for Digital Communications Engineering", Synthesis Lectures on Digital Circuits and Systems, www.morganclaypool.com, ISBN:1598291629, 2007, pp. 97.

[29] J. von Neumann, "Various techniques used in connection with random digits", Applied Math Series, 12, 1951, pp. 3638.

[30] J. Blackledge and N. Ptitsyn, "On the Applications of Deterministic Chaos for Encrypting Data on the Cloud", Third International Conference on the Evolving Internet IARIA Luxembourg, (ISBN: 978-1-61208-008-6 ), 2011, pp. 78-87.

[31] J. Blackledge, S. Bezobrazov, P. Tobin and F. Zamora, "Cryptography using Evolutionary Computing", (IET ISSC13 LYIT Letterkenny), 2013, pp. 1-6.

[32] P. Tobin, J. Blackledge, "Entropy, Information, Landauer's Limit and Moore's Law", (IET ISSC14 UL, Limerick), 2014, pp. 1-6.

[33] R. Frigg, "In what sense is the KSE a measure for chaotic behaviour?", (London School of Economics May), 2003.

[34] A. Ruk et al, "A statistical test suite for the validation of random number generators and pseudo-random number generators for cryptographic applications", NIST http://csrc.nist.gov/rng/rng2.html, 2001.

[35] Random.org, "True Random Number Service", [Online]. Available: http://www.random.org [retrieved: Aug 10, 2016]. 2013.

[36] [Online]. Available: http://jork.byethost7.com/chaosencrypt/

# Enhancing Cloud Security and Privacy: The Unikernel Solution

Alfred Bratterud
Dept. of Computer Science
Oslo and Akershus University
Oslo, Norway
Email: alfred.bratterud@hioa.no

Andreas Happe
Dept. Digital Safety & Security
Austrian Inst. of Tech. GmbH
Vienna, Austria
Email: andreas.happe@ait.ac.at

Bob Duncan
Computing Science
University of Aberdeen
Aberdeen, UK
Email: bobduncan@abdn.ac.uk

***Abstract*—Cloud security and privacy is a very challenging problem to solve. We started a project to explore a new approach to addressing this problem by utilising a unikernel based solution. In this paper, we outline the technical details of such an approach, identifying how this new approach can better address the issues involved. We have demonstrated how this new approach can improve the status quo.**

***Index Terms*—Cloud security and privacy; management control; compliance; complexity**

## I. Introduction

In [1], we provided a high level account of ten security issues, which management (Mgt) need to take account of when using cloud computing systems, and suggested how unikernel-based systems might address many of those issues, as we see in TABLE I below.

TABLE I. ITEMS ADDRESSED BY UNIKERNELS ©2016 [1]

| Issue | Description | Helped by: |
|---|---|---|
| 1 | Definition of security goals | Mgt and Unikernels |
| 2 | Compliance with standards | Mgt and Unikernels |
| 3 | Audit issues | Mgt and Unikernels |
| 4 | Management approach | Mgt and Unikernels |
| 5 | Technical complexity of cloud | Unikernels |
| 6 | Lack of responsibility and accountability | Mgt/Cloud Service Providers |
| 7 | Measurement and monitoring | Unikernels |
| 8 | Management attitude to security | Mgt |
| 9 | Security culture in the company | Mgt |
| 10 | Threat environment | Unikernels can help to enforce good design/architectural decisions |

While these security issues can be successfully addressed by other means, the reality, as evidenced by the recurring success of attackers, is that many companies are failing to apply the necessary rigour needed to resolve these issues in their existing approaches. Year after year, many attacks, which are both simple and relatively inexpensive to defend against, continue to be exploited.

In this paper, we introduce a framework of definitions and metrics for classifying unikernel systems, which we later make use of in the design, testing and assessment of new unikernel based system architectures. We compare a number of other unikernel and microkernel systems in this paper, but because of space constraints, do not address every single system available. In Section II, we discuss the background, motivation for this work, work already carried out and future work proposed. In Section III, we outline some necessary definitions and preliminary observations on unikernels, and in Section IV we consider 6 security observations relating to unikernels. The remainder of the paper is organized as follows: in Section V, we review the relationship between unikernels and microkernels; in Section VI, we discuss the implications of implementation language choice; in Section VII, we present well defined properties of unikernel systems; in Section VIII, we outline our proposed solution. In Section IX, we show how our proposed approach will address those key issues identified in TABLE: I. In Section X, we consider some initial thoughts on attack vectors; and in Section XI, we discuss our conclusions.

## II. Background, Motivation, Work Already Carried out and Proposed Future Work

The authors share a common interest in finding a solution to the challenging problem of cloud cyber security. The minimal resource efficiency of IncludeOS motivated the authors to consider whether there might be a possibility to develop a framework, based on unikernels, to deliver a far more secure system that could be run on cloud, and would offer high levels of security, privacy, audit and forensic trails, good scalability, high resource efficiency, and have the ability to take away the prospect of mis-configuration by users through lack of understanding of how to configure much more complex systems.

In [1], we outlined how the concept might be developed, and in [2], we considered how the proposed framework might be adapted to incorporate the Internet of Things (IoT). This paper outlines in a more formal way, definitions and metrics for classifying unikernel systems, which will be referred to in future work involving design, testing and assessment of new unikernel based system architectures. We next extend the work carried out in [1][2], providing much more detail on how the IoT system might be developed, and further examine how the single responsibility inherent in the unikernel design could be harnessed to provide a far more robust defence against common security problems.

As we develop each part of the framework, we carry out in-house penetration testing to ensure the robustness of the approach. Each part developed is intended to work seamlessly with all of the previous parts, so that the system as a whole will work properly as it is developed and grown. Once it reaches the point where it will interest at enterprise level, we will carry out large scale empirical testing to assess what will happen in the real world. We are developing fuzzing based penetration approaches, adapting tools and sanitizers, hardening tools and whatever else we can use to strengthen the user environment. We have still to develop communication channels, proper and secure audit and forensic trails, specialised storage, and plan to ensure the framework is capable of working under both object oriented styles and the model view controller paradigm.

## III. A PRECURSOR TO FORMAL WORK ON UNIKERNELS

Modern unikernel research, particularly concerning deployment in cloud, is still in its infancy and the literature currently available does not include much in the way of theoretical work or precise definitions, but rather takes a pragmatic approach [3]–[5]. One popular definition states that *"Unikernels are specialised, single-address-space machine images constructed by using library operating systems*; and that *Unikernels provide many benefits compared to a traditional Operating System (OS), including improved security, smaller footprints, more optimisation and faster boot times"* [6]. Without further qualification, directly associating unikernels with security benefits can be hazardous. It is not at all clear what "machine images" or "operating system libraries" are, nor what it means to construct them, and hence it is unclear precisely how unikernels can be said to be more secure. It is our view that stricter definitions are both necessary and achievable. We propose a set of working definitions intended to make the following exposition more precise, and to serve as a theoretical basis of a framework for unikernel based cloud computing.

To this end we can go back over four decades to early work on virtualization of mainframes. Early single address space operating systems, such as Mungi or Opal and many others do not seem to have much traction today. In 1995 [7], there was some early work on the Exokernel system, with some updating over the years, but little widespread use. Microsoft work on library operating systems, Drawbridge [8], saw little use at the time other than for research. It later evolved into the Haven system [9], which was intended for use in the Azure cloud, and also was integrated into Windows 10 as part of the pico-process security architecture.

**Definition III.1.** Popek-Goldberg virtual machine. An environment created by the virtual machine monitor, which is functionally equivalent to the physical machine on a given hardware (HW) platform, as defined in [10].

Popek and Goldberg provide formal definitions of both Virtual Machine Monitor and Virtual Machine, which form the most well known, if not the only, formally defined virtualization platform, which also directly corresponds to modern HW and nomenclature. An x86 Popek-Goldberg virtual machine is a virtual machine running under x86 Popek-Goldberg compliant HW virtualization, e.g., x86 HW with *vt-x* extensions. To give a precise definition of unikernels, we need to define their constituent parts. Our intention is not to provide definitions that encompass all the complexities or functionalities of unikernels, but rather the opposite; just enough to get a precise idea of what unikernels are and what they are not.

**Definition III.2.** Compiled program object, symbol. An n-tuple of machine instructions from a Turing complete instruction set, e.g., Intel x86, or an arbitrary sequence of bytes $b$, i.e., $0 >= b < 2^8$.

**Definition III.3.** Software library, symbol. A *Software library* is taken to be a collection of compiled program objects, $\{O_1, ..., O_m\}$ and arbitrary byte-sequences (e.g., data) $\{D_{m+1}, ..., D_n\}$ providing symbol resolutions, i.e., linkable objects, each corresponding to a *symbol* in the set $\{S_1, ..., S_m, S_{m+1}, ..., S_n\}$

The intuition here is to capture the idea of a library of compiled code, where functions and data are represented as binary objects in, e.g., `libos.so`, `libos.a`, `libos.dll` etc., where functions and static data can be accessed via symbols available to a linker. For the purposes of this paper, we assume the process of linking and symbol resolution are given and well defined.

**Definition III.4.** Software service. Objects, and optionally symbols, from a software library, with the addition of an entry point object $O_0$ corresponding to a symbol $S_0$ (e.g.,`_start`) that may or may not be present in the service, providing the compiled code necessary for a program to be executable on a given HW architecture.

Compiling an executable binary typically includes defining the entry point, e.g., `main` in ISO C, from where to start executing functions provided from a library. Compilers such as `gcc` will typically pre-pend some additional functionality through, e.g., the `_start`-symbol, mapped to code for initializing the C-runtime, including calling global constructors, zero-initializing the `.bss`-segment etc. The symbols are required during link-time but can later be stripped out when they are mapped to memory addresses relative to the binary.

We can now give an operational definition of a library operating system. The term has held different meanings [11][3], and we do not intend the following to be canonical, but merely one that will suffice to precisely define a unikernel for the purposes of our framework.

**Definition III.5.** Library operating system. For a software service $SW$, where the objects $\{O_0, ..., O_n\}$ form the set of objects necessary and sufficient for $SW$ to run on a given HW platform, a library operating system is a software library that can provide $\{O_0, ..., O_n\}$

This definition implies that a library operating system provides all the objects necessary to form a fully functional program, independent of any other software present on a system, except that which may or may not be presented through an instruction level interface, e.g., software that responds to a *trap* on the *Virtual Machine Monitor* in the Popek-Goldberg model.

*1) Definition of a unikernel:* In the context of virtual machines and cloud computing, it makes sense to describe the whole virtual machine as a unikernel [3], as there is in fact no classic boundary between kernel- and user space, and also because any combination of objects that can be pulled from the library operating system individually can be combined with a piece of software to form a unique whole. This piece of completely linked software will have full access to HW on the same level as a classic kernel.

In the context of classic operating system kernels, however, the library operating system designed to produce unikernels may also be called a unikernel [12] in reference to "micro-kernel", "nanokernel", "monolithic kernel" etc. It could be argued that if all the contents of a virtual machine were to be considered a unikernel, there wouldn't really be any point in using the word "kernel".

The following definiton is intended to be sufficiently flexible to allow both interpretations.

**Definition III.6.** Unikernel. Given a library operating system OS, a unikernel $U$ is defined as $U \subseteq OS$ such that $U$ is sufficient and necessary to provide complete linkage to some service $S$ for a given HW platform.

Using an inclusive subset allows both the whole library operating system and any subset to be called a unikernel.

**Definition III.7.** Unikernel machine image A software service $SW, \cup U$ where $U$ is the unikernel for $SW$, they both share the same address space, and with the addition of any facilities necessary to start $SW$ on a given well-defined virtualization platform, e.g., a bootloader in the case of an x86 Popek-Goldberg virtual machine.

**Definition III.8.** Popek-Goldberg unikernel. A Popek-Goldberg virtual machine initialized with a unikernel machine image.

## IV. Six security observations in Unikernel-based systems

We have identified 6 security observations, which are exhibited by unikernel systems:

- Choice of service isolation mechanism;
- The concept of reduced software attack surface;
- The use of a single address space, shared between service and kernel;
- No shell by default, and the impact on debugging and forensics;
- Micro services architecture and immutable infrastructure;
- Single thread by default.

### A. Choice of service isolation mechanism

In the previous paper in this series, the argument was made for why classic virtualization is the preferred platform for secure cloud computing. While many alternatives exist, which are both practical and widely trusted, one cannot reason precisely about their security properties unless they are well defined. In this paper, we make no judgements about their usefulness, but merely note that classic virtualization has had a precise foundation since 1974. We believe that the lack of similar models for other modes of virtualization is due to the fact that Popek-Goldberg virtualization exists at the instruction level, which is necessarily simple in nature as it must be implemented in physical circuitry. Other approaches typically rely on higher level software interfaces, and are thus harder to define precisely. Despite the simplicity of C, it still proves a hard nut to crack for the purposes of formal verification [13].

### B. Reduced software attack surface

Using the above definitions we can now define the software attack surface of a system as the sum of all objects, in bytes.

**Definition IV.1.** Software Attack surface. The number of bytes in a system, physically available for reading, writing or executing as instructions for a given HW architecture.

Physical protection can be seen as a grey area when it comes to microcode, firmware and otherwise mutable HW such as, e.g., field-programmable gate arrays (FPGAs). This definition is intentionally kept general in order to allow further specifications to refine the meaning of "physically available" for a given context. The following example can serve to illustrate how the definition can be used for one of many purposes. Building a classic virtual machine (VM) using Linux implies simply installing Linux, and then installing the software on top. Any reduction in software attack surface must be done by removing unneeded software and kernel modules (e.g drivers). Take TinyCore Linux as an example of a minimal Linux distribution and assume that it can produce a machine image of 24 MegaBytes (MB) in size.

Given this intuition, let $L$ be a collection of compiled program objects for x86, such that $L = \{O_1, ..., O_{2400}\}$, i.e., all the objects provided by TinyCore Linux, totalling 24MB in size, and for simplicity assume the objects are uniformly sized, 1Kb each. Adding a 1MB software service $SW$, which require $\{O_0, ..., O_{1000}\}$ to be executable, we get a software attack surface of 25MB, regardless of how many objects of $L$ were actually needed by $SW$. Assuming a *library operating system* existed that could provide $\{O_0, ..., O_{1000}\}$, a *unikernel* would by definition III.6, provide exactly those objects, forming a 2MB sized unikernel machine image. (2MB + 512 bytes of bootloader code in an x86 HW-VM). Hence the software attack surface of the unikernel VM is reduced by 92%. Conversely, the Linux VM could be said to add 23/1 * 100 = 2300% of unnecessary code, which we will refer to as *bloat* or *increased software attack surface* depending on context.

### C. The use of a single address space

The main objective for postulating a single address space is to imply single process or singular purpose. In a classic kernel, the need for multiple address spaces is prompted by the need to run multiple processes, which must be kept separate to ensure consistency and integrity among them. A classic kernel will typically rely on virtual memory implemented in HW to ensure process isolation and to provide a controlled virtual to physical address translation. Popek-Goldberg virtualization relies directly on this general concept without further extension. Aside from the performance degradation often seen in nested address translation, we take the view that introducing virtual memory and multiple processes inside a Popek-Goldberg virtual machine needlessly complicates an already complex system. In particular, it lays upon the virtual machine the added responsibility of creating and maintaining a process-kernel boundary.

**Definition IV.2.** Single address space. For a computer system, a *single address space* is defined as an interval of positive integers $[a_0, .., a_n]$ where $n$ is a power of two, representing the total addressable memory of a system in a given state, such that dereferencing any address $*a_x$ from anywhere inside the system would access the same physical memory cell.

The intuition is that virtual memory is not employed inside the system, effectively eliminating the possibility of running several disjoint processes. We are not making any assumptions or requirements as to whether or not all addresses are in fact accessible, e.g., physically present or readable / writeable / executable, merely that they point to the same location if any. Note that virtual memory can and will be employed on the virtual machine monitor, to protect one VM from another, but further nesting of virtual memory would violate the single address space principle.

### D. No shell by default and the impact on debugging and forensics

One feature of unikernels that immediately makes it seem very different from classic operating systems is the lack of a command line interface. This is however a direct consequence of the fact that classic POSIX-like command line interpreters (CLI)s are run as a separate process (e.g., `bash`) with the main purpose of starting other processes. Critics might argue that this makes unikernels harder to manage and "debug", as one cannot "log in and see what's happened" after an incident, as is the norm for system administrators. We take the position that this line of argument is vacuous; running a unikernel rather corresponds to running a single process with better isolation, and in principle there is no more need to log in to a unikernel than there is to log in to, e.g., a web server process running in a classic operating system.

While unikernels by definition are a single address space virtual machine, with no concept of classic processes, a text based CLI could be provided (e.g., IncludeOS does provide an example) — the commands wouldn't start processes, but call functions inside the program. From a security perspective we take the view that this kind of ad-hoc access to program objects should be avoided. While symbols are very useful for providing a stack trace after a crash or for performance profiling, stripping out symbols pointing to program objects inside a unikernel would make it much harder for an attacker to find and execute functions for malicious and unintended purposes. Our recommendation is that this should be the default mode for unikernels in production mode. We take the view that logging is of critical importance for all systems, in order to provide a proper audit trail. Unikernels however simply need to provide the logs through other means, such as over a virtual serial port, or ideally over a secure networking connection to a trusted audit trail store.

Lastly it is worth mentioning that unikernels in principle have full control over a contiguous range of memory. Combined with the fact that a crashed VM by default will "stay alive" as a process from the virtual machine manager (VMM) perspective, and not be terminated, this means that in principle the memory contents of a unikernel could be accessed and inspected from the VMM after the fact, if desired. Placing the audit trail logs in a contiguous range of memory could then make it possible to extract those logs also after a failure in the network connection or other I/O device normally used for transmitting the data. Note that this kind of inspection requires complete trust between the owner of the VM and the VMM (e.g., the cloud tenant and cloud provider). Our recommendation would be not to rely on this kind of functionality in public clouds, unless all sensitive data inside the VM is encrypted and can be extracted and sent to the tenant without decrypting it.

### E. Micro services architecture and immutable infrastructure.

Micro services is a relatively new term founded on the idea of separating a system into several individual and fully disjoint services, rather than continuously adding features and capabilities to an ever growing monolithic program. Being single threaded by default unikernels naturally imply this kind of architecture; any need for scaling up beyond the capabilities of a single CPU should be done by spawning new instances. While classic VM's require a lot of resources and impose a lot of overhead, minimal virtual machines are very lightweight. As demonstrated in [14] more than 100,000 instances could be booted on a single physical server and [12] showed that each virtual machine, including the surrounding process require much less memory than a single "Hello World" Java program running directly on the host.

An important feature of unikernels in the context of micro services is that each unikernel VM is fully self contained. This also make them immune to breaches in other parts of the service composition, increasing the resilience of the system as a whole. Add to this the idea of *optimal mutability* (defined below), and each unikernel-based micro service can in turn be as immutable as is physically possible on a given platform. In the next paper in this series we expand upon these ideas and take the position that composing a service out of several micro services, each as immutable as possible, enables overall system architects and decision makers to focus on a high level view of service composition, not having to worry too much about the security of their constituent parts. We take the view that this kind of separation of concerns is necessary in order to achieve scalable yet secure cloud services.

### F. Single threaded by default

While the above definitions do not impose any restrictions on whether or not a unikernel can run several concurrent threads or multiple CPU cores, it is well known that concurrency is a major source of errors accounting for a significant number of vulnerabilities. IncludeOS and MirageOS are both examples of unikernels that are single threaded by default. Efficiency is achieved by event based asynchronous interfaces with no blocking calls. While pre-emptive interrupt handling and concurrency using shared memory are necessary for certain workloads, we take the view that single threaded concurrency free services are by nature less complex and thus less error prone. It is also well known that threaded applications perform worse inside virtual machines than single threaded applications due to the extra layer of context switches necessary to schedule threads inside the VM as well as outside.

Our recommendation is to keep unikernels single threaded by default and rather achieve concurrency by adding more instances, to the extent possible. In a modular library OS one can add threading and re-entrant versions of libraries as optional components without causing bloat or increased complexity to unikernels not requiring concurrency.

## V. Relationship to Microkernels

While there exists a rich fauna of operating system kernel types, the most well known distinction is between monolithic kernels and micro kernels. For this reason we'll briefly explain how unikernels fit in this spectrum. Microkernel operating systems are absolutely minimal in the sense that nothing that doesn't have to be in the kernel is. However, most implementations such as the L4 are still A) multi-process; B) not library operating systems; and C) will typically have a classic style command line, etc., which would make it almost orthogonal to our purpose as it addresses other issues (L4 is focussed mainly on fast Industrial PCs). That being said, they have an advantage over classic kernels when it comes to: A) software attack surface (it can run many programs, but it does not have to); and B) complexity. The simplicity of the microkernel is what made it possible to do formal verification of the Haskell implementation of L4 - and that is a major security benefit.

Our position is that unikernels have the potential to incorporate the "small and simple" from microkernels, while still adding new security features — in particular: 1) The library operating system approach, which guarantees a minimal amount of unnecessary code is introduced; 2) the single-purpose approach; and 3) it is single-threaded by default. This provides a further means of simplification (parallel programming is notoriously error-prone), while also strongly encouraging micro service architecture, which increase resilience of the system as a whole.

## VI. Choice of Implementation Language

**Definition VI.1.** Independent systems language. A Turing complete programming language with facilities to utilize the whole instruction set for a given HW architecture, including writing arbitrary data to arbitrary addresses.

C and C++ are examples of independent systems languages for most modern HW architectures, e.g., x86: the `asm` keyword (i.e., "inline assembly") makes the full instruction set available to the programmer, including privileged instructions such as `hlt`,`in` and `out`, and the pointer data type and (unsafe) type conversion allows arbitrary data to be written to arbitrary addresses. Type safe languages such as javascript, OCaml, Haskell and Python are not independent systems languages by design; type safety can be immediately violated by, e.g., type coercion. The requirement for being an independent systems language is thus incompatible with type safety. To bridge this incompatibility, unikernels written in type safe languages must necessarily contain a portion of code written in an independent systems language. In most cases, such as with MirageOS, this is done in C.

## VII. Well Defined Properties of Unikernel Systems

Based on the previous definitions we can now provide a framework of well-defined properties of unikernel-based systems:

- **Service isolation:**. A well-defined and absolute isolation mechinanism such as Popek-Goldberg virtualization is preferable as 0 bytes of code needs to be shared between services during runtime. Enforcement is performed by HW at the instruction level. Following closely is Xen PVH, which is mostly HW virtualization, but some shared code. Paravirtualization shares a thin yet fairly complex set of software bindings and HW is only used for classic process isolation. One way to quantify this property is the amount of software, in bytes, shared by each service on the virtual machine monitor. Microcode / firmware would be a grey area, but that would be common to all current isolation mechanisms.
- **VM Slimness, Bloat and software attack surface:** For a software service $SW$, requiring objects $A, B$ and $C$ to form a machine image, a system (e.g., unikernel library) that can produce a virtual machine containing exactly $\{SW, A, B, C\}$ without $\{D, E, F, ...\}$ provides *optimal slimness*. Conversely, the amount of code added to the VM in addition to $\{SW, A, B, C\}$ adds *bloat*. As an example, if $\{SW, A, B, C\}$ was 10MB in size and an operating system added 5 MB that would be 50% of bloat. Linux-based virtual machines would easily be 2000% bloated for single-purpose virtual machines, e.g., using a trimmed down Linux micro-core of 24MB used to run a 1MB service, 96% of the machine image would be operating system. IncludeOS instances are typically 1 MB of OS, so if the service could run with IncludeOS that would be 50/50 software and OS, plus a few percent overweight (one typically would not use all the code included, even if one included only the objects needed, unless the objects themselves are each absolutely minimal). Given that 1MB was sufficient to add the required operating system parts, wrapping it in a Linux VM would literally make for 2300% of bloat.

- **System mutability:** To what extent is it possible to change the system once launched? This is hard to quantify, but we propose the following set of properties as "optimal immutability", which a system should strive for:
  1) All data that can be read-only is;
  2) All executable code is write-protected;
  3) Write-able areas of memory (i.e., the heap / working memory) is not executable.

  Enforcement of these rules should be implemented at the lowest level. In IncludeOS, this kind of protection cannot really be enforced on current platforms. Type-safe language unikernels, such as Mirage, have a certain degree of language-level protection, but only in the parts of the unikernel not written in C. We propose a future work on hypervisors where we provide an interface for specifying which parts of the VM that should be read-only, execute- and read/write (but not execute), when the system boots. This way, the hypervisor at ring -1 can set up memory segments inside the VM before it starts, denying even the VM itself the ability to modify read-only parts of memory. Having the CPU enforce these rules will make it useless to inject code into a VM, if one found a way to do it, as jumping to that code would trigger a HW trap.
- **Possibility of internal system misuse:** To what extent does the operating system allow parts of the code to be used for unintended purposes? Having a terminal makes several commands available for "general purpose" or "ad-hoc use" of the code embedded into the system. Not having a terminal, or other similar means of allowing ad-hoc function calls, greatly reduces or entirely removes this possibility.

## VIII. Our proposed solution

By default, in the interests of usability, conventional systems open many more ports than may be needed to run a system. An open port, especially one that is not needed, is another route in for the attacker. We also take the position that the probability of vulnerabilities being present in a system increases proportionally to the amount of executable code it contains. Having less executable code inside a given system will reduce the chances of a breach and also reduce the number of tools available for an attacker once inside. As Meireles [15] said in 2007 *"... while you can sometimes attack what you can't see, you can't attack what is not there!"*. Given the success with which the threat environment continually attacks business globally [16]–[20], it is clear that many companies are falling down on many of the key issues we have highlighted in Section I. It is also clear that a sophisticated and complex solution is unlikely to work. Thus we must approach the problem from a more simple perspective.

### A. Service isolation

A fundamental premise for cloud computing is the ability to share HW. In private cloud systems, HW resources are shared across a potentially large organization, while on public clouds, HW is shared globally across multiple tenants. In both cases, isolating one service from the other is an absolute requirement.

The simplest mechanism for service isolation is simply *process isolation* in classic kernels, relying on HW supported virtual memory, e.g., provided by the now pervasive x86 protected mode. While process isolation has been used successfully in mainframe setups for decades, access to terminals with limited user privileges has also been the context for classic attack vectors such as stack smashing, root-kits etc., the main problem being that a single kernel is being shared between several processes and that gaining root access from one terminal would give access to everything inside the system. As a result, much work was done in the sixties and seventies to find ways to completely isolate a service without sharing a kernel. This work culminated with the seminal 1974 paper by Popek and Goldberg [21] where they present a formal model describing the requirements for complete instruction level virtualization, i.e., *HW virtualization*.

While HW virtualization was in wide use on e.g., IBM mainframes from that time, it wasn't until 2005 that the leading commodity CPU manufacturers, Intel and AMD, introduced these facilities into their chips. In the meantime, paravirtualization had been re-introduced as a workaround to get virtual machines on these architectures, notably in [22]. While widely deployed and depended upon, the Xen project has recently been evolving its paravirtualization interface towards using HW virtualization in, e.g., PVH [23] stating that *"PVH means less code and fewer Interfaces in Linux/FreeBSD: consequently it has a smaller TCB and software attack surface, and thus fewer possible exploits"* [24].

Another isolation mechanism is operating system-level virtualization with containers, e.g., Linux Containter (LXC) popularized in recent years by Docker, where each container represents a userspace operating environment for services that all share a kernel. The mechanism for isolating one container from another is classic process isolation, augmented with software controls such as cgroups and Linux namespaces. While containers do offer less overhead than classic virtual machines, a good example where containers make a lot of sense would be trusted in-house clouds, i.e., Google is using containers internally for most purposes [25]. We take the position that HW virtualization is the simplest and most complete mechanism for service isolation, with the best understood foundations as formally described by Popek and Goldberg, and that this should be the preferred isolation mechanism for secure cloud computing.

### B. Why Use Unikernels?

Using HW virtualization as the preferred isolation mechanism requires an operating system to be embedded into the virtual machine. IaaS cloud providers will typically offer virtual machine images running a classic general purpose operating system, such as Microsoft Windows and one or more flavours of Linux, possibly optimized for cloud by, e.g., removing device drivers that are not needed. While specialized Linux distributions can greatly reduce the memory footprint and software attack surface of a virtual machine, general purpose multi-process operating systems will, by design, contain a large amount of functionality that is simply not needed by one single service. We take the position that virtual machines should be specialized to a high degree, each forming a single purpose micro service, to facilitate a resilient and fault tolerant system architecture, which is also highly scalable.

We argue that the unikernel approach offers potential to meet all our needs, while delivering a much reduced software attack surface, yet providing exactly the performance we require. An added bonus will be the reduced operating footprint, meaning a more green approach is delivered at the same time.

### C. How Does This Compare to a Conventional System?

Looking at what Frederick P. Brooks Jnr. suggests in [26] "Because ease of use is the purpose, this ratio of function to conceptual complexity is the ultimate test of system design. Neither function nor simplicity alone defines a good design", we can see where modern software systems are missing the point. The more complex a system becomes, the more overhead is introduced, leading to greater complexity and unnecessary bloat, draining performance, and exposing vulnerabilities. Conventional cloud systems tend to be over-complicated, unnecessarily bloated, and thus expensive to scale. Unikernels, in [6], "Unikernels are specialized, single-address-space machine images constructed by using library operating systems", meaning they are exactly the right size to carry out their given task — no larger, and no smaller.

Our approach, using unikernels, limits/enforces the software architect to use a given pattern (event-based computing using the single-responsibility-principle, service-oriented architectures, separation of data and processing, and modularity) — which is very good from a software design point of view. We are trying to get people to use "best-of-breed" patterns, and thus develop better software through this limitation.

## IX. How Does This Address Our Ten Key Concerns?

As we saw in the introduction, we identified 10 key security issues needing to be addressed. We believe our unikernel solution can help us address seven of these issues, namely: The definition of security goals; Compliance with standards; Audit issues; Management approach; Technical complexity of cloud; Measurement and monitoring; The threat environment.

### A. The Definition of Security Goals

By design, we will build in a number of sensible security goals to the system. We can also accommodate additional goals, where the user identifies those as appropriate.

### B. Compliance with Standards

Compliance is generally achieved through some form of assurance [27], which generally can be achieved by a compliance process or by audit. Audit is expensive if done well, thus compliance through the use of checklists is the usual method chosen, but brings weaknesses with it [28]. Tightening information flows within the system, and providing rigorous audit trails, maximises assurance, leading to compliance in a much more accurate and cost effective way.

### C. Audit Issues

Many audit issues needing to be addressed [29], especially those surrounding the use of the humble audit trail [30]. In a forthcoming paper, we outline in more detail how our system will tackle this key issue with a much more rigorous approach.

### D. Management Approach

Cloud ecosystems involve far more actors than conventional systems, and many of these actors have differing agendas [31]. Our approach seeks to minimise the impact of third party actors by reducing the opportunity for these actors to adversely influence the effectiveness of the security approach.

### E. Technical Complexity of Cloud

Distributed systems are highly complex. Cloud ecosystems are, by their nature, far more complex [32]. We propose to tackle this issue through simplification of the system architecture, to minimise the software attack surface.

### F. Measurement and monitoring

To achieve a provable level of security [33], it is necessary to measure and monitor what is happening with a system. Our system will, by default, provide a considerable armoury of measurement and monitoring capabilities, which will allow users to be satisfied of the level of security they have achieved, and will continue to achieve through continuous monitoring.

### G. The threat environment

This is a major and very worrying issue, which continues to evolve day by day. Our approach seeks to tackle this through minimising software attack surface, minimising access routes to attackers, and generally making life difficult for the attackers. This area will need ongoing scrutiny by the research community in order to try to keep ahead of the attackers.

## X. Initial Thoughts on Penetration Testing

Penetration testers often refer to the OWASP foundation Top 10 report, see Table II below for details of the most used attack techniques. In its current 2013 installation, two vulnerabilities—A5-Security Misconfiguration and A9-Using Known Vulnerable Components—are directly related to the rich landscape of available server-side functions, which commonly are neither minimized nor properly configured. Recent years have given rise to opinionated frameworks, i.e., frameworks that guide developers with sensible security defaults. Their security measures efficiently reduce threats from common attack vectors, e.g., A1-Injection or A2-Cross-Site Scripting, but those frameworks themselves can introduce vulnerabilities, as OWASP noted with its introduction of A9 as "the growth and depth of component based development has significantly increased the risk of using known vulnerable components". The Unikernel approach implicitly minimizes infrastructure — runtime environment, and libraries as well as operating system shells — and thus reduces exposure to attack vectors A5 and A9. Plus, their single-process paradigm enforces beneficial architecture design decisions, yielding systems with clearer separation-of-concerns. Given the rise of opinionated frameworks, we envision a web-development framework that de-constructs high-level workflows into separate unikernels, structures communication between those, and provides sensible security defaults. We assume that such a system of unikernels can solve complex web-application workflows in a secure manner without negatively impacting developer's productivity during development and debugging, which we next address in much more depth.

TABLE II. OWASP TOP TEN WEB VULNERABILITIES — 2013 [34]

| 2013 Code | Threat |
|---|---|
| A1 | Injection Attacks |
| A2 | Broken Authentication and Session Management |
| A3 | Cross Site Scripting (XSS) |
| A4 | Insecure Direct Object References |
| A5 | Security Misconfiguration |
| A6 | Sensitive Data Exposure |
| A7 | Missing Function Level Access Control |
| A8 | Cross Site Request Forgery (CSRF) |
| A9 | Using Components with Known Vulnerabilities |
| A10 | Unvalidated Redirects and Forwards |

## XI. CONCLUSIONS

We introduced a framework of definitions and metrics for classifying unikernel systems, and began developing a formal approach to describing our framework, and considered how such a theoretical framework might provide a more secure approach to the challenges of cloud security and privacy.

We have proposed a novel means of significantly reducing the software attack surface for a cloud based system, removing in the process many classic attack vectors. We consider the architecture of the proposed system and its resilience to attack in much more depth in our forthcoming publications.

We need to look at, and solve, the challenge presented by audit trail issues, which will require secure internal communication, access logging and log storage, and provision of a strong forensic trail. Once these security basics are in place, we can turn our attention to a robust approach to privacy.

## REFERENCES


[1] B. Duncan, A. Bratterud, and A. Happe, "Enhancing Cloud Security and Privacy: Time for a New Approach?" in *INTECH 2016*, Dublin, 2016, pp. 1–6.

[2] B. Duncan, A. Happe, and A. Bratterud, Enterprise IoT Security and Scalability: How Unikernels can Improve the Status Quo, in *9th IEEE/ACM International Conference on Utility and Cloud Computing (UCC 2016)*, 2016, Shanghai. pp. 16.

[3] A. Madhavapeddy, et al., "Unikernels: Library Operating Systems for the Cloud," *ASPLOS '13 Proc. eighteenth Int. Conf. Archit. Supp Prog. Lang. Oper. Syst.*, vol. 48, pp. 461–472, 2013.

[4] A. Madhavapeddy and D. J. Scott, "Unikernels: Rise of the Virtual Library Operating System," *Commun. ACM*, vol. 57, no. 1, pp. 61–69, 2014.

[5] A. Kantee, "The Rise and Fall of the Operating System," *Login:*, pp. 6–9, 2015.

[6] Unikernel.org, "Unikernels," 2015. [Online]. Available: www.unikernel.org Last accessed: 11 Jan 2017

[7] D. R. Engler, M. F. Kaashoek, and Others, *Exokernel: An operating system architecture for application-level resource management*. ACM, 1995, vol. 29, no. 5.

[8] D. E. Porter, S. Boyd-Wickizer, J. Howell, R. Olinsky, and G. C. Hunt, "Rethinking the library OS from the top down," in *ACM SIGPLAN Not.*, vol. 46, no. 3. ACM, 2011, pp. 291–304.

[9] A. Baumann, M. Peinado, and G. Hunt, "Shielding applications from an untrusted cloud with haven," *ACM Trans. Comput. Syst.*, vol. 33, no. 3, p. 8, 2015.

[10] G. J. Popek and R. P. Goldberg, "Formal Requirements for Virtualizable Third Generation Architectures," *ACM SIGOPS Oper. Syst. Rev.*, vol. 7, no. 4, p. 112, 1973.

[11] M. F. Kaashoek, et al., "Application Performance and Flexibility on Exokernel Systems," *ACM SIGOPS Oper. Syst. Rev.*, vol. 31, no. 5, pp. 52–65, 1997.

[12] A. Bratterud, A.-A. Walla, H. Haugerud, P. E. Engelstad, and K. Begnum, "IncludeOS: A Minimal, Resource Efficient Unikernel for Cloud Services," *2015 IEEE 7th Int. Conf. Cloud Comput. Technol. Sci.*, pp. 250–257, 2015.

[13] G. Klein, et al., "seL4: Formal verification of an OS kernel," *Proc. ACM SIGOPS 22nd Symp. Oper. Syst. Princ.*, pp. 207–220, 2009.

[14] A. Bratterud and H. Haugerud, "Maximizing Hypervisor Scalability Using Minimal Virtual Machines," *2013 IEEE 5th Int. Conf. Cloud Comput. Technol. Sci.*, pp. 218–223, 2013.

[15] P. Meireles, "Narkive Mailinglist Archive," 2007. [Online]. Available: http://m0n0wall.m0n0.narkive.com/OI4NbHQq/m0n0wall-virtualization Last accessed: 05 Jan 2017.

[16] PWC, "Information Security Breaches Survey 2010 Technical Report," pp. 1–22, 2010.

[17] PWC, "UK Information Security Breaches Survey - Technical Report 2012," London, Tech. Rep. April, 2012.

[18] PWC, "2014 Information Security Breaches Survey: Technical Report," Tech. Rep., 2014.

[19] Verizon, N. High, T. Crime, I. Reporting, and I. S. Service, "2012 Data Breach Investigations Report," Verizon, Tech. Rep., 2012.

[20] Verizon, "2014 Data Breach Investigations Report," Tech. Rep. 1, 2014.

[21] G. J. Popek and R. P. Goldberg, "Formal Requirements for Virtualizable Third Generation Architectures," *Commun. ACM*, vol. 17, no. 7, pp. 412–421, 1974.

[22] P. Barham, et al., "Xen and the art of virtualization." *SIGOPS Oper.Syst.Rev.*, vol. 37, no. 5, pp. 164–177, 2003.

[23] D. Chisnall, "Xen PVH: Bringing Hardware to Paravirtualization." *Inf. IT*, 2014.

[24] X. Project, "Xen Project Software Overview," 2016. [Online]. Available: http://wiki.xen.org/wiki/Xen_Project_Software_Overview#PVH Last accessed: 05 Jan 2017.

[25] A. Verma, L. Pedrosa, M. Korupolu, D. Oppenheimer, E. Tune, and J. Wilkes, "Large-scale cluster management at Google with Borg," *Proc. Tenth Eur. Conf. Comput. Syst. - EuroSys '15*, pp. 1–17, 2015.

[26] F. P. Brooks Jr, *The Mythical Man-Month: Essays on Software Engineering, Anniversary Edition, 2/E*. Pearson Education India, 1995.

[27] B. Duncan and M. Whittington, "Compliance with Standards, Assurance and Audit: Does this Equal Security?" in *Proc. 7th Int. Conf. Secur. Inf. Networks*. Glasgow: ACM, 2014, pp. 77–84.

[28] B. Duncan and M. Whittington, "Reflecting on whether checklists can tick the box for cloud security," in *Proc. Int. Conf. Cloud Comput. Technol. Sci. CloudCom*, vol. 2015-Febru, no. February. Singapore: IEEE, 2015, pp. 805–810.

[29] B. Duncan and M. Whittington, "Enhancing Cloud Security and Privacy: The Cloud Audit Problem," in *Cloud Comput. 2016 Seventh Int. Conf. Cloud Comput. GRIDs, Virtualization*. Rome: IEEE, 2016, pp. 119–124.

[30] B. Duncan and M. Whittington, "Enhancing Cloud Security and Privacy: The Power and the Weakness of the Audit Trail," in *Cloud Comput. 2016 Seventh Int. Conf. Cloud Comput. GRIDs, Virtualization*. Rome: IEEE, 2016, pp. 125–130.

[31] B. Duncan and M. Whittington, "Company Management Approaches Stewardship or Agency: Which Promotes Better Security in Cloud Ecosystems?" in *Cloud Comput. 2015*. Nice: IEEE, 2015, pp. 154–159.

[32] B. Duncan, D. J. Pym, and M. Whittington, "Developing a Conceptual Framework for Cloud Security Assurance," in *Cloud Comp. Tech. Sci. (CloudCom), 2013 IEEE 5th Int. Conf. (Vol 2)*. Bristol: IEEE, 2013, pp. 120–125.

[33] B. Duncan and M. Whittington, "The Importance of Proper Measurement for a Cloud Security Assurance Model," in *2015 IEEE 7th Int. Conf. Cloud Comput. Technol. Sci.*, Vancouver, 2015, pp. 1–6.

[34] OWASP, "OWASP Top Ten Vulnerabilities 2013," 2013. [Online]. Available: https://www.owasp.org/index.php/Category:OWASP_Top_Ten_Project Last accessed: 05 Jan 2017.

# CloudMediate

## Peer-to-peer Media Aggregation for Augmented Reality

Raimund K. Ege
Department of Computer Science
Northern Illinois University
DeKalb, USA
email: ege@niu.edu

*Abstract*—**Augmented Reality strives to produce a world composed from virtual models and multiple multi-media streams, and enables complete immersion into the result via modern mobile hand-held or wearable devices. In this paper, we present a conceptual media aggregation framework that is flexible, powerful and scalable to identify, establish and manage connections to media stream source (virtual and real) and produces an adaptable world view, which is then made available to consuming devices with attitude feedback. The framework is structured into three layers: presence, integration, and homogenization layers that work together in a peer-to-peer (p2p) manner to facilitate the delivery of multimedia data. Each layer features cloud-based mediator components, each mediator transforms an input stream into an output stream. This mediation process is context-aware, adaptive and dynamically structured.**

***Keywords-augmented reality; virtual reality; peer-to-peer systems; multi-media content delivery.***

## I. INTRODUCTION

The proliferation of mobile and wearable devices has enabled access, at least on a physical level, to a multitude of disparate but often related information, while scaling geographical barriers. This information, in the form of multimedia streams is produced, stored on and accessed from various kinds of heterogeneous devices. Our goal is to select suitable input streams, correlate and combine them into a virtual world. The virtual world can then be made available to clients, again rendered onto suitable mobile and wearable devices.

Fig. 1 shows our overall idea of how CloudMediate operates. The left side of the figure symbolizes the multitude of potential input streams. While audio and video streams are most common, our approach allows arbitrary streams of data from any sensor. The right side of the figure shows consumption of streams by mobile devices. The common smartphone might be one example of such a display device. Wearable devices, such as headsets and virtual glasses are the target of our approach. Both sides are connected by a cloud-hosted network of intermediaries that normalize, correlate and combine input streams into consumable output streams.

We use the term "mediator" to describe these intermediaries. We chose this term in analogy to the "Mediator" behavioral pattern that address the responsibilities of objects in an application and how they communicate [1].

In this paper, we describe a framework for peer-to-peer media aggregation for augmented reality that features a three-layer architecture for multimedia mediation. The paper is organized as follows: Section 2 presents some related work and briefly covers some differences and similarities between our architecture and existing ones. Section 3 describes our overall architecture and each layer and what functions are performed therein. We also discuss the different classes of mediators in those layers. Section 4 covers the CloudMediate web-based control interface that allows peers to register and sign up with their multi-media stream. The section also introduces our mobile application for portable and wearable devices to allow a peer user to become immersed in the resulting augmented virtual reality. We conclude with an outlook to our future work.

## II. BACKGROUND

Virtual Reality devices are emerging rapidly in the market place. Every major vendor of systems and hardware has introduced mobile and wearable gadgets to support virtual and augmented reality. From simple holders for smart phones, to headsets from market leaders such as Samsung and Google (even eye glasses, e.g., Google GLASS). Software to enable these devices is becoming more commonplace. The

Figure 1. CloudMediate Structure.

application developer kits are becoming ever more powerful to harness the dynamic features of these devices.

Multimedia data requires special attention to throughput, timeliness and other quality of service factors. There is a need for architectures to deal with buffering and the intermittent connection associated with mobility. Our approach to enabling high quality access is to build a layered framework of mediators [2]. Lower-layer mediators connect to the actual data sources, while higher-layer mediators provide a logical schema of information to applications. Mediators are typically employed in a situation where the client data model does not coincide with the data model of the potential data sources. They are facilitators that search for likely resources and ways to access them. They provide a mapping of complex models to enable interoperability between client and source(s). Many mediator systems have been proposed for a variety of applications, a major problem often encountered is how to seamlessly query and integrate data from heterogeneous data sources [3].

In peer-sourced augmented reality systems, the management of the multi-media source and establishment of trust is essential [4]. In our prior work [5] [6], we investigated the authentication of participants in peer-to-peer networks, the establishment and management of trust, and the use of such media sources in building content management systems. An important lesson was that while modern mobile devices are compute-capable, cloud-based components add additional heft and authority to a seamless and smooth creation of a truly immersing virtual and augmented reality experience [7][8][9].

## III. MEDIATOR ARCHITECTURE

We approach the task of delivering multi-media streams from their producers to the consumers be decomposing it into small steps according to an overall architectural framework. The architectural framework features three layers: Presence, Integration and Homogenization as shown in Fig. 2.

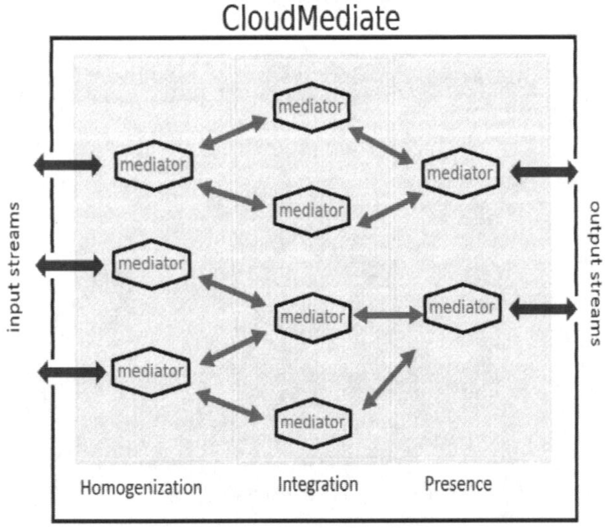


Figure 2. Layers of Architecture.

The Presence layer is closest to the device that consumes the output stream. The Homogenization layer is closest to the device that produces the input stream. The integration layer correlates Presence and Homogenization mediators.

Each layer is composed of several cloud-based mediators. Different classes of mediator are employed within each layer. Fig. 3 shows the top of the mediator class hierarchy.

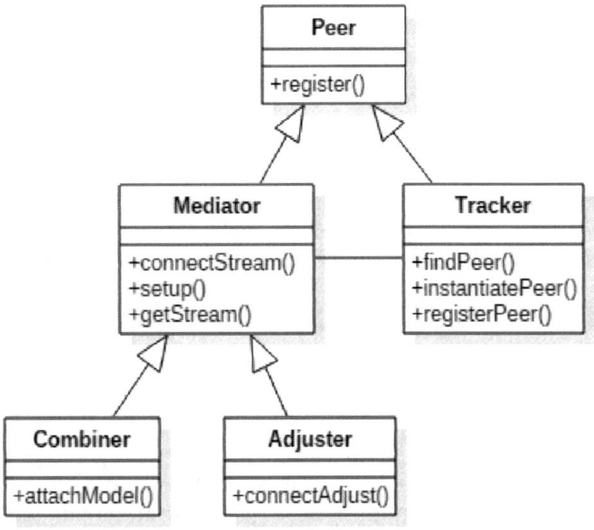


Figure 3. Mediator Class Hierarchy.

Each mediator has an input and an output side and transfers and negotiates on three kinds of information; the schema of the data stream, the data stream itself, and some quality of service (QoS) information specific to the stream. The nature of mediation varies from a simple combination of input streams, to correlation of virtual and augmented streams, and up to reformatting of a stream based on attitude information.

The central class is Mediator: it manages the input/output connections. It is a subclass of Peer, which handles peer setup and registration. A special Tracker peer is responsible for keeping track of all peers. It accepts registrations from other peers and facilitates peer lookup. It can also instantiate new peers to create a path from incoming media streams to output streams through the layers of our framework.

Two subclasses of Mediator are shown here: Combiner is able to attach a virtual reality model to input streams to correlate multiple input streams into a single output stream; Adjuster connects to an attitude stream of an output stream device. As the device attitude changes, it adjusts the perceived attitude geometry of the output stream.

### *A. Homogenization Layer*

In our architecture, each homogenization layer mediator is directly associated with an incoming multi-media data stream from a mobile device.

In addition to the actual data sensed, it must be packaged with the exact time of recording. Multiple streams of sensor data are combined into a multi-media stream which interleaves its content streams plus provides meta-data to ensure their proper sequencing and correlation. It is important that the container format used to wrap the content streams is flexible enough to accommodate not only the stream data but also extensive amounts of reference information used to combine the streams. We are using an extension of the WebM project [10] format. The WebM container format is an open standard and allows us to collate an unlimited number of video, audio, pictures and subtitle tracks into one stream. We add the capability of identifying reference elements at identified points in time and at locations.

Video data is the key stream type captured via video sensors, i.e., cameras, available on the wearable devices carried by a peer. Video is captured as a sequence of video frames. Each frame carries a time stamp as major meta reference data. Equally important is the location of video capture, lens parameters and attitude, i.e., which way the camera points. Our container format allows us to group sequential video frames into video sequences that share a common location. We represent the location with a "Normal Vector".

Fig. 4 shows how a normal vector captures not only the location of a video plane but also its relative position. The normal vector is represented via 2 points: its origin and extent points. Both points are captured in absolute latitude and longitude coordinates. While the distance between origin and extent point of the normal vector is not normally relevant, we use the length of the vector as a guide to the size of the video frames being referenced. A longer vector indicates a larger area shown in the video. We use the length of the normal vector when attaching multiple streams into a virtual reality frame.

Audio data is captured by microphones and sequences into frames that are referenced with a time stamp. While it would be possible to also capture and store directional information, which might be meaningful in the case of a directional microphone, we are able to deduce that information from the normal vector stored for video frames recorded at the same time on the same device. Of course, if the wearable device only records video, then such directional information is not available. We are considering this extension for future work. The audio data with its correlated reference metadata is also wrapped into the same container as the video data.

Any other data, such as gathered from special purpose data sensors, is equally framed and referenced. Examples of such data might be the heart rate of the person wearing the device, the temperature of the surroundings, or movement & acceleration data measured. Our container format allows a free-form type designator that enables sensors of any kind, as long as their sensed data can be digitized and framed.

### B. *Integration Layer*

The mediators that comprise this layer feature multiple incoming streams and usually just one outgoing stream. The task of the mediator is to correlate and combine the input streams into a coherent output stream.

Figure 4. Normal Vector.

The meta information contained in the inputs' container guides the combination. The simplest correlation is for 2 video input streams that is based on the time and location of each stream. The attitude of each individual stream is carried in its normal vector. The output stream contains the adjusted meta information for the combined video.

Our container format also allows the carrying of virtual reality model data. Actually, such data is similar in nature to "real" data, but is derived not from sensors but from virtual reality models of the surroundings that the wearers of the wearable devices inhabit. To allow clear distinction of sub-streams within the container, each sub-stream carries a unique stream identifier, which is correlated to a stream dictionary that holds relevant information about the sub-stream. The complete stream dictionary is embedded into the multi-media stream at regular intervals.

### C. *Presence Layer*

The mediators in this layer are created by the Tracker peer (see Fig. 3) based on a client's request. The primary functions performed in this layer are:

1. Identify and process an input media stream.
2. Connect to location and attitude streams from a peer client.
3. Continuously adjust and re-compute an output media stream to the peer client.

Based on a peer client request, a suitable mediator is instantiated in the cloud to handle that request. It is connected to input and control streams. The mediation of input stream involves geometric conversions to adjust the spatial location and dimensions to produce a life-like presentation. The rendering of the resulting augmented reality is adjusted to conform to the attitude of output device: this enables a peer client to view the resulting stream in the same geo space as its recording device.

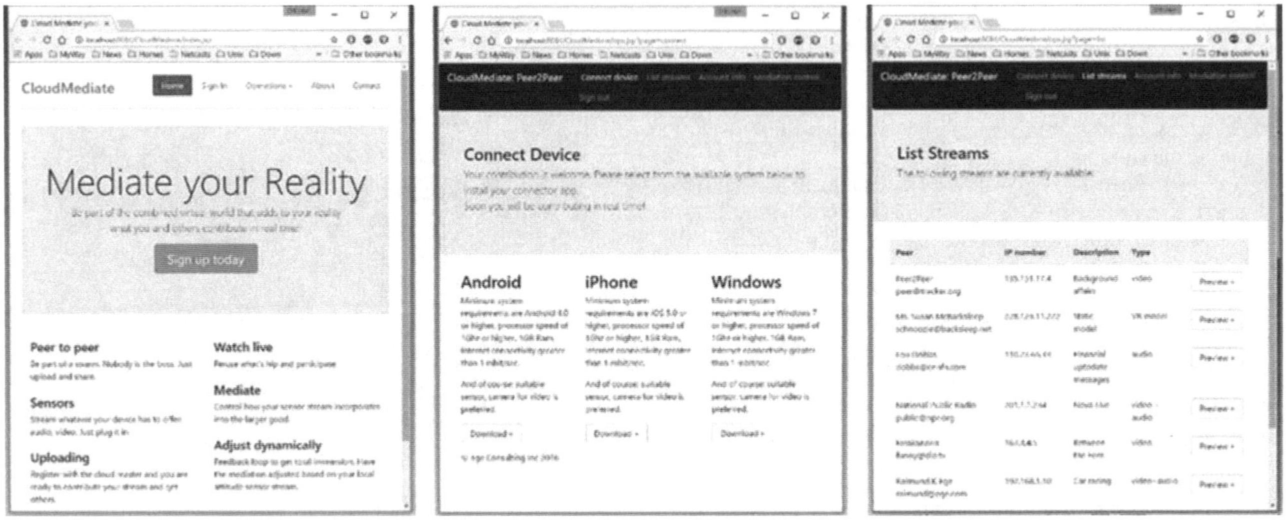


Figure 5. CloudMediate Web-Control Interface.

QoS management is essential to efficiently access pertinent information at the required level of quality. This function attempts to meet the level of quality required by user. The continuous nature of the QoS management is especially important in the event that the client device is mobile. Resources are scarce on mobile devices and the availability of a resource may vary significantly and unpredictably during the runtime of an application. In the absence of resource guarantees, applications need to adapt themselves to the prevailing operating conditions.

## IV. PROTOTYPE: CLOUDMEDIATE

The features provided by our architecture framework are illustrated by our reference prototype implementation. It is anchored by the CloudMediate web-based control interface that allows peers to register and sign up with their multi-media stream. Fig. 5 shows screenshots. The left part shows the central welcome and sign-up screen.

Users can sign up and sign in, which then makes the peer-to-peer features available. The following operations become available: "Connect Device", "List Streams", "Account Info" and "Mediation Control". Only control functions are available via the web interface. Actual stream production, connection and consumption and is handled via custom apps that can be downloaded. "Connect Device" (center screen shot) allows users to download a suitable app for their device. While the screenshot shows Android, iPhone and Windows, we currently have only an Android prototype under development. The "List Streams" operation displays all streams that are currently controlled by the CloudMediate system, that is all the input streams offered up by all peer clients, plus the output streams of all active mediators from all three layers of our framework. The "Account Info" operation allows the peer to see its own capabilities. The "Mediation Control" operation allows a peer to adjust parameters and settings of its own streams.

The final component of our prototype framework is our proof-of-concept client peer implementation for the Android platform. Fig. 6 shows the login screen of our Android prototype client peer application. The "login" screen allows the peer to authenticate with its OpenID credentials. The user enters userid and password, plus the URL of a boot strap tracker peer. If the peer is recognized into the content delivery network, the tracker peer transmits all available streams to the new peer.

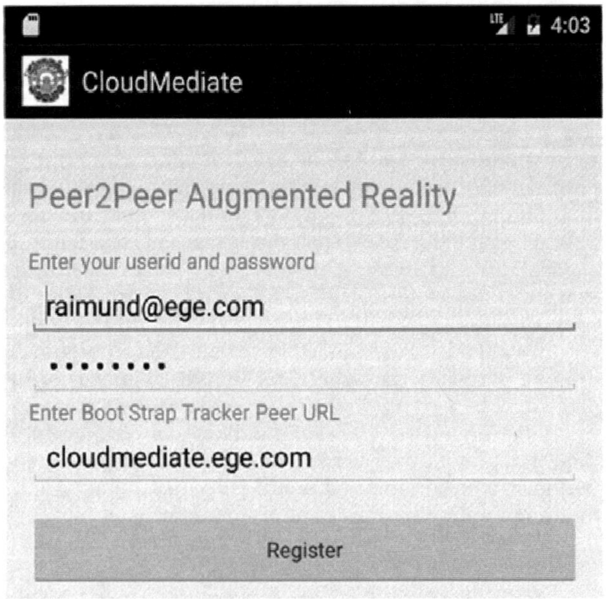


Figure 6. Android App Login Screen.

While the main app activity allows a peer to consume an available stream (see Fig. 8), our prototype also allows a peer to serve up its streams. Fig. 7 shows how a peer connects its input sensors in the mediator network. Any streams that are gathered by the peer device can be made available. In the example shown, video, audio and location streams are available and can be selected.

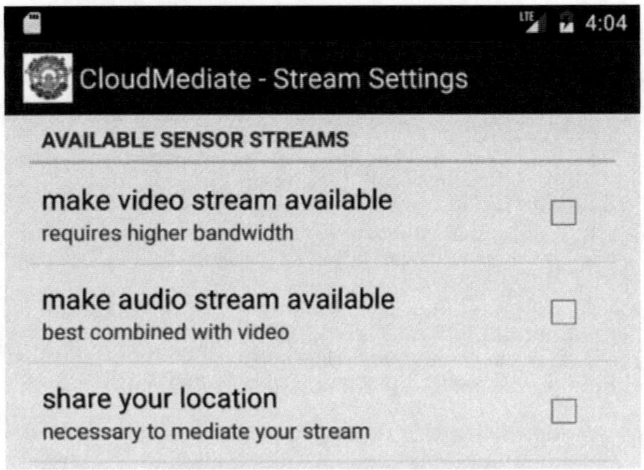


Figure 7. Android App Stream Setting.

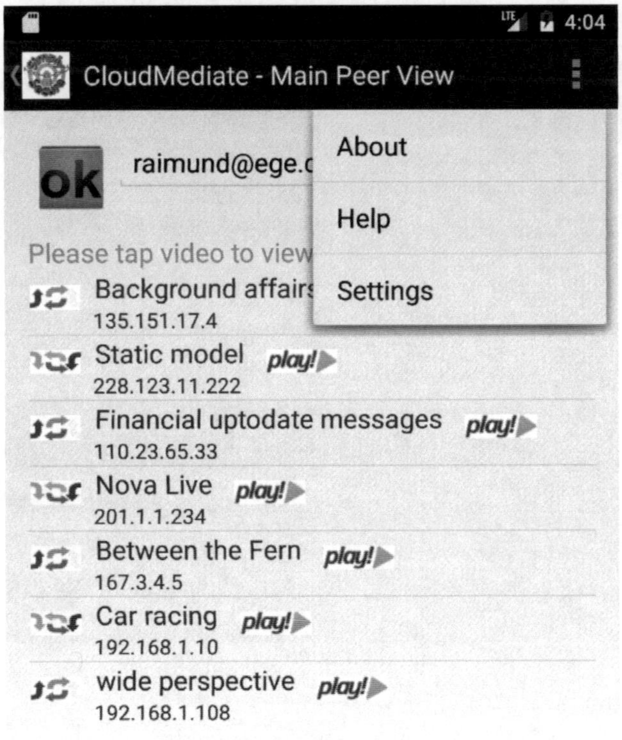


Figure 9. Android App Stream Selection.

The "stream selection" (Fig. 8) screen shows the currently available streams in the prototype application. As before, not all streams are available to the new peer: only those that display the "play" button can be used by this peer based on its trust level. Once the "play selected video stream" button is pressed, and a sufficient read-ahead buffer has been accumulated, the video stream starts playing on the Android device.

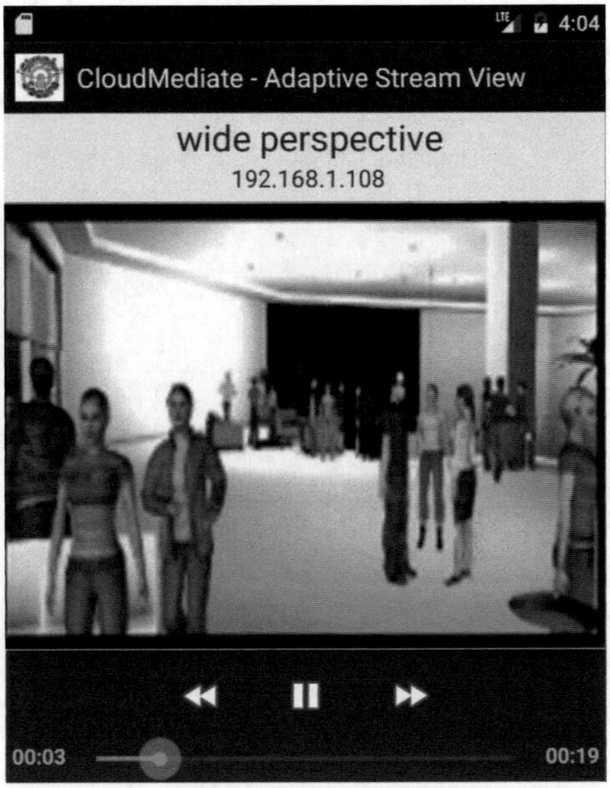


Figure 8. Android App Stream View.

The screen capture in Fig. 9 shows the video stream being displayed. The video shown here is derived from a scene generated by a virtual reality rendering producer peer. The on-screen control allows the user to control the video display.

## V. Conclusion and Future Work

The interchange of data between client and heterogeneous sources requires an efficient and dynamic approach to mediation. The framework described in this paper features three layers of mediators: presence, integration, and homogenization. We gather multi-media sources from sensors and tag them suitable for adequate correlation and mediation. Peers join a content delivery network and establish trust relationships among each other. Cloud-based media streams – mediated based on their associated metadata - are embedded into a reference virtual reality model and rendered into a geo-referenced attitudinal output media stream suitable for a heads-up display.

The advantage of our mediation process is its adaptive and dynamic nature. The framework is designed to uniquely determine how to fulfill each query while taking properties of delivery into consideration. Our mediation architecture is a work-in-progress and there are many research issues that will be encountered during the course of this project, they include but are not limited to, defining of communication protocols with specific focus on how to deal with real-time data and mobility (e.g., temporary loss of connectivity in mobile devices), security issues involved with the distribution and access of data across a p2p network, and how to intelligently decompose and integrate XML schemas and streams while avoiding loss of information.

Our goal for future research is to enhance the media mediation capabilities of our cloud-based peer components. We envision a rich augmented reality world that is populated by many dynamic input streams.

## REFERENCES


[1] E. Gamma, R. Helm, R. Johnson, and J. Vlissides, Design Patterns: Elements of Reusable Object-Oriented Software, Addison-Wesley Professional, 1994.

[2] R. Ege, L. Yang, Q. Kharma, and X Ni, "Three-Layered Mediator Architecture Based on DHT" Proceedings of the International Symposium on Parallel Architecture, Algorithm and Networks (I-SPAN), Hong Kong, China, pp. 313-318, 2004.

[3] S. Giesecke, J. Bornhold, and W. Hasselbring, "Middleware-Induced Architectural Style Modelling for Architecture Exploration", Proceedings of 2007 Working IEEE/IFIP Conference on Software Architecture (WICSA'07), pp. 44-47, 2007.

[4] S. Aukstakalnis, Practical Augmented Reality, Addison-Wesley Professional, 2017.

[5] R. Ege, "Secure Trust Management for the Android Platform," International Conference on Systems (ICONS 2013), Seville, Spain, pp. 98-103, 2013

[6] R. Ege, "Peer to Peer Media Management for Augmented Reality," International Conference on Networking and Services (ICNS 2015), Rome, Italy, pp. 95-100, 2015.

[7] R. Azuma et al., "Recent Advances in Augmented Reality," IEEE Computer Graphics and Applications (CGA) 21(6), pp. 34-47, 2001.

[8] D. Wagner, G. Reitmayr, A. Mulloni, T. Drummond, and D. Schmalstieg, "Real-Time Detection and Tracking for Augmented Reality on Mobile Phones," IEEE Transactions on Visualization and Computer Graphics, 16(3), pp. 355-368, 2010.

[9] A. Morrison et al., "Collaborative use of mobile augmented reality with paper maps," Journal on Computers & Graphics (Elsevier), 35(4), pp. 789-799, 2011.

[10] The WebM Project - About WebM. http://www.webmproject.org. [retrieved December 19, 2016]

# Using $k$-Core Decomposition to Find Cluster Centers for $k$-Means Algorithm in GraphX on Spark

Sheng-Tzong Cheng, Yin-Chun Chen, and Meng-Shuan Tsai
Computer Science and Information Engineering
National Cheng Kung University
Tainan, Taiwan
email: stcheng@mail.ncku.edu.tw, darkerduck@gmail.com, and stoya35893@hotmail.com

***Abstract*—Big data analysis is getting more and more attention these days. In social network applications, a large amount of data is in a graph structure form. As a result, more computation time is required for graph data analysis. In 2014, a framework of in-memory computing, Spark, was proposed for big data analysis. Through reusing the data in memory to solve the long computation time issue, Spark finishes a task in a shorter time compared to Hadoop. In addition, GraphX, a Spark API (Application Interface), provides a graphical interface and makes graph data analysis simple and efficient. This study presents an improved *k*-mean clustering method by integrating *k*-core decomposition, which is an important algorithm in community detection to find the center of each cluster. We implement the clustering algorithm with GraphX to get better performance and results compared to the original *k*-mean clustering method.**

***Keywords*—cloud computing; GraphX; Spark; k-core decomposition; graph-based k-means**

## I. INTRODUCTION

With the massive growth of computational data, cloud computing has become one of most popular disciplines in recent years. A typical example of cloud computing system like Hadoop [15], is based on MapReduce model [16] and Google file systems [16] to collect and analyze huge data.

For big data, analysis is the most important work. Techniques, such as machine learning, are used to train data and retrieve the most important parts form the data. Data reuse is also common in many iterative machine learning and graph algorithms, including PageRank [15], $k$-Core decomposition [3], and $k$-Means clustering [17]. However, for the framework of MapReduce, iterations of data computation become the critical bottleneck of the performance. Therefore, AMP (Algorithms Machines People) Lab at the University of California, Berkeley, proposes a new architecture, Spark [1], that not only improves the data processing over a parallel in-memory system, but also reuses inter-mediate results across multiple computations. Empirically, a program on Spark could run up to 100 times faster than that on Hadoop MapReduce.

Graph is a useful form to represent a massive amount of data in analysis, such as social network, biological information, business model, road and map, and collaboration network. However, traditional MapReduce framework makes it difficult to describe the graph-parallel computation in distributed system. Fortunately, Spark provides useful APIs (Application Interfaces) for GraphX [2] and MLib (Machine Learning Library). When users run applications on Spark, the APIs make the code development easy to use and build some algorithm efficiently. MLib provides machine learning algorithms. GraphX is a new large-scale distributed graph-parallel framework, such as Pregel [2], Graphlab [2], and PowerGraph [2], to provide useful graph algorithms. It also allows users to develop applications faster. In this paper, we consider the graph data analysis by using GraphX on Spark.

Graph clustering is one of the crucial problems in graph data analysis. It is used to group the vertices of a graph into clusters with as few edges as possible between them. It is related to unsupervised learning to divide a data set into some small classes without *a priori* information on how the classification should be done. $K$-Means clustering [17], which is an algorithm for graph clustering, uses vectors of characteristics to transform data into some clusters to find the nearest center. It usually gives $k$ virtually random points as the initial centers of clusters. For each point, it finds the minimum Euler distance to a center. Then, each point is assigned to the cluster containing the nearest center. Before the next iteration, each cluster can re-compute a new center. The iteration repeats until there is no change for centers. In this work, we consider the $k$-Means algorithm for the graph clustering in GraphX.

The $k$-Core decomposition has been proposed to find the strongest communicators in a graph. Recently, $k$-Core decomposition for analysis of large networks has been reported [3]. We observe that the performance and results can be improved further if we combine the $k$-Core decomposition with the graph-based $k$-Means, in which the $k$-Core is used to find centers and the $k$-Means is used to find clusters. The contribution of this paper is to engineer the integration of $k$-Means clustering with $k$-Core decomposition for graph data analysis in GraphX on Spark. The rest of the paper is organized as follows. Background is given in Section II. The problem description and the system design are stated in Section III. Implementation details and experiment results are illustrated in Section IV, and conclusion remarks are drawn in Section V.

## II. BACKGROUND

### A. Spark

Spark is an open-source cluster computing system. It is the highest-level project in Apache Software Foundation. In November 2014, the world record of data sorting in the Sort Benchmark Competition was broken by Spark, while the previous record was made by Hadoop. As Hadoop took seventy-two minutes to finish the job, Spark only took less than thirty minutes to complete the sorting. Furthermore, it only used 207 sets of amazon E2 i2.8*large virtual machines, significantly less than 2100 sets used by Hadoop.

In the original data flow of Hadoop MapReduce, the reduce function has to be performed after each map function. Spark critically improves the performance by changing the original inflexible data flow (of Hadoop MapReduce) to a new flexible framework in which several map functions could be done in memory before the reduce function is invoked. In this way, it can avoid many times of operations in the reduce stage and data is not required to write back to disk.

## B. GraphX

Spark API provides a Pregel-like framework [4] to deal specifically with graphs. To compute graphs with strong correlation between the nodes, it needs to adjust Graph construction for running on a classic data-processing platform. GraphX combines two graph processings, Pregel and Graphlab [4], to make a new graph-parallel framework. GraphX is developed directly on Spark to obtain better performance than Graphlab.

*1) VertexRDDs, EdgeRDDs, and Route Table:* These three data structures are the most important components to compose a graph in GraphX. When a dataset of graph is stored into GraphX, the graph will be initialized to an edge table, which describes the information about a node linking to another node with a value. After that, it generates a vertex table by using the class named Graph.

A vertex table is always the place for storing and computing the result, such as collecting all data, generating sub-graphs, joining vertices to give new data, and filtering some vertices, etc. Two kinds of operators for user programing are possible. One operator is to view a loose graph as a table and allow users to modify data without strong relation. The other operator is to view a graph as a tight graph in which vertex relations are required to re-compute when a update is propagated. New subgraphs may be generated then.

*2) Graph Parallelism*: Google developed a super-step algorithm framework [4] for graph-parallelism in 2010. It is widely used to build graphs in distributed computing systems, because of convenience and efficiency just like using MapReduce. Users only need to complete three functions for super-steps.

This model follows the bulk synchronization to finish the computation. There are four steps for one process and the final step can only stop when every node is inactive. It is also the condition to start running the application for the next round.

Four steps are described as follows.

*a)* A node receives some messages and transforms the status from inactive to active.

*b)* Active nodes aggregate all messages to get a result for itself.

*c)* If the result does not need to update to nodes, then change the status from active to inactive; otherwise, send message to other nodes.

*d)* Repeat steps *a* to *c* until there is no message sending to nodes.

In GraphX, the algorithm starts to send an initial message to all of vertices. If vertices need to update their data, the vertices will turn the status to active just like step (1). Second, they filter all active vertices and compare with neighbors to decide whether messages shall be sent or not. They use triplet to compare the data in two vertices. In step (2), all messages in a vertex will be stored as a list that performs sequential processing to get a result. This result will be compared to the original data to control the status and data. In the end, GraphX will generate a new graph with some new RDDs (Resilient Distributed Datasets)for this result.

## C. k-Means Clustering

This is a well-known data-clustering algorithm. Upon given every node vector of characteristics and the value of $k$, the algorithm can separate the set of data into $k$ clusters [5]. In the basic mode, operations define the original data with characteristics, grouping those values, and vectorization. The dataset will be divided into $k$ clusters, given $k$ random centers with the same dimension. Secondly, each node finds a nearest center by Euler distance so that primitive clusters are formed. Thirdly, new centers are identified by averaging the sum of nodes in each cluster. Repeat these three steps. In traditional algorithm follows the math model: $S$ is the center set, and $D(x, y)$ is the distance between $x$ and $y$ for $y \in S$

$$\mathrm{m(S)} = \arg\min_{S} \sum_{i=1}^{k} \sum_{y \in S_k, x \neq y} D(x, y),\ k = 1, \dots, N \quad (1)$$

## D. k-Core Decomposition

In graph theory, $k$-Core decomposition [6] is usually used. It is a $O(m)$ algorithm where $m$ represents the number of edges in non-parallel computing. Its main goal is to find a strong subgroup, whose members play the role of communicators in the graph. Every node in the sub-graph needs to be at least degree of $k$. In this paper, we extend the $k$-Core decomposition to the graph computation in parallel.

## E. Modularity

In recent years, the concept of "quality for graph clustering," proposed by Newman, has been widely used as a measure of performance [7]. Researchers usually use it to optimize the community that splits the network. If each community has dense relationship within the group and sparse relationship outside of the group, the value of modularity will be higher.

The modularity defined by $\mathrm{Q} = \dfrac{\text{(edges within communities − expectation of these edges)}}{\text{sum of all degrees}}$.

$Q$ lies in the range $[-1/2, 1)$. Without loss of generality, we assume that a graph has $n$ nodes and $m$ edges. Let the adjacency matrix for the graph be represented by $A$, where the element $A_{vw}$ of matrix equals to zero meaning there is no edge between vertices $v$ and $w$; otherwise, the element equals to one that means there is an edge between two vertices. The degree of vertex $v$ is represented by $d(v)$.

Consider a graph is split into $k$ communities $\{C_i\}_{i=1}^{k}$, and $Q$ can be written as

$$\mathrm{Q} = \frac{1}{2\mathrm{m}} \sum_{\mathrm{i}=1}^{\mathrm{k}} \sum_{vw \in C_i} A_{vw} - p(v, w) \quad (2)$$

where, $p(v, w) = \frac{d(v)d(w)}{2\mathrm{m}}$.

We can rewrite (2) to

$$Q = \sum_{i=1}^{k}\left( \sum_{vw\in C_i} \frac{A_{vw}}{2m} - \frac{1}{2m}\sum_{vw\in C_i} \frac{d(v)d(w)}{2m} \right)$$
$$= \sum_{i=1}^{k}\left( \sum_{vw\in C_i} \frac{A_{vw}}{2m} - \left(\sum_{v\in C_i} \frac{d(v)}{2m}\right)^2 \right) \quad (3)$$

Modularity indicates how good the result is. The value of modularity often drops in the range from 0.3 to 0.7, which means the result is moderate. For the experiment in section IV.B.3 about the social circle in Facebook, we can see that a graph can get a high value of modularity when the number of clusters equals 9. In this paper, we use modularity as the performance index to conduct experiments.

## III. System Design

In this section, we give the problem description and focus on the details of our system design. First, we clarify our problem. Then, we discuss the steps of system flow chart. Finally, the algorithm is given in details.

### A. *Problem Description*

When people use graph to represent the real-world data, graph representation and graph clustering become crucial issues. Graph clustering focuses on finding the sub-graph with high relatives. It relies on the edges to reflect the relation and connection of vertices. Normally, the matrix is considered as the data structure for graph clustering. However, as a graph becomes larger, the matrix computation makes the performance worse.

Similarly, an adjacency matrix is not suitable for the classic *k*-Means algorithm. In fact, the number of edges in real-world graph is far less than the square of the number of vertices. Using the row of a huge sparse matrix to be feature vector makes *k*-Means algorithm heavy. It will compute many huge vectors, but they have many useless values leading to resource waste. Therefore, in this paper, we only use the idea of "finding the minimum distance sum to *k* center of clusters" and rebuild the *k*-Means algorithm with the *single source shortest path* algorithm and *k*-Core decomposition.

### B. *Scheme Overview*

Fig. 1 shows the system flow chart to express our graph-based *k*-means algorithm. We run the code in Spark, which provides strong and flexible framework to deal with distributed parallel computing. It hides complex details of application development so that programmers can write functions with operations such as Map and Reduce. The GraphX adopts the graph-parallel processing model into Spark and transforms the big graph into some RDD table. The Pregel-like super-step module is a simplified coding for the iterative graph algorithms. Now, we explain the system systematically and introduce properties with Spark and GraphX in steps.

*1)* Spark connects to HDFS (Hadoop Distributed File System). If programmers want to run the project in parallel-computing mode, they should put the data into HDFS, which is a Hadoop database. Spark uses HDFS for not-local data to get better performance.

*2)* GraphX needs to generate edge RDD first for graph generation.

*3)* We separate graph generation from initializing the values. The values are initialized in the beginning of loops every time.

*4)* K-means algorithm is to select the nearest center for clustering the data set. In this paper, we choose the single source shortest path module for finding nearest center for each vertex. Given *k* centers, run single source shortest path for each vertex to find which center is the nearest center for this vertex.

*5)* *K* clusters are obtained from the result of step 4. Then, run the *k*-Core decomposition for each cluster. In the end, this step will find *k* new centers. The reason why we use *k*-Core decomposition to find the center of clusters is originating from the property: a core with the value of *k* is a group in which every member is connecting to at least *k* members. The vertex in-group with the biggest original degree value will be picked as the center.

*6)* Repeat steps *3* to *5* until the group of centers remains unchanged.

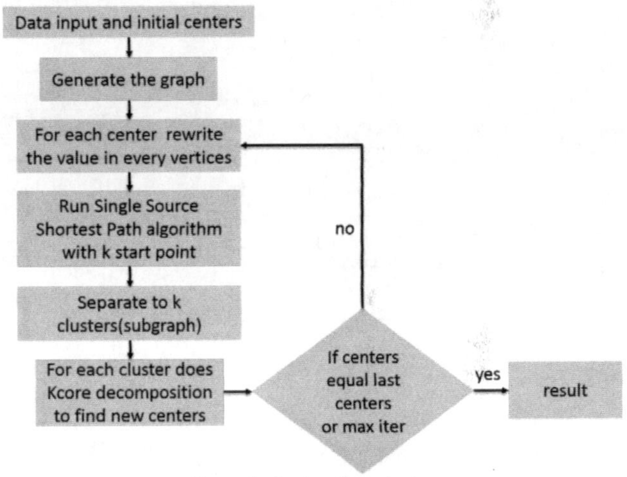


Figure 1. System flow chart.

### C. *k-Core Decomposition*

In this section, we describe the details of implementing k-Core decomposition on GraphX. The k-Core decomposition has the following property:

$$\forall u \in V : k - core(u) = k \leftrightarrow \begin{cases} \text{There exist a maximum subgraph } V_k \\ \text{such that } \forall v \in V_k : deg(v) \geq k, \text{ and} \\ \text{There is no subgraph } V_{k+1} \\ \text{such that } \forall v \in V_{k+1} : deg(v) \geq k+1 \end{cases} \quad (4)$$

This algorithm is mainly to find a sub-graph with the strongest relationship of *k*. It means every member in this sub-graph has at least *k* neighborhoods. Furthermore, there is no greater sub-graph where every member has more than *k* neighborhoods. Therefore, if we find a vertex that has the highest degree in this sub-graph, it will be a good candidate for the center in a cluster.

We tried to implement two versions with two different methods. The time complexity of both methods is $O(|V|^2)$. We can use a pair likes (a, b) to be data in a vertex table and the data will be changed to an integer value, K, representing the number of cores as the output.
Fig. 2 presents the pseudo code of *k*-core decomposition.

```
Procedure k-core decomposition
  Input
   Graph: data in vertex is (degree, bool)
  Output
   Graph: data in vertex is K
  Pseudo Code
   While
      Initial the Pregel send initial MSGs to all node
      Graph.Vertex update (intitial MSGs)
      MSGs = message merge (all message sent)
      While messages.count > 0
         Graph.Vertex update (messages)
         MSGs = message merge (all message sent)
      End while
      K += 1
   End while
   Vertex update stage(messages)
      If (message.bool ) messages.degree =
  max(origin, new degree)
      Message.bool = origin && new bool
   Message send stage
      If ( ! v1.bool || ! v2.bool)
         empty
      Else if(v1.degree == k && v2.degree > k)
         Send to v2 (1,true)
         Send to v1 (0,false)
      Else
         Iterator.empty
   Message merge stage
  (Sum, a.bool && b.bool)
```

Figure 2. Pseudo code for k-Core decomposition.

GraphX uses triplets to compare two nodes that need updates. The time complexity of the methods is $O(|V|^2)$.

## IV. Implementation and Experiment

In this section, we describe the experimental environment and illustrate the results obtained for modularity and run time. We use the same terminology for the original *k*-means algorithm to compare the performance of the original algorithm with that of our revised method.

### A. *Experiment environment and setting*

In the experiment, we consider a peer-servicing cloud-computing platform, which contains six homogeneous virtual machines. The hardware and software specifications are detailed in Tables I and II, respectively. In Table III, the setting of our configuration of Spark is given. Because some RDDs are only used once, we do not need the original setting of memory fraction (0.75), which means the memory splits most of the space for storing RDD. When the system executes several iterations, the driver's java garbage collection is always too late to recycle the resource. We observe that the driver's memory stores a lot of DAG (Directed Acyclic Graph) and RDD in memory and therefore, only little space is left for allocating work. It may block the operation of iterative loop, so that we reduce the fraction from 0.75 to 0.4 and increase the memory for drivers.

TABLE I. RECEIVER ENVIRONMENT

| Item | Content |
|---|---|
| OS | Ubuntu 15.10 Desktop 64bit |
| Spark | 2.0.0 |
| Java | 1.7.0_101 |
| Scala | 2.11.8 |
| Maven | 3.3.9 |

TABLE II. HARDWARE SPECIFICATION OF RECEIVER

| Item | Content |
|---|---|
| CPU | Intel(R) Xeon(R) E5620 @2.40GHz x 2 |
| RAM | 8 GB |
| Hard Drive | 80GB |
| Network Bandwidth | 1Gbps |

TABLE III. CONFIGURATIONS OF SPARK

| Item | Content |
|---|---|
| Number of executor | 6 |
| Memory size of the driver | 6GB |
| Memory size of each executor | 6GB |
| Memory fraction | 0.4 |
| Running mode | Standalone |

### B. *Experiment Results*

We conduct experiments on three real-world datasets from SNAP [8] and UCI Network Data Repository [9]-[13]. Each dataset is represented as a graph with vertices and edges. To revise the original *k*-means algorithm, we transfer the data to an adjacency matrix, because the algorithm requires the vertices' features for clustering. Each column can be considered as features of a vertex in the adjacency matrix. The vertices connecting to same vertex should be assigned to the same cluster. After finishing clustering, we calculate the modularity to evaluate the performance of both our revised method and the original *k*-means with adjacency matrix. Spark has a software version of the common *k*-means algorithm in Mlib, which is an API for machine learning.

The runtime of an experiment does not include the time of transferring original data to a matrix nor the time of calculating the modularity. From the experimental results, we see that even though the runtime of our proposed method is longer than the common *k*-means in Mlib, the value of modularity is much higher than the original *k*-means. All of the experiments started with centers randomly picked.

*1) The dolphin social network*

This is a famous social network dataset for graph clustering. There is a network of frequent associations between 62 dolphins in a community living off Doubtful Sound, New Zealand [9]. In Fig. 3 (a), we can see that the modularity gets higher when the number of clusters increases. For example, our method gets an averaged value of modularity up to 0.3924 upon splitting to five clusters. Comparing the results reported in [14], they get the highest scores on four clusters. Although the case of four clusters is not the best result for our method, our proposed method still gets an averaged Q to 0.387703. This is helpful for observing a big group in real world.

In Fig. 3 (b), the runtime of our proposed method gets significantly high from 5 to 6 (for the number of clusters). Taking into account the modularity, the optimum case for the number of clusters is five.

*2) The social cycle in Facebook*

In this section, the dataset is much bigger than the datasets in the formal two experiments. The dataset is provided by J. McAuley and J. Leskovec [11]. They collected data from using an APP (Application) named social circle. There are 4039 vertices and 88234 edges. One edge between two vertices means two vertices are friends. In Fig. 4 (b), we can see that the runtime does not grow up when the data size increases if the memory is still enough to handle the experiments. This result also proves that Spark is fit for large-size data rather than small-size data.

The Stanford website [8] not only provides the dataset for researchers but also provides some basic analytic results. The average clustering coefficient they provided is 0.6055. In our method, we can find when the $k = 4, 7, 8, 9, 10$, the average modularity is higher than 0.6055 and the highest modularity is appearing when $k = 9$, which is the same number of clusters for the data on website. We think this data has a clear relationship between groups, because both methods obtain good result. In our method, when $k$ is 5 or 6, the performance is worse than the case when $k$ is 4. It is because that the four-cluster structure is similar to the nine-cluster graph. We can see from Fig. 4 (a) that the modularity reaches a local peak when $k$ is 4 .

*3) Gnutella Network*

This is the experiment with Gnutella peer-to-peer file sharing network from August 2002. Nodes represent hosts in the Gnutella network topology and edges represent connections between the hosts [12][13]. There are 8717 vertices and 31525 edges in the graph. Compared to the second experiment, this graph has double the number of vertices but the number of edges is much less. On Stanford website [8], we can see that for this kind of graphs with strongly-connected components, only a small group can reach each other. It also has bad coefficient in clustering. In $k$-means with adjacency matrix, the modularity is almost approaching zero, however, as shown in Fig. 5 (a), our proposed method still gets the modularity average higher than 0.2. Although this result is slightly less, our method still performs well for $k$-means with loose grouping dataset.

For runtime shown in Fig. 5 (b), our proposed method is faster than $k$-means with adjacency matrix for the cases when $k$ is from two to six. Actually, the edges are less dense so that the $k$-mean algorithm spent time in computing many bad features. We observe that when the data size grows, $k$-means algorithm not only needs a large space and time to transfer data for adjacency matrix but also needs more time to divide the graph into small clusters.

## V. CONCLUSIONS AND FUTURE WORK

In this paper, we proposed a graph-based $k$-means algorithm on Spark. Given a dataset, a graph could be structured and fed into this algorithm for solving the clustering problem. We also implemented the $k$-core decomposition with GraphX API to find the centers of clusters.

By spending more runtime, our proposed method would be able to find clusters with higher modularity. If we take the time for data processing into account, the total elapsed time of our method will be approaching to that of $k$-means. It is because the matrix structure used by k-means needs more processing time especially for the sparse matrix of many vertices with few edges. We find that $k$-core decomposition still is a good method for finding centers of clusters.

The initial random centers have a large effect on the performance of the $k$-means algorithm and our proposed method. Runtime can be greatly reduced if the two methods start with good initial points. Furthermore, even if the two methods start with the same initial centers, they probably have big difference in the clustering and the result value of modularity. We also find that vertices with many neighbors have great dominating effects. If we can select initial centers nearby these vertices, we can gain a better result.

Future work is to improve the performance of our proposed method further. The distributed $k$-core decomposition could be improved by integrating with Pregel algorithm. The original Pregel algorithm wastes a lot of time in sending initial iterators that have impact on the performance of GraphX. We plan to use the internal code of GraphX Pregel API to reconstruct the $k$-core decomposition.

## REFERENCES

[1] M. Zaharia, et al., "Spark: cluster computing with working sets" Hot Cloud, vol. 10, 2010, pp.10-10.

[2] R. Xin, J. Gonzalez, M. Franklin, and I. Stoica "GraphX: A Resilien t Distributed Graph System on Spark", AMPLab, EECS, UC Berkele y 2013

[3] W. Khaouid, M. Barsky, V. Srinivasan, and A. Thomo, "K-Core Deco mposition of Large Networks on a Single PC," Proc. VLDB Endowm ent, vol. 9, no. 1. 2015.

[4] G. Malewicz, et al., "Pregel: a system for large-scale graph processin g," Proc. 2010 ACM Intl. Conf. on Management of data, 2010.

[5] J. Hartigan and M. Wong, "A k-means clustering algorithm," Applie d Statistics, vol. 28, 1979, pp. 100-108.

[6] A. Montresor, F. Pellegrini, and D. Miorandi, "Distributed k-core dec omposition," IEEE Trans. Parallel Distrib. Syst., vol. 24, no. 2, 2013, pp. 288–300.

[7] M. Newman, "Modularity and community structure in networks," Pr oc. Natl. Acad. Sci. USA, vol. 103, no. 23, 2006, pp. 8577-8582.

[8] Stanford Large Network Dataset Collection, http://snap.stanford.edu/data/index.html [Jul, 6, 2016].

[9] D. Lusseau, et al., "The bottlenose dolphin community of Doubtful S ound features a large proportion of long-lasting associations," Behav ioral Ecology and Sociobiology," vol. 54, 2003, pp. 396-405.

[10] W. W. Zachary, "An information flow model for conflict and fission in small groups," J. Anthropological Research, vol. 33, 1977, pp. 452 -473.

[11] J. McAuley and J. Leskovec, "Learning to Discover Social Circles in Ego Networks," NIPS, 2012.

[12] J. Leskovec, J. Kleinberg, and C. Faloutsos, "Graph Evolution: Dens ification and Shrinking Diameters," ACM Trans. Knowledge Discov ery from Data, vol. 1, no. 1, 2007.

[13] M. Ripeanu, I. Foster, and A. Iamnitchi, "Mapping the Gnutella Netw ork: Properties of Large-Scale Peer-to-Peer Systems and Implication s for System Design," IEEE Internet Computing Journal, 2002.

[14] D. Lusseau and M. E. J. Newman, "Identifying the role that individu al animals play in their social network," Proc. R.SOC.LONDON B, 271:S477, 2004.

[15] "Hadoop," http://hadoop.apache.org/.

[16] "MapReduce," http://research.google.com/archive/mapreduce.html.

[17] J. Hartigan and M. Wang, "A K-Means Clustering Algorithm," J. Royal Statistical Society, vol. 28, no.1, 1979, pp. 100-108.


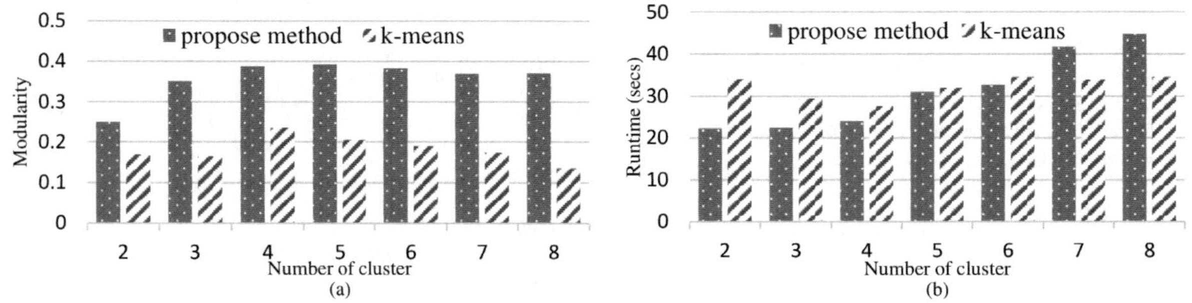


Figure 3. Modularity and runtime of dolphin social network.

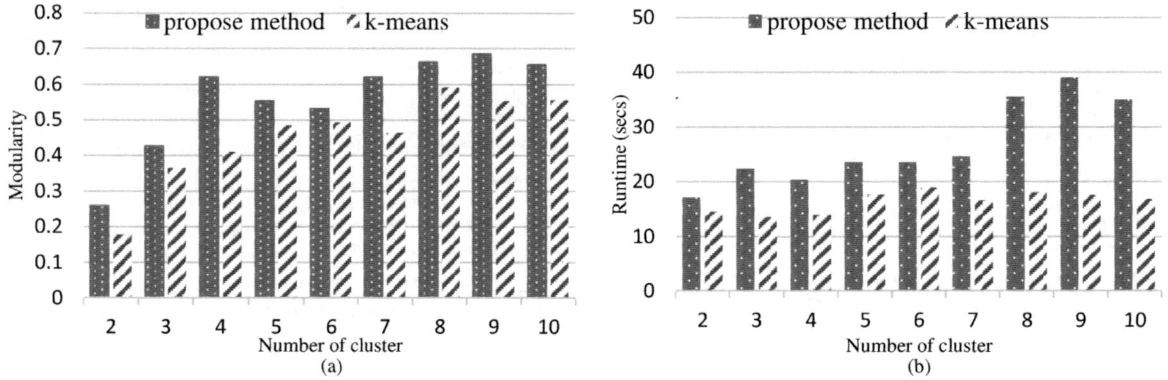


Figure 4. Modularity and runtime of Facebook social network.

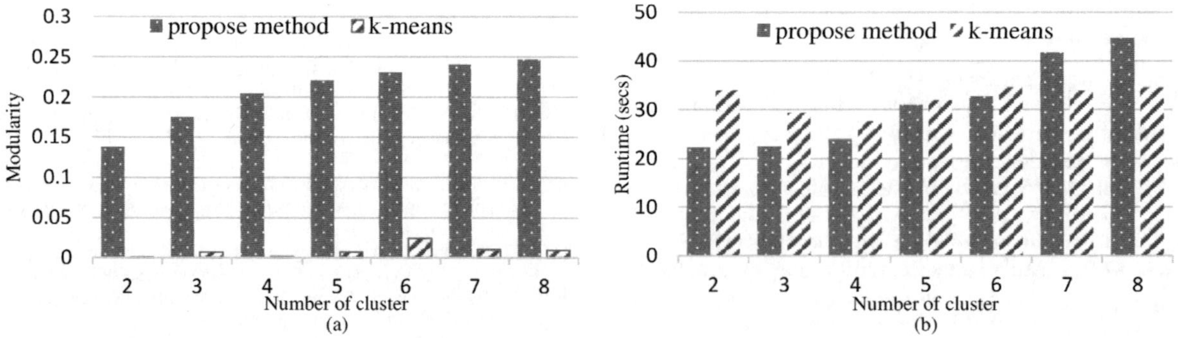


Figure 5. Modularity and runtime of Gnutella network.

# Data Placement Based on Data Semantics for NVDIMM/DRAM Hybrid Memory Architecture

Gaku Nakagawa, Shuichi Oikawa
Department of Computer Science
University of Tsukuba
Tsukuba, Ibaraki, Japan
e-mail: {gnakagaw, shui}@cs.tsukuba.jp

***Abstract*— Non-Volatile Dual Inline Memory Module (NVDIMM) makes it possible to expand the main memory with non-volatile memory. However, constructing the main memory only with NVDIMM is unrealistic because NAND Flash, the most promising candidate as NVDIMM device, has several shortcomings about write access. The hybrid memory architectures with NVDIMM and Dynamic Random Access Memory (DRAM) is a method to hide the shortcoming of NAND Flash. In the architecture, we can offload write-hot data to DRAM. In this paper, we utilize data semantics to determine data placements on NVDIMM/DRAM hybrid memory architecture. The architecture requires distributing data between NVDIMM and DRAM. Data semantics (i.e., meaning of data) is useful for the decision for the data placements. As a proof-of-concept, we executed a simulation experiment to determine data allocation between NVDIMM and DRAM based on the data semantics. As a result, we could suppress write access to the NVDIMM area under only 0.2% of the DRAM area.**

***Keywords-memory management; nvdimm; non-volatile memory.***

## I. INTRODUCTION

Non-Volatile Dual Inline Memory Module (NVDIMM) [1] makes it possible to expand the main memory with non-volatile memory. NVDIMM is an interface standard to connect between solid state drive and Dual Inline Memory Module (DIMM) slots [1]. Now, we can access SSDs (Solid State Drives) only via an input/output bus, such as Serial ATA (Serial Advanced Technology Attachment) and PCI-Express (Peripheral Component Interconnect) [2]. With the NVDIMM standard, we can access SSD via a memory bus. It reduces the latency between Central Processing Unit (CPU) and SSDs. Thus, NVDIMM makes it possible to use SSD as part of the main memory.

Constructing the main memory only with NVDIMM is unrealistic. It is required to combine NVDIMM and the existing DRAM. NAND Flash, the most promising candidate as NVDIMM device, has two shortcomings related to write access. One is that the write access latency is much larger than that of DRAM. The other is limited write endurance. Thus, if we place data with many write access (write-hot data) on NVDIMM, the system will lose its performance and durability. The hybrid memory architectures with NVDIMM and DRAM are methods to hide the shortcomings of NAND Flash [3] – [5]. In the architectures, we can offload write-hot data to DRAM.

NVDIMM/DRAM hybrid memory architecture requires distributing data between NVDIMM and DRAM. It is ideal that there are write-hot data on the DRAM area and write-cold data on the NVDIMM area. A simple way is data migration based on the number of write access. In the way, all new data is placed on NVDIMM area. If the memory manager detects write-hot data on NVDIMM area, it moves the detected data to the Non-Volatile Memory (NVM) area. However, the simple method has a problem. With this method, the memory manager cannot detect write-hot data before actual write access concentrations.

In this paper, we utilize data semantics to resolve this problem. Data has its meaning in each program context (data semantics). The semantics have their characteristics about write access (i.e., write-hot or write-cold). With the characteristics, we can determine the appropriate placement area for each data.

As a proof-of-concept, we executed a simulation experiment to determine data allocation between NVDIMM and DRAM based on the data semantics. As a result, we could suppress write access to the NVDIMM area under only 0.2% of the DRAM area.

The paper is organized as follows. Section II shows the usefulness of data semantics for data placement on NVDIMM/DRAM hybrid memory architecture. Section III shows an evaluation experiment for a proof-of-concept. Section IV shows the summary of this paper.

## II. DATA PLACEMENT BASED ON DATA SEMANTICS

NVDIMM/DRAM hybrid memory architecture requires determining data placement between NVDIMM and DRAM. Data semantics is useful information for the decision. Each program places its data in its memory area. The data have semantics in each program context, such as numeric data, string data, some data structures, and so on. Each data semantic has its write access characteristics. For example, a pointer that indicates the head of a linked list has the possibility to be updated. In contrast, the string data that contains command line arguments does not have the possibility to be updated. We can predict whether data is write-hot or write-cold based on the write access characteristic of the data. With that prediction, we can determine the appropriate placement area for each data.

Current operating systems do not know the data semantics in user processes because they do not take care of the data meaning. In this research project, we proposed a method to determine the data placement at programming language runtime level. In the method, a programming language runtime manages data placement between the allocated NVDIMM area and DRAM area based on the data semantics. The proposed method focuses on class types in the target program as the data semantics.

## III. Simuralation Experiment

For a proof-of-concept, we executed a simulation experiment for data placement based on data semantics. We modify an existing Java language runtime to distribute data between 2 separated areas: pseudo-NVDIMM area and DIMM area. In the experiment, we did not use any NVDIMM device. The NVDIMM area was standard DRAM. Thus, the results did not take into account the characteristics of NVDIMM. The simulation software is implemented based on Jikes Research Virtual Machine (Jikes RVM). The base version of Jikes was 10709.

In the simulation, the language runtime corrects the characteristics of write access to each class type. The runtime determines the write-hot classes based on the corrected information. It determines data placement based on the list of write-hot classes, i.e., it places the write-hot class instance on DRAM area. The runtime often makes a miss decision. They may place the write-hot data to NVDIMM. The runtime detects the write-hot objects, as well as the write-hot class. If it found a write-hot object on the pseudo-NVDIMM area, it moves the object to the DRAM area. Also, it detects the write-cold objects on DRAM area. When the runtime finds them, it moves the detected object to the pseudo-NVDIMM area. We executed a benchmark software on the simulation software. We adopted the Jython benchmark from the DaCapo benchmark suite [6], version 2006-10-MR2.

Fig. 1 describes the number of write accesses to each memory area in chronological order. The blue and red lines represent the number of write accesses to NVDIMM and DRAM respectively. The green dotted line describes the sum of the number of write accesses to the two areas. The data shows that the number of write accesses to the pseudo-NVDIMM was much lower than that of DRAM area. The number of write accesses to the pseudo-NVDIMM area was only 0.2.

Fig. 2 describes the data distribution between the DRAM area and the pseudo-NVDIMM area. The data shows that there was much data on the pseudo- NVDIMM area. The maximum size of the DRAM area was 8.2 MiB. The average size of the DRAM area was 6.1 MiB. The maximum size of the pseudo-NVDIMM area was 29.9 MiB. The average size of the pseudo- NVDIMM was 27.3 MiB.

The results show that we can reduce the number of write access to the pseudo-NVDIMM area with data semantics. The number of write accesses to the pseudo- NVM area was much less than that to the DRAM area while the runtime placed much data on the pseudo- NVDIMM area than on the DRAM area.

## IV. Summary

In this paper, we propose a new approach for the data placement decision on the hybrid memory architecture. The proposed approach utilizes the data semantics to resolve the problem. Data has data semantics in the program context. The semantics have their characteristics about write access. With the characteristics, we can determine the appropriate placement area for each data. The results of a proof-of-concept evaluation show that the proposed method has significant merits for the data placement problem related to the NVDIMM/DRAM hybrid memory architecture.

There are several future works. The important one is an experiment on cycle-accurate computer architecture simulators. In this paper, the accuracy of the experiment is not sufficient because we did not use any real NVDIMM devices. For a detailed discussion, we need a more accurate evaluation. An experiment on the simulator that reproduces memory access behavior (i.e., cycle-accurate simulator) would be useful for that.

## References


[1] JEDEC Solid State Technology Association, "JEDEC Announces Support for NVDIMM Hybrid Memory Modules". [Online]. Available from: https://www.jedec.org/news/pressreleases/jedec-announces-support-nvdimm-hybrid-memory-modules, 2016.11.1.

[2] David A. Patterson and John L. Hennessy, "Computer Organization and Design", Fourth Edition. Morgan Kaufmann Publishers Inc., 2008.

[3] G. Dhiman, R. Ayoub, R. Tajana, "PDRAM: A Hybrid PRAM and DRAM Main Memory System," in Proc. of the 46th Annual Design Automation Conference (DAC' 09), pp. 664–669, 2009.

[4] P. Zhou, B. Zhao, J. Yang, Y. Zhang, "A durable and energy efficient main memory using phase change memory technology," in 6th Annual International Symposium on Computer Architecture (ISCA '09 ), ACM, pp. 14–23, 2009.

[5] W. Zhang and T. Li, "Exploring Phase Change Memory and 3D Die-Stacking for Power/Thermal Friendly, Fast and Durable Memory Architectures," in Proc. of PACT' 09, IEEE, pp. 101–112, 2009.

[6] S. M. Blackburn, R. Garner, C. Hoffmann, A. Khang, K. Mckinley, R. Bentzur, et al., "The DaCapo Benchmarks: Java Benchmarking Development and Analysis," in Proc. of the 21st annual ACM SIGPLAN conference on Object-Oriented Programing, Systems, Languages, and Applications, ACM, pp. 169–190, 2006.

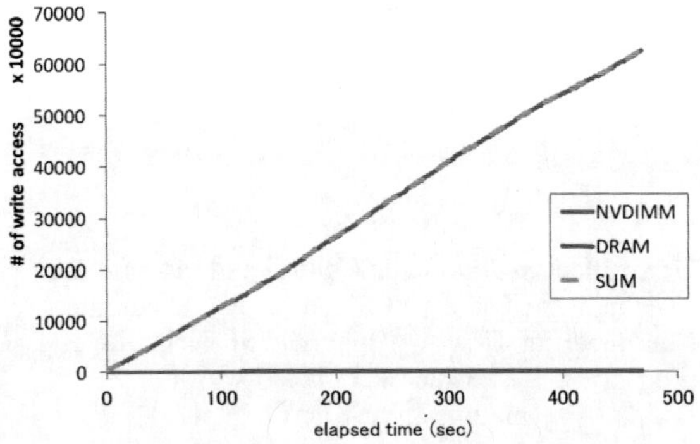


Figure 1. Change of write access

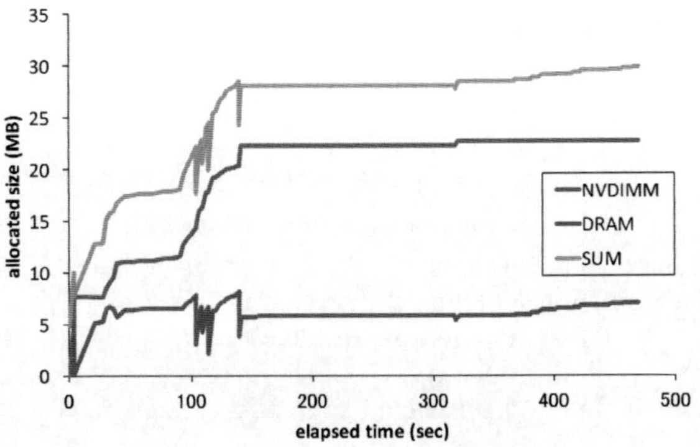


Figure 2. Change of memory allocation size

# A Load Balancing Mechanism Based on Fuzzy Nonparametric Analysis of QoS Parameters

Dmytro Halushko, Oleksandr Rolik
Department of Automation and Control in Technical Systems, National Technical University of Ukraine "Kyiv Polytechnic Institute"
Kyiv, Ukraine
e-mail: dmytro.halushko@lll.kpi.ua, o.rolik@kpi.ua

Volodymyr Samotyy
Department of Automatic Control and Information Technology, Faculty of Electrical and Computer Engineering, Cracow University of Technology
Cracow, Poland
e-mail:vsamotyy@pk.edu.pl

***Abstract* – Load balancing enables the increase the productivity and quality of services being provided by data centers. It is suggested to use virtual machines for a more flexible allocation of data center resources. The proposed two-step method provides a statistical evaluation of service quality without any assumptions about the probability characteristics of the processes occurring in the data center. The result of this evaluation is used in load balancing between several virtual machines. The proposed method is implemented in the management system for the SLA-defined service quality management. The results of this implementation are presented in the paper.**

***Keywords* – *QoS; fuzzy logic; nonparametric statistics; zonoids; load balancing.***

## I. INTRODUCTION

Data centers provide a scope of services to their customers. Quality of Service (QoS) is specified in the Service Level Agreement (SLA) and directly dependents on the volume of Internet Technology (IT) resources they have allocated, the number of users using this service, etc.

In order to avoid losses due to non-compliance of SLA, the data center manager monitors the quality of provided services. When quality degrades considerably, then the volume of resources that support these services needs to be increased. However, an excessive increase in the volume of resources leads to financial losses for the data centers. Therefore, it is necessary to implement a continuous monitoring of the allocated resource volume in such a way that the quality of this service will correspond to the stipulations in the SLA with a minimum number of allocated resources. Service Level Management and allocation of resources are managed by control systems of the data center. For the distribution of tasks or user requests to the data centers, load balancers interacting with management systems are used.

The remainder of the paper is organized as follows: in Section II, the related work is discussed. The method which enables to determine the quality of service provided is described in Section III. In Section IV, the application of estimated QoS value in load balancing is described. Theoretical calculations have been confirmed by the experiments, results of which are shown in Section V. The paper is concluded with Section VI, where the results and future research directions are addressed.

## II. RELATED WORK

In [1], the authors propose a load balancing algorithm to optimally distribute the incoming tasks in the cloud data centers. In [2], the authors propose a virtualization framework that makes background load balancing more flexible and less resource intensive. The authors of article [3] formulate a load balancing problem as a robust optimization problem, that minimizes the worst-case cost of a given data center's services. Another approach to solving this problem is described in [4]. The authors propose to differentiate the SLA agreements with different kinds of hosting, using several criteria.

In [5], the authors propose a method for aggregating quality metrics of an IT infrastructure component to estimate its functioning. The method is based on the graph-representation of the IT infrastructure and a non-parametric statistic. It enables to aggregate the parameters which have different types and which impact the quality of component functioning in generalized parameters. This method solves the problem of generalization of element parameters by representing them in a single parametric space with the possibility of projection to the quality axis. This generalization takes into account the probabilistic side of consideration of elements not being attached to any distribution by using non-parametric models.

One should also take into account the geolocation of the data center servers. The authors in [6] propose to manage the data center's servers by activating or deactivating certain servers in data center. This approach takes into account the fact that not all servers of data centers are located at the same place.

## III. FUZZY NONPARAMETRIC ANALYSIS OF QOS

A data center is composed of many computation and storage nodes. Each node has a series of IT resources, such as central processing unit (CPU), random access memory (RAM), physical memory, network bandwidth, etc.

The proposed two-step method provides a statistical evaluation of QoS without any assumptions about the probability characteristics of the processes occurring in the data center.

## A. *Defining of the IT resources that affect the functioning of data center's services*

Assume that the provider offers users a set $S = \{s_i\}$, $i = \overline{1,K}$ of services. For each service, one or several identical virtual machines (VM) $V_{j,i}$, $j = \overline{1,M_i}$, $i = \overline{1,K}$, where $M_i$ is the maximum number of VM, can be allocated for the maintenance of the $i$-th service. Each VM supports only one service.

Resources from a $R_m$, $m = \overline{1,L}$ are allocated to each virtual machine, where $L$ represents the number of different types of resources at the data center. The volume $r_{m,i}$, $m = \overline{1,L}$, $i = \overline{1,K}$ of resources of the $m$-th type is allocated to each VM supporting the $i$-th service. The volume of allocated resources to each VM supporting the $i$-th service is defined by requirements of the $i$-th, $i = \overline{1,K}$ service. In the course of operation, each VM $V_{j,i}$, $j = \overline{1,M_i}$, $i = \overline{1,K}$ actually involves the volume $r^*_{m,i}$, $m = \overline{1,L}$, $i = \overline{1,K}$ of the $m$-th resource type. The size $r^*_{m,i}$ dynamically changes and depends on the number of users of the $i$-th service and the type of user requests.

For each $i$-th service from a set of services $S$ within process of Service Level Management (SLM) quality indicators are defined. The measure values $q_{b,i}$, $b = \overline{1,D_i}$, $i = \overline{1,K}$ of quality approved by the customer are agreed upon in SLA, where $q_{b,i}$ is a value of the $b$-th indicator of quality of the $i$-th service, and $D_i$ is the number of indicators of quality of the $i$-th service. The services should be monitored to ensure the specifications in the SLA level of QoS. For this purpose, the control system defines the actual values $q^*_{b,i}$, $b = \overline{1,D_i}$, $i = \overline{1,K}$ of quality indicators, and compares them to the approved values. SLM is aimed at the constant maintenance of service quality at the approved level.

$$q_{b,i} - q^*_{b,i} \to 0, \forall b,i . \qquad (1)$$

As each service is provided by several VMs $V_{j,i}$, $j = \overline{1,M_i}$, $i = \overline{1,K}$, it is rather labor-consuming to trace the current measure values $q^*_{j,b,i}$, $j = \overline{1,M_i}$, $b = \overline{1,D_i}$, $i = \overline{1,K}$ of quality of each VM which provides the $i$-th service with subsequent assessment of the final quality level of apply the service provided by the data center. Therefore, authors proposed to use the indirect method of a quality evaluation of services by applying the methods of non-parametric analysis and fuzzy logic. Use of fuzzy logic in case of a quality evaluation of services is caused by the fact that the assessment by the user of the services is received by the service provider with use of the linguistic variable accepting values from "it is very bad" to "perfect".

The essence of a method is that, on the basis of the saved-up statistics for VM providing the $i$-th service, the dependence of values $q^*_{b,i}, \forall b,i$ of quality indicators on values $r^*_{m,i}, \forall m,i$ of the involved volumes of the data center resources is established. The management of services quality comes down to the fact that the management system permanently makes determination of the involved volumes $r^*_{m,i}$ of resources of each VM $V_{j,i}$, $j = \overline{1,M_i}$, $i = \overline{1,K}$. Then the management system estimates the current level $q^*_{j,b,i}$ of the $b$-th, $b = \overline{1,D_i}$ quality indicator of service, provided by VM $V_{j,i}$, $j = \overline{1,M_i}$, $i = \overline{1,K}$ and causes the decision on management of the level of services. At the same time, two controlling mechanisms on the maintenance of the level of services within SLA level are applied. One mechanism is based on the scope of changes of the resources allocated for service maintenance. In this work, an increase or reduction of the number of VM providing services is performed. Other mechanisms use load balancing for VM. At the same time, for each $i$-th service, $i = \overline{1,K}$ a new load balancer is initiated, which is a component of the management system.

In the absence of assumptions about the nature of the dependencies between the value $q^*_{j,b,i}$, $j = \overline{1,M_i}$, $b = \overline{1,D_i}$, $i = \overline{1,K}$ of the service quality and the values $r^*_{m,i}$, $m = \overline{1,L_i}$, $i = \overline{1,K}$ of used resource types, as well as the possibility of the existence of any kind of relationship between the quality of service provided by separate VMs and the total quality of service provided by data center, it is expedient to apply expert estimation, the fuzzy logic apparatus and the apparatus of nonparametric analysis.

As in this paper homogeneous servers are being considered, and VMs $V_{j,i}$, $j = \overline{1,M_i}$, which provide the $i$-th service, have identical characteristics, then the dependence established between an indicator of quality $q^*_{j,b,i}$, and volume of the involved resources $r^*_{m,i}$ the index $j$ can be excluded.

Geometric estimation of nonparametric statistics is used in analysis of dependences between values of volumes $r^*_{m,i}, \forall m,i$ of resources which consume VMs providing the $i$-th service and values of indicators of quality $q^*_{b,i}$, $b = \overline{1,D_i}$, $i = \overline{1,K}$ of the $i$-th service which it provides. The projection of the zone responding to a certain value of the linguistic QoS variable establishes connection of measured values of quality with the VM resources.

## B. *Converting the quality indicators to fuzzy variables*

By means of a fuzzy logical conclusion [7] the dependence between values $q^*_{b,i}$, $b = \overline{1,D_i}$, $i = \overline{1,K}$ and integral quality estimation $Q_i$, $i = \overline{1,K}$, of the $i$-th service which is also fixed within SLA is established. The integral quality estimation $Q_i$, of the $i$-th service is usually described by a linguistic variable and linguistic value, which correspond to the quality estimation of the user.

Integral quality estimation $Q_i$ of the $i$-th service and indicators of quality $q^*_{b,i}, \forall b$ of the $i$-th service are described by linguistic values from sets of $\{l^Q_{i,\omega}\}$, $i=\overline{1,K}$, $\omega=\overline{1,\Omega_i}$ and $\{l^q_{b,i,\gamma}\}$, $\gamma=\overline{1,\Gamma_{b,i}}$, where $\Omega_i$ is the amount of the linguistic values corresponding to integral quality estimation of the $i$-th service, $\Gamma_{b,i}$ is the amount of the linguistic values describing the quality indicators $q_{b,i}$, $b=\overline{1,D_i}$ of the $i$-th service $i=\overline{1,K}$. To each $l^Q_{i,\omega}$, $\omega=\overline{1,\Omega_i}$ and $l^q_{b,i,\gamma}$, $\gamma=\overline{1,\Gamma_{b,i}}$ are mapped to fuzzy sets $\Psi^Q_{i,\omega}$ and $\Psi^q_{b,i,\gamma}$ respectively.

At the fuzzification stage, a degree of belonging $L^q_{b,i,\gamma}$ of the values $q_{b,i}, \forall b,i$ to fuzzy sets $\Psi^q_{b,i,\gamma}$ $\gamma=\overline{1,\Gamma_{b,i}}$ is defined.

For each service $s_i$, $i=\overline{1,K}$, the $L_i$-dimentional space is defined where to each axis the type $R_m$, $m=\overline{1,L}$ of the data center's resource is mapped. At points of such space, the value of coordinates corresponds to a certain value of the volume of the involved resources $r^*_{m,i}$ of VM.

For all fuzzy values $l^q_{b,i,\gamma}, \gamma\in[1,\Gamma_{b,i}]$ the $P_{b,i}$ reference points having property (4) are chosen.

$$L^q_{b,i,\gamma'} \square\ L^q_{b,i,\gamma''}, \qquad (4)$$

where $\gamma',\gamma''\in[1,\Gamma_{b,i}]$ and $\gamma'\neq\gamma''$. Such points set reference area in space for the fuzzy set $\Psi^q_{b,i,\gamma}$.

For such point set the central ordered regions of the given depth $\alpha$ is constructed. Due to a number of useful properties described in the definitions [8] of central ordered regions, the most suitable notation is zonoid [9] – a convex polyhedron with such useful properties as:

- the affinity equivariance that "binds" the location estimate to elements;
- the completeness of information that provides a unique evaluation;
- the continuity in depth (depth defines the region centrality);
- the distribution that ensures stability of the solution to the input data;
- the bulge that simplifies the calculation of degree of belonging.

The zonoid has an appearance of a convex polyhedron and is set by formulas:

$$Z(\alpha)=conv\{U_1,U_2,\ldots,U_P\}, \qquad (5)$$

for $\alpha\in]0,\frac{\mathrm{B}}{P}]$, and

$$conv\left\{\frac{1}{\alpha\square P}\sum_{\beta=1}^{\mathrm{B}}U_{p_\beta}+\left(1-\frac{1}{\alpha\square P}\right)U_{p_{\mathrm{B}+1}}\right\}, \qquad (6)$$

for $\alpha\in[\frac{\mathrm{B}}{P},\frac{\mathrm{B}+1}{P}]$, where $\mathrm{B}\in\{1,2,\ldots,P-1\}$, $\{p_1,p_2,\ldots,p_{B+1}\}\subset\{1,2,\ldots,P\}$, and $\{U_1,U_2,\ldots,U_P\}$ – points on the basis of which the zonoid is constructed, $P$ – the number of such points.

To define the degrees of belonging $L^q_{b,i,\gamma}$ within the point in time $t$, there is a point $U_{i,b}(t)$ in space, corresponding to the current values of the involved VM resources in point $t$:

$$U_{i,b}(t)=\{r^*_{i,b,1}(t),\ldots,r^*_{i,b,L_i}(t)\}. \qquad (7)$$

For each linguistic value $l^q_{b,i,\gamma}$, $\gamma=\overline{1,\Gamma_{b,i}}$ the smallest Euclidean distance $d_{b,i,\gamma}$ from a point $U_{i,b,\gamma}(t)$ to the zonoid corresponding to this linguistic value is defined. The value $L^q_{b,i,\gamma}$ is estimated by the formula:

$$L^q_{b,i,\gamma}=1-\frac{1}{\max\{d_{b,i,1},d_{b,i,2},\ldots,d_{b,i,\Gamma_{b,i}}\}-d_{b,i,\gamma}}, \qquad (8)$$

where $\Gamma_{b,i}$ – amount of the linguistic values describing quality indicators $q_{b,i}$, $b=\overline{1,D_i}$ of the $i$-th service.

*C. Reduction of service quality indicators, specified in the SLA, to a single integral quality indicator*

In order to establish the dependence of an integral quality indicator $Q_i$, $i=\overline{1,K}$, from all quality indexes $q_{b,i}$, $b=\overline{1,D_i}$ of the i-th service, the fuzzy database is used. Rules of such base are represented as follows:

$$IF \wedge\left(L^q_{b,i,\gamma}\mid\gamma\in[1,\Gamma_{b,i}]\right) THEN\left(l^Q_{i,\omega}\mid\omega\in[1,\Omega_i]\right), \qquad (9)$$

for $b=\overline{1,D_i}$.

Indicate $L^Q_{i,\omega}$ as the degree of belonging to the fuzzy set $\Psi^Q_{i,\omega}$, $\omega=\overline{1,\Omega_i}$. Its value is defined as the minimum of all values derived from the fuzzy database rules (9) corresponding to fuzzy value $l^q_{b,i,\gamma}$.

*D. Calculation of the integral quality indicator of service*

At a defuzzification stage for the $i$-th service the numerical value of its integral quality indicator $Q_i$ is calculated by a formula:

$$Q_i = \frac{\int_{x=0}^{1} x \cdot F_i(x)\,dx}{\int_{x=0}^{1} F_i(x)\,dx}, \qquad (10)$$

where $F_i(x)$ is calculated by the formula:

$$F_i(x) = agg\left(imp\left(L^Q_{i,\omega}, \mu_{i,\omega}(x)\right)\right), \qquad (11)$$

where $\mu_{i,\omega}$ is the membership function of integral quality indicator $Q_i$ to the fuzzy set $\Psi^Q_{i,\omega}$, $i=\overline{1,K}$, $\omega=\overline{1,\Omega_i}$.

## IV. LOAD BALANCING

Two control mechanisms are implemented in the management system "SmartBase ITS Control", developed by the National Technical University of Ukraine "Kyiv Polytechnic Institute" for the SLA-defined service quality management. The first of them assumes a change of the number of VMs providing the *i*-th service, and the second – the VM load balancing.

The algorithm of "SmartBase ITS Control" management system during quality management of the *i*-th service consists in the following.

For each VM $V_{j,i}$, $j=\overline{1,M_i}$, $i=\overline{1,K}$ the current quality of the provided service is defined. For this purpose, the value of the involved volumes of resources $r^*_{m,i}$, $m=\overline{1,L}$, $i=\overline{1,K}$ is defined for each VM.

Proceeding from value $r^*_{m,i}$, $m=\overline{1,L}$, $i=\overline{1,K}$ taking into account expressions (6)–(8) the values $L^q_{b,i,\gamma}$, $b=\overline{1,D_i}$, $\gamma \in [1,\Gamma_{b,i}]$ are calculated.

The calculated values $L^q_{b,i,\gamma}$, are substituted in rules (9) of fuzzy database and degree of belonging to $L^Q_{i,\omega}$, $\omega=\overline{1,\Omega_i}$ is defined.

To find a numerical value of an integral quality indicator $Q_i$ of the *i*-th service for *j*-th VM, the center of mass is determined by a formula (10) which represents the result of aggregation of belonging functions $\mu_{i,\omega}$, bound above by the values $L^Q_{i,\omega}$ determined by formula (11).

If for all VMs $V_{j,i}$, $j=\overline{1,M_i}$, $i=\overline{1,K}$, the received values of integral quality indicators $Q_i$ are lower than stipulated within SLA, then the manageent system makes the decision to increent the number of VMs that provide the *i*-th service.

If for all VMs $V_{j,i}$, $j=\overline{1,M_i}$, $i=\overline{1,K}$ the received values of integral quality indicators $Q_i$ exceed the stipulations within SLA, then the decision to decrement the consumption of resources of the data center is made. Specifically the number of available VMs for the *i*-th service is decremented.

If the received values of integral quality indicators $Q_i$ are in norm limits, then the balancer distributes the user's requests between VMs $V_{j,i}$, $j=\overline{1,M_i}$, $i=\overline{1,K}$ in proportion to values $Q_i$ for each VM.

## V. EXPERIMENTAL RESULTS AND ANALYSIS

As the experimental service, a Web service, which works using the HTTP protocol had been selected (denoted as $s_1$). The indicator of HTTP-service quality is the time of reaction of the server for the user's request.

As there are no well-defined standards for the time of any given loaded page, it had been decided to follow the recommendations by [14] and to follow the recommendations by Yandex. In said recommendations, it was stipulated that the quality of HTTP service is considered excellent if a server response time is less than 3 seconds, satisfactory – from 3 to 6 seconds, and unsatisfactory if the time of the server response is longer than 6 seconds.

The VM resources are determined by the parameters that are indirectly influencing HTTP server response time. Based on the paper [14], it was defined, that the time of the page loading, and the quality of HTTP-service are influenced by following resources: the involved processor time, the free RAM, and throughput of the communication channel.

For carrying out an experiment, three homogeneous virtual machines $V_{1,1}, V_{1,2}, V_{1,3}$. are deployed. On VMs the Apache Server and Java were installed. As test service the Atlassian Jira was selected. It is rather resource-intensive service. It is rather resource-intensive service therefore even insignificant increase in the number of the users' requests for such service leads to noticeable increase in the value of resources spent by VMs. At the initial point in time, only one virtual machine is active. Other machines are in the sleep mode to decrease data center resource consumption.

As VMs are homogeneous, the data center operators are able to increase quickly the number of machines, if necessary. CPU load (parameter $r_{11}$), free RAM (parameter $r_{21}$) and bandwidth of network interface (parameter $r_{31}$) are resources that may be allocated for service $s_1$ for $V_{1,1}, V_{1,2}, V_{1,3}$.

The workload is formed by Apache Jmetter during the experiment. From 1 to 100 users' requests per second have been emulated. The emulation results without load balancing are displayed in Fig. 1.

Fig. 1 shows that the load time increases dramatically on the 20th second approximately. This is due to the increase in the number of users' requests from 1-25 to 75-100.

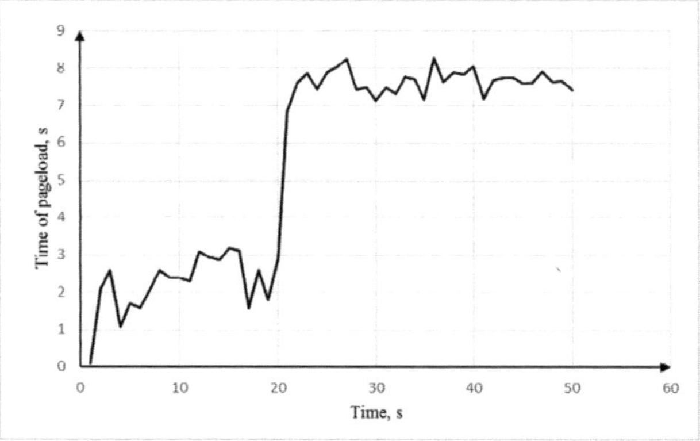


Figure 1. Emulation results without management system

The results of the same experiment, while using the management system, are shown in Fig. 2.

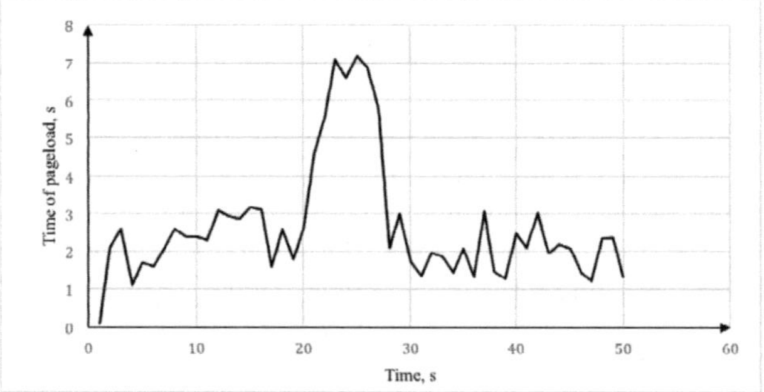


Figure 2. Emulation results with management system

When the management system has determined that there are not enough resources for providing service quality, it launches an additional virtual machine. This happens after 20 seconds. Then, the load balancer begins distributing users' requests between the virtual machines evenly.

With a more uniform VM workload increase, the management system allowed to exclude unwanted delays completely. Fig. 3 shows the simulation results without control, but with a uniform workload increase.

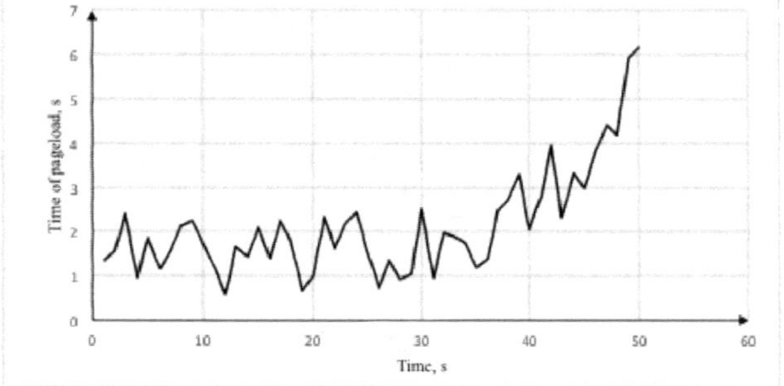


Figure 3. Emulation results with a uniform workload increase without management system

Fig. 4 displays the simulation results with the activated management system, as proposed in the paper, with a uniform workload increase.

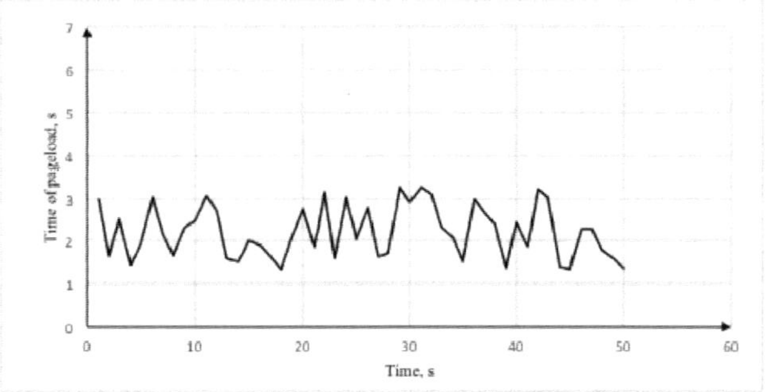


Figure 4. Emulation results with a uniform workload increase with management system

Simulation results have shown that the proposed load balancing method works satisfactorily when the number of user's requests changes slightly. When a workload increases sharply up to the critical point, the management system needs some time to adjust to the new conditions.

This problem arises from the fact that the new virtual machines need time to turn on. And even the fact that they are in the sleep mode, but are not turned off completely, did not allow them to react quickly enough to sudden changes in the server's workload.

If one of the backup virtual machines is left enabled, but the load balancer for it is disabled, so that it does not send requests until the moment when the active virtual machines fully cope with the current workload, the response to sudden workload surges will be more rapid.

Only providing unlimited resources would completely eliminate the problems associated with the sharp increase in workload at the servers, which is not feasible. But it is possible to use the methods described in [2] to decrease the reaction time.

## VI. CONCLUSION AND FUTURE WORK

In this work, a load balancing management system for data center servers based on the current quality of service is proposed. It is suggested to use virtual machines for a more flexible allocation of data center resources.

The advantage of this method of load balancing is that a balancer determines the need for additional resources, being based not on the number of resources involved, but on the value of the integral quality indicator of services. The proposed two-step method provides a statistical evaluation of QoS without any assumptions about the probability characteristics of the processes occurring in the data center.

In contrast to the method proposed in [5], the method described in this paper allows to determine in advance the time when there is a need for additional resources for the given service. In [3], the authors have proposed a load balancing algorithm, which operates at a consistently high workload at the servers. The disadvantage of this method is the increased consumption of data center resources at low workloads. In [4], the authors have proposed to define SLA service compliance of service quality on the proposed criteria. In this study a similar method has been suggested. But the use of fuzzy inferencing, when aggregating the quality indicators overall, integral quality indicator provides a more accurate assessment of the service quality.

HTTP-service experiments were carried out as an example for showing operability of the proposed management system. The experiments have shown the efficiency of this method. The quality of the service under consideration did not go beyond the norm in the experiments.

However, the authors of this work have not considered the problems described in [2], and [6]. The balancing method proposed in this paper, in combination with the algorithms described in [2], and [6], will improve the current method. Also, the time of VM switching on will be reduced.

## REFERENCES


[1] A. Kumar and M. Kalra, "Load balancing in cloud data center using modified active monitoring load balancer," International Conference on Advances in Computing, Communication, & Automation (ICACCA) (Spring), pp. 266—270, 2016.

[2] J. Duan, "A data center virtualization framework towards load balancing and multi-tenancy," IEEE 17th International Conference on High Performance Switching and Routing (HPSR), pp. 14—21, 2016.

[3] T. Chen, Y. Zhang, and X. Wang, G. B. Giannakis "Robust geographical load balancing for sustainable data centers," IEEE International Conference on Acoustics, Speech and Signal Processing (ICASSP), pp. 3526—3530, 2016.

[4] O. Shpur, B. Strykhalyuk, and O. Morushko, "The optimal distribution of optical resources between data centers for providing the required level of QoS," the 13th International Conference on Modern Problems of Radio Engineering, Telecommunications and Computer Science (TCSET), pp. 649–651, 2016.

[5] O. Rolik, P. Mozharovskyy, V. Vovk, and D. Zaharov, "Constructing quality metrics for IT infrastructure components using the nonparametric statistics," Visnyk NTUU "KPI" Informatics, operation and computer science, vol. 53, pp. 160–169, 2011.

[6] L. Gu, D Zeng, A Barnawi, S Guo, and I. Stojmenovic, "Optimal Task Placement with QoS Constraints in Geo-Distributed Data Centers Using DVFS," IEEE Transactions on Computers, vol. 64, issue. 7, pp. 2049—2059, 2015.

[7] E.H. Mamdani, "Applications of fuzzy logic to approximate reasoning using linguistic synthesis," IEEE Transanctions on Computers, vol. 26, no. 12, pp. 182—1191, 1977.

[8] Y. Zuo and R. Serfling, "General notions of statistical depth functions," Ann. Statist, vol. 28, no 2, pp. 461—482, 2000.

[9] G. Koshevoy and K. Mosler, "Zonoid trimming for multivariate distributions," The Annals of Statistics, vol. 25, no. 5, pp. 1998—2017, 1997.

[10] K. Mosler, T. Lange, and P. Bazovkin, "Computing zonoid trimmed regions of dimension d>2," Computational Statistics and Data Analysis, vol. 53, issue 7, pp. 2500—2510, 2009.

[11] K. Mosler, "Multivariate dispersion, central regions and depth," New York. : Springer, p. 291, 2002.

[12] L.A. Zadeh, "Fuzzy Sets," Information and Control, vol. 8, pp. 338—353, 1965.

[13] Abu M. T. Osman, "On the direct product of fuzzy subgroups", Fuzzy Sets and Systems, vol. 12, pp. 87—91, 1984.

[14] Giovanni Giambene, "Resource management in satellite networks", Optimization and Cross-Layer Design, pp. 67—94, 2007

# Dynamic Virtual Machine Allocation Based on Adaptive Genetic Algorithm

Oleksandr Rolik, Eduard Zharikov
Department of Automation and Control in Technical Systems, National Technical University of Ukraine "Igor Sikorsky Kyiv Polytechnic Institute"
Kyiv, Ukraine
email:o.rolik@kpi.ua, email:zharikov.eduard@acts.kpi.ua

Sergii Telenyk, Volodymyr Samotyy
Department of Automatic Control and Information Technology, Faculty of Electrical and Computer Engineering, Cracow University of Technology
Cracow, Poland
email:stelenyk@pk.edu.pl, email:vsamotyy@pk.edu.pl

***Abstract* – The widespread use of the virtualization paradigm in modern data centers has increased the necessity of improving the management efficiency of virtual machine allocation on physical machines (PM). Modern service providers offer a large number of virtual machine types and settings. The density of virtual machine placement per physical server also complicates the solution of this problem. Under these conditions, for solving such kind of problems, the adaptive genetic algorithm (AGA) is proposed. The proposed algorithm uses parametric and algorithmic adaptation simultaneously by selecting the values for a genetic operator's parameters and by selecting the probabilities of applying these operators. The AGA is evaluated for the solution of virtual machine allocation problem and demonstrates efficiency compared to the classical and the controlled versions of genetic algorithm.**

***Keywords – data center; genetic algorithm; virtual machine; resource management***

## I. INTRODUCTION

Data center resource management is an important and urgent problem at the present time. The growth in the number and complexity of modern data centers leads to an increasing number of virtual machines (VMs) and opens new challenges for management process automation. The Infrastructure as a Service (IaaS) paradigm enables customers to dynamically request the needed number of virtual machines based on their business requirements. One of the main tasks of managing resources in IaaS is the VMs allocation on the physical servers of the infrastructure. The VMs allocation process must be performed in a way that results in a reduction in the number of physical servers and a decrease in the energy consumption.

The use of genetic algorithms (GA) and their benefits compared with heuristic methods to solve data center resource management problems is shown in [1]. Classical genetic algorithms (CGA) have their own specifics as GA simultaneously use several types of genetic operators: unary, binary, and multiple. It is difficult to choose the strategy to generate values of probabilities for the use of certain operators so that their application gives positive results for the entire period of the GA. In addition, each operator has a set of parameters that influence the results of the algorithm, and to find the optimum values of these parameters is a rather difficult task.

In [1], a managed genetic algorithm (MGA) is proposed. It allows the adjustment of the parameters of the algorithm at all stages of the problem solving. In addition, the MGA does not suffer from the problems of the classic GA, such as degeneration of the population, getting into local extremes, etc. The main disadvantages of MGA are the need for the participation of an administrator and its application to a narrow class of problems. The solution to these problems of GA in general is not possible, therefore it is necessary to develop an effective strategy for the selection of the operator's parameters and for determining the probability of applying these operators for the entire period of the GA.

The remainder of the paper is organized as follows: in Section II, the related work is discussed, in Section III the problem of genetic algorithm adaptation is analyzed and an AGA is presented, in Section IV a particular case of the VMs allocation in the data center with a homogeneous configuration of the PMs is considered. This problem is proposed to be solved using an AGA. In this section, the results obtained by classical genetic algorithm, modified genetic algorithm and adaptive genetic algorithm for solving the considered problem are compared. Section V concludes the paper discussing the results and future research directions.

## II. RELATED WORK

As stated in [2][3][4], there is a significant effort of research in the data center resource management field including resource provisioning, resource allocation, resource brokering, resource scheduling, resource mapping, and resource capacity planning. There are a lot of cloud computing frameworks and systems proposed that have specific mechanisms to provide and monitor resources, including those using heuristics and new methods such as load prediction mechanisms, considering imbalance of workload and virtual machine interference.

Genetic algorithms are widely used for solving computational problems of resource allocation in data centers, and produce sufficient productive solutions [5][6]. In these studies, one needs to determine the list of issues that need to be figured out when using the GA to solve the problems of different dimensions and constraints.

During the last decade, many approaches to various VM placement problems have been proposed. In [7], the authors propose to model the server consolidation problem as a vector packing problem with conflicts using techniques inspired by grouping genetic algorithm. The algorithm has been tested in various scenarios and it allows to minimize the number of servers used for hosting applications within datacenters. Besides, it maximizes the packing efficiency of the servers utilized.

In [8], the authors consider the virtual machine packing problem as a multi-objective optimization problem and propose to solve it by using genetic algorithm as one of the meta-heuristics. The authors have implemented a virtual machine packing optimization mechanism based on genetic algorithm for a virtual cluster management system.

A hybrid genetic algorithm, using best fit decreasing strategy, was proposed in [9] to deal with infeasible solution due to the bin representation. The authors have proposed a new approach based on correcting infeasible chromosomes to prevent overflow of the bin. Hence, the new proposed chromosomes were suitable for the application of the genetic operators. They contributed to the execution time reduction. The proposed algorithm was evaluated on the VM placement problem and it lead to the usage of a minimum number of physical machines.

Energy consumption in the communication network is another subject of research related to the virtual machine placement problem. The approach based on genetic algorithm, that considers the energy consumption in both the servers and the communication network in the data center, was proposed in [10]. But the authors' assumption about network topology does not strictly correspond to the real data center networks.

To solve the VM placement problem in a cloud data center, the authors in [11] proposed to adopt a genetic algorithm using the future workloads prediction with Brown's quadratic exponential smoothing. But their online self-reconfiguration approach for reallocating VMs is focused on serving three types of Web transactions, namely browsing, shopping and ordering transactions.

To address fine-grained virtual machine resource allocation and reallocation problem, a two-level control system has been proposed in [12] to manage the mappings of workloads to VMs and the mappings of VMs to physical resources. An improved genetic algorithm with fuzzy multi-objective evaluation has been proposed to efficiently solve the VM placement problem, which is formulated as a multi-objective optimization problem of simultaneously minimizing total resource wastage, power consumption and thermal dissipation costs.

In [13] [14], the idea of genetic operator adaptation and adjustment of the probabilities of their use was proposed. The disadvantage of these approaches is that the adaptation of only one crossover operator was proposed. Another disadvantage is that the possible approaches to adaptation are used independently of each other.

As a rule, for the adaptation of the GA for specific tasks, a certain control parameter is used [15][16]. The effectiveness of the deterministic control has been proven for some tasks [13], but its generalization is problematic. Adaptive control [17] uses feedback to determine how the parameters should be changed. With adaptive control [14], it is necessary to introduce additional information that allows to adjust the behavior of the operators.

Today, the main efforts of GA researchers are focused on the adaptation of only one parameter. The most complete combination of management forms [16] was presented in [18], where the adaptation was performed simultaneously on three parameters: probability of mutation, crossover, and population size. Other forms of adaptive algorithms are presented in [19][20][21].

## III. The Adaptive Genetic Algorithm

The main feature of the proposed algorithm is the use of two adaptation strategies, so the process of obtaining the solution is a cyclical repetition of two stages. In the first stage, using the parametric adaptation, the algorithm selects the most productive settings for each of the operators. In the second stage, the parameter of performance is estimated and the algorithm selects the most efficient type of operator taking into account the results of algorithmic adaptation. If the resulting solution does not satisfy the specified criteria, the process is repeated from the first step.

The general formulation of the problem of genetic algorithm adaptation can be reduced to minimizing a function $F$ that serves as a criterion for GA adaptation and depends on parameters such as: types of operators to be used in the evolutionary process, the frequency of use of these operators and the values of the parameters with which the operators are applied. Let us define the adaptation function as $F(M, C, \alpha_M, \alpha_C, \beta_M, \beta_C)$, where $M$, $C$ are the parameters that govern the use of mutation and crossover operators, and take values from the set {0, 1}, and the equality of the parameter to 0 means that the operator does not take part in the evolutionary process, and the equality of the parameter to 1 means that the operator takes part in the evolution process; $\alpha_M, \alpha_C$ are frequencies of the use of operators $M$ and $C$ respectively which take values from the interval [0; 1]; $\beta_M, \beta_C$ are the sets of possible values of mutation and crossover operators.

Finding an explicit form of the function $F$, even for simple cases, requires a huge amount of computation that would negate all the benefits of GA. The use of structural adaptation within the solution of IT infrastructure management tasks is impossible, so when carrying out adaptation it is proposed to use some information regarding the properties of the function $F$. In the evolutionary process, such information will be the types of operators and parameters of these operators.

Genetic algorithms use several types of operators such as unary (mutation), binary (crossover), and multiple (multi-point crossover). Each type of operator has a set of parameters that affect its behavior, and GA begins with specific parameter values.

Suppose the set of types of operators is given as $D=\{d^1,...,d^z,...,d^Z\}$, where $z=\overline{1,Z}$ is the number of types of operators used in the GA. One such example is the modified crossover operator or the modified mutation operator. Each type of operator $d^z, z=\overline{1,Z}$ has a set of parameters $X(d^z)=(x_{z,1},...,x_{z,k},...,x_{z,Y})$, $k=\overline{1,Y}$. For example, the modified mutation operator has two parameters, which correspond to probabilities $p_{10}$ and $p_{01}$, and crossover has only one parameter that is the number of crossover points.

To generate new generations, the GA uses genetic operators with parameters that correspond to its type. The parameters take their values from some set or interval. For modified mutation operator, the parameter's values will be selected from the interval [0, 1], whereas the parameter of crossover operator can take any positive integer value, less than $(n-1)$.

The parametric adaptation applied to increase the chances of survival and reproduction of the operators with the parameter values, showed the best results. Consider the AGA, which uses the types of operators from the set *D*. For each type of operator $d^z \in D$, $z=\overline{1,Z}$ the population of parameter values is constructed. For example, if modified mutation operator and modified crossover operator are defined for AGA, then $(alter\_rate, p_{10}, p_{01}) \in \{(0.1; 0.1; 0.9), (0.7;0.8;0), (0.4;0.1;0.1)\}$ is a fixed set of operator instances for mutations and $(c) \in \{(1),(2),(n-1)\}$ is fixed set of operator instances for crossover.

Let us denote a set of operators used by AGA as $O=\{op_1,...,op_h,...,op_H\}$, $h=\overline{1,H}$, where *H* is a number of operators in AGA.

The behavior of each operator is adjusted by changing its parameters using an evolutionary procedure for each operator. The evolutionary procedure operates in the space of possible values of the operator. After starting the AGA, changes in parameter values are made for each operator. Since relatively small search space is optimized, a GA is also used for the search of a set of the operator's values, leading to an improvement of the AGA results. GA is used for each individual operator. Let us denote as operator's stage of GA (OGA) the GA that implements searching of the best operator's values.

The population for each operator will consist of chromosomes, which are a set of possible values of the operator's parameters. A single-point crossover is used to generate new populations. The OGA that is used to search the best values in the space of a single type of the operator is running as the GA procedure and is referred to as the main stage of GA (MSGA). The MSGA is working on the direct solution search. The resulting solution obtained by the use of OGA is the initial data for MSGA. In this case, AGA is viewed as a set of the OGA and the MSGA cycles.

The algorithmic adaptation task is solved at the MSGA stage. This task is to increase the probability of use of operators that provide the best solutions. To evaluate the work of the operators, we introduce the following concepts.

The *event* – the use of a specific genetic operator. *Absolute improvement* – an event when the value of the objective function of the new generation is greater than the value of the objective function of previous generations. *Improvement* – the new generation has a better objective function value than the parent's one. *Stabilization of decision* – the value of the objective function of the new generation is slightly different from the parent's one for a number of epoch. *Degeneration* – the next generation has a worse value of the objective function than the parent's one, and none of the generations are better than the parental.

Let us introduce the parameters of performance, showing the efficiency of the operator in the current generation, and being used as a feedback for the evolutionary process. Based on the values of the performance indicators, the AGA corrects the values of probabilities of using the operators. The parameter of performance for the operator $op_h$, $h=\overline{1,H}$ is defined as a function of four variables $\pi_{op_h}(ae,e,pw,w)$, where *ae* is the number of absolute improvements, *e* is the number of improvements, *pw* is the amount of stabilized solutions, *w* is the amount of degeneration. The total number of events on the step of the AGA is defined as $N=ae+e+pw+w$.

The performance parameter is introduced in order to determine which of the operators provides the best solution in the current step of AGA. The frequency of using operators is taken into account with the relative frequencies of occurrence of a certain type of events. When $N>0$ the relative frequency is calculated as follows: for an absolute improvement – $\varphi_{ae}=ae/N$; improvement – $\varphi_e=e/N$; stabilization of decision – $\varphi_{pw}=pw/N$; degeneration – $\varphi_w=w/N$.

In this paper, we adopted the following procedure for comparing the performance parameters, which will be formulated as follows based on the example of the two operators. An operator will be more productive if it has a performance setting characterized by a large number of absolute improvements. If the number of absolute improvements is the same, the comparison is made on the number of improvements. If the number of improvements is also the same, the comparison is made on flat events. If this comparison does not allow to select the best operator, then the more productive will be the operator with less amount of degeneration. If there is an equal number of degenerations, then the mutation is used.

To determine the order of use of the operators we introduced the concept of reward. For each operator $op_h \in O$, $h=\overline{1,H}$ the award $\rho(op_h)$ is assigned, which increases as a result of the accumulation of positive experience. Primarily the operator with the greatest reward is used. The value $\rho(op_h)$, $h=\overline{1,H}$ is constantly updated, and the experience gained during recent tests is seen as more urgent.

Let $\chi(op_h)$, $h=\overline{1,H}$ be the rank of operator $op_h$ assigned depending on the performance such that the most productive type of operator gets the highest rank. Moreover, the assignment of the rank is made after completion of the OGA. The awards are updated at the end of each AGA epoch in accordance with formula (1)

$$\rho(op_h)=\delta\rho(op_h)+\beta+\gamma\chi(op_h), h=\overline{1,H}, \quad (1)$$

where $\delta$ is the attenuation factor that is constant in the set $\{0, 1\}$. And $\delta=0$ for the operator, that just came into the work, and $\delta=1$ means that all previous experience of the operator is fully taken into account. The amplification factor $\gamma$ is to recognize the best operators. The coefficient $\beta$ having a value less than $\gamma$, is commonly used to ensure that the operator is required to be used in AGA step.

An example for the two operators: crossover and mutation, as well as limitations on the duration of the periods as the amount of epoch is shown below.

Step 1: The setting of the stop condition of the algorithm, which may be the number of epochs of genetic algorithm or the algorithm duration.

Step 2. The initialization of the initial population randomly within the constraints (3)–(5) and the following rule: when accessing the population, each time its individuals are sorted in descending order of objective function value. The best representative of the population is saved as a stored solution. The best population is remembered as a stored population. Initially, the primary population is the stored population.

Step 3: The initialization of the population of the operator's values randomly subject to the restrictions imposed for each type of operator. For example, for the mutation parameters and the crossover the following values may be used $(alter\_rate, p_{10}, p_{01}) \in \{(0.1; 0.1; 0.1), (0.2;0.2;0.2), (0.3;0.3;0.3)\}$ and $(c) \in \{(1),(2),(3)\}$ respectively.

Step 4. The use of each value of the respective types of operators to generate intermediate populations, with the help of the objective function to select values which allow to achieve the greatest performance indicators for each of the type of operators. For example, for mutation it may be $(alter\_rate, p_{10}, p_{01})=(0.1; 0.1; 0.1)$, for crossover it may be $(c)=(1)$.

In the case of improvement of the obtained results, the stored population is changed using the results obtained by means of the most productive of the two operators, and the stored solution is overwritten. If the performance of two operators is identical, the mutation operator has to be chosen. If this does not improve the initial solution, proceed to Step 3 and use OGA to adjust the values of the parameters using the crossover operator.

If it was not possible to improve the parameters of the operators by using crossover, then apply mutation to avoid possible falling into local extremes. The use of mutation parameter to adjust the values of parameters of the operators is made on a cycle by using the following rules. The rule for crossover is to increment the number of crossover points, and if the number of points is equal to $(n-1)$, to take the next number of crossover points equal to 1. The rule for mutation is to increase each of the values of mutation parameters by 0.1, and if the value of any of the parameters is 0.9, the next value is set to 0.1. If the decision is not improving, the algorithm finishes and the resulting solution is taken as the most productive.

Step 5: The ranks assigning to operators, calculation of awards, the use of the operators $M$ times (the total number of MSGA steps is equal to $2\times M$ in the first epoch, and $3\times M$ in all subsequent) in descending order of reward value. If the use of the operator has improved the decision, the solution must be used as a new stored solution to the problem, and then continue with the improved population.

Step 6. After a predetermined number of AGA steps, the value of performance options is updated and the most productive operator is chosen. For example, if the operator $(alter\_rate, p_{10}, p_{01})=(0.1; 0.1; 0.1)$ has been proven to be the most productive, it needs to be saved and used in the next epochs. Overwrite the stored solution.

Step 7. If the conditions of the AGA stop are not met, then go to step 3 and start a new epoch. On the stage of the OGA work, the most productive values for all types of operators must be chosen. For example, if $(alter\_rate, p_{10}, p_{01})=(0.2; 0.2; 0.2)$ and $(c)=(1)$ for mutation and crossover respectively, then in MSGA step the work on population will be carried out for the three operators (the mutation operator $(alter\_rate, p_{10}, p_{01})=(0.1; 0.1; 0.1)$ passes from the previous epoch). At the end of MSGA, count and compare the performance parameters, and choose the best of the three operators and go to the next epoch (Step 3).

Step 8. If the conditions of the AGA stop are fulfilled, then finish the job, use the current stored solution as a solution to the problem, otherwise go to step 3 and continue to work to complete the stop conditions.

In this paper, we used the combined stopping condition of the algorithm, which includes a predetermined time and the number of evolution periods in which the optimization result is not improving, and the growth of the objective function stops. GA aims to improve the outcome during the allotted time.

## IV. Experimental Results and Analysis

### A. *Formulation of the problem*

The authors consider a particular case (policy) of the VMs allocation in the data center with a homogeneous configuration of the PMs and propose to solve this problem using the adaptive genetic algorithm presented above. The VM allocation on the physical servers of the IT infrastructure relates to the problem of consolidation of computing resources. The case of using homogeneous PM configurations is chosen because it can be implemented within a single cluster, which may be considered as a unit of control in a data center. The mathematical model of the VMs allocation on the PMs is represented as follows.

The data center contains a set of PMs $N=\{N_1,\ldots,N_n\}$, where $n$ is the number of PMs. $K=\{K_1,\ldots,K_m\}$ is a set of VMs that should be allocated to the PMs, where $m$ is the number of VMs. Each PM $N_i$, $i=\overline{1,n}$, is characterized by two parameters that determine its computing capacity: $\Omega_i$ is the CPU capacity of the PM $N_i$, and $\Gamma_i$ is the RAM capacity of the PM $N_i$. Each VM $K_j$, $j=\overline{1,m}$, has the computational resource requirements: $\omega_j$ is the CPU time, and $\gamma_j$ is the RAM size. It is necessary also to determine the VM allocation matrix, $R=\|r_{ji}\|$, with the size of $m\times n$, where

$$r_{ji}=\begin{cases}1, \text{if VM } K_j \text{ is allocated on PM } N_i,\\ 0, \text{otherwise.}\end{cases} \quad (2)$$

The matrix $R$ is a solution to the problem and determines the allocation of $K$ VMs on the set $N$ of PMs. The authors consider that all PMs in set $N$ have identical specifications and, consequently, the same computing resources, so they assume that $\Omega_i = 1$ and $\Gamma_i = 1$ for all $i=\overline{1,n}$, that is

$$\{\Omega_i, G_i\}|_{N_i}=\{1,1\}, \text{ for all } i=\overline{1,n}. \quad (3)$$

This assumption allows the authors to make a transition from the measurement of PM computing resources in absolute values when the memory is measured in gigabytes and CPU frequency in GHz to a relative value. Then, the VM needs are defined as part of the PM's resources, recalculated in relation to the maximum possible value of 1. The number of resources allocated to a virtual machine is determined by the application requirements. The necessary resources for the VM are recalculated with respect to the physical server and they are part of it.

The authors consider also that resource needs of each VM do not exceed the capabilities of the PM

$$\omega_j \le 1 \text{ and } \gamma_j \le 1, \text{for each } j=\overline{1,m}. \quad (4)$$

When solving the problem of VMs allocation for all PMs from $N$, the following resource constraint must be satisfied

$$\sum_{j=1}^{m} r_{ji}\omega_j \le 1 \text{ and } \sum_{j=1}^{m} r_{ji}\gamma_j \le 1, \text{ for } i=\overline{1,n}. \quad (5)$$

Further, the authors introduce the vector $\vec{y}=\langle y_i\rangle$, $i=\overline{1,n}$, where

$$y_i=\begin{cases}1, \text{ if at least one VM is allocated on } N_i,\\ 0, \text{ otherwise.}\end{cases} \quad (6)$$

Then the optimum criterion for solving the problem of VM placement on PMs will be

$$\min \sum_{i=1}^{n} y_i, \quad (7)$$

that is the PMs should be filled with VMs so that the minimum number of PMs are involved.

When the criterion (7) is satisfied the total cost S of the data center and PMs maintenance and energy supply will be minimized.

The objective function can be represented as follows:

$$S=\sum_{i=1}^{n} s_i y_i, \quad (8)$$

where $s_i$ is the maintenance and energy supply costs for the $i$-th PM.

In the case when the PMs in the data center have identical specifications (i.e., homogeneous), the expression (8) becomes

$$S=s\sum_{i=1}^{n} y_i, \quad (9)$$

where $s$ is the maintenance and energy costs per PM.

Taking into account the previous description, the problem of $K$ VMs allocation can be summarized as follows: it is necessary to place the VMs on data center PMs so that either the expression (8) or (9) reaches a minimum value.

The authors consider two cases, namely, the initial placement of the VMs and also their change in placement during the execution. The algorithm restarts when unused resources are detected in PM. If the number of unused resources on a PM is greater than the threshold, then that server is added to a consolidation list. The algorithm restarts if the total number of unused resources on the physical servers, included in the consolidation list, exceeds the resources of one PM. As a result, it is proposed to run the AGA not for all PMs, but for PMs in the consolidation list. All migrations initiated by the AGA at the previous stage must be completed. The selection of the threshold value is not considered in this work.

### *B. Evaluation*

Experimental studies were performed on the data center resource allocation problem solution using three algorithms: the classical genetic algorithm, the managed genetic algorithm [1] and the adaptive genetic algorithm presented in this paper.

At the same time, studies were conducted for different ratios of the number of VMs and PMs resources. For this study, we considered three options for resource ratios that are close to reality:

- the case of disproportionate resource requirements when in relative units the requested amount of CPU time is much higher than the requested amount of

RAM, i.e., $\omega_j >> \gamma_j$, for all $j=\overline{1,m}$. This type of problem occurs when a large number of applications require complex calculations;

- the case of disproportionate resource requirements when requested units of CPU is much less than the requested amount of RAM, i.e., $\omega_j << \gamma_j$, for all $j=\overline{1,m}$. This problem occurs when the VMs with applications that require large amounts of data processing are located on the servers;
- the most common practical case is when the amount of the requested CPU and RAM for all VMs are distributed randomly in the range [0.05; 0.6].

The ranges of computer resources requested by VM for the different experiments are presented in Table 1.

TABLE I. THE RANGES OF COMPUTER RESOURCES REQUESTED BY VM

| Experiment number | RAM limitation | CPU limitatiom |
|---|---|---|
| 1 | 0.3—0.45 | 0.05—0.15 |
| 2 | 0.45—0.6 | 0.05—0.15 |
| 3 | 0.05—0.15 | 0.3—0.45 |
| 4 | 0.05—0.15 | 0.45—0.6 |
| 5 | 0.05—0.6 | 0.05—0.6 |

In [1], it has been proved that when the number of VMs is less than fifty the heuristic and genetic algorithms give approximately the same results, but with the increased number of VMs the genetic algorithm provides a better quality performance.

The evaluation of the quality of CGA, MGA and AGA algorithms is performed in terms of the number of the PMs released (turned off). As it is assumed that the physical servers are homogeneous, they consume the same amount of energy. It is assumed that to allocate each VM initially, a separate PM is deployed. Next, using the proposed algorithms placement of VMs on PMs are optimized with the assessment of the maximum number of released PMs for each of the algorithms. To compare the success of each algorithm according to the criterion (7), the authors assessed the number of unused physical servers, which were turned off. It is obvious that, as a result of each algorithm work for VM consolidation, the more PMs are turned off, the better.

Fig. 1 illustrates the dependence of the number of the PMs released on the problem dimension (number of VMs) in the case when the requested number of CPU and RAM for all VMs is randomly distributed in the range [0.05; 0.6]. The x-axis denotes the number of VMs, the y-axis denotes the number of PMs released.

For comparing the MGA and the AGA results, the concept of additional released PMs $N_B$ is introduced. The value $N_B$ is defined as the difference between the number of PMs $N_{CGA}$, released as a result of CGA, and the number of PMs $N_{MGA}$ and $N_{AGA}$ released using the MGA and the AGA respectively.

Thus, Fig. 2 shows a winning of the MGA and the AGA regarding the CGA as a function of a number of additional PMs released $N_B$ from the dimension of the problem for different ratios of the resources requested.

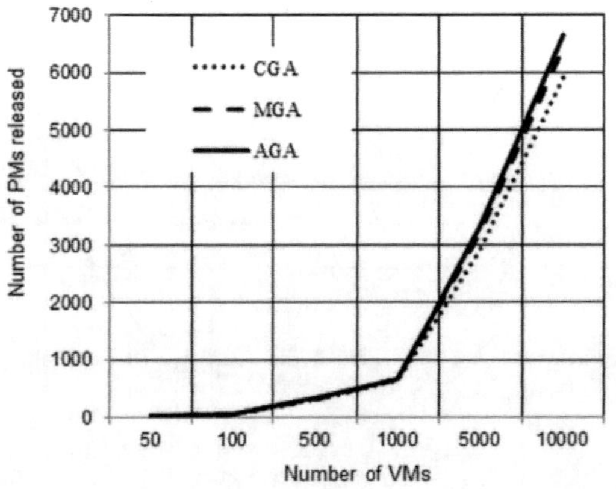


Figure 1. Dependence of the number of PMs released, from the problem dimension.

The x-axis represents the number of VMs that need to be placed on the PMs, y-axis represents the number of additional PMs released for each of the algorithms.

The data for the experiments were generated randomly with a uniform distribution law. The experimental results are shown in Fig. 2.

The analysis of the results shown in Fig. 2 leads to the following conclusions: (1) the use of the MGA and AGA is more effective than the use of the CGA; (2) the AGA always allows to get the best results on the VMs allocation, regardless of the experimental conditions; (3) in the case of dispersion over a wide range of requirements [0.05; 0.6] (Fig. 2 b), the use of the AGA is the most effective.

## V. CONCLUSION AND FUTURE WORK

One of the most important problems in the modern virtualized environment is an allocation of virtual machines on physical servers. Taking into account the large number of types and virtual machine settings that modern service providers offer, as well as the high density of virtual machines per physical server the solution for this problem is complicated.

In this work, the virtual machine allocation problem is solved by using the adaptive genetic algorithm. The proposed adaptive genetic algorithm uses parametric and algorithmic adaptation simultaneously by selecting the values for genetic operator's parameters and by selecting the probabilities of applying these operators. The authors' added contribution regarding existing genetic algorithms is to apply the adaptation, which consists in the change of probability of using GA operators and in the change in the parameter values of these operators depending on the nature of the problems and on the results obtained during the problem solving.

The adaptive genetic algorithm is evaluated for virtual machine allocation problem solution and demonstrated efficiency compared to classical and controlled versions of the genetic algorithm. It is shown that the proposed algorithm allows for an equal number of epochs to get better results.

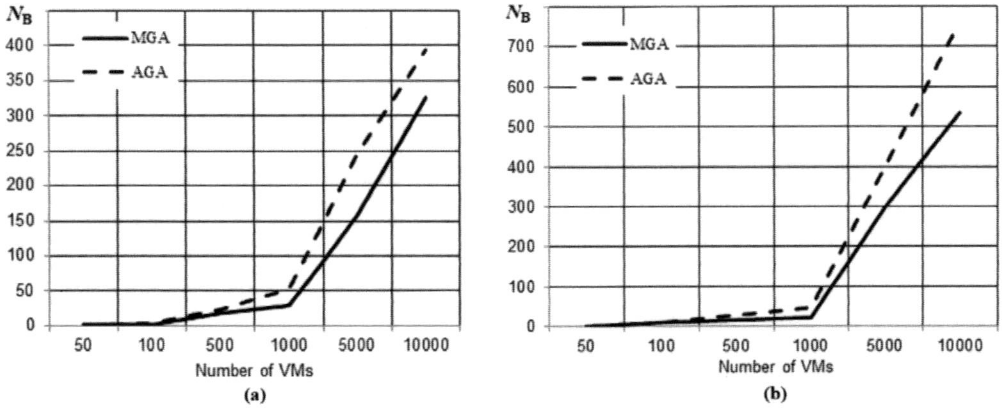


Figure 2. The dependence of the number of additionally released PMs on the dimension of the problem, when the requirements for the requested resources are in the ranges: (a) to the CPU – [0.05; 0.15], to the RAM – [0.3; 0.45]; (b) to the CPU – [0.05; 0.6], to the RAM – [0.05; 0.6]

For future work, the authors plan to develop the provisions of the adaptive genetic algorithm, to make recommendations on configuring the algorithm's parameters for specific kind of tasks, and apply an adaptive genetic algorithm for solving other tasks of the data center management.

## REFERENCES

[1] S. Telenyk, O. Rolik, P. Savchenko, and M. Bodaniuk, "Managed genetic algorithm in problems of virtual machines allocation in the data center," Scientific Journal of ChSTU, No 2, pp. 104-113, 2011

[2] A. Hameed et al., "A survey and taxonomy on energy efficient resource allocation techniques for cloud computing systems," Computing, pp. 1–24, 2014.

[3] S. H. H. Madni, M. S. A. Latiff, Y. Coulibaly, and S. M. Abdulhamid, "Resource scheduling for infrastructure as a service (IaaS) in cloud computing: Challenges and opportunities," Journal of Network and Computer Applications, vol. 68, pp. 173–200, 2016.

[4] S. Singh and I. Chana, "A Survey on Resource Scheduling in Cloud Computing: Issues and Challenges," Journal of Grid Computing, pp. 1–48, 2016.

[5] S. Telenyk, O. Rolik, M. Bukasov, S. Androsov, and R. Rymar, "Control of Data Centers' Load and Resources Virtual Hosting," Scientific Journal of the Ternopil State Technical University, Vol 14, No 4, pp. 198–210, 2009.

[6] S. F. Telenik, A. I. Rolik, M. M. Bukasov, and S. A. Androsov, "Genetic algorithms of decision of tasks of management resources and loading of centers of processing of data," Automatic. Automation. Electrical engineering complexes and systems, No 1 (25), pp. 106–120, 2010.

[7] S. Agrawal, S. K. Bose, and S. Sundarrajan, "Grouping genetic algorithm for solving the server consolidation problem with conflicts," In GEC '09: Proceedings of the first ACM/SIGEVO Summit on Genetic and Evolutionary Computation, New York, NY, USA, pp. 1-8, 2009.

[8] H. Nakada, T. Hirofuchi, H. Ogawa, and S. Itoh, "Toward virtual machine packing optimization based on genetic algorithm," In IWANN '09: Proceedings of the 10th International Work-Conference on Artificial Neural Networks, Berlin, Heidelberg, pp. 651-654, 2009.

[9] M. A. Kaaouache and S. Bouamama, "Solving bin Packing Problem with a Hybrid Genetic Algorithm for VM Placement in Cloud," Procedia Computer Science, Volume 60, pp. 1061-1069, 2015.

[10] G. Wu, M. Tang, Y. Tian, and W. Li, "Energy-Efficient Virtual Machine Placement in Data Centers by Genetic Algorithm," Neural Information Processing, Volume 7665 of the series Lecture Notes in Computer Science, Springer, pp. 315-323, 2012.

[11] H. Mi et al., "Online self-reconfiguration with performance guarantee for energy-efficient large-scale cloud computing data centers," Proc. of the IEEE International Conference on Services Computing, pp. 514–521, 2010.

[12] J. Xu and J. Fortes, "Multi-objective virtual machine placement in virtualized data center environments," Proc. of the IEEE/ACM International Conference on Green Computing and Communications & 2010 IEEE/ACM International Conference on Cyber, Physical and Social Computing, pp. 179–188, 2010.

[13] T. Back, "Optimal Mutation Rates in Genetic Search," Fifth International Conference on Genetic Algorithms: University of Illinois at Urbana-Champaign, July 17–21, pp. 2–8, 1993.

[14] W. Spears, "Adapting Crossover in Evolutionary Algorithms," Proc. Of the 4th Annual Conference on Evolutionary Programming: San Diego, California, March 1–3, pp. 367–384, 1995.

[15] Z. Michalewich, "Genetic Algorithms + Data Structures = Evolution Programs," Berlin: Springer, 1996.

[16] Z. Michalewich and D. Fogel "How to Solve It: Modern Heuristics," Berlin: Springer, 2002.

[17] B. Julstrom, "What Have You Done for me Lately? Adapting Operator Probabilities in a Steady-State Genetic Algorithm," Proc. of the Sixth International Conference on Genetic Algorithms: University of Pittsburgh, July 15–19, pp. 81–87, 1995.

[18] J. Lis and M. Lis, "Self-adapting Parallel Genetic Algorithms with the Dynamic Mutation Probability, Crossover Rate and Population Size," Proc. of the 1st Polish National Conference on Evolutionary Computation. Oficina Wydawnica Politechniki, Warszawskiej, pp. 324–329, 1996.

[19] A. Kosorukoff, "Using incremental evaluation and adaptive choice of operators in a genetic algorithm," Proc. of the Genetic and Evolutionary Computation Conference: (GECCO-2002), New York, USA, July 9–13, p. 688, 2002.

[20] M. Pelikan, D. Goldberg, and S. Tsutsui, "Combining the strengths of Bayesian optimization algorithm and adaptive evolution strategies," Genetic and Evolutionary Computation Conference: (GECCO-2002), New York, USA, July 9–13, pp. 512–519, 2002.

[21] D. Thierens, "Adaptive mutation rate control schemes in genetic algorithms," Congress on Evolutionary Computation: CEC'02, Honolulu, Hawaii, May 12–17, pp. 980–985, 2002.

# Software License Optimization and Cloud Computing

Anne-Lucie Vion - Noëlle Baillon
Orange SA
Paris, France
email: annelucie.cosse@orange.com
email: noelle.baillon@orange.com

Fabienne Boyer - Noël De Palma
Univ. Grenoble Alpes, LIG, CNRS
Saint-Martin-d'Hères, France
email: fabienne.boyer@imag.fr
email: noel.depalma@imag.

*Abstract-* **In this article, we propose a review of Software Asset Management (SAM) state of the art and existing tools oriented in the Cloud perspective; it seems that Software identification, through its complete virtualized lifecycle, is a major lock in efficient control. In this context, we propose a model and process architecture to cope with this complexity. We underline innovative graph modeling benefits in this contribution. We use a simple, but vivid example to prove the validity of our model.**

***Keywords-Software Asset Management; SAM; License optimization; Software uses.***

## I. INTRODUCTION

Software Asset Management (SAM) enables tracking software uses with the finest possible granularity. The aim is to constantly reconcile the real uses with the usage rights acquired from software providers in order to optimize and control the risks of non-compliance (i.e., counterfeiting). The current economic climate underlines this particularly burning issue, as each non-compliance situation is heavily penalized in financial aspects.

In this paper, we consider SAM processes in the context of emerging technologies, namely virtualization and Cloud environments. This change from traditional architectures to cloud environments, virtualized to the extreme, is still a virgin territory. Cloud environments add many degrees of complexity. Among others, tracking software becomes more challenging because the installation is disconnected from true physical infrastructure. Altogether, the complexity of software lifecycle management, the multiplication of actors in this cycle and the lack of efficient tools, lead to an understandable disconnection between software usages, associated hardware and the related licensing model. Also, because cloud environments tend to automate software lifecycle management, SAM processes are expected to be automated as well. On the contrary, automation is currently circumscribed to asset management in traditional architecture.

Going further, in cloud environments (Fig. 1), SAM is not only assets management, but also service management, which must be done in real time taking into account the fast rhythm of changes: services are provisioned, configured, reconfigured and decommissioned in a matter of minutes. Compliance risks are increased by the ease and speed of provisioning, which can bypass traditional centralized processes. In such conditions, SAM controls are difficult to implement.

| | Yesterday | Tomorrow |
|---|---|---|
| Software Cycle | Long cycle | Real time |
| Total costs | Calculable | Hidden and additional costs |
| Provisioning | Centralized | Built to be decentralized |
| Expenditure | Organized | Lower financial visibility |
| Licensing | Complex rules | Complex rules combination |
| Usage | Understandable | i.e., BYOD, multiplexing |
| Assets nature | Software | Cloud Services |
| Virtualization | 1 software-1 hardware | Multiple layers: hardware disconnection |

Figure 1. Complexity factors brought about by cloud architecture.

The idea that will be developed in this paper is that turning to the Cloud is not changing the object of SAM, but altering how SAM processes should be designed. The contributions are the following. We propose (i) an architecture for SAM in the cloud, (ii) the related SAM management workflow, (iii) some major implementation choices and (iv) a preliminary evaluation.

The remaining of this paper is organized as follows. Section 2 presents a synthesis of the state of the art and our related SAM maturity scale, Section 3 describes our global architecture for managing software, a model for managing installations and usages on PaaS (Platform as a Service) layer and discusses the choice of graph database to support our SAM model. Section 4 presents our first evaluation result, and we conclude in Section 5.

## II. STATE OF THE ART

This section discusses the state of the art regarding SAM solutions. We firstly recall the theoretical SAM models and then describe the existing SAM tools. We end this section with a short discussion on the "cloud-ready" dimension of SAM processes.

### A. Theoretical SAM Models

One of the first studies leading to SAM considerations, in 1999, was proposed by Holsing and Yen [1] through a software asset probation model and identification of five problem areas, which actuate the need for software management: ethical, legal, technical, managerial and economic.

In 2004, Ben-Menachem and Marliss [2] introduced the "paradigm of change" based on methods, tools and procedures for accurate overall Information Technology (IT) inventory management. Thereby, they underline that investments in the creation and maintenance of a dedicated software inventory is a sine qua non prerequisite to proper long-term SAM.

In 2011, McCarthy and Herger [3] proposed a solution in four points to combine IT, processes and business in SAM perspectives: Discover software assets, mainly consisting in achieving a scan of installed licenses; Reconcile purchased assets, enables performing a procurement inventory; implementing contract management; producing business intelligence reporting "audit readiness" and compliance.

SAM tools are widely used in a lot of computing environments. In 2014, for Gocek, Kania and Malecki [4], these tools refer to software programs that discover and collect information about software instances deployed in monitored environments. As software owners continue to shift toward complex software licensing schemes, SAM tools will continue to play increasingly major roles.

### B. SAM Tools

Several studies [5][6][7] show that people around the world, all face the same difficulties to compare existing SAM tools. This is mainly due to the exuberant marketing made by publishers about features that appear similar between existing tools and the lack of a model to classify them. The scope is absolutely not defined between traditional architecture and the cloud environment, as if the way to manage software assets in both environments was similar. We can add that multiplication of tools is also due to multiplication of actions to manage: i.e., management tools often perform discovery activities and inventory. However, they rarely gather sufficient details on software inventory to allow making informed decisions about their elimination or even just to compare to usage rights acquired by contracts.

We have developed the following SAM maturity scale, illustrated in Fig. 2, to compare the existing SAM tools regarding the features they provide. In Fig.2, four levels are defined on a **vertical axis** about SAM maturity.

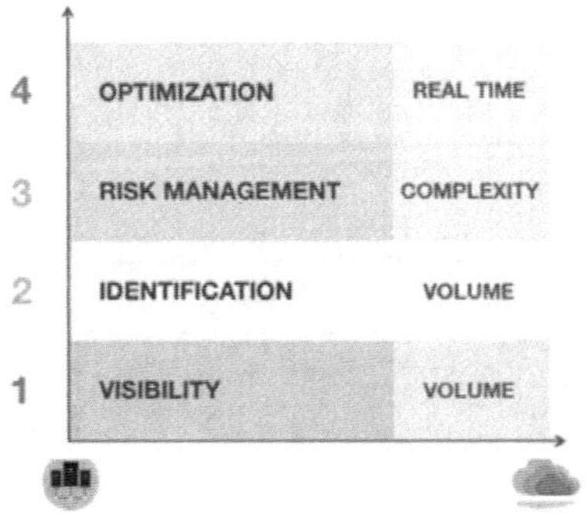


Figure 2. SAM processes maturity scale

(1) *VISIBILITY:* this level precisely identifies resources. In other words, SAM tools providing this level of feature allow (i) recognizing each device with its physical features, (ii) identifying the virtual machines and the resources allocated to them, and (iii) discovering any software installed on any physical or virtual devices.

(2) *IDENTIFICATION*: this level consists in translating any resource in its associated assets. In other words, it translates software installation in terms of related licenses and products user rights. It can be identifying a product as a trial version or circumscribed to a particular scope; diagnose that it belongs to a software suite or that it is an option whose use is conditioned by the use of the basic product.

(3) The third level, *RISK MANAGEMENT* consists in reconciling data provided by the two previous levels: VISIBILITY and IDENTIFICATION. In other words, the goal is to compare product usage rights with real uses. Mainly, the aim is to prevent two different risks: the first one is a legal one, counterfeiting: using software without license or with wrong way of licensing (nowadays, more often due to the complexity of licensing models). The second is a financial risk, over-deployment: not using licensed software, or the license covers more usage rights than needed.

(4) *OPTIMIZATION*: through the accurate view of installations, usages and assets provided by the previous levels, it becomes possible to identify ways to improve license spends, and in fine to automate this optimization process in a real time manner.

Fig. 3 illustrates the current state regarding existing SAM tools. We can notice that the four levels previously introduced do not have the same maturity. A lot of tools are really efficient at the VISIBILITY level, in terms of discovery of resources on equipped resources. Among others, we can cite BladeLogic [8], Open Computer Software Inventory New Generation [9] (OCS), System Center Configuration Manager [10] (SCCM).

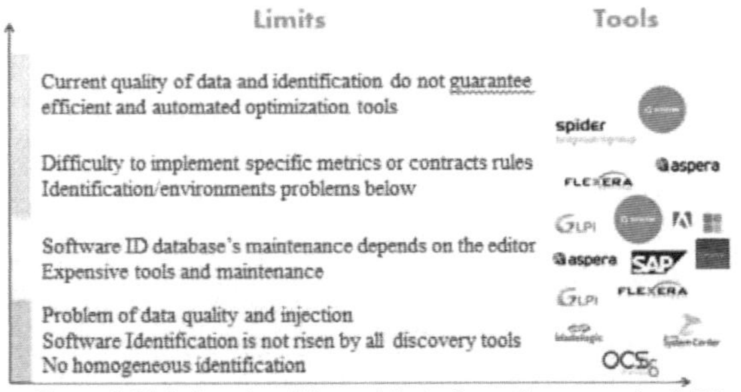


Figure 3. Main functionalities and limitations of most popular SAM tools

More problematic is the second level, especially because matching between information from contracts, usages and technical view from first level is, at least, not easy. At this IDENTIFICATION level, we find tools like GLPI (Gestion Libre Parc Informatique) [11] that manage resources discovered in the first step, but are not able to truly identify product usage rights. Contrary, tools proposed by Aspera [12], Snow [13] or editors' own solutions are able to manage product user rights (PUR) and, for some of them, able to identify some risks of over/under deployments (Snow, Spider [14], Aspera). However, these tools are expensive, especially database updates, and do not offer complete lifecycle tracking.

It is important to mention that software identification mainly relies on tags (i.e., SoftWare Identification Tag (SWID tag) [15]) that record unique information about an installed software application, including its name, edition, version, whether it's part of a bundle and more. The structure of SWID tags is specified in the international standard ISO/IEC 19770-2:2015 [16], which defines an XML (eXtensible Markup Language) data structure aiming to the precise identification of software, regardless of the platform and the device on which it is installed.

Finally, regarding the last level, in the current situation, despite the numerous risk management tools, the treatments are still approximate and optimization difficult to automate.

### C. *Synthesis*

One of the business benefits of cloud computing is its agility and speed-to-market. Services are provisioned, configured, released in a matter of minutes. Thus, while traditional SAM processes assume long lifecycles (usually, we can consider 5 – 8 years for a software, it leads to long cycles of contract, discovery, inventory and reconciliation), cloud accelerates these processes up to real-time requirements.

A second issue to consider is the different levels of services and multiplication of hidden costs in cloud environments. These hidden costs may include cost of migration, integration with IT systems, premium support services, new storage requirements, data extraction cost, service renewal costs, etc.

Moreover, we underline that if SaaS (Software as a Service) seems to reduce or even delete infringement risks (supposed to be indexed on real usage), this use is in fact restricted in many cases and is not often negotiable. In such cases, SAM should have appropriate controls to ensure compliance with all requirements and limitations (geographical scope, Restriction on shared accounts, on non-employees/providers, partners, etc., time, transactions volume). It leads to multiplications of complex rules, not only based on hardware metrics, but directly on usages, sometimes more difficult to identify.

As said in Business Software Alliance (BSA), 2014 [17] cloud services are often considered as operational expenses and not as capital expenditures. It leads to several problems: (1) less involvement in the contracting phase, (2) loss of control of operational dependencies, (3) loss of known limits to final costs, (4) lack of financial visibility, and (5) increased license compliance risks.

## III. PROPOSITION OF A SAM MODEL FOR THE CLOUD

### A. SAM Control Loop

Our SAM proposal takes into account the complete software lifecycle, considering that each step feeds a SoftWare DataBase (SWDB) and that every step is accompanied by one or more SAM control (or SAM check-points). All possible information related with the use of software should be captured and stored in order to implement all the required usage controls.

Through the check-points, the SAM processes analyze the current situation in real-time and confront the use of services with the license stock. SAM processes also take potential optimization decisions, creating a control loop.

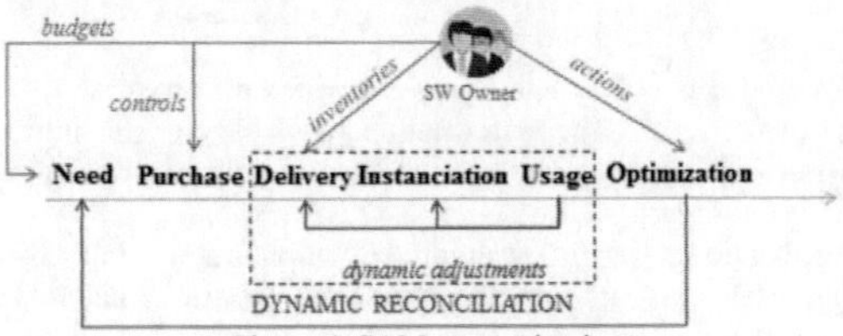


Figure 4. SAM retroaction loop

In its basic form, the software lifecycle that we consider is composed of 5 + 1 steps as shown in Fig. 4 and Fig. 5 – Fig.9; some steps can be played several times:

1) *Need's Expression*: the consumer justifies his need and choice of software.

2) *Purchasing*: this step encompasses sourcing processes, negotiation, contract, billing etc. At this stage, we get a Stock Keeping Unit (SKU) identifying the purchased software and its own [product] usage rights (PUR) created by the manufacturer and acquired during purchasing processes.

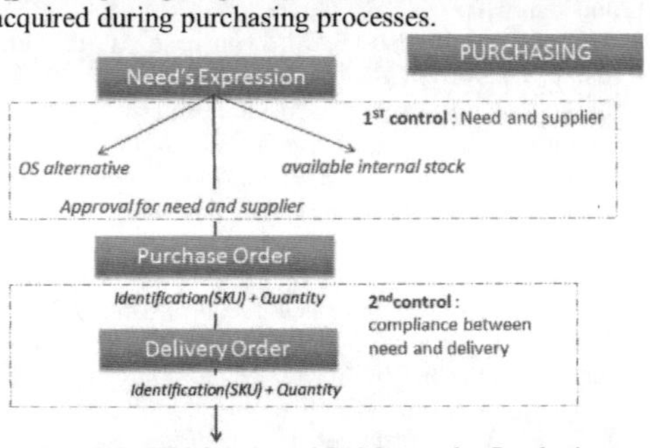


Figure 5. SW lifecycle and SAM controls - Purchasing

3) *Delivery*: this step corresponds to the software receipt via downloading platforms, preparation for installation on user platform, entry into a software catalogue. Through this step, we get a SWIG Tag containing the software's SKU created by the manufacturer and extendable with client-specific information. SWID tag will be the default software identifier.

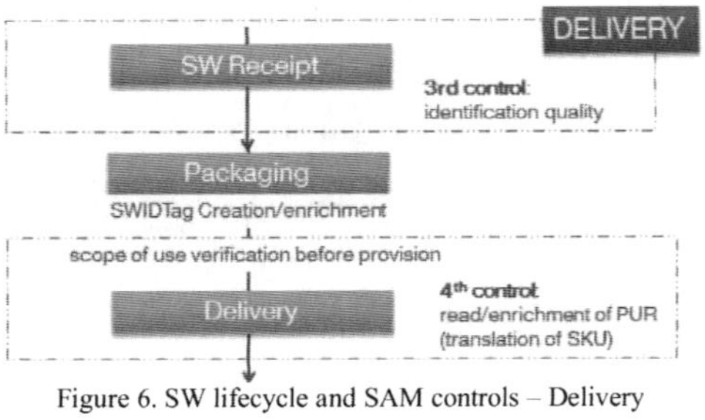


Figure 6. SW lifecycle and SAM controls – Delivery

4) *Instantiation*: The software is installed in an environment (for instance, a given Cloud), in other words, the software is able to be used.

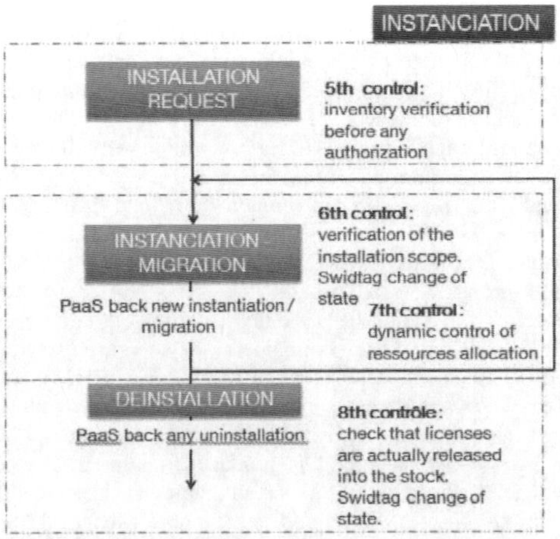


Figure 7. SW lifecycle and SAM controls - Instantiation

5) *Usage*: a user consumes a service/software. Here, we have to identify the cases where multiple users consume the same service simultaneously and translate this in terms of use (multiplexing, multidevice , etc.)

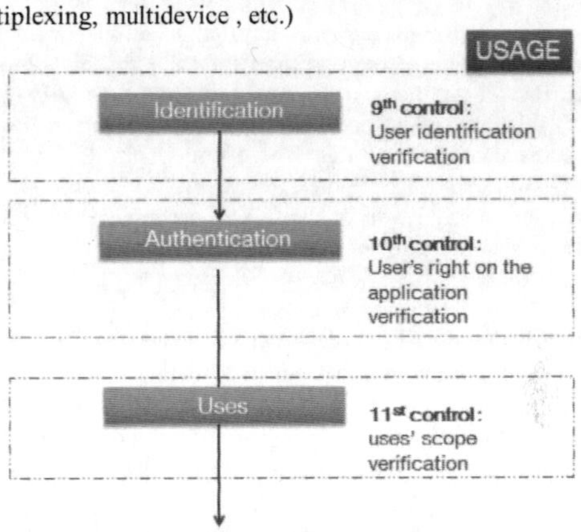


Figure 8. SW lifecycle and SAM controls - Usage

6) *Optimization:* this corresponds to confronting the need/contract/installation/use with the license stock according to a measure of consumption previously defined (metric). Here, we can create a model of costs for any measure of use and identify the most suitable scenario of consumption or of customer billing.

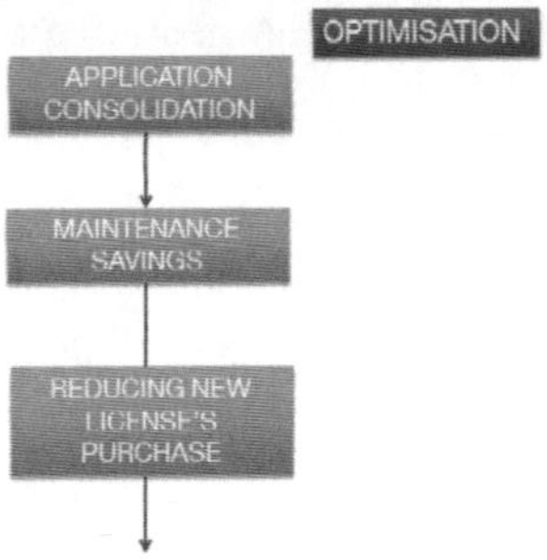


Figure 9. SW lifecycle and SAM controls - Optimization

## *B. Instance and usage capture*

### *1) Focus on Instantiation*

To implement SAM check-points over the instantiation step, we need to make assumptions on the targeted cloud environments, especially in terms of the PaaS layer that will be used to deploy services. In a first design, we consider clouds managed through the well-known and commonly used Cloud Foundry [18] PaaS. We consider that it will be possible to apply our model to a variety of PaaS, as long as they allow instantiation/usage's capture. In further works, we will extend to Infrastructure as a Service (IaaS) layers.

Deploying an application through the Cloud Foundry (CF) PaaS layer is done by running a *push* command from a Command Line Interface (CLI), either as part of the CF build packs or through a service broker:

*Build pack.* User pushes app bits (i.e. artefact: .jar, .war, tgz, etc.) from desktop/CLI selecting one of the supported stack (i.e., Ubuntu)

*Service broker* pushes a docker image reference (public or private registry), or a container specification reference

In both cases, a droplet is produced, taking into account dependencies configuration. As a result, app instances are started and run the image within quotas (Random Access Memory (RAM), Computer Process Unit (CPU), etc.). Among others, between *push* and application's availability, CF uploads and stores the application files, and examines and stores the application's metadata (for SAM purposes the SWID Tag enriched by all relevant contractual information during delivery step)

Before one can retrieve any application or service information, one must retrieve the Cloud Controller (using the Service Broker Application Programming Interface (API)). The brain of this controller knows services and applications as well as their instances and settings. The Cloud Controller exposes a Rest (Representational State Transfer) API for all this information through which the SAM processes can get the necessary knowledge to perform their tasks.

### *2) Focus on usage*

To implement SAM check-points over the USAGE step, we need to get the knowledge of which applications are used. We decided to achieve this first through the application rights verification. In more detail (Fig. 10), we summarize the steps performed when a user wants to use an application in our context:

1. The user wants to access the cloud application via the user portal
2. The user is identified and authenticated via a User Identification and Information System Access libraries
3. The system checks permission of the authenticated user to access the applications via the Application rights library and if yes, return a certificate. This step allows collecting usage information, especially the moment when a certificate for using the application is issued or withdrawn. The lifecycle of this certificate allows determining the time of using the application and all its software components.
4. Embedding cookies and certificates, the user can start to consume application

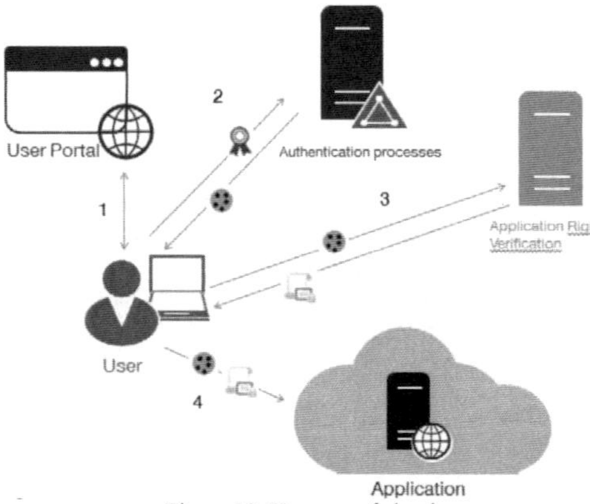


Figure 10. Use case of cloud app access

An application may embed several software services, so it is necessary to cross the information on usage with internal software cartography to be able to determine and affect usage directly to software.

Application's usages cannot be summarized only by a number of access or minutes spent. We consider that it also covers consumed resources (i.e., CPU, RAM, bandwidth, event p/s, flow p/s, etc.).

Open-source tool Abacus [19] provides usage metering and aggregation for Cloud Foundry services. This is implemented as a set of REST micro-services that collect usage data, apply metering formulas, and aggregate usage at several levels within a Cloud Foundry organization. Runtime provider (CF Bridge) submits application usage events (other runtime providers submit other runtime usage events); external services providers submit service usage events that are received and stored by Abacus, metered, accumulated, aggregated to provide usage reports and summaries.

We should recall that SAM's purpose is to confront contractual provision (PUR) with observed usages. Since we assume usage capture, we should focus on this aim to direct our implementation choices. Indeed, how we store the collected information (instantiation + usage) influences comparison and optimization operation's efficiency and relevance.

## *C. Feeding the database*

Each step previously described feeds a software database (SWDB). Following software lifecycle, we can represent every data injection summarized in Fig. 11:

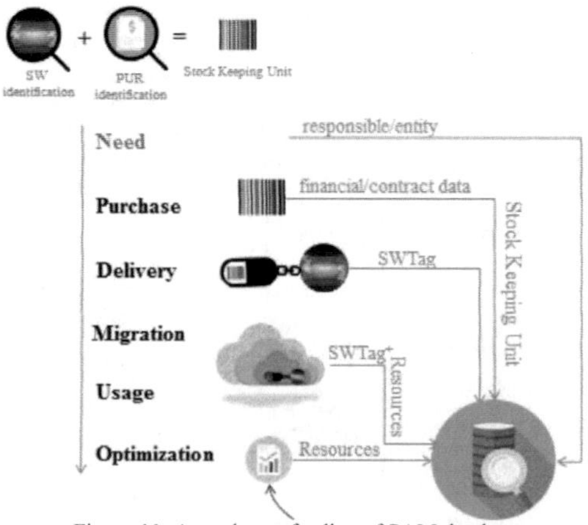


Figure 11. Asynchrone feeding of SAM database

To implement this database, we adopted a graph-oriented database. The lack of flexibity is the biggest weakness of relational databases when the data structure may vary like for SAM topic. Their scheme cannot support the dynamic real time, and uncertain nature of data, new technologies and platforms. Graph data models are centered on relationships. Just by connecting nodes and relationships, it can generate sophisticated models that fit closer to our problem (cohesive picture between contracts, usages and installations) when relational databases require us to infer connections between entities using special properties such as foreign keys, or out-of-band processing like map-reduce disconnecting the evolving schema and the actual data model.

Each node in the graph database model contains a list of relationship-records. These relationship records are organized by type and direction and may hold additional attributes (Fig. 12). Whenever one runs the equivalent of a JOIN operation, the database just uses this list and has direct access to the connected nodes, eliminating the need for expensive search / match computation.

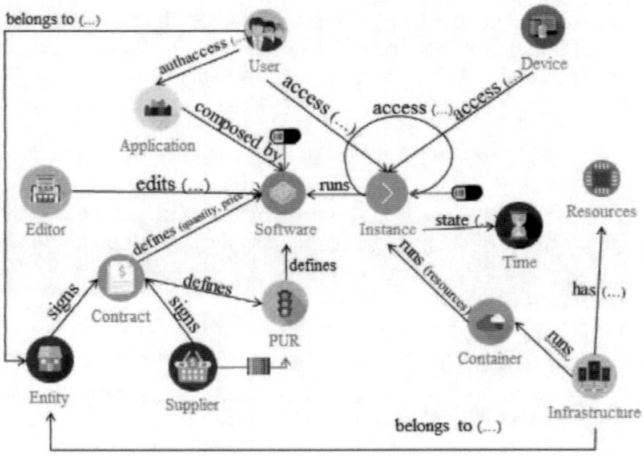


Figure 12. Graph modelization of SAM in Cloud

Graph representation makes the comparison between all software dimensions easier: looking at this model, software is logically linked to contracts, instances and user. The global picture seems to be cohesive and we can identify Software lifecycle, likewise tag's cycle. It can be read like: "Entity signs (a) Contract, which defines Software run by (a/n*) Instance(s) etc."

## IV. EVALUATION

In our preliminary evaluation, we focused on the purchase-delivery-instantiation-usage phases of our SAM model, omitting the optimization phase that remains a future work. Our objective was to validate the fact that our graph model can be managed through a capture of PaaS usages (Cloud Foundry/Abacus in our experience). To achieve this experience, we considered a well-known software: an Oracle database.

We choose the Oracle Database Enterprise Edition (Oracle DB EE) example for several reasons: (1) It is a vivid example for the SAM community; one of the most often mentioned for the complexity of its license management. (2) Oracle DB licenses can be defined by several types of metrics, oriented on material (i.e., CPU) or user (i.e., Named User Plus). (3) It will allow us to increase complexity of our use cases such as: integrating controls between product's link (options – standard product) and constraints of uses.

In this theoretical evaluation, we will follow the Software lifecycle proposed in Fig.4 and Fig.5-Fig.9 and refer to the Fig.2 SAM processes maturity scale: visibility, identification, risk management and optimization.

### 1) *Purchasing*

For the purpose of our example, we will skip the first phase of need/choice/approval, and directly start with purchasing processes.

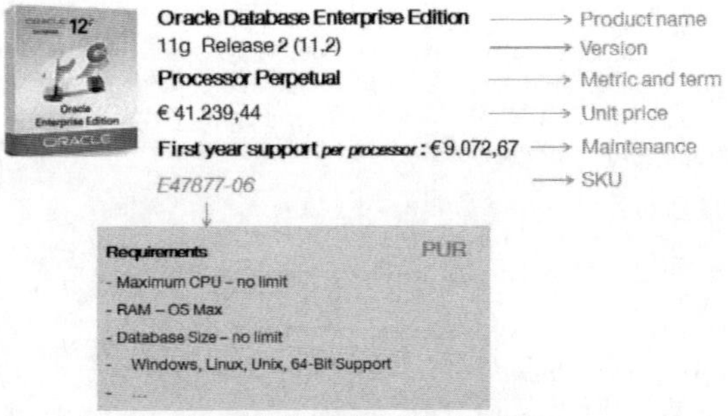


Figure 13. Example of Oracle's offer

Fig. 13 can be an extracted from "License Store's" catalogue proposing the product we need and are planning to buy.

Few elements (above) are necessary to identify precisely this offer and determine the level of grants (PUR) given by this way of licensing. These elements have to be collected in the purchase order and reconciliated with data from the delivery order. In the graph: The first step is to create our product, with a label 'Software' and several attributes found in the purchase order. In the same way, we create a label 'Retailer' and 'Editor' to identify a node 'License Store' and 'Oracle':

```
CREATE (m:Software { name : 'Oracle Database', version : '11g Release 2
(11.2)', sku:'E47877-06', category: 'Database'})
CREATE (z:Supplier {name : 'License Store'})
CREATE (n:Editor { name : 'Oracle' })
```

Then, we create several nodes with label 'PUR', which represents scope of usage, metrics, environments, etc. The idea is to create nodes, independent from products (not node properties) to allow further comparison between product, version, etc. or identify similar metrics.

```
CREATE (o:PUR {metric: 'processor', term : 'perpetual'})
CREATE (p:PUR {name: 'requirement', maximumCPU : 'no limit', RAM :
'OS max', DatabaseSize : 'no limit'})
CREATE (q:PUR {name: 'OperatingSystem', windows : 'yes', unix : 'yes',
linux : 'yes'})
```

Then, we create relations between nodes:

(1) Between an editor and product (EDITS): 'Oracle' edits 'Oracle Database'.

(2) Between a product and PUR (DEFINES): 'Oracle DB' is licensed under processor metric/ or can run on windows/Unix/Linux/etc.

(3) Between a supplier and a product (DISTRIBUTES): 'License Store' distributes 'Oracle DB'. This relation is important because contains all information about the contract: financials, number, maintenance, etc. This link may be multiple (unique relations), as many as the number of contract.

This process and collect are essential to fulfill the Identification requirements: PUR are translated in the SKU, this SKU enriches the SWIDTag delivered during provisioning processes; it guarantees the link between a contract and Software/ Software and Instance.

*2) Provisionning*

After Global sourcing processes, our Oracle Database is right now under exploitation teams' responsibility. The software can be packaged/enriched (i.e., tag) according to company's rules or considered like included in an Application before being instantiated.

In our case, let us create a label Application and a node 'HumanRessources' which we'll include in our Database.

The relations 'CONTAINS' is enriched by properties like a project's id or application's project manager:

```
CREATE (n:Application {name :'HumanRessources', responsible :'Tom'})
MATCH (a:Software),(b:Application)
WHERE a.name = 'Oracle Database' AND b.name = 'HumanRessources'
CREATE (b)-[r:CONTAINS {id_project : '1234R'}]->(a)
```

*3) Instantiation*

To fulfill the step 1 (visibility) of the maturity scale, we need to have an exhaustive view of infrastructure resources and instantiation. The PaaS handles infrastructure resources (Virtual Machine (VM), networking, storage), database instantiation, Subscription to shared services, application deployment, installation, configuration, application monitoring, application log collection and interaction with app-ops (inventory/CMDB, monitoring/alerting)

CF allows identifying allocated resources. Our experience is here restricted to PaaS layer, it would be necessary to reach underlying infrastructure (i.e., VMware, OpenStack etc.) to obtain IaaS resources. All this chain allows to keep and know information about the allocated ressources in each stage.

In our example, the application, which contains our database has been deployed on the cloud via a "push" command and ran as an instance. We stress that this instance contains metadata like SWIDTag enclosed during the provisioning. A key part is now to create links between instance and product which we bought. Everything is based on the use of SKU number. The instance knows and updates all SWIDtags of its components (i.e., Fig 14). This allows to create the link between the product in catalogue and the installed product.

| Balise | Description |
|---|---|
| entitlemet_required_indicator | true if activated/serialized<br>false if evaluation/not licensed |
| product_title | Oracle Database EE |
| product_version<br>• name<br>• numeric | <br>• chaine version<br>• numeric |
| software creator<br>• name<br>• regid | <br>Oracle<br>regid.1977.oracle |
| software licensor<br>• name<br>• regid | <br>Oracle<br>regid.1977.oracle |
| software_id | E47877-06 |
| tag_creator<br>• name<br>• regid | <br>Oracle<br>regid.1977.oracle |
| • license_linkage<br>• activation_status | evaluation/serialisez/actived/abonnement/no license |

Figure 14. SWID Tag example for Oracle DB EE

```
MATCH (i:Instance),(a:Software)
WHERE i.software_id= a.sku
CREATE (i)-[c:INSTANCES]->(a)
```

*4) Uses*

The Oracle DB is expected to be accessed by both humans and software (automated applications encompassing the optimization phase of the SAM model as described previously in the paper). Different queries can be performed on the different links of the database.

The link ACCESS/AUTHACCESS has properties that characterize the use (scope, duration, consumed resources, etc.) captured by CF and accumulated/aggregated by Abacus. The capture fulfills the step 2 of the SAM processes maturity scale.

```
MATCH (s:Software {name:'Oracle Database'})<-[:INSTANCES]-
(i:Instance)
RETURN s, i
```

*"Show me all 'INSTANCES' relation(s) to 'Oracle Database'"* will provide all instances related to Software. As we can identify the Product Usage Rights (via the SWIDTag/SKU) by a direct link between Software/PUR and Software/Instances, we can fulfill first part of the step 3 (SAM processes maturity scale): the risk management (here: counterfeit risk).

```
MATCH (i:Instance {name:'HumanRessources'})<-[:ACCESS]-(user)
RETURN i, user
```

*"Show me all 'ACCESS' relation(s) to 'HumanRessources"* will provide all access/authaccess related to Software. As we can identify the Product Usage Rights (via the SWIDTag/SKU) by a direct link between Software/PUR and Software/Access, we can fulfill second part of the step 3 (here: over-deployment risk).

*5) Basic control of inventory's consistency*

Obviously, a lot of queries would be necessary to implement true SAM analysis. For the purpose of our example, let us study quickly three of the most basic, but also the most important:

- *What I bought ?*

```
MATCH (e:Entity)-[g:SIGNS]-(c:Contract)-[r:DEFINES]->(s:Software)
MATCH (p:PUR)-[h:DEFINES]->(s) WHERE p.name='Metric'
RETURN e.name AS Entity, s.name AS Software, s.SKU AS SKU,
sum(r.quantity) AS Quantity, p.metric AS Metric,
c.date AS Date ORDER BY e.name, s.name, c.date
```

This query returns a table: the number of bought licenses order by software and metric with a list of contract per software

- *What I instanciated ?*

This query returns a table: the number of instances per software ordered by metric with collection of application containing this software.

```
MATCH (v:VM)-[t:RUNS]->(i:Instance)-[r:RUNS]->(a:Application)-
[c:COMPOSEd_BY]->(s:Software)
RETURN s.category AS Category,s.name AS Software, s.SKU AS SKU,
count(t) AS InstanceNumber, collect(distinct(a.name)) AS Application
```

- *Am I compliant ?*

This last query consists in a verification of the 'Processor' metric (typical for Oracle). Basically, we have to multiply the number of cores per processor of the physical machine hosting the DB by the number of processors and by a coefficient given by Oracle for each processor. It returns a table of licenses ordered by the software, and he number of bought/instanciated (according to Oracle licensing rules).

```
MATCH (s:Software) WITH s
MATCH (m:Machine)-[*]->(a:Application)-[co:COMPOSEd_BY]->(s)
MATCH (r:Resources)<-[h:HAS]-(m:Machine)
WITH s,((toFloat(r.core))*(toFloat(r.corefactor))*(toFloat(h.quantity))) AS
nbL, m,r
RETURN s.name as Software,s.SKU as SKU,
SUM(nbL) AS ProcessorLicenses
```

#### 6) SAM Optimization

Optimization consists, first, in automating the rise of alerts. When a countfeiting situation is detected (piracy, but mainly editor's metric misunderstanding) or when the use reaches or exceeds a fixed threshold or the level of inventories, then, purchasing/activating new licenses could be automated to adjust the license stock, in real time.

When the visibility and identification steps are mastered, optimization might consist of operating simulations: usage/instantiation captures, may reveal some possibility to renegociate a contract in a more favorable (financial) way: i.e., to change the Oracle DB negociated metric (currentlypProcessor) into another metric (i.e., Access), more appropriated to observed uses, or to project a future software/license uses based on current observed situation. This will be developped in further works.

## V. CONCLUSION

Software is not like other IT assets that can be considered as just software installation or in its intangible dimension provided by the license that defines the scope of use. Both dimensions of the software should always be considered in managing this asset. Virtualization and Cloud technologies add a new degree of complexity in the first dimension (material) when installation is disconnected from true physical infrastructure. Altogether, the complexity of software lifecycle management, the multiplication of actors in this cycle and the lack of efficient tools, lead to a disconnection between the software material and intangible dimensions.

We point out in the article the problem of software identification through its complete lifecycle and proposed a reference model or architecture for SAM to cope this complexity. This reference model also help getting a clear understanding on how SAM can be applied in the cloud computing domain. Using the Oracle DB example, we assess that our model works on simple, but vivid SAM cases, and that choice of a graph model is relevant.

Next steps will be (1) to increase complexity of the model, by implementing more complex licensing rules (2) to show more complex interface and queries allowing realistic SAM controls and optimization; (3) to measure cost of interception of SW tags; (4) to measure cost of interception of usages. Regarding step (2), considering elastic applications will be a major step.

## REFERENCES

[1] F. N. Holsing, and D. Yen, "Software Asset Management: Analysis, Development and Implementation", *Information Resources Management Journal (IRMJ) 12(3)*, pp.13, 1999

[2] M. Ben-Menachem, and G.S. Marliss, "Inventory Information Technology System: Supporting the « Paradigm of Change »", *IEEE Software*, pp.34-43, 2004

[3] M. McCarthy, and L.M. Herger, "Managing Software Assets in a Global Enterprise", *IEEE International Conference on Services Computing*, (pp. pp.560–567), 2011

[4] P. Gocek, P. Kania, B.Malecki, M. Paluch, and T. Stopa, "Obtaining software asset insight by analyzing collected metrics using analytic services", *US9424403 B2*, Available from https://www.google.com/patents/US9424403, 2014

[5] J. Disbrow, "Software vedor auditing trends : What to watch for and how to respond", *Gartner (DOI G00230816)*, 2012

[6] J-D. Lovelock, Worldwide IT Spending Forecast", *Gartner (DOI: G00323753)*, 2016

[7] C. Rudd, ITIL V3 Guide to Software Asset Management. Broché, 2013

[8]www.bmcsoftware.fr/it-solutions/asset-management.html, September, 2016

[9] www.ocsinventory-ng.org/fr/, September, 2016

[10]www.microsoft.com/fr-fr/server-cloud/products/system-center-configuration-manager/, September, 2016

[11]www.glpi-project.org/, September, 2016

[12]www.aspera.com/fr/, September, 2016

[13]www.snowsoftware.com/fr, September, 2016

[14]www.brainwaregroup.com/en/solutions/software-asset-management/spider-licence/, September, 2016

[15] www.tagvault.org, September, 2016

[16] ISO/IEC 19770-2:2015

[17]A.Hughes, Seizing Opportunity Through License Compliance. BSA, Software Alliance, 2016

[18] www.cloudfoundry.org/, September, 2016

[19]https://github.com/cloudfoundry-incubator/cf-abacus, January 2017

# Policy Based Context Aware Service Level Agreement (SLA) Management in the Cloud

Mhammed Chraibi
Abdelilah Maach
Dept of Computer Engineering
Ecole Mohammadia d'Ingénieurs
Universite Mohammed 5, Rabat, Morocco
e-mail: M.Chraibi@aui.ma

Souhail Meftah
Hamid Harroud
School of Science and Engineering
Al Akhawayn University in Ifrane
Ifrane, Morocco
e-mail: S.Meftah@aui.ma

***Abstract*—The lack of security and the inexistence of Quality of Service tracking mechanisms limit the success of cloud computing as a new technology, even if it demonstrates great capabilities of solving a number of problems that almost all organizations suffer from. This paper presents a novel way of expressing Service Level Agreements (SLAs) and tracking them to assure the client about the security and Quality of Service that are provided by the Cloud Service Provider. Allowing the client to combine specific security and Quality of Service metrics with context information within SLAs, when they are expressed as software policies, increases tremendously their expressiveness and precision.**

***Keywords—Security; Quality of Service; Service level Agreement; software policies;***

## I. INTRODUCTION

Cloud computing as a technology is changing the way Information Technology (IT) is seen by private, public, and independent organizations. None of them can survive in today's environment without heavily relying on IT. Therefore, all of them are looking for innovative ways to have their data and applications run. The quality of IT management might give them the edge that they need over the competition. Cloud computing, with the advantages it brings is, for many organizations, the most viable alternative. Having their data and applications managed by experts guaranteeing security and Quality of Service (QoS) on a pay per use basis is an incredible opportunity. Unfortunately, the fear of losing control of data and information that is not hosted locally anymore is stopping the organizations from migrating their IT to the cloud.

Our research group firmly believes that, if organizations were provided with the means to express their security and QoS needs and were able to track how well the cloud service provider is doing in taking care of those needs, they would be more willing to migrate to the cloud. The research we present in this paper consists of proposing software policies as a way to represent and manage Service Level Agreements (SLAs). The SLAs are the contract between the client and the Cloud Service Provider (CSP). The SLAs must allow the clients to express in terms of metrics what QoS and what security mean for them. In addition to that, software policies, the way we designed them, allow the integration of context information. Context awareness does not only increase the expressiveness of SLAs, but it also allows them to tackle any metrics identified to increase security and Quality of Service.

In this paper, we start by describing what we mean by context information within the cloud environment. Then, in Section III, we present our policy based, context aware Service Level Agreements design. In Section IV, we explain the reasons why we opted for a middleware to incorporate the management of SLAs in the cloud. Then, in Section V, we discuss the testing of the prototype that we built as a proof of concept. Finally, in the conclusion, we describe the future work.

## II. CONTEXT AWARENESS IN CLOUD COMPUTING

The definition of the context of an application within the cloud is an exercise that has not been done by many researchers. The reason behind this is the fact that every application within the cloud has a different role and a different context. When the cloud is used for offloading, the context of the processing done in it relates to the domain where the application operates. In this section, we will see how context information is used to improve QoS in terms of efficiency, performance, or security.

### A. *Context information for performance improvement*

Mobile Cloud Computing, for example, is currently a research hotspot. Scientists are looking into ways to allow mobile applications run their processing and data analysis in the cloud. They are aware that one of the major challenges facing them, the moment they consider offloading as an alternative, is the performance of the network. CloudAware is a context aware framework that contains a context manager entity responsible for collecting and analyzing network data to predict the status of the network at a point in time and make sure that the processing and communication of the data is done in a reasonable amount of time [1]. The context manager, once it has received the data from network sensors and other tools, performs a set of intelligent data mining operations in order to predict the future situation of the network [1]. This leads to the improvement of the overall network performance.

### B. *Context information for security management*

Context aware role based access control is the solution described by [2]. The use of context information in order to provide a personalized service and "dynamic adaptation" of access control requires collecting continuously context data. To move into useful information, a few steps are described, such as:

- Context pre-processing
- Context analyzing
- Context providing

The huge amount of data received from the different context acquiring tools (both hardware and software) is considered big data. Therefore, intelligent, machine learning algorithms are utilized by [2] in order to filter and have readily available context information. Such quality context information allows for state of the art role based access control without adding a big load to the overall system performance.

### C. Multiplicity of cloud context providers

Within a cloud environment, any context aware platform, middleware, or application needs to be able to handle incoming context data from a wide variety of sources. Depending on the nature of the source, different processing of the data may be done to be transformed into information that will be used in order to perform the appropriate actions. In [3], the authors raise the point that heterogeneity of incoming context data must be handled and they review the literature and analyze the way it is done. In the framework that they present, named MobiLife, the context data is all received by an entity called the context provider. That entity has three main responsibilities:

- It receives data from the different context sources, analyzes it, checks the ontology being used
- It advertises the availability of the context information
- It responds to requests of context information

Such a central entity is necessary because of the different sources of context data. They also mention how new needs of modeling of context data are there since context aware applications do not rely anymore on location only as it was the case previously.

## III. CONTEXT AWARE SERVICE LEVEL AGREEMENTS FOR SECURITY AND QUALITY OF SERVICE

SLAs are the contract that exists between the cloud service provider and the cloud application. The accuracy of the SLA is the key to a healthy relationship between those entities. Therefore, there is a need for a way that allows the detailed expression of SLAs and monitoring to know if the SLAs are being respected or not. In this section, we present our policy specification language that is used to represent SLAs. Then, we go deeper into the metrics that the policy specification language must allow the SLAs to express. Finally, we show examples of SLAs and how they are represented.

### A. SLA Specification Language

In a previous work, our team developed a policy specification language that allows the expression of policies to manage security in quickly changing environments [4]. Figure 1 shows the structure of the Service Level Agreement using our policy specification language.

The first Attribute of the SLA is the ID. It represents a unique identifier to each Service Level Agreement. It allows the tracking and modification of SLAs. It is the only attribute that is not assigned a value by the client. Second, every SLA has a Subject. It is the entity responsible for enforcing the policy's action. Usually, the subject is a Policy Enforcement Point (PEP) that wraps the client application. More details about the PEP are given in Section IV.

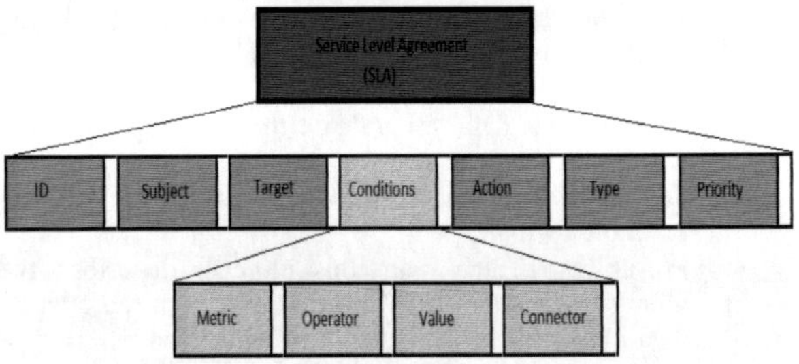


Figure 1. SLA policy based structure

The next attribute is the Target. It is the entity on which the action defined by the SLA is executed. Obviously, every Service Level Agreement contains the action itself that is triggered in case the conditions are met, and a priority that allows conflict resolution between policies. Finally, every SLA has a type. Obligation SLAs are triggered when a change in the context happens and a notification is generated. On the other hand, Authorization policies are triggered when a request, from the client application, is received asking to verify if an SLA is being respected or not.

The condition set, as shown in Figure 1, is composed of four different attributes. The major attribute is the metric that is being evaluated. It also contains the value against which the metric is compared. The comparison is done through an operator such as: greater, smaller, equal. Finally, since an SLA can have a set of conditions, they are linked using connectors. These connectors are based on First Order Logic (FOL) in order to allow for as much flexibility as possible.

### B. SLA Metrics

SLAs describe for both parties (the client and the cloud provider) expectations and act as a roadmap for change in the cloud service. Actually, just as an IT project needs a roadmap that comprises a set of clearly defined deliverables, an SLA is also crucial for working with cloud infrastructure. In fact, to develop a consistent and an effective SLA, a list of important criteria needs to be mentioned [5]. The following are some of the most important criteria:

- Availability: describes the percentage of the availability of the service agreed upon during working and non working days. For example: 99.9% during work days, 98.5% for nights/weekend.
- Performance: this element describes the maximum response times for a specific service.
- Security/privacy of the data: this element is related to the section described above concerning the confidentiality, integrity, availability, and accountability of the data stored within the cloud. An example of a rule regarding security is: encrypting all stored and transmitted data.
- Disaster Recovery expectations: this element describes the commitment sated by the cloud provider to ensure the recovery of data in case of disaster that may affect the main data center.

- Location of the data: this element describes the location where data are stored. This rule should be consistent with local legislation.
- Access to the data: this rule defines the way the client will be using to access its data. An example of this rule would be: data retrievable from provider in readable format.
- Portability of the data: this element describes the identity of another provider that may own the client's data whenever the main provider encounters a problem. In fact, it is possible for the cloud provider to not mention any other cloud provider.
- Change management process: this part deals with process a service should go through to be updated or add new functionalities.
- Exit strategy: this part describes how smooth the exit from the data center of the cloud provider is.

While going through the literature, we have identified two major categories of metrics that can be expressed within SLAs. The first category contains metrics to assess the Quality of Service offered by the CSP, while the second one contains metrics that are used to assess the security of the environment offered by the CSP. In both categories, we could subdivide the metrics based on the level of service offered by the CSP: Software as a Service (SaaS), Storage as a Service, Platform as a Service (Paas), and Infrastructure as a Service. In Figure 2, we classify the metrics that we can assess when we are considering the Quality of Service offered by the CSP.

Since security is one of the most important aspects that clients consider before making the decision to move the management of their data and services to the cloud, we have identified, in Figure 3, the different metrics that need to be expressed in an SLA to assure clients of the security of their assets.

Identifying the different metrics that need to be specified and detailed in SLAs is an important step that will allow us to design our policies. In fact, our team is still working and making progress in detailing the metrics and bringing them to a lower level of granularity. In the next section, we present two policy based SLAs in order to show the way they are represented using our policy specification language.

### C. *Examples of SLAs*

Figure 4 shows two policies that represent SLAs. We intentionally decided to give the example of a QoS SLA and the example of a security SLA.

From the first policy, the user is enforcing the fact that as agreed with the CSP, in case of maintenance work, the services of the client applications must not be down for more than 2 hours and it has to be between 3 and 5 AM. This example shows clearly how a policy can be used to combine metrics extracted from Service Level Agreement with context information (in this example, time) to express the users preferences in terms of Quality of Service. The second policy, on the other hand, deals exclusively with a security issue management. The user wants to be notified in the case of an intrusion detection where the latency of response is more than 80ms. The choice of then 80ms is specific to the client's own knowledge about the application. Finally, from the two examples, we demonstrate how clients can express their Quality of Service requirements and security requirements using software policies. These policies are a representation of the Service Level Agreement between the client and the cloud service provider.

In the next section, we will show the architecture of our system and explain how the policy based SLA management system fits within the cloud environment.

## IV. SLA MANAGEMENT WITHIN THE CLOUD

### A. *Opting for a Middleware Solution*

Our policy based security management system was previously used within the context of mobile computing. When we started thinking of re-modeling it to adapt to the needs of cloud environment, the question of how to insert the software in the cloud was raised. When we were dealing with mobile environments, one of the major concerns that arose was the amount of processing needed by the system versus the mobile device's computing power and battery life. We are not the only ones who struggled with such an issue. In [8], the authors show that there is a direct impact of offloading on energy saving in mobile devices. Computation offloading is defined as "sending heavy computation to resourceful servers and receiving the results from these servers" [9]. In other words, instead of having the heavy computations take place at the level of the mobile device, given that there is an Internet connection available, and a safe medium to transmit the data and instructions, the computations can be delegated to a powerful server (or the cloud). The results can then be sent back to the mobile device. In the same line, researchers have proposed frameworks for developing software to make use of offloading.

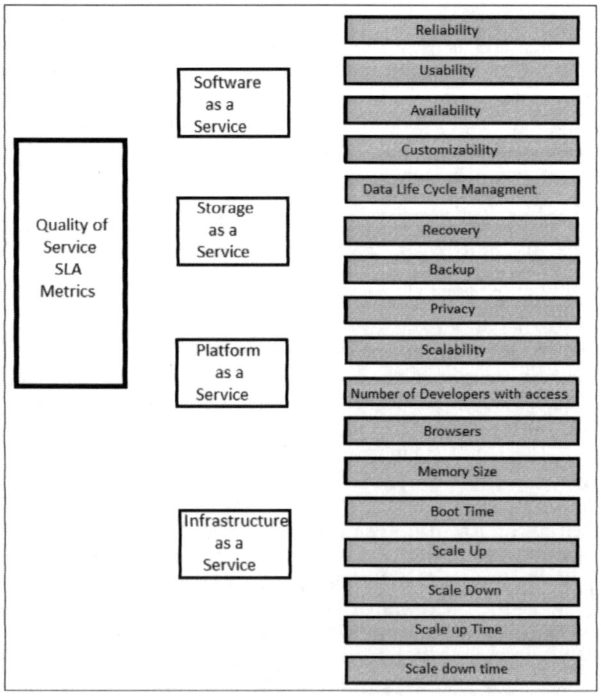


Figure 2. Quality of Service SLA metrics [6]

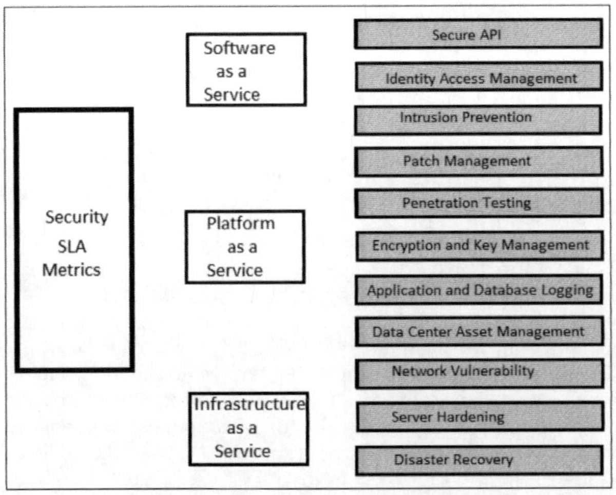


Figure 3. Security SLA metrics [7]

In [10], for example, a framework was tested to considerably reduce execution time of different types of applications given that a fast and reliable network connection is available between the mobile device and the server.

Learning from that experience, we decided that the policy based security management in the cloud should offload client applications from SLA management and the processing it incurs. Using a middleware is the best way to offer to cloud client applications. Since both the middleware and the applications are run by the same physical platform, the issue of latency in response that existed in mobile environments [11][12] does not exist anymore. Figure 5 shows how our system fits within the cloud.

### B. *Middleware Architecture*

The middleware contains three main components, as we can see from Figure 5. We have described in detail each one of them in our previous work [4]. The major tasks performed by each one of them are summarized as follows:

- Tool Abstraction Layer (TAL): This component is responsible for collecting context data. This context data can be obtained by software tools just like it can be obtained by Radio Frequency IDentification (RFID) readers or other hardware tools. The tool abstraction feeds the received data to the context and services management system.

- Context and services management system receives data from the TAL and transforms it into useful (needed) context information. It does so by processing the data through the following services:
  - Data transformation services
  - Data dissemination services
  - Data filtering services
  - Data aggregation services
  - Duplicate removal services
  - Data replacement services

  The way the services are managed is also through policies.


```
<?xml version="1.0" encoding="UTF-8"?>
<aui>
 - <SLA>
     <id>4</id>
     <type>obligation</type>
     <subject>client1_PEP</subject>
     <target>client1_NotificationManager.exe</target>
     <action>SendNotification.Code4111()</action>
     <priority>8</priority>
     <audit>yes</audit>
     <active>yes</active>
   - <conditions>
       <condition>Maintenance_status equal Ended AND</condition>
       <condition>System_timezone equal GMT AND</condition>
       <condition>Server_downLength greater 2hrs OR</condition>
       <condition>Server_downHour Less 3AM OR</condition>
       <condition>Server_downHour greater 5AM</condition>
     </conditions>
   </SLA>
 - <SLA>
     <id>5</id>
     <type>obligation</type>
     <subject>client1_PEP</subject>
     <target>client1_NotificationManager.exe</target>
     <action>SendNotification.Code4112()</action>
     <priority>6</priority>
     <audit>yes</audit>
     <active>yes</active>
   - <conditions>
       <condition>IntrusionDetection_Status equal True AND</condition>
       <condition>IntrusionDetection_latency greater 80ms OR</condition>
     </conditions>
   </SLA>
</aui>
```


Figure 4. QoS and Security SLA example

- Policy management system contains the following:
  - Policy Decision Point (PDP): Entity responsible for checking the data provided in a request or a context change notification against the client's policies. The PDP then enforces the action of the policy or not.
  - Policy manager: Entity responsible for adding policies, removing policies, or updating policies.
  - Policy conflict manager: Entity responsible for resolving conflict between different policies whose conditions are met and that need to be triggered.
  - Policy information base: this entity is a repository where all policies are stored.

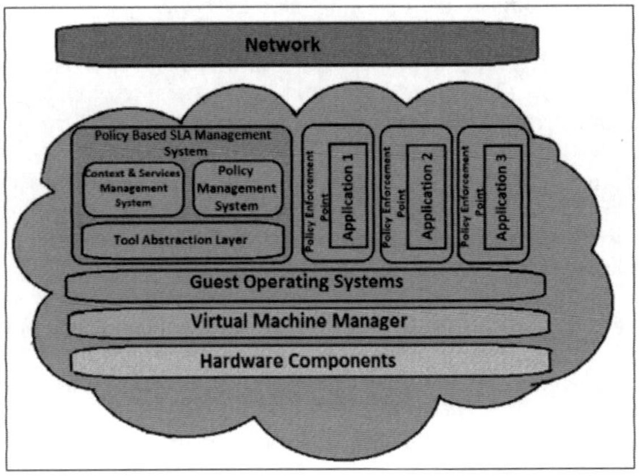


Figure 5. Policy based SLA management system in the cloud

- Policy Enforcement Points (PEP): are wrapping entities that have access to enforce policy actions on the target entities. This access is provided by the client applications through method calls.

Our team has developed a prototype for the middleware and we started proceeding with the evaluation and testing, as we show in the next section.

## V. SLA MANAGEMENT MIDDLEWARE EVALUATION AND TESTING

The International Organization for Standardization (ISO) and the International Electrotechnical Commission (IEC), in the standard ISO/IEC 9126, later on revised to ISO/IEC 25010:2011, identified the different criteria to evaluate the quality of a software as being: Functionality, Reliability, Usability, Efficiency, Maintainability, and Portability [13]. In this section, we will discuss how our middleware performs in each one of those categories keeping in mind that we are talking about a prototype meant for the sole purpose of building a proof of concept.

### A. Functionality

The Policy based security management system is responsible for managing and enforcing the SLA policies provided by the client application. In that sense, once the policies are obtained from the client, they are stored in the policy information base and retrieved for evaluation when a request pertaining to the client is received. In our software, only the policies that have as a target the client's application are retrieved, each one of the conditions is checked against the data in our context base and a decision on whether the action of the policy is to be triggered or not is made. Therefore, the middleware fulfills the functionality for which it was designed in terms of suitability and accuracy.

The quality of the context information is managed by the software policies that deal with the requests incoming from the different software tools that provide us with raw data. There are some cases, where a piece of data comes only from one source where it might be given by the CSP itself. For example, the data about availability of the cloud services is posted every month on the website of the cloud service provider. We have not yet identified a tool that can provide us with such an information. Therefore, our context base is fed with data coming from the website of the service provider. Since this process is public, it is up to the client to choose whether to rely on the accuracy of that data in order to formulate their policies of Service Level Agreements. Finally, the policy based security management middleware still fulfills its functionality.

The system is reliable because no external entity can interfere with its processing. The policy management entity and context management entity only receive requests that come from the Policy Enforcement Point, which is part of the middleware. Therefore, the system is reliable and will perform the expected actions the way it was designed to.

### B. Reliability

In the context of the discussion, the real threat to reliability is the interaction between the PEP and the client application, and the way the PEP intercepts the incoming requests, models them and forwards them to the policy decision point. The communication protocol between the PEP and the client application (it is also the process by which an application registers to the services of the middleware) is part of the future work. As for metrics such as maturity, and fault recovery we will only be able to test for them when we deploy on the cloud.

### C. Maintainability

When we were thinking of the maintainability of the middleware, only one thing came to mind: we have designed the software for maintainability. Policy based systems are by definition maintainable. Since they are managed by policies, to maintain the software all that is required is remove the obsolete policies and replace them with updated versions. In terms of Analyzability, the accountability tag on the policies (audit tag) allows the system to keep track of all the policies whose actions have been triggered. Once new policies are in place it is straight forward to design requests that will test the impact of the policies on the system. Several scenarios have been described before showing how we can use requests to test the policies; therefore, we can say that the system is changeable and stable. As for testability, we have run several performance tests and the results are shown below.

### D. Usability & Portability

The programming language and programming platform that we have used are synonyms of portability. The JAVA language and J2EE environment need no introduction and one of their major advantages is portability. As for usability, the client applications, once they have submitted their security policies, their interaction will remain with the Policy enforcement point. A graphical user interface is being developed in order to allow the clients to express their business rules and have them translated into software policies. The user interface is meant to be as user friendly as possible. All the translation into the policy attributes and XML will be transparent to the user.

### E. Efficiency (Performance)

One of the major motivations behind opting for the middleware as a way to include the policy based SLA management middleware in the cloud is to offload the tracking and management of SLAs from the client applications. The moment we think about offloading, we want to know how much extra processing time will incur when the services of our middleware are being used. For performance testing, Table 1 shows the platform that we have used.

TABLE I. TESTING ENVIRONMENT

| | |
|---|---|
| **CPU** | Intel core i5 3221M 2.5Ghz |
| **RAM** | 4 GB |
| **Operating System** | Windows 8 professional (64bits version) |
| **IDE** | Netbeans 8.0.2 |

In the first scenario, we wanted to investigate the impact of having multiple clients in our system on the performance of the system with regards to the requests received for a specific client. In the scenario, we have designed 100 policies and we sent 20 requests. During the first run, all the 100 policies belong to client 1. Then, we keep only 80 policies from client 1 (the one to whom the requests are directed) and we add 20 new policies from 4 other clients and we see the impact it has on the average request processing time. We continue using the same technique and, at each step, we reduce the number of policies of client 1 by 20 and increase the other clients' policies by 20. The results are shown in Figure 6.

We see from the graph that the processing time per request decreases with the number of client policies. The more policies we have, the more conditions we check the request against and therefore the more processing time is required. What is interesting for us to see is compare these results with the equivalent ones in the previous figures. That comparison can give us an idea about the impact of having multiple clients versus having one single client on the overall performance.

In the second scenario, we send 20 requests when client 1 owns 60 policies, when he/she owns 40 policies, and when he/she owns 20 policies. Figure 7 shows the average response time when the user is the only client in the environment versus when the environment is shared.

When we first look at Figure 7, we are surprised to see that the response time in shared environment is less than the one in the environment where a client is alone. But the tendency changes as we increase the number of policies. This is explained by the nature of policies. It just happens that the policies used in the first test (20 requests, 20 policies in a non-shared environment) contained more conditions leading to a higher processing time. When we increase the number of policies, it normalizes the number of conditions within a

| Client 1 policies/ other client policies | Response time (ms) |
|---|---|
| 100/0 | 128 |
| 80/20 | 127 |
| 60/40 | 112 |
| 40/60 | 62 |
| 20/80 | 47 |

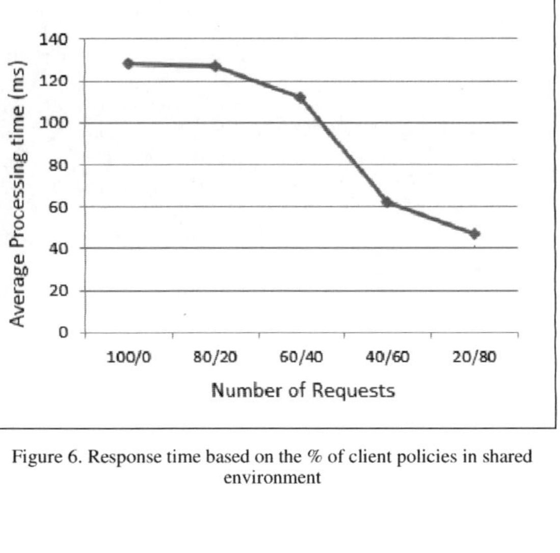


Figure 6. Response time based on the % of client policies in shared environment

policy and makes the performance in shared environments less than the one in non-shared environments. The reason behind that is the time that is used in selecting the client policies.

## VI. CONCLUSION

Policy based management has proven efficient in many environments. First, we have used policies to manage security in mobile environments. Then, we adapted our work to the context of security management in the cloud. Here, we are modeling and testing the management of Service Level Agreements. Next, we are investigating policy based management in mobile cloud computing. Also, the next step in our project is to devise a set of policies that would express the needs of Quality of Service and security for a real life client. At the university, we have a private cloud which is the ideal environment for us to perform the necessary set of tests in order to see how the system performs.

| Number of Policies | Response time (ms) Shared Environment | Response time (ms) Non Shared Env |
|---|---|---|
| 20 | 47 | 69 |
| 40 | 62 | 73 |
| 60 | 112 | 104 |

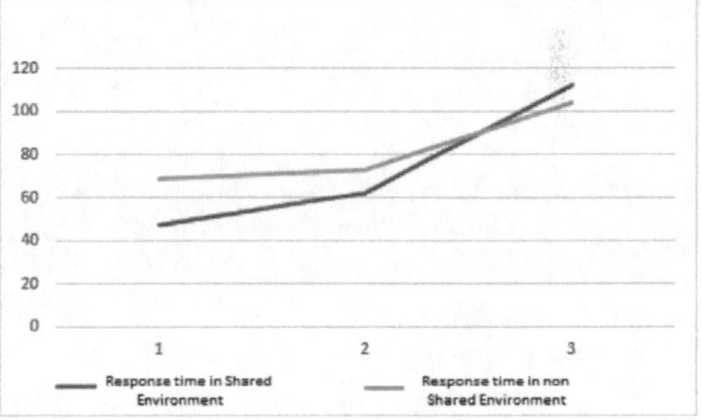


Figure. 7. Performance in shared environment Vs non-shared environment

## REFERENCES

[1] G. Orsini, D. Bade, and W. Lamersdorf, "Cloudaware: Towards context adaptive mobile cloud computing," in IFIP/IEEE IM 2015: 7th Intern.Workshop on Management of the Future Internet (ManFI), 2015.

[2] S. Hiray and R. Ingle, "Context-aware middleware in cyber physical cloud (CAMCPC)". Proceedings of the 2013 International Conference on Cloud & Ubiquitous Computing & Emerging Technologies (CUBE)", Pune, India, 15–16 November 2013, pp. 42–47.

[3] N. Gupta and A. Agrawal, "Context Aware Mobile Cloud Computing: Review", 2nd International Conference on Computing for Sustainable Global Development (INDIACom), pp. 1061–1065, 2015

[4] M. Chraibi, H. Harroud, and M. Maach, "Personalized security in mobile environment using software policies", UBICOMM 2011 : The Fifth International Conference on Mobile Ubiquitous Computing, Systems, Services and Technologies, Nov 2011, Lisbon, Portugal.

[5] http://www.facilities.ac.uk/j/free-cpd/155-slas-and-service-specifications, retrieved: December, 2016

[6] M. Alhamad, T. Dillon, and E. Chang, "Conceptual SLA framework for cloud computing", 4th IEEE International Conference on Digital Ecosystems and Technologies, 2010, doi:10.1109/dest.2010.5610586

[7] M. Hoehl, "Proposal for standard Cloud Computing Security SLAs - Key Metrics for Safeguarding Confidential Data in the Cloud", Used from:

https://isc.sans.edu/forums/news/Proposal+for+standard+Cloud+Computing+Security+SLAs+Key+Metrics+for+Safeguarding+Confidential+Data+in+the+Cloud/893991/studies on magneto-optical media and plastic substrate interface", IEEE, retrieved: December, 2016

[8] K. Kumar and Y. Lu, "Cloud computing for mobile users: Can offloading computation save energy?" IEEE Comput, pp. 51–56, 2010

[9] K. Kumar, J. Liu, Y. Lu, and B. Bhargava, "A Survey of Computation Offloading for Mobile Systems", In the Journal of Mobile Networks and Applications, Springer, pp. 129–140, 2012.

[10] E. Cuervo, "MAUI: Making Smartphones Last Longer with Code Offload", Proc. 8th ACM MobiSys, 2010

[11] C. Shi, K. Habak, P. Pandurangan, M. Ammar, E. Zegura, and M. Naik, "Cosmos: Computation offloading as a service for mobile devices", ACM MobiHoc, 2014

[12] H. Flores, S. N. Srirama and R. Buyya, "Computational offloading or data binding? bridging the cloud infrastructure to the proximity of the mobile user", Proceedings 2nd IEEE International Conference on Mobile Cloud Computing, Services, and Engineering, 2014

[13] http://www.iso.org/iso/catalogue_detail.htm?csnumber=35733, retrieved: December, 2016

# Advancing the Micro-CI Testbed for IoT Cyber-Security Research and Education

William Hurst, Nathan Shone & Abdennour El Rhalibi,
Department of Computer Science
Liverpool John Moores University
Byrom Street
Liverpool, L3 3AF, UK
{W.Hurst, N.Shone, A.Elrhalibi}@ljmu.ac.uk

Andreas Happe
AIT Austrian Institute of Technology, Austria
andreas.happe@ait.ac.at

Ben Kotze
Department of Electrical, Electronic and Computer Engineering,
Central University of Technology, Free State, South Africa
bkotze@cut.ac.za

Bob Duncan
Computer Science
University of Aberdeen
Aberdeen, UK
Email: bobduncan@abdn.ac.uk

***Abstract*— Physical testbeds offer the ability to test out cyber-security practices, which may be dangerous to implement in a real-life scenario. They also provide a means to educate students and researchers on effective cyber-defence practices. However, the majority of existing non-virtualised physical testbeds are costly, inaccessible, and are often location constrained. As such, modern education and research for control system security is becoming increasingly reliant on virtualised labs and tools. Any learning or research undertaken using these tools, however, is based around the limitations and characteristics of such tools, as well as any assumptions made by their developers. Virtual testbeds are not perfect. Additionally, the accuracy of data resulting from emulations and models may be further decreased if used outside of their intended usage scenario. As such, this paper presents a discussion on the effectiveness of physical testbeds over simulation approaches. In addition, an approach for the design and construction of a replicable, cost-effective testbed for cyber-security education and training is presented.**

***Keywords—Testbed, Cyber-Security, Education***

## I. INTRODUCTION

Simulation-based testbeds are used to construct data for cyber-security experimentation, testing and education purposes [1]. A virtualised approach offers significant cost savings and a self-paced and active approach to learning. However, it has several key limitations including: no hands-on experience, no real-world training with specific equipment and no experience in identifying and interpreting incorrect or uncharacteristic data. Simulation is effective at representing *'correct'* behaviour. However, critical infrastructure systems need to be protected against situations where they are exposed to extreme abnormal events. Unfortunately, in such circumstances, systems do not always behave in the way expected or respond in the same consistent manner. Similarly, it is therefore difficult to accurately model how a system's erratic behaviour might cascade and impact other parts of the infrastructure.

Additionally, a simulation testbed approach is constructed through the developer's mental model of how the system functions. In result, the data generated is constructed. Whereas, in a physical approach, data is, instead, captured. This can be for example, communication, control and physical system characteristics in a unified environment [2]. Both simulation data and captured data are used for research purposes [3]. Captured, also known as observational data, is generally irreplaceable and tends to offer further realistic analysis over simulation approaches. Yet, simulation is mainly used, as testing in '*real*' scenarios has the potential to impact human well-being [4]. For that reason, testbed projects are often presented to bridge the cyber-physical divide and offer a safe environment for cyber-security testing and training [5]. However, many existing approaches, as outlined in the related research section, are either costly, not-replicable or involve an element of simulation in their design.

The research presented in this paper provides an ideal solution. The practical element involved in the Micro-CI project introduces a level of realism that is difficult to match through simulation alone. As such, this project provides innovative research opportunities for the testing and development of security enhancements in a real-life scenario. This is evaluated through a cyber-attack case study, to demonstrate the capability to construct different data set types. As such, the aim of the research is to have a practical output; a fully working critical infrastructure testbed named Micro-CI. The goal is to demonstrate the suitability of the datasets generated by the Micro-CI testbed for the following advantages.

- Pedagogical benefits: Research has shown that practical learning opportunities are vital to students becoming comfortable with cyber-security concepts. In addition, users will learn the functioning of infrastructures and their security systems through reverse engineering. A lack of experience produces immaturity for systems understanding, in an era where cyber-security experts are in high demand [6];
- Cost effectiveness: Project has been designed to be as cost effective as possible. We estimate that at the time of writing the paper, replicating the experiments can be achieved for under £100;
- Portability and Dataset: As the project components are on a miniaturised bench-top scale, it enables them to be packed away, stored and transported with ease. Projects can still be moved and/or stored whilst partially assembled. We envision that the testbed can be purchased

and assembled by other researchers in the future. In addition, as outlined later in the paper, the amount of real data which can be generated in a relatively short time period offers advantages over larger testbed constructions.

The remainder of this paper is organised as follows. Section 2 presents an insight into the motivation behind this work and a discussion on related projects. Section 3 details the approach taken for the Micro-CI testbed development. Section 4 presents an evaluation and the paper is concluded in Section 5.

## II. BACKGROUND

Internet of Things (IoT) is growing as a new model for the expansion of the Internet, and can be held as the next revolution in distributed systems and pervasive computing technologies. It is predicted that in the next decade, it will transform everything in people's everyday lives due its major influence on so many areas of the industry: critical infrastructure, education, healthcare, city management, business, innovation, community, cultural heritage and many more. In this new emerging technology, IoT would be effortlessly assimilated within data science infrastructures, producing data and generating knowledge. Traditionally, data was stored upon few centralised hosts. All connections to them were protected by perimeter security, connected clients themselves were input/output devices with very limited capabilities. Security mostly focused upon the few centralised components.

### A. *The Cyber-Threat*

As technology moved onwards, things became decentralised. Desktop computers, with their myriad of installed software systems and applications, and often lacking professional administrative care, became a new battle ground. In hindsight, this was an evolutionary step that led to even more decentralised networks; the current manifestation being the internet of things (IoT) and connected industrial control systems (ICS). Initially, these were attacked too, e.g., Stuxnet [15] or reports of attacks against honeypots posing as nuclear power plants. However, recently, they have also become weapons that endanger other systems too – they are now commonly part of large distributed high-bandwidth distributed denial of service (DDoS) attack botnets [16]. There's an abundance of insecure IoT and ICS devices, fitting to a common cloud-theme. For example, one can currently buy a botnet-as-a-sevice for around $7500 for a 100000 device botnet.

While decentralisation is still the best hope in the face of state-based offensive actors, its security implications still need further analysis. With the rise of desktop computers, attackers started to pivot between captured desktops, utilising retrieved credentials to move between networks and gain further data. To prevent these attacks, security on and between desktops was improved. Personal firewalls and malware detection tools were deployed on desktops; network segregation and traffic scanning was performed between them. This reduced the available attack surface.

IoT and ICS now introduce even more communication paths, while the IoT/ICS devices themselves are sometimes lacking resources for essential security tasks. This allows attackers to traverse more freely between devices while the devices themselves are worse protected when compared to traditional computers and servers. The latter is not just due to reduced performance; IoT devices employ different hardware architectures, some of the most commonly used architectures lack hardware support for basic hardware security techniques such as memory protection. This is related to the monetary and power consumption related requirements. While desktop computers are always connected to a power outlet and may (now) cost a substantial amount of money, IoT devices are power limited or run on battery-power and must not cost more than a couple of dollars. Power utilisation might be of higher importance than security.

Another distinction is their usage pattern. Desktops are personal computers, named due to their direct usage through human users. IoT/ICS devices are often not directly monitored by users. While security problems can ultimately be of the highest consequences, they might not be detected immediately. Even if faults are detected, end users might not have the means of easily updating those systems. While a desktop computer is built by commodity hardware and runs (mostly) standard software, IoT and ICS devices are often build for a special purpose and employ special software. If the vendor ceases product support, the device will gain additional security problems that might not be solvable over time.

Educational material must adapt to this new reality. In particular, they should focus on the distributed nature of deployed systems and not on a single high-value target. The interaction between the control system and distributed "*cheap*" and insecure sensors should be part of any testbed. Simulation of update mechanisms and transport mechanisms that are not standard Ethernet cables should be included to resemble the real world. We fear, that without an adequate testbed the next generation of defensive IT professionals will have an even harder task as the current generation already has.

The growing cyber-threat has led to a switch in research focus from physical protection to digital infrastructure security measures. However, this cyber-security research is hampered by a lack of realistic experimental data and opportunities to test new theories in a real-world environment.

### B. *Related Projects*

For that reason, projects such as SCADAVT, have developed simulation-based testbeds, which builds upon the CORE emulator, for building realistic SCADA models [7]. In their approach, Almalawi *et al.*, develop a framework to construct a water distribution system [7]. The testbed consists of SCADA components, including the Modbus/TPC slave and master, and the Modbus/TPC HNI server. Functioning together, the testbed employs the use of the dynamic link library (DLL) of EPANET to simulate the water flow within the system. The testbed combines the use of existing techniques to produce a novel testbed application. The system tested through a case study involving a DDoS attack to demonstrate that convincing data-construction is possible. Software-based simulation data, such as this approach, is often used to test theoretical cyber-security systems; however, the data is constructed through emulators.

Examples of simulation approaches include a SCADA-testbed constructed using TrueTime, and Matblab Simulink. In their research, Farooqui *et al.*, discuss the effectiveness of TrueTime, which is used for simulating controller task network transmissions and continuous plant dynamics [8]. To evaluate their testbed, two varied DoS attack scenarios are conducted. The first is an attack on the PID Controllers, the second involves the generation of false control signals for a specific actuator node. Whilst, the research is noteworthy, in that TrueTime can be used to model network data to a detailed level. This means that a close evaluation of the effects of 2 different DoS attacks can be understood when affecting the normal system behaviour. There is, however, no comparison with a physical application presented. Meaning that, the mental model of the researchers is being evaluated.

PentesterLab, is an online tool for educating users on exploiting SQL injections in a PHP-based website [9]. The idea is to educate how the technique can be used for gaining access to administration pages. Unlike the above simulation approaches, PentesterLabs, has a focus on education and teaching about the techniques used to implement an attack. Whilst beneficial for an attack, there is a limited realism as the application is set to a predefined attack scenario.

Other projects do recognise the need to integrate physical components into testbed developments. For example, Van Leeuwen *et al.*, propose a methodology, which is a hybrid testbed combining real and simulated components [10]. The idea, much like the research presented in this paper, is to develop a testbed, which is transportable and functions on a single unified-platform. The main challenge faced by the hybrid approach, as detailed, is that the simulated components must be able to cope with the real-time functionality of the physical components. To compensate for this, estimation algorithms are implemented in order to support the real-time functionality of the simulation.

This type of approach is referred to as cyber-physical, where an amalgamation of both simulation tools and physical components are merged to develop a testbed. One of the more advanced cyber-physical-based testbeds is detailed by Siaterlis *et al.*, who present an emulation-capable testbed construction termed EPIC [11]. The testbed is able to recreate the cyber-part of interconnected critical infrastructures and makes use of multiple software simulators to represent physical components. The testbed demonstrates effective results under cyber-security experimentation. However, the technical construction of the testbed means that it would not be an ideal tool for pedagogical use and the replicability would be unfeasible.

Physical testbed constructions are common place, but often are bespoke and expensive to recreate. Heracleous *et al.*, for example, detail the design and construction of a critical infrastructure testbed, which is able to emulate the operation and faults commonly found in a water supply system, such as leaks or pump and value faults [12]. Specifically, the testbed emulates a small-scale version of a city water supply system. The system, makes use of tanks, pipes, pumps and valves to process the water. A SCADA system is in place to act as the control system software. However, whilst the testbed is an effective achievement, the large-scale implementation of the device, with for example 15000 m3 tanks in place, means that replicability costs would be high and not accessible to the average researcher. The nature of the testbed also means that it is confined to one critical infrastructure type and is not adaptable to additional critical infrastructure varieties or indeed capable of experiments on networked critical infrastructures.

### C. *Discussion*

To summarise, by using simulation-based techniques, a hands-on learning experience is missed. This can be an integral experience for understanding effective cyber-security practices and techniques. It also means that the development of new and innovative cyber defence systems are tested against mental models as opposed to a real-world scenario. In addition, the background research presented above, has also led us to believe, that while effective physical testbeds are in existence, there is limited access and replicability for researchers and students. As such, we consider also the following main challenges related to cyber-security education.

- Traditional school education is limited, even security certifications are seldom hands-on. While applicable for managerial roles, this is not sufficient for technical personnel;
- Traditional virtual machine-based labs focus upon single high-value targets. This does not resemble the IoT with its multitude of connected devices. Some labs, e.g., Offensive Security Certified Professional (OSCP), do offer advanced functions in this pivotal area, but they mostly focusing upon segregated networks;
- Traditional protection techniques are not 100% fitting for IoT. Hardware architectures sometimes lack basic hardware requirements for security techniques, e.g., IoT CPUs often lack a Memory Management Unit (MMU) and thus cannot perform memory protection. Power usage is more important than security;
- Typical web-application centric testbeds do focus on web-application technologies. Within IoT and ICS there is a development back to insecure technologies like telnet, etc.;
- IoT and ICS have the same update problem as mobile devices. For example, the process for automatically installing updates. These update procedures can be attacked by offensive actors.

As such, in the following section, our approach is put forward for the development of a hackable and replicable testbed for cyber-security training and education.

## III. APPROACH

The testbed will be developed based on the Semantic sensor networks (SSN) [17], which was proposed by the W3C semantic sensor network incubator group (SSN-XG) [18], to describe and discover IoT devices and their data.

### A. Previous Implementation

In our past work, we presented the design of a rudimentary water distribution plant testbed [13]. As illustrated in Figure 1, there are two reservoir tanks, which are fed by two pumps moving water from external sources. The remote terminal unit is used to monitor the outgoing flow rate and water level, to dynamically adjust the pump speed ensuring adequate replenishment of the reservoir tanks. However, vulnerabilities exist in the system, meaning that it is possible for an external source to cut off the water supply or flood the reservoir tanks.

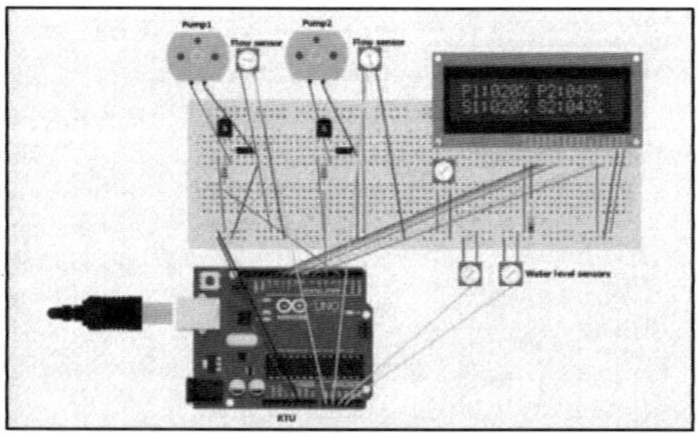

Figure 1. Physical wiring schematics

This can be achieved by switching off or speeding up either of the pumps used to control the water flow. The practical implementation of the testbed includes the following physical components: an Arduino Uno Rev. 3 as the RTU, two 12v peristaltic pumps as the water pumps, two liquid flow meters, two water level sensors, two amplification transistors, diodes, resistors and an LCD. In the schematics shown in Figure 1, potentiometer symbols have been used in place of sensors; this is due to the limited symbols available in the blueprint software. As the maximum output of the Arduino is only 5v, transistors amplify this to the 12v required by the pumps. Lastly, the diodes are used to ensure the current can only travel in one direction, thus preventing damage to the Arduino.

The hardware specification used is modest, meaning there is scope for future expansion; yet is sufficient in size to produce realistic infrastructure behaviour datasets for research purposes. The construction is displayed in Figure 2. For the purpose of this experiment, the Arduino board remains connected to a PC via a USB cable (although this could be replaced with a network connection for similar experiments). The system is also inactive. Through this USB connection, a serial connection is established to supply a real-time data feed, which is recorded and preserved by the PC (as illustrated in Figure 2).

Figure 2. Testbed Construction

The metrics collected in this instance include: Water level sensor1/2 readings, Flow meter1/2 readings and Pump1/2 speeds. These readings are taken from each sensor every 0.25 seconds (4Hz) and written to the serial data stream.

### B. Implementation

The above testbed can be used for simple data collection, which in turn can be used to understand simple cyber-attack behaviours, such as Distributed Denial of Service (DDoS) attacks [14]. However, to advance this, the testbed must be open to penetration testing experimentation and further realistic attack scenario creation. To achieve this, we incorporated an Internet of Things approach. Specifically, the testbed was made Internet-ready with the integration of a webpage which allows for the control of the individual device components. The framework layout is presented in Figure 3.

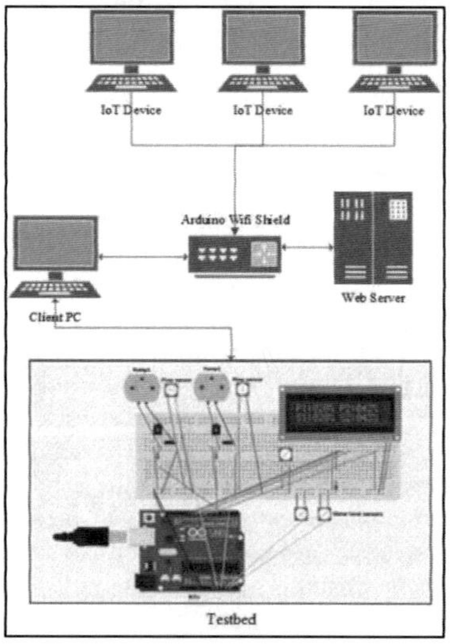


Figure 3. IoT Framework

To begin with, a webpage, which can be used to control a light on the Arduino board and a basic HTML page with buttons to turn it on an off was set up. This enables the possibility to add pumps/flow controls/etc. and control them through the web page. Other IoT devices can connect to the webserver through the Arduino Ethernet shield, which is where security and penetration testing can take place. The Arduino Ethernet shield provides access to the web server and the testbed. The Client PC displays the control screen for the testbed. Figure 4 displays the IoT setup, where the phone in the middle (which can also be replaced with a raspberry pi instead) represents the web server (1) and it is accessed through the Arduino's wifi shield (2). The laptop and second phone (3) represent other IoT devices which can connect to the webserver, if given the correct IP address. At this stage it becomes possible to integrate security, firewall and intrusion detection systems to identify unauthorised access of the web page.

Figure 4. Testbed Extension

Specifically, the proposed system focuses on a water distribution plant; however, the design is extendable and testbeds can be extended to incorporate other infrastructure types, such as an ecologically-aware power plant.

## IV. EVALUATION

This testbed is evaluated through the demonstration of a Distributed Denial of Service attack.

### A. *Test Case Scenario*

The metrics collected in this instance include: Water level sensor1/2 readings, Flow meter1/2 readings and Pump1/2 speeds. These readings are taken from each sensor every 0.25 seconds (4Hz) and written to the serial data stream.

To examine the quality of the data produced by the Micro-CI implementation, a dataset was recorded over the period of 1 hour. During this time, the testbed was operating under normal parameters (i.e. no cyber-attacks were present). Essentially, this means that the pump speeds are configured to slowly continue filling the tanks at a controlled speed until full (even if no water is being used) and to cover the current rate of water consumption (if possible). The outflow (water being consumed) is a randomly applied value within a specific range (to make usage patterns more realistic). In this instance, the water source pipe is 60% smaller than the outflow pipe, which allows for a more accurate representation of overflow.

The initial configuration of the testbed was as follows: Tank1 is 65% full, Tank2 is 69.9% full, Outflow1 is functioning at 20 + (1-35)% of capacity and Outflow 2 is operating at 30 + (1-35)% of capacity. A small sample of the data obtained at 00:10.5 of run time is shown in Table 1. From this dataset, we can see that there is no significant variation present in the data. We can also see that all the metrics maintain consistent trends in operation.

TABLE I – PHYSICAL TESTBED DATA SAMPLE (%)

| Sample (*t*) | P1 | P2 | P3 | P4 | P5 | P6 |
|---|---|---|---|---|---|---|
| **00:10.5** | 65.0 | 69.9 | 47.3 | 55.4 | 81.9 | 85.1 |
| **00:10.7** | 65.0 | 69.9 | 39.4 | 48.5 | 74.1 | 78.8 |
| **00:11.0** | 65.0 | 69.9 | 39.4 | 53.4 | 74.1 | 83.1 |
| **00:11.2** | 65.0 | 69.9 | 33.6 | 50.5 | 69.0 | 81.1 |
| **00:11.5** | 65.0 | 69.9 | 41.4 | 39.7 | 76.0 | 70.2 |

Components:

- P1 - Water Level 1 - this depicts the water level in tank one.
- P2 - Water Level 2 - this depicts the water level in tank two.
- P3 - Water Flow 1 - this refers to the flow rate through pipe one.
- P4 - Water Flow 2 - this refers to the flow rate through pipe two.
- P5 - Pump Speed 1 - this is the operating speed of pump one which controls the flow of water from tank one.
- P6 - Pump Speed 2 - this is the operating speed of pump two which controls the flow of water from tank two.

For this case study, data for the water distribution plant is recorded whilst operating under normal conditions. This allows for the building of a behavioural norm profile for the system, in order to identify anomalies. Within the testbed, during the DDoS attack, only intermittent readings from the sensors are received, forcing it to make drastic (and therefore uncharacteristic) changes to the pump speeds, rather than gradual as when operating as normal. In this cyber-attack dataset, a DDoS attack is launched against the RTU's communications channel, so it is only able to get sensor readings intermittently. Whilst no new values are readily available, the RTU will continue to maintain the previous pump speed.

In Figure 5, the components are displayed along the x-axis, with labels 1 to 6. The y-axis displays the operating capacity of the component. The exact behaviour induced by this experiment was relatively unknown. The results obtained showed that one tank kept filling whilst the other maintained the same level. As such, Figure 5 displays box plots of the distribution values for the testbed data for normal behaviour.

Figure 6 displays the alteration in data when in a cyber-attack scenario. The change in behaviour, as a result of the attack, can be seen in the average value changes in the datasets, as previously for the simulation dataset. Particularly a change in the output for P5 is visually apparent.

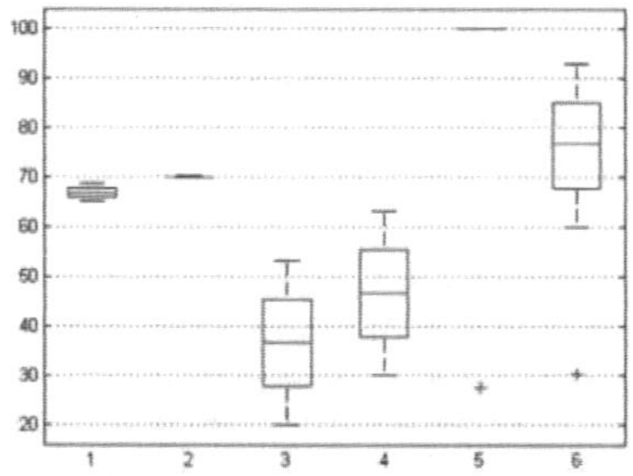


Figure 5. Distribution values for Testbed Normal Data Plot

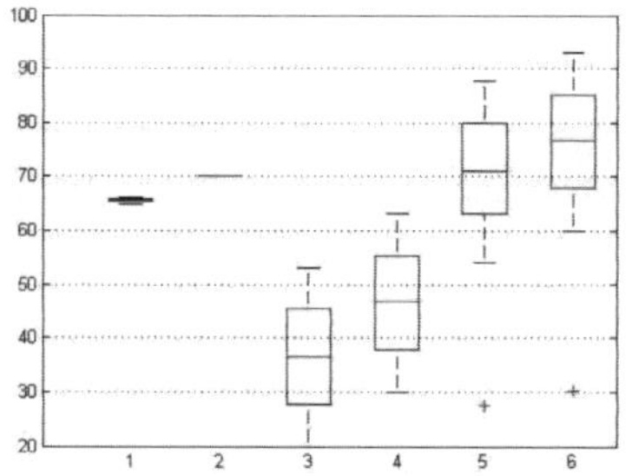


Figure 6. Distribution values for Cyber-Attack Data Plot

The data constructed during normal operation and under cyber-attack is used to assess the potential of the data to be used for cyber-security training and research. The data is evaluated using data classification techniques to identify the nature and timing of the conducted cyber-attacks.

## V. CONCLUSION AND FUTURE WORK

One of the most effective aspects of the Micro-CI testbed, as demonstrated in this paper, is its expandability. This means the scale of the testbed can be expanded to incorporate additional components and sensors. One of the aims of this project is to devise a testbed, which is suitable for cyber-security training and research. It is our belief that the use of real-life data is more suitable for cyber-security research, than that of simulation only. However, as with all solutions, there are some drawbacks to our approach. The first is that the use of low cost hardware reduces the level of accuracy that can be achieved. For example, the Arduino Uno uses an ATMega microcontroller, which is only capable of recording 4-byte precision in double values. This can present problems if precision is a crucial part of the research being undertaken. This can be mitigated by purchasing more expensive hardware. Another limitation is that in comparison to simulation software, the practical approach may require a greater level of improvement to students' skillsets (which is not a detrimental attribute), and a longer initial construction time, to accomplish a working implementation.

## REFERENCES

[1] S. Badri., P. Fergus., and W. Hurst., Critical infrastructure automated immuno-response system (CIAIRS), In Proceedings of the IEEE International Conference on Control, Decision and Information Technologies, 2016

[2] A. Ashok., P. Wang., M. Brown., and M. Govindarasu., Experimental evaluation of cyber-attacks on Automatic Generation Control using a CPS Security Testbed, In Proceedings of the IEEE Society General Meeting on Power & Energy, 2015

[3] Boston University Libraries, Research Data Management, What is 'Research Data'?, reference, available at [http://www.bu.edu/datamanagement/background/whatisdata/], access 08/12/2016

[4] G. Bernieri., F. Del Moro., L. Faramondi., and F. Pascucci., A testbed for integrated fault diagnosis and cyber security investigation, In Proceedings of the IEEE International Conference on Control, Decision and Information Technologies, 2016

[5] P. Singh., S. Garg., V. Kumar., and Z. Saquib, A testbed for SCADA cyber security and intrusion detection, In Proceedings of the IEEE Conference on Cyber Security of Smart Cities, Industrial Control System and Communications, 2015

[6] B. Somekh., C. Lewin., D. Saxon., D. Woodrow., et al., Evaluation of the DfES ICT Test Bed Project, The Qualitative Report, Coventry: Becta, 2007

[7] A. Almalawi., Z. Tari., I. Khalil., and A., Fahad, SCADAVT-A framework for SCADA security testbed based on virtualization technology, In Proceedings of th 38th IEEE Conference on Local Computer Networks, 2013

[8] A. A Farooqui., S. S. Haider Zaidi., A. Y Memon., and S. Qazi., Cyber Security Backdrop: A SCADA testbed, In Proceedings of the IEEE Computing, Communications and IT Applications Conference, 2014

[9] PentesterLab, available at [https://pentesterlab.com/] accessed 08/12/2016.

[10] B. Van Leeuwen., V. Urias., J. Eldridge., C. Villamarin., and R. Olsberg, In Proceedings of the IEEE International Carnahan Conference on Security Technology, 2010

[11] C. Siaterlis., B. Genge., and M. Hohenadel., EPIC: A Testbed for Scientifically Rigorous Cyber-Physical Security Experimentation., IEEE Transactions of Emergining Topics in Computing, 2014

[12] C. Heracleous., E. E. Miciolino., R. Setola., F. Pascucci., D. G. Eliades., G. Ellinas., C. G. Panayiotou., and M. M. Polycarpou., Critical Infrastructure Online Fault Detection: Application in Water Supply Systems, In Proceedings of the Springer Journal on Critical Information Infrastructures Security, vol 8985, pp 94-106

[13] W. Hurst., N. Shone., Q. Shi., and B. Bazli., Micro-CI: A Critical Systems Testbed for Cyber- Security Research, In Proceedings of The Eighth International Conference on Emerging Networks and Systems Intelligence, At Venice, Italy, Volume: Special Session on Big Data Analytics in Critical Systems (BDA-CS), 2016

[14] K. Alieyan., M. M. Kadhum., M. Anbar., and S. Ul Rehman., et al., An overview of DDoS attacks based on DNS, In Proceedings of the IEEE International Conference on Information and Communication Technology Convergence, 2016.

[15] Bill Miller and Dale Rowe. A survey SCADA of and critical infrastructure incidents. In Proceedings of the 1st Annual conference on Research in information technology (RIIT '12). ACM, New York, NY, USA, 51-56, 2012.

[16] Marjan Kuchaki Rafsanjani and Neda Kazeminejad. Distributed denial of service attacks and detection mechanisms. J. Comp. Methods in Sci. and Eng. 14, 6, 329-345, 2014.

[17] Compton M et al., The SSN ontology of the W3C semantic sensor network incubator group, Web semantics: science, services and agents on the World Wide Web, vol 17. Elsevier, London, 2012

[18] Semantic Sensor Network Incubator Group. https://www.w3.org/2005/Incubator/ssn/. Retrieved Dec 2016

# Development of a Secure Cloud Based Learning Environment for Inclusive Practice in Mainstream Education

Nigel Beacham
Computing Science
University of Aberdeen
Email: n.beacham@abdn.ac.uk

Bob Duncan
Business School
University of Aberdeen
Email: bobduncan@abdn.ac.uk

***Abstract*—The use of IT based systems in mainstream education brings a particular focus to bear on security. When these systems involve the use of cloud, the challenge increases exponentially. There are a great many benefits to be gained from cloud use, and therefore, we argue that developing a suitable approach to provide a secure cloud based learning environment, which would be used to facilitate use for inclusive practice in mainstream education would be a worthwhile goal. We demonstrate how to develop such an approach, which we believe could provide a more effective approach than traditional technology based approaches.**

***Keywords–Inclusive education; security; privacy;cloud system.***

## I. INTRODUCTION

Educational systems are complex socio-technical systems and we need to consider what makes this so. Introducing educational services through the cloud can open pupils and staff to further exploitation, which we need to investigate [1][2]. We must bear in mind that the use of technical solutions alone can never succeed. Any solution must be addressed from a social engineering perspective, which considers the political, personal and social aspects. This paper addresses this important issue from this different perspective in order to address both the special needs of all involved, the special security and privacy issues raised by using a cloud based solution, and the other security and privacy factors, which must be taken into account.

Proper security and privacy for any web based system is challenging. When cloud systems are used, these challenges become considerably more difficult to address successfully. Thus, in Section II, we discuss the motivation for this work. In Section III, we discuss the educational needs and requirements, which must be satisfied in order to deliver the aims and goals of the work. In Section IV, we outline the security requirements needed to deliver the goals and aims of this work, and in Section V, we explain how achieving these security requirements will meet the security goals of the project. We discuss our conclusions and future work in Section VI.

## II. MOTIVATION

Virtual Learning Environments (VLE)s tend to be perceived as providing tools for specific individuals and not as tools for everybody [3]. They tend to be used for what is suggested as inclusion; to facilitate a pupil's ability to participate in learning [4]. We argue that such tools allow the pupils to access learning materials and/or curriculum, and in doing so, can allow pupils to sometimes integrate within the classroom [5]. To be seen as fully inclusive, they should be made available for everybody, including teachers, parents, support staff and other agencies, if appropriate. Instead of the emphasis being on the use of VLEs to allow individuals to participate, there needs to be a greater emphasis on the way all those in the class use VLEs to allow all to participate. Consequently, at present, little is understood about the way VLEs can be made available and used for everybody. Looking at current practices using VLEs, they tend to be used by pupils in schools under the control of teachers, despite teachers tending not to use VLEs themselves as part of their teaching practice. With a huge variety of VLEs available, teachers often lack confidence, awareness and knowledge of VLEs, particularly in how best to use them in the classroom [6]. Naturally, it can take teachers extra time and effort to consider how to use VLEs within the classroom for those pupils who are deemed as requiring such support. VLEs tend to be made available only to those children within their school who require them, and only to those areas the educational system deems require their use [7].

Even when VLEs are made available to a pupil outwith the school, they are often reported as failing to work appropriately and many VLEs are only available for use within a particular class. There are also numerous reports of many materials in VLEs residing on the shelf, often unused. Where VLEs have been used effectively in schools, it is unclear how useful they were, the impact they had on the children's learning, whether it is used in terms of integration or inclusion, and whether the tools were available from home and outside the school. Whether VLEs are made available or not, it can leave pupils excluded in class and also at home. New ways of observing and analysing the way VLEs are used need to be explored and better understood [8]. Whilst many children see technology as just part of life, some pupils see the computer and the use of VLEs as essential in all aspects of their learning. This is particularly evident from those pupils with disabilities, who have access to VLEs through assistive technologies and computers at home that support their needs, as opposed to those available in school. For other pupils, some may not wish to use VLEs as part of a differentiated task but as part of 'normal' class work. Furthermore, savvy teachers and pupils consider the limitations of some VLEs as being restrictive, especially when similar open source tools are free.

The impact of technology on learning is much more difficult to determine than first thought. Factors inside and outside school can impact on the use of VLEs for learning. For example, barriers within schools can prevent the use of open source tools, while outside school, they are widely and freely available to all [9]. We believe that a cloud based approach can fulfil many of the practical requirements that must be addressed. Principal among these is the adaptable approach, with rapid scalability, and the ability to tailor resource usage to the demands of teaching in order to optimise operating costs. The use of cloud facilities also removes the barriers associated with rolling out large scale computing projects using traditional distributed hardware and software. This means the system could quickly and easily be scaled out to service not just a single school, but many schools within a region, or indeed across a country. We cover many of these technical points in later sections. Thus, our discussions throughout this paper are based on the premise that we will use a cloud based approach. We are acutely aware that pupils can be open to exploitation and grooming within VLEs, not just at school, but also in home and community environments. We are aware that pupils, teachers and administrative and support staff must be made ready for the step change in approach needed to ensure a high level of cloud-based security as the main mechanism by which we can ensure security and privacy inside the VLE. The lessons learned from this robust approach to security and privacy in this VLE can provide pupils with the foundation for a key skill in protecting the secure development of their personal on-line future. In the next section, we address the educational needs and requirements, which must be delivered in order to develop a successful system.

## III. The Educational Needs and Requirements

It is likely that teachers may lack preparedness in understanding the proper use of tools and techniques to monitor and retain a secure and safe VLE, a vital part of ensuring the successful running of a safe and secure environment, so this must form part of the preparation for the use of such a system [9]. We must also consider current VLE limitations in the context of Transformability theory.

Transformability theory is a framework for transforming learning capacity [10]. It provides a way of conceptualising learning capacity and how to improve it through the teaching practices used by teachers and schools [11][12][13]. Underpinning the theory are the three principles: co-agency; everybody; and trust. Co-agency relates to teachers, pupils, parents and support services being a joint enterprise. Everybody relates to teachers, pupils, parents and support services being responsible and committed to all pupils in a learning community. Trust relates to building close trusting relationships between teachers, pupils, parents and support services. This theory not only provides a lens within which to research, reflect and inform the ways Assistive Technology (AT) and Information and Communications Technology (ICT) are generally used to enable meaningful participation in learning, but can guide teachers on what to do, and not to do, in their practice with cloud-based VLEs to improve security.

In educational terms, AT focuses on providing access to materials and the curriculum [4]. Research on the development and use of AT tends to centre on investigating how tools improve access. This is only one of a number of aspects, which need to be addressed to improve the capacity to learn. Other aspects include the role AT plays in enhancing collaboration, achievement, acceptance and recognition of learner diversity, and furthermore how effective using a particular AT is to facilitate collaboration, achievement and acceptance and recognition of diversity. It is these aspects, which tend to be ignored, and as many teachers will know, make an important difference in improving learning capacity. An inclusive pedagogical approach draws attention to these additional aspects. Theories such as transformability help inform teachers not only to use AT to improve access to the materials and the curriculum but also to address the other crucial aspects of learning capacity [14][15].

Thus, we need a theoretical framework to extend inclusive education practices to security – in effect using a transformability theory approach. By this means, we can ensure that not just technical staff are aware of preparedness in cloud-based security, but everybody in the learning ecosystem does too. This co-agency approach between pupils, parents, teachers, administrators and technical staff is vitally important and is required to keep pupils and staff safe, not just for the duration of their learning, but as a solid foundation to ensure their lifelong online protection. This will also help us to satisfy the need to develop closer trust within learning communities as a whole, and to ensure everybody perceives and benefits from being recognised, accepted and included [16].

## IV. Security Requirements to be Addressed

The well recognised security requirements of any enterprise are confidentiality, integrity and availability (CIA). Duncan and Whittington [17], suggest that we should also add the goals of sustainability, resilience and ethics. The traditional approach to satisfy the CIA requirements, are access control, plus encryption, for confidentiality; transaction monitoring, possibly with encryption, for integrity; and redundancy for availability. Long term sustainability comes from providing a system that works, achieving the goals set for it, providing value for money, and does so in a reliable fashion. Resilience comes from providing a system that is resilient to unexpected shock; and a business continuity mechanism or policy, can assist with this task. Ethical behaviour on the part of all the actors in a cloud ecosystem can be delivered where all parties are properly accountable, and through their individual ethical behaviour, demonstrate they will not try to gain personal advantage at the expense of others within the ecosystem.

These goals are generally well understood by enterprises, and are often approached using technical solutions. However, in any business environment, the business architecture comprises a combination of people, process and technology [18], not by technology alone. The people of any business are generally recognised as being the weakest link, and whether it is a FTSE100 world class enterprise, a government organisation, a small firm, or an educational body, the fact remains that the people in the organisation present the largest threat. When we talk about people in the context of this paper, we refer to the description for everybody in Section II, above. To this, we must add all the agents involved in the cloud ecosystem, and of course, the attack community. The bad guys have long recognised that the weakest part of any IT system is actually the users of that system, which is why they have long been developing and polishing the very successful practice of social engineering. Thus, proper user training must be undertaken.

Since cloud computing is enabled by use of the internet, then web based applications present some of the most successful attack vectors for the bad guys. While web vulnerabilities are well understood, we can see from data collected by the Open Web Application Security Project (OWASP) [19], who publish a top ten list of web security vulnerabilities every three years, that these attacks continue to be perpetrated successfully year on year. OWASP provide the most comprehensive list of the most dangerous vulnerabilities and a number of very good mitigation suggestions. The last three OWASP lists for 2007, 2010 and 2013 are provided in TABLE I, below.

TABLE I. OWASP TOP TEN WEB VULNERABILITIES — 2013 - 2007 [19]

| 2013 | 2010 | 2007 | Threat |
|---|---|---|---|
| A1 | A1 | A2 | Injection Attacks |
| A2 | A3 | A7 | Broken Authentication and Session Management |
| A3 | A2 | A1 | Cross Site Scripting (XSS) |
| A4 | A4 | A4 | Insecure Direct Object References |
| A5 | A6 | - | Security Misconfiguration |
| A6 | - | - | Sensitive Data Exposure |
| A7 | - | - | Missing Function Level Access Control |
| A8 | A5 | A5 | Cross Site Request Forgery (CSRF) |
| A9 | - | - | Using Components with Known Vulnerabilities |
| A10 | - | - | Unvalidated Redirects and Forwards |

These lists are based on the result of analysis of successful security breaches across the globe, and highlight the most easily breached areas in web based systems. It illustrates the worst ten web vulnerabilities in computing systems globally. While these vulnerabilities are relatively easy to address, it is concerning that they continue to recur year after year. Thus, these should all be addressed. There are likely to be additional potential vulnerabilities, which also must be considered, not necessarily only technical issues such as we have illustrated above. Duncan and Whittington [17], identified ten key management issues, which also must be addressed. Often these are not properly thought through by management.

The ten key management security issues identified are: The definition of security goals; Compliance with standards; Audit issues; Management approach; Technical complexity of cloud; Lack of responsibility and accountability; Measurement and monitoring; Management attitude to security; Security culture in the company; and the threat environment. Further details on each of these key areas of potential weakness are provided in [17]. As quickly as security researchers come up with solutions to new vulnerabilities, the bad guys, in turn, come up with successful attacks against these fixes. This continual "arms race", means that it is also essential to ensure a proper monitoring system forms part of the design framework. Also, since cloud provides easy scalability of resources to track the demand curve, it will also be necessary to have a system that can track the addition of new instances, the shutting down of instances no longer required, and the extraction of suitable audit trail and system logging data for forensic examination purposes in the event of a breach. These security requirements we propose go much further than conventional technical approaches in use until now. It is clear from recent annual security breach reports such as [20][21][22], which clearly demonstrate the security and privacy problems still faced today. The same attacks continue to be successful year on year. Looking at this five year summary of Verizon reports shown in TABLE II below, we can see the result of failing to use a complete solution to the security problem:

It is clear that a more complete solution must be used, and we have outlined the essential components of such a system. A cloud service provider might well have a secure and effective technical cloud solution, but it will be useless if cloud users are compromised by a successful social engineering attack.

TABLE II. VERIZON TOP 5 SECURITY BREACHES — 2010-2014 (1=HIGHEST) [23][24][25][26][20]

| Threat | 2010 | 2011 | 2012 | 2013 | 2014 |
|---|---|---|---|---|---|
| Hacking | 2 | 1 | 1 | 1 | 1 |
| Malware | 3 | 2 | 2 | 2 | 2 |
| Misuse by company employees | 1 | 4 | 5 | 5 | 5 |
| Physical theft or unauth. access | 5 | 3 | 4 | 3 | 4 |
| Social Engineering | 4 | 5 | 3 | 4 | 3 |

## V. HOW THIS MEETS SECURITY GOALS

There are many challenges, which must be met by cloud based systems, meaning a far more rigorous approach is needed. A fundamental requirement is the use of a proper monitoring system [27]. Without one, it will be almost impossible to tell that a system has been breached. With no proper audit trail and sufficient forensic evidence, it will be extremely difficult to understand precisely which data has been accessed, modified, ex-filtrated or deleted. The popular approach to cloud cyber security generally centres around technical solutions. For the reasons stated in Section IV, this will always prove inadequate in the face of adversaries with ever improving skill levels and attack tool sets. Thus, our proposed framework must incorporate some addition components. Cloud can necessarily create and destroy instances at will, in order to scale up, or down, as demand dictates, so it will be necessary to have some level of control and monitoring system to log each new instance as it is created, or deleted, and should constantly monitor the instance throughout its life-cycle, to ensure it continues to function as expected, and has not been compromised by an attack.

The controller function should be created in a separate server from the running instances. The data logs and any audit trail should be stored in another separate secure server running immutable database software to guard against attack. Neither of these systems should run any other software, and should not be exposed to public access on the internet. Each should run behind a strong firewall, and should be protected by intrusion detection software. In addition, the main system should also run behind a secure cloud firewall, and should also run intrusion detection software. Access should be delivered via multi-step authentication, to protect against common password attack strategies. There are three ways to do multi-step authentication:

1) Something the user knows (e.g., a password, partial password, pass phrase, or personal identification number (PIN), challenge response (the user must answer a question, or pattern), or security question);
2) Something the user has (e.g., wrist band, ID card, security token, mobile phone with built-in hardware token, software token, or mobile phone holding a software token);
3) Something the user is or does (e.g., fingerprint, retinal pattern, signature, face, or voice identifier).

The minimum use of two of the categories with three or more questions to be successfully answered before access is granted, provides an extremely secure level of access control, without the use of passwords. We have outlined how there are many more threats than just those that can be solved by technical means alone. These additional threats are very effective, yet relatively simple to guard against. The approach we have outlined here is not technically difficult to achieve, nor expensive to implement, yet these steps, taken in concert with conventional technical solutions, can prove invaluable in the fight against attack. This section considers the above security threats from the perspective of transformability theory and its three underlying principles. Transformability theory has as its underlying philosophy 'Learning without Limits'. Based on this premise, we suggest that security threats should be faced in a similar fashion — 'Security without Barriers'. From a social perspective the more barriers are erected, the less secure communities will be. Thus, it is important to develop a culture of ethical hacking between agencies. A culture that ensures everybody is involved and included so they acquire the knowledge and skills to keep them safe from, and prepared for, cyber security threats. Core to this is the need to develop trust within the community so focus can be targeted outside, in the knowledge that inside, the community is soundly built.

Threats caused by e.g., pupils targeting their peers by sending SMSs, emails and tweets, etc., need to be confronted and addressed immediately and openly within the learning environment. The perpetrator, their parents and other necessary agencies need all to be aware. This may not reduce the stress on the targeted pupil but does identify and expose the perpetrator and their behaviour. Such an approach requires everybody's participation, trust and involvement. Action needs to focus on improving respect and acceptance with the outcome of changing behaviour. Physical threat or unauthorised access can be reduced when working with and through others. Working on activities requiring the synchronisation of two or more agents can reduce the likelihood a third party will obtain unauthorised access. We encourage more use of computer-supported collaborative learning (CSCL)[28][29], approaches and tools. Social engineering threats ultimately tend to target entire communities rather than individuals within.

## VI. CONCLUSION

We have outlined the problems faced when considering the use of a cloud based technology solution in mainstream education, and in particular where the learning environment is used for inclusive practice. We argue for a more inclusive approach to ethical hacking; providing an environment that encourages security without barriers; all of which can be used for communities as well as a society built on trust. Transformability theory provides a framework, which introduces a positive mind-set that together, communities such as those within education, can address security threats within both educational systems and any socio-technical system. It provides a common language from a social engineering perspective to discuss and deal with threats; and provides a way to measure and monitor environments for threats in the future. Such an approach will be developed and piloted and provide useful knowledge in the implementation of cloud-based security.

As we move towards virtual and augmented collaborative learning environments such as Second Life, inclusive pedagogies must have more dynamic security. Many real-world social skills are replicated in these virtual and augmented worlds [30]. It is therefore important that inclusive pedagogies are adaptable for physical and virtual learning environments, including considering the role AT can play in enabling meaningful participation in learning within such multi-dimensional environments. To date, few ATs can be integrated effectively within groupware systems in mainstream education.

## REFERENCES


[1] S. K. Beach, "Usable cybersecurity: Human factors in cybersecurity education curricula, " Natl. Cybersecurity Inst. J., 2014, p. 5.

[2] N. Sultan, "Cloud computing for education: A new dawn?" Int. J. Inf. Manage., vol. 30, no. 2, 2010, pp. 109–116.

[3] G. Attwell et al., "Personal learning environments-the future of eLearning?" Elearning Pap., vol. 2, no. 1, 2007, pp. 1–8.

[4] L. Florian and J. Hegarty, ICT and special educational needs: a tool for inclusion. McGraw-Hill Education (UK), 2004.

[5] N. Beacham and K. McIntosh, "Student teachers' attitudes and beliefs towards using ICT within inclusive education and practice," J. Res. Spec. Educ. Needs, vol. 14, no. 3, 2014, pp. 180–191.

[6] N. Sclater, "eLearning in the cloud," Int. J. Virtual Pers. Learn. Environ., vol. 1, no. 1, 2012, pp. 10–19.

[7] S. Hubackova, "Pedagogical foundation of eLearning," Procedia-Social Behav. Sci., vol. 131, 2014, pp. 24–28.

[8] E. Wiebe and D. Sharek, "eLearning," in Why Engagem. Matters. Springer, 2016, pp. 53–79.

[9] N. Beacham, "Developing NQTs e-pedagogies for inclusion," Institution University of Aberdeen, May 2011.

[10] S. Hart, A. Dixon, M. Drummond, and D. McIntyre, "Learning without limits," in Sage Handb. Spec. Educ., 1st ed. Open University Press, 2008, ch. 38, pp. 499–514.

[11] L. Florian and J. Spratt, "Enacting inclusion: A framework for interrogating inclusive practice," Eur. J. Spec. Needs Educ., vol. 28, no. 2, 2013, pp. 119–135.

[12] L. Florian, K. Young, and M. Rouse, "Preparing teachers for inclusive and diverse educational environments: Studying curricular reform in an initial teacher education course," Int. J. Incl. Educ., vol. 14, no. 7, 2010, pp. 709–722.

[13] C. Forlin and D. Chambers, "Teacher preparation for inclusive education: Increasing knowledge but raising concerns," Asia-Pacific J. Teach. Educ., vol. 39, no. 1, 2011, pp. 17–32.

[14] S. Riddell, "Social justice, equality and inclusion in Scottish education," Discourse Stud. Cult. Polit. Educ., vol. 30, no. 3, 2009, pp. 283–296.

[15] T. Mortimore, "Dyslexia in higher education: Creating a fully inclusive institution," J. Res. Spec. Educ. Needs, vol. 13, no. 1, 2013, pp. 38–47.

[16] M. Ainscow and A. Sandill, "Developing inclusive education systems: The role of organisational cultures and leadership," Int. J. Incl. Educ., vol. 14, no. 4, 2010, pp. 401–416.

[17] B. Duncan and M. Whittington, "Enhancing cloud security and privacy: The power and the weakness of the audit trail," in Cloud Comput. 2016 7th Int. Conf. Cloud Comput. GRIDs, Virtualization. Rome: IEEE, 2016, pp. 125–130.

[18] PWC, "UK information security breaches survey - Technical Report 2012," London, Tech. Rep. April, 2012. [Online]. Available: www.pwc.com Last accessed: Jan 2017

[19] OWASP, "OWASP top ten vulnerabilities 2013," 2013. [Online]. Available: https://www.owasp.org/ Last accessed: Jan 2017

[20] Verizon, "2014 Data breach investigations report," Tech. Rep. 1, 2014. [Online]. Available: http://www.verizonenterprise.com/resources/reports/rp_Verizon-DBIR-2014_en_xg.pdf Last accessed: Jan 2017

[21] PWC, "2014 Information security breaches survey: Technical report," Tech. Rep., 2014.

[22] Trustwave, "Trustwave global security report," Tech. Rep., 2013. [Online]. Available: https://www2.trustwave.com/2013GSR.html Last accessed: Jan 2017

[23] W. Baker et al., "Data breach investigations report," Tech. Rep., 2010.

[24] Verizon, "2011 Data breach investigation report: A study conducted by the Verizon RISK team in cooperation with others," Verizon/USSS, Tech. Rep., 2011.

[25] Verizon, N. High, T. Crime, I. Reporting, and I. S. Service, "2012 Data breach investigations report," Verizon, Tech. Rep., 2012.

[26] Verizon, "Verizon2013," Tech. Rep., 2013.

[27] B. Duncan and M. Whittington, "The importance of proper measurement for a cloud security assurance model," in 2015 IEEE 7th Int. Conf. Cloud Comput. Technol. Sci., Vancouver, 2015, pp. 1–6.

[28] Wikipedia, "Computer supported collaborative learning," 2017. [Online]. Available: https://en.wikipedia.org/wiki/Computer-supported_collaborative_learning Last accessed: Jan 2017

[29] S. Järvelä and A. F. Hadwin, "New frontiers: Regulating learning in CSCL," Educ. Psychol., vol. 48, no. 1, 2013, pp. 25–39.

[30] A. Dix, J. Finlay, G. Abowd, and R. Beale, "Evaluation techniques," Hum. Comput. Interact., 2004.

# Corporate Governance, Risk Appetite and Cloud Security Risk: A Little Known Paradox. How Do We Square the Circle?

Bob Duncan
Computing Science
University of Aberdeen
Email: bobduncan@abdn.ac.uk

Yuan Zhao
Accounting and Finance
University of Aberdeen
Email: y.zhao@abdn.ac.uk

Mark Whittington
Business School
University of Aberdeen
Email: mark.whittington@abdn.ac.uk

***Abstract*—In today's corporate world, the notion of corporate governance has taken a more important role in the management of large corporates. There is a growing consensus that large corporates ought to take more of a stewardship approach to running a company in a clear attempt to move away from the agency theory approach, with all its attendant problems and issues. A fundamental component of corporate governance concerns the adequate recognition of risk faced by the organisation and dealing with it appropriately. Traditional corporate IT risk is well understood, as are the mitigation strategies needed to address this important area. Large corporates also understand risk theory well, and how finding the right balance between risk and profitability is key to ensuring profitability can be maximised while ensuring long term sustainability and resilience are also achieved. We assert that the cloud computing paradigm, while economically attractive to corporates, provides such a step change from traditional IT paradigms, that new risks have evolved, which are not well understood, leading to the possibility of unintended exposure to these sometimes considerable risks. We propose a different approach to the quantification of these risks, which we believe will provide a more robust approach to understanding the potential exposure they face when using cloud.**

***Index Terms*—Corporate governance; corporate stewardship; risk appetite; cloud security risk.**

## I. INTRODUCTION

Achieving effective information security in the cloud is not a trivial process. There are many challenges to overcome, and sometimes those challenges arise from the most unexpected places. There are a great many influences, which bear down on the successful outcome of meeting this important goal, and often, a number of these influencing factors are not aligned.

This presents managers with something of a paradox when it comes to satisfying all the demands placed upon them, particularly when it comes to satisfying the rules of good corporate governance, managing risk effectively and balancing this with the primary goal of a company, which is to maximise the resources of that company for the benefit of the shareholders. This fiduciary responsibility of management to the shareholders has been a fundamental tenet of good corporate management for a very long time.

However, there is also a recognition that a company needs to be managed responsibly in a sustainable way to ensure the continued existence of the company, such that it be capable of withstanding sudden market shock, in other words is resilient to market forces, and added to this is the requirement to act in a responsible, accountable and ethical manner.

A modern requirement of a company is that there is now a recognition that information forms a key element of the resources of that company, and that it is therefore necessary to safeguard this information properly. This is further reinforced following the introduction of, sometimes punitive legislation [1][2], to ensure that companies achieve this goal.

For those member states of the EU, and for the UK post Brexit, there is a new "Bogey man" on the horizon — the forthcoming General Data Protection Regulation, which is scheduled to be brought into law in May 2018. This will require a considerable number of changes to be implemented in corporate systems in order to comply with this legislation. The level of fines proposed takes compliance fines to a new high, and will definitely attract the attention of board members.

In Section II, we discuss some background on all these issues. In Section III, we consider how the Financial Services Sector approach cyber risk, in Section IV, we consider why this might be important for company cloud users. In Section VI, we consider how this might work; and in Section VII, we discuss our conclusions.

In the next section, we will take a look at these important areas to see what we can learn.

## II. BACKGROUND

We start by looking at Corporate Governance, followed by Risk Appetite, IT Risk and Cloud Security. This first area we look at will be Corporate Governance.

### A. *Corporate Governance Literature*

We can trace some of these issues back to the early 1930s, when Berle and Means [3], commented how setting up a large company was now beyond the means of any single person, which would lead to the popularity of the large company, where we would see the concept of the separation of management and ownership. This, in turn, would ultimately lead to the evolution of Agency Theory [4]. One of the fundamental flaws of Agency Theory is the inability to control greed, and this became one of the fundamental weaknesses of this theory, leading to the uncontrolled growth of management remuneration.

In the UK, the financial de-regulation, which took place in the 1980s, would lead to extremes of corporate financial excess, including corporate scandals, such as the Bank of Credit and Commerce International (BCCI), Maxwell and the controversy over directors' pay. Government responded to this by commissioning the 1992 Cadbury Report [5]. This resulted in the introduction of the "Combined Code", to which all large UK corporates should adhere, by reporting in their annual return whether they "comply or explain" with the recommendations of the report. A year later, Jensen [6], wrote about the effect of technological innovation and internal control systems failures. Jensen and Chew [7] investigate the effects of the takeover boom of the 1980s. The Combined Code was subsequently updated [8]–[11].

Still in the UK, UK corporate governance continues to evolve with incremental but increasing awareness of corporate responsibilities to more than just shareholders and also a widening recognition of risk and societal impact — all relevant to cloud security. One recent example of this wider trend would be the Modern Slavery Act (2015) requiring an annual statement with a home page link explaining the steps the company has taken to expose and take out slavery in their supply chain [12]. This has some relevance as minor web breaches probably are not consequential to shareholders especially if not disclosed, in a similar way slavery is probably even advantageous — perhaps we are slowly moving away from shareholder dominance.

In the US, after the introduction of the Sarbanes-Oxley Act (SOX) in 2002 [1], Bauer et al [13], Bratton [14], Brickey [15], Holmstrom [16], Mitchell [17] and Rosen [18] all wrote about the implications for corporate governance. In the UK, Higgs [19], updated the Combined Code, and the effects of SOX were also addressed for the Financial Reporting Council [20]. The Organisation for Economic Co-operation and Development (OECD) [21] published its principles of corporate governance. Further updates to the code took place [22]–[25], and the next significant change occurred in 2012, when the Financial Reporting Council (FRC) recommended a new Stewardship Code be adopted [26].

It is worth pointing out that there is a fundamental difference between the approach adopted by the UK and the US. The UK have adopted a principles based approach, whereby general principles are established, and companies are required to "comply or explain" in their annual report. This means there is little need to constantly change legislation to keep up. By contrast, the US have adopted a rules based regime, whereby very specific legislation is enacted to determine what corporates must do. While the goals and requirements are generally clear, it has spawned a high-end legal and accounting industry, which constantly seeks to probe and push the boundaries in order to gain advantage, while retaining the ability to achieve compliance. Thus, the US government must constantly rewrite and update the rules to keep pace with these continuous attempts to subvert the rules — a considerable ongoing task. Regulators too, will have a more challenging task to keep on top of all these attempts to subvert the rules. Duncan and Whittington [27] provide some useful background on this area, including corporate legislation and standards compliance issues.

The clear and evolving message to come through from all these changes is that there is now a much greater emphasis on the need to identify and address risk properly. The global financial crash of 2008 really brought home the importance of effective risk management. Banks, in particular, had been "going through the motions" rather than really paying attention to the possibility that some of these risks were very real, and the consequences of failing to address them properly would have a catastrophic impact on not just their own business, but the global economy as a whole. It is also the case that financial regulators were themselves pretty much caught asleep on the job. Thus, we will next look at risk appetite.

### B. Risk Appetite

Risk appetite can be described as the amount and type of risk that an organisation is willing to take in order to meet their strategic objectives. Risk needs first to be properly identified, and the consequent financial implications properly measured or estimated should the risk identified arise. The probability of occurrence of each risk identified, must also be calculated. Such identified risks must then either be accepted, mitigated against, or declined, depending on the risk appetite of management. Usually, there is a correlation between risk and reward. The more profit that can be generated, usually the greater the risk the organisation is exposed to. Often, this risk considerably exceeds the potential amount of profit to be generated.

All companies generally have developed a mission statement, or vision statement. Where financial goals or targets are identified, it will be necessary to identify the risk requiring to be taken to achieve such goals and targets. This identifies the minimum required risk that must be taken in order to meet the goals or targets. If the risk required is unrealistic, i.e., too high, then the goals or targets should be adjusted, otherwise this will automatically lead the company to accept dangerous levels of risk.

In any event, the risk capacity of the company must be identified, as must the risk tolerance. These are not the same thing. Risk capacity tries to identify the extent to which the investment strategy can withstand negative events without seriously affecting the achievement of the goals or targets of the company. Whereas risk tolerance considers the extent to which a company is willing to risk a less favourable outcome in pursuit of a possible greater outcome. This can be considered a psychological trait, and if company managers happen to have have a high tendency towards the psychopathic spectrum of behaviour, there is a greater chance of a mismatch arising between risk capacity and risk tolerance, leading to a less well considered attitude towards the real risk being undertaken [28].

This leads management to seek an economic equilibrium between profit and risk, such that they can maximise profit constrained by their understanding of risk. Where the company is run by prudent management, they will usually decide to accept those risks, which they understand really well, mitigate risks, which they are prepared to accept, but where they mitigate the extent of the risk accepted, possibly by the use of insurance, to minimise their exposure, and decline all risk they do not understand. This will usually lead to a safe performance, if somewhat unexciting. Duncan and Whittington [29], argued that where the management approach to running the company is biased towards the traditional agency based management approach, rather than a stewardship approach, the company is likely to have a higher risk appetite. Successful use of this high risk approach can lead to complacency over time, resulting in a more cavalier assessment of risk within the company, which can ultimately lead to hubris developing, leading to the acceptance of much higher risk levels than have been understood. When this approach goes wrong, the results can be catastrophic [30].

Risk culture in a company evolves from a system of values and behaviours present in that company, which will shape the risk decisions of management and employees. An important element of risk culture is the development of a common understanding of a company and its business purpose or aims.

### C. IT Risk

In large corporates, the area of IT risk in traditional distributed systems is generally very well understood. There are some very good security standards, such as the joint International Organization for Standardization (ISO) and the International Electrotechnical Commission (IEC) (ISO/IEC), ISO/IEC 27000 [31], Control Objectives for Information and Related Technologies (COBIT) [32], and the Payment Card Industry Data Security Standard (PCI DSS) [33], which are well adopted by large corporates. Indeed, by 2012 [34], some two thirds of FTSE100 companies were either fully or partially compliant with the ISO/IEC 27000 series of security standards. While this is a laudable approach, it must be considered that compliance alone will not guarantee security [27].

The attack community are continually developing and exploiting new vulnerabilities, and thus a stringent and robust approach to system monitoring must be in place. There is little point in having a certificate to show compliance, if the company fails to detect a breach. Many breaches are not picked up until some time later. The risk emanating from this can turn out to be expensive. Recently, ASUS settled for $400,000 after they were sued by the Federal Trade Commission (FTC) [35], because they were not providing updates for their insecure routers. The new EU General Data Protection Regulation (GDPR) will come into force in May 2018. It will increase this (monetary) problem for companies with a maximum monetary penalty of up to 4% of global turnover.

### D. Cloud Security

Often, companies will seek to prove they have achieved security through assurance. This assurance is usually achieved by compliance with standards, or by audit. However, one of the difficulties with cloud computing is that there are over 30 standards bodies who have been working on cloud security standards, and we are yet to see a fully comprehensive cloud security standard evolve [27]. There are difficulties too, with the method of compliance audit undertaken [36], which can have a considerable impact on the effectiveness of the audit exercise.

The fact that we have no complete cloud security standard is a major issue, meaning large corporates might be missing the potential to identify the increased risk arising from running their own software on the cloud. In the multi-tenancy, multi layer, environment of cloud computing, many forget that the solid corporate firewall they have so carefully developed for their corporate distributed systems does not extend to the cloud environment.

There is much we can learn from the approach taken by one of the most exposed market sectors to cyber risk — the financial services sector. This market sector is a prime target for cyber attacks. Liquid cash, particularly in electronic form is much easier to attack than large physical objects. Thus, in the next Section, we consider the approach taken to evaluating cyber risk in the financial services sector. These risks are well understood, and the risk models developed are now very advanced, and highly accurate.

## III. CYBER RISK IN THE FINANCIAL SERVICES SECTOR

Cyber risk has attracted increasing awareness for financial risk management in recent years. Financial intermediaries such as banks, investment companies, and insurance companies are the prime targets for cyber crimes. Figure 1 shows the average cost of cyber crimes incurred by companies of a specific industry, started from financial services, energy and utilities, and followed by defence and aerospace, and technology. The financial service sector has undergone a tremendous technological transformation, resulted from the adoption of digital banking, Financial Technology (FinTech), mobile applications, cloud computing, etc.

### A. Cyber Risk in Financial Risk Management

It is of great importance to quantify cyber risk for financial risk management. Four types of risk - credit, liquidity, market, and operational — can affect the potential outcome / performance of financial investments for companies. Value at Risk (VaR) is a popular approach among modelling techniques used by financial institutions to quantify the market risk of investment. However, the model can not foresee a 'black swan event', a low-probability occurrence with high-value impact. Cyber VaR can be used to model the cyber risk, with consideration for cyber black swan events. A cyber VaR model can be used to estimate the likely loss of an organisation in the event of cyber attacks during a time period. The components of the VaR framework consist of the existing vulnerabilities of

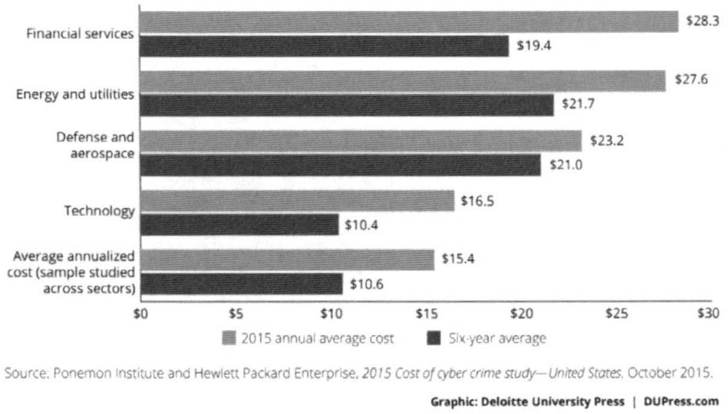


Fig. 1. AVERAGE ANNUAL COMPANY COSTS OF CYBERCRIME IN $MILLIONS

a system, the maturity of defending the system, the frequency of successful breaches, the tangible and intangible assets of the company, the types of attachers and their attacking motivations, etc. The adoption of cyber VaR can be helpful for a company to quantify the potential loss of a cyber attack.

### *B. Crypto-Currency in the Financial Sector*

Crypto-currency, which is a form of virtual currency that uses crypography for security, may present increasing threat that negatively impact the cyber security of finance. Based on new applications of information technology, these virtual currencies attempt to remove money and banking from the control of sovereign governments, and they represent one of the most disruptive innovations ever in consumer finance. The underlying distributed ledger technology has many other potential applications in diverse areas such as property registration, accounting and auditing, gambling and financial derivatives.

The potential threat of this emerging technology motivates a better understanding of crypto-currency. It has essentially resulted from a technical experiment, with no monetary value. It has grown to an industry with more than 510 crypto-currencies with market value of $5.5 billion, composed of bitcoins. Although crypto-currencies have the advantage of higher efficiency and transparency for conducting transactions, reducing banking fees and bringing technological innovation to the financial industry, they are also used by cyber-criminals as they are not connected to any central banks and not regulated in many countries.

In the next Section, we explain why this model could be relevant to corporate cloud users.

## IV. WHY IS THIS RELEVANT TO CORPORATE CLOUD USERS?

In order to properly identify what risk is in the case of using cloud computing, users should first start with their prior evaluation of IT risk in regard to their existing distributed non-cloud setup. Since they will have been running these systems for a very long time, it is likely that the risks will be well understood. However, where a company assumes that because they understand these existing risks well, they will be well able to handle cloud risk, they will be placing themselves in considerable danger.

However, once they make the decision to move to cloud, simply moving software systems across to the cloud and assuming all past risks will continue as they have traditionally been identified, is a fallacy, and could lead them into a false sense of security. IT risk does not equal cloud risk. Any cloud ecosystem is far more complex than a traditional distributed IT system, and there are far more actors in the cloud ecosystem, meaning it is far more difficult to ensure a proper lavel of security can be achieved.

Many modern companies present an attractive target and will be subject to a raft of attacks, from a variety of different sources. These attacks will come from state sponsored actors, industrial espionage, hacktivists, specialist criminal gangs, and talented amateurs.

State sponsored actors will be exceptionally well resourced, will be very highly skilled, with the capability to breach systems, and leaving a minimal footprint. They are extremely hard to detect, and difficult to protect against, but may only be interested in keeping an eye on what the company is up to, in order to provide their government with the means to understand how other countries are progress in what may be a competitive market for their country. Thus, stealing cash is not likely to be high on their priority list.

Those who perpetrate industrial espionage generally have a view to getting their hands on new technology, either to sell to a rival, or to simply sell on the black market. They will generally be well skilled, independently well resourced from past espionage activities, and highly persistent. While that may have a long term impact on the company, they are less likely to be looking to steal cash.

Hacktivists are often very skilled, highly motivated towards their cause, although less well resourced than the previous groups. They usually are not concerned with stealing cash, but are concerned with exposing perceived wrongdoing by the target company. They are primarily motivated to cause maximum embarrassment, sometimes will seek to disrupt physical systems to highlight their cause, but generally are not interested in staling cash. Where they disrupt systems, the knock on damage could be substantial.

Specialist criminal gangs can range from well resourced and well skilled groups, down to small scale criminals, who will often "rent an attack" from the dark web. The primary goal of these groups is to steal cash, or to obtain intelligence, which will enable them to steal the cash at a later time. They tend to be very resourceful, highly skilled at social engineering attacks, and can often buy in the attack tools they require from the dark web.

The amateur group can range from very talented amateurs down to complete amateurs just trying to breach large systems in order to boast about it. The really talented ones are much harder to catch. While they can be very skilled, and have limitless patience and time to spend on the attacks, they often are poorly resourced, which can inhibit their activities. The complete amateurs can be problematic from the damage they sometimes cause as they try to get into systems, or after they get there. The majority are not after cash, but the really talented ones can cause a huge amount of disruption.

So, with all these different actors constantly trying to get into company systems, why is the financial services sector of interest to cloud users? It is simply the fact that they have been targets of attack for a very long time, due to the very liquid nature of their business. Over the past decades, they have become very skilled in developing risk attack models to evaluate the risks they face, and are getting really good at it.

Equally, large companies often invest cash surpluses to maximise revenue production while they accumulate cash in preparation for their next expansion pus, thus in the process becoming greater targets. The attack actors have become adept at gathering a wide range of business intelligence in addition to learning how to analyse and understand financial statements, thus are able to pick better targets to attack.

Thus, companies must learn how best to evaluate properly they very real risks they face. In the next section, we consider how they might go about achieving this.

## V. Finding the Balance

Risk is a fundamental part of any company. The main goal of any company is to maximise the generation of profit in a sustainable way. In order to achieve this goal, it is necessary to define what the target return will need to be. This provides the risk requirement needing to be accepted in order to achieve the desired outcome.

Assuming this risk requirement to be both practical and achievable, the management of the company will then evaluate all the risks in order to understand what they are taking on, not just to achieve the goals of the corporation, but to satisfy the requirements and obligations incumbent upon them, such as compliance with legislation, regulation, standards, best practice and accepted ethical standards of doing business. Enterprises need to be sustainable in the long run and resilient to shock. Each of these requirements can cause a conflicting pull on company management to ensure the best outcome can be achieved.

Not all risks must be taken by a company. Rather, they need to evaluate which risks to accept, which to mitigate, and which to decline, in order that they can satisfy all the requirements placed upon them. Clearly, some level of compromise will need to be made in order to find a suitable balance.

The best approach for achieving this balance is first to understand fully the extent of each risk, and to assess properly whether they are prepared, or need to accept each risk. By identifying those they must accept, if they understand the risk properly, they will be better placed to evaluate whether each risk should be accepted in full, in part, or rejected.

The use of a good evaluation model will provide a better means of achieving this goal more easily. This is why we suggest adopting the financial services VaR model on IT risk as a foundation for adapting it to also cover cloud risk.

## VI. How Will it Work?

The application of cyber VaR would be of help to establish the minimum standard on covering the limits and risk assessment of cyber security. Based on the literature [37][38], the current challenge of quantifying and validating cyber VaR is the lack of quality data. Another shortcoming of the VaR measure is that it can be 'useless' for small probabilities with a significant outcome event. In finance literature, the Monte Carlo simulation and other measures have been proposed to tackle this. To address the impact / size of the outcome, the tail event or extreme event is defined as the largest percentage of losses measured relative to the respective VaR. Thus, the extreme event for cyber risk can be considered for risk management of cyber security.

## VII. Conclusion

We have demonstrated how traditional and well understood approaches to IT security risk do not work well with trying to identify and evaluate cloud cyber risk. We have highlighted how cloud risks differ from traditional distributed systems, and illustrated weaknesses in existing approaches. We have looked at how cyber risk is tackled in the financial services sector, and suggest how adapting the proposed cyber risk VaR model might help to improve cloud cyber risk assessment, thus helping companies to find a better balance between risk and reward.

We note that the National Institute of Standards and Technology (NIST) and the Cloud Security Alliance (CSA) have both introduced new updated approaches to cloud cyber risk. These and other national organisations are co-operating more with the ISO, who have produced a number of risk standards, such as ISO 31000 on corporate risk, ISO/IEC 27005 on information security risk management. We propose to review how their approach has been updated and will seek to discover whether any of these changes might be implemented into our system.

We are in the process of agreeing a plan to carry out a pilot development of this proposed system, and to compare its performance against existing approaches to evaluate how well it performs, with a view to providing the means of assessing the best level of risk awareness that is possible.

## References


[1] Sox, "Sarbanes-Oxley Act of 2002," p. 66, 2002. [Online]. Available: news.findlaw.com/hdocs/docs/gwbush/sarbanesoxley072302.pdf Last accessed: Jan 2017

[2] Crown, "Data Protection Act 1998," 1998. [Online]. Available: http://www.legislation.gov.uk/ukpga/1998/29/contents Last accessed: Jan 2017

[3] A. A. Berle and G. G. C. Means, *The modern corporation and private property*, 1932. [Online]. Available: https://books.google.co.uk/books?id=mLdLHhqxUb4C Last accessed: Jan 2017

[4] M. C. Jensen and W. H. Meckling, "Theory of the firm: Managerial behavior, agency costs and ownership structure," *Int. Libr. Crit. Writings Econ.*, vol. 3, no. 214, pp. 191–246, 2008.

[5] A. Cadbury, "The financial aspects of corporate governance," HMG, London, Tech. Rep., 1992. [Online]. Available: http://www.ecgi.org/codes/documents/cadbury.pdf Last accessed: Jan 2017

[6] M. C. Jensen, "The modern industrial revolution, exit, and the failure of internal control systems," *J. Finance*, vol. 48, no. 3, pp. 831–880, 1993.

[7] M. C. Jensen and D. Chew, "US corporate governance: Lessons from the 1980's," *Harvard Univ. Press*, no. December 2000, pp. 1–47, 1995.

[8] R. Greenbury, "Directors' remuneration - Report of a study group chaired by Sir Richard Greenbury," HMG, London, Tech. Rep., 1995. [Online]. Available: http://www.emeraldinsight.com/journals.htm?articleid=848139&show=abstract Last accessed: Jan 2017

[9] R. Hampel, "Committee on corporate governance," London, Tech. Rep., 1998.

[10] S. Turnbull, "Corporate governance: Theories, challenges and paradigms," *SSRN Electron. J.*, pp. 1–97, 2000.

[11] P. Myners, "Institutional investment in the United Kingdom: A review," HMG, London, Tech. Rep., 2001.

[12] H. Gov, "Transparency in supply chains etc. A practical guide," 2015. https://www.gov.uk/government/uploads/system/uploads/attachment _data/file/471996/Transparency_in_Supply_Chains_etc__A_practical _guide__final_.pdf Last accessed: Jan 2017

[13] R. Bauer, N. Guenster, and R. Otten, "Empirical evidence on corporate governance in Europe: The effect on stock returns, firm value and performance," *J. Asset Manag.*, vol. 5, no. 2, pp. 91–104, 2004.

[14] W. W. Bratton, "Enron, Sarbanes-Oxley and accounting: Rules versus principles versus rents," *Soc. Sci. Res.*, vol. 48, no. 4, pp. 1023–1056, 2003.

[15] K. Brickey, "From Enron to WorldCom and beyond: Life and crime after Sarbanes-Oxley," 2003. [Online]. Available: http://heinonlinebackup.com/hol-cgi-bin/get_pdf.cgi?handle=hein.journals/walq81&section=19 Last accessed: Jan 2017

[16] B. Holmstrom and S. N. Kaplan, "the State of U.S. corporate governance: What's right and what's wrong?" *J. Appl. Corp. Financ.*, vol. 15, no. 3, pp. 8–20, mar 2003.

[17] L. E. Mitchell, "The Sarbanes-Oxley Act and the reinvention of corporate governance?" *Villanovo Law Rev.*, vol. 48, no. 4, pp. 1189–1216, 2003.

[18] R. E. Rosen, "Risk management and corporate governance: The case of Enron," *Conn. Law Rev.*, vol. 35, no. 1157, pp. 1157–1184, 2003.

[19] Financial Reporting Council, "The combined code on corporate governance," HMG, London, Tech. Rep. July, jan 2006. [Online]. Available: http://doi.wiley.com/10.1111/1467-923X.00209 Last accessed: Jan 2017

[20] Financial Reporting Council, "The Turnbull Guidance as an evaluation framework for the purposes of Section 404(a) of the Sarbanes-Oxley Act," Financial Reporting Council, London, Tech. Rep., 2004.

[21] G. Clinch, B. Sidhu, and S. Sin, "OECD principles of corporate governance," Organisation for Economic Co-Operation and Development, Tech. Rep. 4, may 1999. [Online]. Available: http://www.oecd.org/corporate/ca/corporategovernanceprinciples /33977036.pdf Last accessed: Jan 2017

[22] Financial Reporting Council, "The combined code on corporate governance," Financial Reporting Council, London, Tech. Rep. July, 2006.

[23] Financial Reporting Council, "Review of the 2003 combined code: Summary of responses to the review," Financial Reporting Council, London, Tech. Rep., 2006.

[24] Financial Reporting Council, "Review of the implementation of the 2006 combined code: Regulatory impact assessment," Financial Reporting Council, London, Tech. Rep., 2008.

[25] Financial Reporting Council, "The UK corporate governance code," Financial Reporting Council, London, Tech. Rep. September, 2010. [Online]. Available: http://www.nonexecutivedirector.co.uk/images/files/ UKCorporateGovernanceCodeSeptember2012.pdf Last accessed: Jan 2017

[26] Financial Reporting Council, "The UK stewardship code," Financial Reporting Council, London, Tech. Rep., 2012.

[27] B. Duncan and M. Whittington, "Compliance with standards, assurance and audit: Does this equal security?" in *Proc. 7th Int. Conf. Secur. Inf. Networks*. Glasgow: ACM, 2014, pp. 77–84.

[28] J. W. Barnard, "Shirking, opportunism, self-delusion and more: The agency problem today," *48 Wake For. Law Rev.*, pp. 745–770, 2013.

[29] B. Duncan and M. Whittington, "Company management approaches — stewardship or agency: Which promotes better security in cloud ecosystems?" in *Cloud Comput. 2015*. Nice: IEEE, 2015, pp. 154–159.

[30] N. M. Brennan and J. P. Conroy, "Executive hubris: The case of a bank CEO," *Accounting, Audit. Account. J.*, vol. 26, no. September, pp. 172–195, 2011.

[31] ISO, "ISO/IEC 27000:2009," 2014. [Online]. Available: www.iso.org

[32] IT Governance Institute, *Cobit 4.1*, 2010.

[33] PCI Security Standards Council LLC, "Data Security Standard: Requirements and Security Assessment Procedures," PCI Security Standards Council, Tech. Rep. November, 2013.

[34] PWC, "UK information security breaches survey - Technical report 2012," London, Tech. Rep. April, 2012. [Online]. Available: www.pwc.comwww.bis.gov.uk Last accessed: Jan 2017

[35] FTC, "ASUS settles FTC charges that insecure home routers and "cloud" services put consumers' privacy at Risk," 2016. [Online]. Available: https://www.ftc.gov/news-events/press-releases/2016/02/ asus-settles-ftc-charges-insecure-home-routers-cloud-services-put Last accessed: Jan 2017

[36] B. Duncan and M. Whittington, "Reflecting on whether checklists can tick the box for cloud security," in *Proc. Int. Conf. Cloud Comput. Technol. Sci. CloudCom*, vol. 2015-Febru, no. February. Singapore: IEEE, 2015, pp. 805–810.

[37] C. Biener, M. Eling, and J. H. Wirfs, "Insurability of cyber risk: An empirical analysis," Geneva Pap. Risk Insur. Issues Pract., vol. 40, no. 1, pp. 131–158, 2015.

[38] P. Pandey and E. A. Snekkenes, "A performance assessment metric for information security financial instruments," in Information Society (i-Society), 2015 Intl. Conf. on, 2015, pp. 138–145.

# Security and Privacy Requirements Engineering Methods for Traditional and Cloud-Based Systems: A Review

Argyri Pattakou and Christos Kalloniatis

Privacy Engineering and Social
Informatics Laboratory,
Department of Cultural
Technology and Communication,
University of the Aegean
University Hill
GR 81100 Mytilene, Greece
Email: a.pattakou@aegean.gr, chkallon@aegean.gr

Stefanos Gritzalis

Information and Communication Systems
Security Laboratory,
Department of Information
and Communications Systems Engineering,
University of the Aegean
GR 83200 Samos
Greece
Email: sgritz@aegean.gr

***Abstract*—As the software industry experiences a rapid growth in developing information systems, many methodologies, technologies and tools are continuously developing in order to support the system implementation process. However, as security and privacy have been considered important aspects of an information system, many researchers presented methods that, through a number of specific steps, enable system designers to integrate security and privacy requirements at the early stage of system design. Different security and privacy engineering methods have been presented in order to be applied in traditional or cloud architectures. This paper reviews a number of security and privacy requirements engineering methods in both areas and presents a comparative study between these methods.**

***Keywords–security; privacy; requirements; engineering methods; traditional architectures; cloud computing.***

## I. INTRODUCTION

For many decades, as the software industry has been constantly growing, the main interest of software engineers was to deliver new software releases rapidly, with no bugs and with the appropriate functionality. Under these circumstances, new tools, methodologies and technologies have been introduced in order to support system analysis and design, as well as software implementation. However, in the last decade, the software engineers community has realized that security and privacy are very important aspects in software engineering and, as a result, all the development software systems have to ensure security and privacy of the stored data [1]-[6].

As the interest of software engineers was mainly in developing new software, security and privacy was considered during implementation stage more as an ad-hoc process rather than an integrated process at the system design level. However, each late detection of possible security or privacy vulnerabilities has been proven to be extremely costly and time-consuming. Indeed, many researchers argue that security and privacy requirements have to be considered at the system analysis and design stage as security and privacy constraints might affect software functional requirements. In this direction, we need mechanisms in order to elicit and analyse security and privacy requirements through a number of well-defined steps.

However, as the software industry was faced with a lack of integrated security and privacy requirements engineering methods, many researchers focused on introducing methods that support the elicitation of security and privacy requirements during the system design process. A requirement engineering method in the area of security and privacy can support engineers to define critical assets and the threats against them, to identify with accuracy security or/and privacy goals and to examine any kind of conflicts between them in order to come up with a clear and resistant set of security or/and privacy requirements.

Security and privacy requirements engineering methods have been built based on different approaches because, for each method, security and privacy requirements can be derived from different processes. For instance, some methods were introduced as goal-oriented methodologies as security and privacy goals might affect functional goals while other methods put as central issue potential risks and threats in order for security and privacy requirements to be derived. Different approaches can cover possible limitations or gaps among methods, as well as provide a variety of options to system analysts and designers in order to select the method that best fits the system into consideration.

During the last decade, literature has presented a number of security and privacy requirements engineering methods that support system designers and developers to implement secure and privacy-aware information systems hosted in traditional architectures. Some methods consider security or privacy requirements separately, but some other methods consider privacy as a subset of security. Recent literature efforts [6]-[8] emphasize the need for parallel examination of security and privacy requirements under the same unified framework, as a possible security breach might affect users privacy and vice versa. However, few steps have been taken in this direction [9].

On the other hand, as cloud computing architecture introduces special characteristics, security and privacy requirements methods have to be developed in order to cover these special needs [10]-[12]. However, as the cloud computing area still suffers from a lack of integrated requirements engineering methods, methods that were initially introduced for traditional architecture systems were extended in order to be applied in cloud systems as well [13]. But, at the moment, a method for cloud architecture that supports the parallel examination of security and privacy concepts has not been introduced.

In this paper, we present a number of security and privacy requirements methods that have been introduced in the last decades in order to support system design and analysis in traditional or cloud architectures. Also, we present a comparative study among methods that demonstrates the need for designing a framework that will consider security and privacy together under a holistic unified approach. Section 2 presents a set of security and privacy requirements engineering methods for traditional architectures and a comparative study among them. Section 3 is referring to security and privacy requirements engineering methods that can be applied in a cloud environment and Section 4 concludes the paper.

## II. Security and Privacy Requirements Engineering Methods in Traditional Architectures

### A. Security and Privacy Requirements Engineering methods

*1) Security Quality Requirements Engineering (SQUARE) Methodology:* SQUARE methodology [14] was introduced because the software industry was missing an integrated model for eliciting and analyzing security requirements. The proposed methodology is a risk-driven method that supports the elicitation, categorization, prioritization and inspection of the security requirements through a number of specific steps. SQUARE also supports the performance of risk assessment in order to verify the tolerance of the system against possible threats. The final output of this method is a document that includes all the necessary security requirements that are essential in order for the security goals of the system to be satisfied. The methodology introduces the terms of security goal, threat and risk but does not take into consideration the assets and the vulnerabilities of the system. The application of SQUARE methodology requires the participation and the cooperation between stakeholders and the requirements engineering team in order to identify with accuracy all the necessary security requirements at the early stage of the development process. SQUARE does not refer to the elicitation of privacy requirements.

*2) Model Oriented Security Requirements Engineering (MOSRE):* As many research efforts conclude that considering non-functional requirements after system design can be proved very costly, P. Salini and S. Kanmani introduced a security requirements engineering framework (MOSRE) [15] for Web applications that considers security requirements at the early stages of the development process. The framework covers all phases of requirements engineering and suggests the specification of the security requirements alongside with the specification of system requirements. The authors suggest the identification of the objectives, stakeholders and assets of the Web application during the inception phase. The elicitation phase includes the identification of non-security goals and requirements in parallel with security goals, the identification-categorization-prioritization of threats and system vulnerabilities and a risk assessment process in order to elicit the final security requirements. Next phases include the analysis and modeling, the categorization-prioritization and the validation of the final security requirements. The framework does not support the elicitation of privacy requirements.

*3) Security Requirements Engineering Framework (SREF):* Haley et al. [16] introduced a problem based approach in order to elicit and analyze security requirements. The authors describe an iterative process of four steps. During these steps, security goals can be identified after the identification of functional (business) requirements. The identification of security goals includes the identification of system assets and a threat analysis. Risk assessment is also supported during the identification of security goals. However, in order to elicit security requirements from these security goals, the authors of Security Requirements Engineering Framework (SREF) [16] take security requirements as constraints for functional requirements of the system under consideration and these constraints satisfy one or more security goals. The authors also encourage the use of problem diagrams to capture functional requirements with such constraints. The framework includes the notion of trust assumptions and the construction of satisfaction arguments by system analysts in order to validate security requirements. Privacy requirements are not considered by this framework.

*4) Eliciting Security Requirements from the Business Process Models :* N. Ahmed and R. Matulevicius introduced an asset based approach in order to elicit security goals from business process models and translate them into security requirements [17]. The method consists of two stages. At the first stage, an early analysis is performed in order to determine business assets that must be protected against security risks and security goals. At the second stage, the elicitation of security requirements is performed during examination of the security risk of business assets in five contextual areas: access control, communication channel, input interfaces, business services and data store. The final result is the elicitation of security requirements and the generation of business rules that satisfy security goals of the system under consideration. This framework does not support categorization, prioritization and validation of security requirements.

*5) Security Requirements Engineering process (SREP):* Mellado et al. presented SREP method [18] in order to provide a unified framework that considers concepts from requirements engineering and security engineering as well. Security Requirements Engineering Process (SREP) is an iterative and incremental security requirements engineering process and is aiming to integrate security requirements at the early stages of software development life cycle [19]. SREP is an asset-based method, as well as a threat and risk driven method and it is based on the integration of Common Criteria [20] into the software life cycle in order to specify security requirements and validate that products meet security goals. The main idea of the proposed framework is that the unified process is divided into four phases: Inception, Elaboration, Construction and Transition. Each phase might include many iterations of nine activities (definitions, identification of assets, security objectives and threats, risk assessment, elicitation of security requirements, categorization-prioritization, inspection and repository improvement) but with different emphasis depending on what phase of the lifecycle the iteration is in [18]. Also, the authors propose the use of Security Resources Repositories to store sets of requirements that can be reused in different domains. Privacy requirements have not been considered by the authors.

*6) Secure Tropos:* Tropos methodology [21] was introduced by Castro et al. in order to cover system requirements during the whole software development process. However, Tropos methodology gives a strong focus on the early stage of system analysis. The framework includes five development phases: early requirements, late requirements, architectural design, detailed design and implementation. However, security concepts have not been considered in any of theses phases. Thus, Mouratidis et al. extended Tropos methodology in order to accommodate security concepts during the requirements analysis. The extension is called Secure Tropos [22] and utilizes only the early and late requirements phases of Tropos framework. Secure Tropos introduces the concept of security constraints. According to the authors, security constraints are a set of conditions, rules and restrictions that are imposed on a system and the system must operate in such way that none of them will be violated [22]. In the early requirements phase, a security diagram is constructed in order to represent the connection between security features, threats and mechanisms that help the satisfaction of security goals. The security diagram is taken into consideration at the late requirements phase in order for the designers to impose security constraints to the system-to-be. The enforcement of security constraints in different parts of the system can facilitate the disclosure of possible conflicts between requirements.

*7) KAOS:* In 2000, KAOS [23] was first introduced as a goal-oriented requirements engineering method in order to elaborate requirements from high level goals. According to the authors, the fulfillment of goals might be blocked by some exceptional agent behaviors that are called obstacles. In KAOS method, these obstacles have to be identified and resolved, through the elaboration of scenarios between software and agents, in order to produce a reliable system [24]. However, due to the fact that KAOS methodology considers only functional requirements, authors extended KAOS [25] in order to elaborate security requirements as well. The main idea of the extended framework is to build two models. A model of the system-to-be, that will describe the software and the relations between goals, agents, objects, operations and requirements and an anti-model that will capture possible attackers, their goals and system vulnerabilities in order to elicit all possible threats and security requirements to prevent such treats. Security requirements that derived by the anti-model as countermeasures have to be integrated in the original model.

*8) PresSure:* In 2014, Fabender et al. introduced a problem-based methodology, which is called presSure [26]-[27] in order to identify security needs during requirements analysis of software systems. The identification of security requirements is based on functional requirements of a system-to-be and on the early identification of possible threats. The methodology supports the modeling of functional requirements through problem diagrams. At next stage and after identifying the critical assets of the system and the rights of the authorized entities, possible attackers and their abilities have to be determined. Based on that information, a set of graphs is generated in order to visualize flows of possible threats related to the attackers access to critical assets. Security requirements derived from the analysis of these graphs. For each identified asset, every functional requirement is related with possible threats and security requirements.

*9) LINDDUN:* LINDDUN [28] was first introduced in 2010 by Deng et al. as a privacy threat analysis framework in order to support the elicitation and fulfillment of privacy requirements in software-based systems. According to the LINDDUN methodology, after designing a data flow diagram (DFD) of the system, privacy threats are related to the listed elements of the DFD. Threats in LINDDUN are categorized in seven types: Linkability, Identifiability, Non-repudiation, Detectability, Information Disclosure, Content Unawareness, Policy and consent Non-compliance. The method uses privacy threats trees and misuse cases in order to collect the threat scenarios of the system. Trough these misuse cases, privacy requirements can be extracted. Also, LINDDUN supports the prioritization and validation of privacy threat through the process of risk-assessment, before eliciting the final privacy requirements and before selecting the appropriate privacy-enhancing technologies. The authors of LINDDUN also map privacy-enhancing technologies to each privacy requirement in order to support system designers to select the appropriate techniques that satisfy privacy requirements.

*10) SQUARE for privacy:* After noting that, apart from security, privacy needs more attention during developing software systems, the authors of SQUARE methodology [14] adapted their approach in order to support the elicitation of privacy requirements at the early stages of software development process [29]. The extended framework includes the same steps as the original SQUARE method in conjunction with the Privacy Requirements Elicitation Technique (PRET) [30], a technique that supports the elicitation and prioritization of privacy requirements. This technique uses a database of privacy requirements based on privacy laws and regulations. However, the authors note that the database needs to be updated as the laws change and conclude that a new integrated tool is needed in order to support the elicitation of security and privacy requirements in parallel.

*11) PriS:* PriS [31] has been introduced by Kalloniatis et al. as a goal-oriented approach in order to integrate privacy requirements into the system design process. The main idea of this methodology is that privacy requirements are considered as organizational goals and adopts the use of privacy-process patterns in order to describe the impact of privacy goals to the affected organizational processes, to model the privacy-related organizational processes and to support the selection of the system architecture that best satisfies these processes. Thus, the authors of PriS cover the gap between system design and implementation phase. According to PriS, the identification of privacy goals is based on eight privacy concepts namely authentication, authorization, identification, data protection, anonymity, pseudonymity, unlinkability and unobservability.

*12) Secure Tropos and PriS metamodel:* According to the above methodologies, most of the approaches in requirements engineering tend to consider security and privacy separately or consider privacy as a subset of security. However, a number of research efforts [6]-[7] support that security and privacy are two different concepts that have to be examined separately but under the same unified framework. Under these circumstances, Islam et al. [9] introduced a model-based process that considers security and privacy concepts in parallel at the early stage of system analysis. This process integrates two different engineering methods. Secure Tropos is used as the main method in order to identify and analyse security requirements of the system under consideration. However, as privacy concepts are not considered through this method, Secure Tropos is extended integrating the PriS solution. Thus, security and privacy requirements can be identified and analysed in order to meet the goals but also the appropriate architecture and implementation technique can be selected in order for privacy goals to be satisfied.

### *B. A Comparison of Security and Privacy Requirements Engineering Methods*

Many different approaches in the area of security and privacy requirements engineering have been presented in the previous section. Table 1 summarizes and compares the aforementioned methodologies. A table entry that is labeled with Y or N means that the relevant criterion is considered or not by the relevant method.

A first remark is that most methods consider explicitly security or privacy requirements in order to design secure systems. On the other hand, the extension of KAOS method considers privacy as a subset of security. However, as privacy has separate aspects than security and a security incident might have a serious impact in user's privacy and vice versa, security and privacy requirements have to be examined in parallel under the same framework in order to design secure systems[6]-[8]. The meta-model presented by Islam et al. [9] is able to support security and privacy requirements as it combines concepts from Secure Tropos and PriS methodologies that deal with security and privacy issues separately.

It is worth noting that all the aforementioned methodologies can be applied at the early stage of system analysis and design as a late reconsideration of security and privacy requirements can be extremely costly and time-consuming. LINDDUN, PriS methodology and therefore Secure Tropos and PriS metamodel include steps in order to fill the gap between system design and implementation stage and to support developers to select the most appropriate implementation technique.

Each methodology has been build by using a different approach. MOSRE, Secure Tropos, KAOS, PriS and the Secure Tropos and PriS meta-model have been introduced as goal-oriented methodologies as security and privacy requirements are considered as organizational goals that have to be satisfied by the system into consideration. On the other hand, SQUARE methodology and SQUARE extension for integrating privacy requirements have been based on risk analysis results. It is worth noting that even if SQUARE method supports the identification of system threats and the corresponding vulnerabilities, the assets of the system that have to be secured are not considered by the method. On the contrary, the proposed methods by Ahmed et al. [17], MOSRE, SREF and SREP support risk analysis on business assets in order to elicit security requirements. Additionally, as many methodologies have integrated steps in order to support threat identification, SREP and LINDDUN put threat analysis in the center of their attention in order to elicit security or privacy requirements. SREF and presSure have been introduced as problem-based methods as the analysis and the elicitation of security requirements comes from the analysis of problem diagrams.

Regarding the categorization/prioritization criterion, it could be noticed that for many methods this step is a logical extension of a risk analysis process. A categorization and prioritization of security or privacy requirements is an important aspect of many approaches, as, during this process, system designers have to decide if the implementation cost of a requirement is comparable with the value of the secured asset. SQUARE, MOSRE, SREP, LINDDUN and PriS support categorization/prioritization of requirements. Additionally, most of the approaches, SQUARE, MOSRE, SREF, SREP, PriS and the Secure Tropos with PriS metamodel include steps for requirements inspection. Finally, MOSRE, Secure Tropos, PriS and Secure Tropos with PriS meta-model examine the existence of any conflicts between requirements and security or privacy goals.

Table 2 presents the security and privacy requirements that each method aspires to cover. Where $\sim$ is labeled, that means that the author of the method does not specify the requirements.

## III. SECURITY AND PRIVACY REQUIREMENTS IN CLOUD COMPUTING ENVIRONMENT

In the recent years, as cloud computing has rapidly grown, many research efforts have been presented that consider security and privacy into the development process. Almorsy et al. [10] introduced a Model-Driven Security Engineering at Runtime (MDSE@R) approach for multi-tenant cloud-based applications. MDSE@R supports different tenants and service providers security requirements at runtime instead of design time by externalizing security from the application. More specific, service providers may impose some security controls as mandatory but multi tenants can also add extra security requirements at runtime at their own instance of the application. Fernandez et al. [11] presented a method on how to build a cloud Security Reference Architecture (SRE). An SRE is an abstract architecture that describes functionality without implementation details and includes security mechanisms to the appropriate places in order to provide a degree of security. This approach includes threat identification and uses misuse patterns in order to describe how an attack can be performed. Through this process, it can be verified that security patterns have been selected correctly and have been placed properly in the cloud architecture. In 2015, Perez et al [12] presented a data-centric authorization solution, namely SecRBAC, in order to secure data in the cloud. SecRBC is a rule-based approach that provides data managing authorization to CSP through roles and object hierarchies. The authorization model uses advanced cryptographic techniques in order to protect data from CSP misbehavior also. In 2016, Mouratidis et al. [13] extended Secure Tropos requirements engineering approach for traditional software systems in order to enable modeling of security requirements that are unique in cloud computing environment and to support the selection of the appropriate cloud deployment model as well as the cloud service provider that best satisfies security requirements of the system under consideration. In 2013, Tancock et al. [32] presented the architecture of a Privacy Impact Assessment (PIA) tool in order to identify and evaluate possible future security and privacy risks on data stored in a cloud infrastructure. The risk summary that derives from PIA tool takes into consideration aspects like who the cloud provider is, what is the trust rating and what security and privacy mechanisms are used. As threat modeling is an important aspect for developing secure systems, Cloud Privacy Threat Modeling (CPTM) methodology [33] was proposed in order to support the identification of possible attacks and to propose the corresponding countermeasures for a cloud system through a number of specific steps. However, CPTM was designed in order to support only EU data protection directives

TABLE I. COMPARISON OF SECURITY AND PRIVACY ENGINEERING METHODS

| *Method* | Requirements | Approach | Stage | Assets | Risk Assessment | Categorization/Prioritization | Threats | Req. Inspection | Conflicts Identification |
|---|---|---|---|---|---|---|---|---|---|
| SQUARE | Security | Risk driven | Early Design | N | Y | Y | Y | Y | N |
| MOSRE | Security | Goal oriented | Early Design | Y | Y | Y | Y | Y | Y |
| SREF | Security | Problem based | Early Design | Y | Y | N | Y | Y | N |
| N. Ahmed et al. | Security | Asset based | Early Design | Y | Y | N | N | N | N |
| SREP | Security | Threat based | Early Design | Y | Y | Y | Y | Y | N |
| Secure Tropos | Security | Goal oriented | Early/Late Design | Y | N | N | Y | N | Y |
| KAOS | Security | Goal oriented | Early Design | N | Y | N | Y | N | N |
| PresSure | Security | Problem based | Early Design | Y | N | N | Y | N | N |
| LINDDUN | Privacy | Threat driven | Early/Late Design | N | Y | Y | Y | N | N |
| SQUARE for privacy | Privacy | Risk driven | Early Design | N | Y | Y | Y | Y | N |
| PriS | Privacy | Goal oriented | Early/Late Design - Implementation | N | N | Y | N | Y | Y |
| Secure Tropos with PriS | Security/Privacy | Goal oriented | Early/Late Design - Implementation | Y | N | N | Y | Y | Y |

*Y=Yes, N=No

TABLE II. SECURITY AND PRIVACY REQUIREMENTS PER METHOD

| *Method* | *Requirements* |
|---|---|
| SQUARE | CIA |
| MOSRE | CIA, Authentication, Authorization, Auditing |
| SREF | CIA, Accountability |
| N. Ahmed et al. | CIA, Authentication, Authorization |
| SREP | ~ |
| Secure Tropos | CIA, Access control, Non-repudiation, Authentication, Accountability |
| KAOS | CIA, Privacy, Authentication, Non-repudiation |
| PresSure | CIA |
| LINDDUN | Unlinkability, Anonymity, Pseudonimity, Plausible deniability, Undetectability, Unobservability, Confidentiality, Content awareness, Policy & consent compliance |
| SQUARE for privacy | ~ |
| PriS | Identification, Authentication, Authorization, Data protection, Anonymity, Pseudonimity, Unlinkability, Unobservability |
| Secure Tropos with PriS | All SecureTropos and PriS requirements |

**CIA=Confidentiality, Integrity, Availability

and as a result the methodology presented a number of weaknesses in threat identification. Thus, A. Gholami and E. Laure [34] extended CPTM methodology in order to be complied with various legal frameworks. As it is hard for an organization to choose the appropriate cloud deployment type (public, private, hybrid or community), K. Beckers et al. presented a method that can support requirements engineers to decide which cloud deployment model best fits the privacy requirements of the system under consideration [35]. This approach is based on a threat analysis in parallel with the privacy requirements that the system shall satisfy and some other facts and assumptions about the environment like the number of stakeholders on each deployment scenario and the domains that have to be outsourced into a cloud.

Despite the fact that all these contributions develop different kind of mechanisms or processes that consider security and privacy issues in the context of cloud computing, most of them present a number of limitations. Some of them are related to specific cloud service models. MDSE@R is referred to a Software as a Service service (SaaS) model while the method for building a Security Reference Architecture is referred to an Infrastructure as a Service (IaaS) service model. On the other hand, most of the proposed frameworks, methods or processes in the context of cloud computing deal exclusively with security or privacy issues or in some cases privacy is considered as a subset of security. For instance, MDSE@R, secRBAC and SecureTropos consider only security issues while the Privacy Assessment Impact Tool (PIA), CPMT and the method for selecting the appropriate cloud deployment model focus explicitly on privacy issues. In our previous work [8], we presented the reasons why security and privacy have to be considered as two different concepts but have to be examined under the same unified framework. This framework has also been presented in our work. Nevertheless, one of the most important issues is that most of the proposed frameworks that are based on the idea of cloud computing integrate security and privacy controls during implementation phase and not earlier in requirements phase. But, such practices might create late corrections in security and privacy requirements which means additional cost and severe delays in project delivery.

As cloud computing is a new and continuously developing environment, many research efforts have been presented over the last decade that highlight the need of adopting security and privacy mechanisms from the early stage of development life cycle. Nevertheless, until today security and privacy in the context of cloud computing is still performed as an ad-hoc process rather than an integrated process in the development life cycle. As it is mentioned above, Mouratidis et al. [13] presented a requirements engineering method in order to model cloud security requirements at the design level but no privacy requirements have been considered. Under these circumstances, literature presents a lack of integrated methods that through a number of specific steps could be able to support the parallel elicitation and analysis of cloud security and privacy requirements from the early stage of system design. It is worth noting that a security and privacy requirements engineering method at the design level should include steps in order to fill the gap between analysis and implementation phase in order to support system developers to select the appropriate technologies that best satisfy security and privacy requirements.

## IV. Conclusion and Future work

In this paper, we presented a set of security and privacy requirements engineering methods that have been introduced by several researchers. Our research has focused on two areas: on those methods that aim to support software engineers to design and develop information systems hosted in traditional architectures and on those methods that can be applied in cloud systems.

As already mentioned, different security and privacy requirements engineering methods have been introduced in the past as software engineers community agree that security and privacy is still an integral part of the information systems design process. Referring to traditional architectures, there are different approaches that each method has been based on. For instance, security or privacy requirements can be derived from the determination of security or privacy goals, from the results of a risk analysis or from problem diagrams. Additionally, as it is clear from the above analysis, most researchers deal with security or privacy issues separately, a fact that can cause possible conflicts and late reconsiderations in functional requirements.

On the other hand, cloud computing is a more demanding structure as it introduces special characteristics like multi-tenancy and on-demand services. Special characteristics introduce new security and privacy concepts that software engineers have to take into account during system designing and developing. However, even though cloud computing presents a rapid growth last decade, all methods that have been presented by researchers present limitations while it is noting the lack of integrated methods that support the elicitation and analysis of security and privacy requirements in parallel.

The purpose of this research is to demonstrate that in cloud computing area there is a lack of integrated requirements engineering methods that consider security and privacy as two different concepts that have to be examined in parallel under the same unified framework. This study along with our previously proposed conceptual framework [8] will be the base for developing a new methodology in the cloud computing area that will consider security and privacy under the same unified framework.

## References


[1] I. M. Alharbi, S. Zyngier, and C. Hodkinson, "Privacy by design and customers perceived privacy and security concerns in the success of e-commerce," Journal of Enterprise Information Management, vol.26, no.6, 2013, pp. 702-718

[2] R. Cullen, "Culture, identity and information privacy in the age of digital government", Online Information Review, vol.33, no.3, 2009, pp. 405-421

[3] Z. Karake Shalhoub, "Trust, privacy, and security in electronic business: the case of the GCC countries", Information Management Computer Security, vol. 14, no.3, 2006, pp. 270-283

[4] M. Meingast, T. Roosta, and S. Sastry, "Security and privacy issues with health care information technology", Engineering in Medicine and Biology Society, 2006. EMBS'06, 28th Annual International Conference of the IEEE, 2006, pp. 5453-5458

[5] S. E. Sarma, S. A. Weis, and D. W. Engels, "RFID systems and security and privacy implications", International Workshop on Cryptographic Hardware and Embedded Systems, Springer Berlin Heidelberg, 2002, pp. 454-469

[6] S. Gritzalis, "Enhancing Web privacy and anonymity in the digital era", Information Management and Computer Security, vol. 12, no. 3, 2004, Emerald Group Publishing Limited, pp. 255-288

[7] C. Kalloniatis, E. Kavakli, and S. Gritzalis, "Addressing privacy requirements in system design: The PriS method", Requirements Engineering Journal, vol. 13, no.3, 2008, pp. 241- 255

[8] A. Pattakou, C. Kalloniatis, and S. Gritzalis, "Reasoning About Security and Privacy in Cloud Computing under a Unified Meta-Model", In Proceedings of the Tenth International Symposium on Human Aspects of Information Security Assurance, HAISA 2016, pp. 56

[9] S. Islam, H. Mouratidis, C. Kalloniatis, A. Hudic, and L. Zechner, "Model based process to support security and privacy requirements engineering", International Journal of Secure Software Engineering (IJSSE), 2012, vol.3, no.3, pp. 1-22

[10] M. Almorsy, J. Grundy, and A. S. Ibrahim, "Adaptable, model-driven security engineering for SaaS cloud-based applications", Automated software engineering, vol.21, no.2, 2014, pp. 187-224

[11] E. B. Fernandez, R. Monge, and K. Hashizume, "Building a security reference architecture for cloud systems", Requirements Engineering, 2015, pp. 1-25

[12] J.M.M. Perez, G. M. Perez, and A. F. Gomez-Skarmeta, "SecRBAC: Secure data in the Clouds", IEEE Transactions on Services Computing, 2016

[13] H. Mouratidis, N. Argyropoulos, and S. Shei, "Security Requirements Engineering for Cloud Computing: The Secure Tropos Approach", Domain-Specific Conceptual Modeling, Springer International Publishing, 2016, pp. 357-380

[14] N. R. Mead and T. Stehney, "Security quality requirements engineering (SQUARE) methodology", ACM, 2005, vol.30, no.4, pp. 1-7

[15] P. Salini and S. Kanmani, "Model oriented security requirements engineering (MOSRE) framework for Web applications", Advances in Computing and Information Technology, Springer Berlin Heidelberg, 2013, pp. 341-353

[16] C. Haley, R. Laney, J. Moffett, and B. Nuseibeh, "Security requirements engineering: A framework for representation and analysis", IEEE Transactions on Software Engineering, 2008, vol. 34, no. 1, pp. 133-153

[17] N. Ahmed and R. Matulevicius, "A Method for Eliciting Security Requirements from the Business Process Models", In CAiSE (Forum/Doctoral Consortium), 2014, pp. 57-64

[18] D. Mellado, E. Fernandez-Medina, and M. Piattini, "A common criteria based security requirements engineering process for the development of secure information systems", Computer standards interfaces, vol.29, no.2, 2007, pp. 244-253

[19] B. Fabian, S. Grses, M. Heisel, T. Santen, and H. Schmidt, "A comparison of security requirements engineering methods", Requirements engineering, 2010, vol.15, no.1, pp.7-40

[20] Infrastructure, Public Key, and Token Protection Profile, "Common criteria for information technology security evaluation." National Security Agency, 2002

[21] J. Castro, M. Kolp, and J. Mylopoulos, "Towards requirements-driven information systems engineering: the Tropos project", Information systems, vol.27, no.6, 2002, pp. 365-389

[22] H. Mouratidis, "A natural extension of tropos methodology for modelling security", 2002

[23] A. V. Lamsweerde and E. Letier, "Handling obstacles in goal-oriented requirements engineering", IEEE Transactions on Software Engineering, vol.26, no.10, 2000, pp. 978-1005

[24] S. Pachidi, "Goal-Oriented Requirements Engineering with KAOS", 2009

[25] A. V. Lamsweerde, "Elaborating security requirements by construction of intentional anti-models", Proceedings of the 26th International Conference on Software Engineering, IEEE Computer Society, 2004

[26] S. Fassbender, M. Heisel, and R. Meis, "Functional requirements under security pressure", Software Paradigm Trends (ICSOFT-PT), 9th International Conference on IEEE, 2014

[27] S. Fabender, M. Heisel, and R. Meis, "Problem-Based Security Requirements Elicitation and Refinement with PresSuRE", International Conference on Software Technologies, Springer International Publishing, 2014, pp. 311-330

[28] M. Deng, K. Wuyts, R. Scandariato, B. Preneel, and W. Joosen, "A privacy threat analysis framework: supporting the elicitation and fulfillment of privacy requirements", Requirements Engineering, 2011, vol.16, no.1, pp. 3-32

[29] A. Bijwe and N. R. Mead, "Adapting the square process for privacy requirements engineering", 2010

[30] S. Miyazaki, N. Mead, and J. Zhan, "Computer-aided privacy requirements elicitation technique", Asia-Pacific Services Computing Conference, APSCC'08, IEEE, 2008

[31] C. Kalloniatis, E. Kavakli, and S. Gritzalis, "Addressing privacy requirements in system design: the PriS method", Requirements Engineering, vol.13, no.3, 2008, pp. 241-255

[32] D. Tancock, S. Pearson, and A. Charlesworth, "A privacy impact assessment tool for cloud computing", Privacy and security for Cloud computing, Springer London, 2013, pp. 73-123

[33] A. Gholami, A. S. Lind, J. Reichel, J.E. Litton, A. Edlund, and E. Laure, "Privacy threat modeling for emerging biobankclouds", Procedia Computer Science, 2014, vol. 37, pp. 489-496

[34] A. Gholami and E. Laure, "Advanced cloud privacy threat modeling", arXiv preprint arXiv:1601.01500, 2016

[35] K. Beckers, S. Fabender, S. Gritzalis, M. Heisel, C. Kalloniatis, and R. Meis, "Privacy-Aware Cloud Deployment Scenario Selection", In International Conference on Trust, Privacy and Security in Digital Business, 2014, September, pp. 94-105, Springer International Publishing

# Trust Managemement Parameters in Cloud Computing Environments

Zafeiroula Georgiopoulou
Department of Digital Systems,
University of Piraeus
Piraeus, Athens
e-mail: roulageorgio@ssl-unipi.gr

Costas Lambrinoudakis
Department of Digital Systems,
University of Piraeus
Piraeus, Athens
e-mail: clam@unipi.gr

**Abstract— In cloud computing environments, successful trust management can compensate the countermeasures that have been adopted for mitigating the security and privacy risks that the cloud comes across. This paper identifies the parameters that a trust model should include. These parameters are presented together with a detailed analysis of how, each of them, could be applied/utilized by the trust model for quantifying the trust of the cloud providers to their users.**

***Keywords- Cloud Computing; Trust; Trust Managemen;' Trust Models; Privacy; Trust metric***

## I. INTRODUCTION

Cloud computing is a technology that has emerged in all aspects of modern Information Technology infrastructure providing comparative advantages to organizations. However, this deployment and cloud tenancy create major security concerns and loss of trust that mainly comes with the loss of physical perimeter control. During the previous years, several scientists have addressed the issue of proper trust management [1].

A fine-tuned trust management would be a very good countermeasure for many security and privacy risks in cloud environments. The main reason for such a conclusion is that having in place proper trust management mechanisms, users can select providers based on their requirements and trustworthiness and, at the same time, providers can reject or accept users based on how trustful they are.

The novelty of the trust management model proposed in this paper is that it allows cloud providers to monitor in real-time the users of their services. Based on our previous literature review research [1], we propose a list of trust parameters, together with an in depth description of how trust management can be applied per parameter. Furthermore, the proposed model includes a trust metric that will be capitalized for quantifying trust [3].

The structure of the paper is as follows: The next section defines the trust modeling parameters that should be considered for facilitating proper trust management of the users by the cloud providers. Section III explains how the aforementioned trust parameters could be combined in order to produce the "trust metric" that will quantify the trust of cloud providers to their users. The last section concludes the paper and provides pointers for future work.

## II. TRUST PARAMETERS

Defining the correct trust parameters is a key point for successful trust management. They should take into account all the aspects and factors of a cloud architecture that could affect trust. The proposed list of trust parameters follows next.

### A. *Trusted Access Points*

A user typically connects to the cloud from a pre-defined range of devices. By device we mean any electronic device that a cloud user could employ for accessing cloud services (Laptops, desktops, mobile phones, tablets, etc.). The range of devices that have been already used for connecting to the cloud, and thus fulfill the security policy criteria of the provider, will be referred as "Trusted Access Points".

A trust security policy should take into account the access point and extra attention should be paid in the case of new devices. In favor of "Trusted Access Points", a table with the principal characteristics per device, as listed next, should be maintained in a central repository within the perimeter of the cloud provider.

*a) User ID: Uniquely identifies every user in the cloud.*

*b) Unique Device ID: Uniquely identifies each device that a client is utilizing to access the cloud. This unique identifier is the result of a salted encrypted combination of the Device Type and its MAC address.*

*c) Type: Categorization of device (Mobile, Laptop, Desktop, Tablet etc.)*

*d) Operating System: The device's operating system will be stored since it affects the security parameters. For instance, an Android device is considered less safe from a Windows Server device.*

*e) Date of Last Connection: Information on the date and time that a specific device accessed the cloud.*

All the above will be maintained from a "Trusted Access Point Agent", which will monitor the devices employed by each user.

Every time that a user requires to access the cloud an identification / authorization process will be invoked specifically for the purposes of the "Trusted Access Point". The identification part aims to verify if the user's device has been already whitelisted, by checking a central repository named "Trusted Access Points". If the user attempts to access the cloud with an unknown device, a security flag will be raised, initiating a process that will check whether the specific device can be included in the Trusted Access Points repository or not.

The unknown devices must be identified and should fulfill the security policy's minimum requirements. For instance, mobile devices can be prohibited from the security policy [4].

### B. Location

Determining the geo-location of a device is the process of defining, in a precise manner, the latitude/longitude coordinates of the device together with some other characteristics like country, city, address, zip code and time zone. Based on Isaca's definitions [5], Geolocation data are generated and collected either in an active mode, referred as user-device-based geolocation, or in a passive mode, referred as table look-up or data correlation server-based geolocation. Table 1 [5] summarizes these modes and the technologies that each mode employs.

TABLE I. MODES OF GEOLOCATION DATA GENERATION AND COLLECTION

| Mode | Collection Method | Technologies Involved |
|---|---|---|
| Active: User—Device-based | • Uses firmware and software on user's computer or wireless device<br>• Location determined via GPS chip and/or triangulation using cellular tower information<br>• Request-response model | • GPS<br>• Assisted GPS (A-GPS)<br>•Wi-Fi—Wireless positioning<br>• 3G/4G<br>•Mobile applications—iPhone, Android devices, BlackBerry® |
| Passive: Data-lookup—Sever-based | Involves use of third-party geolocation service providers, e.g., Quova®, NetGeo,Bering Media<br>• Based on nonlocation-specific IP address acquired from user device or service set identifiers (SSIDs) for wireless networks<br>• Correlation with stored IP or SSID databases obtained from purchase records, user-provided information, network analysis of trace routes and domain name system (DNS) host names | • IP location—Whois lookup, DNS LOC, geographic names in domain name user or application information, timing data using ping inference based on routing data, e.g., traceroute monitoring of Internet service provider (ISP) networks<br>• 3G/4G<br>•Wi-Fi—Wireless positioning |

A far as privacy issues are concerned, the proposed model will need the IP Geolocation. Assuming that an accurate method for retrieving the location of a cloud client exists, we will consider how this affects the trustfulness of the client, justifying the fact that a trust security policy should take into account geolocation information [5]-[8].

A user usually accesses the cloud from specific locations. This range of locations will be referred as "Trusted Geolocation Coordinates". To maintain this information, the main characteristics of each user location, as listed next, will be recorded in a central repository within the perimeter of the cloud provider.

a) *User ID: Uniquely identifies every user in the cloud*

b) *Location: Latitude and longitude coordinates of each user location*

c) *IP address: The IP address that the user is utilizing to access the cloud*

d) *City: The City from which the user is accessing the cloud*

e) *Zip: The Zip code of the user's access location*

f) *Time Zone: The Time Zone of the user's location*

g) *Last Access: Information about the date and the time that a user accessed the cloud for the last time form a specific location.*

All the above will be maintained from the "Location Agent". Then, an allowed zone of latitude/longitude coordinates will be defined that a user could be pinpointed. This zone comes from the combination of coordinates and an acceptable distance that has been specified at the initial configuration of the model. Every time a user accesses the cloud an identification and authorization method regarding geolocation characteristics is initiated. The identification process checks a central repository named "Trusted Geolocation Coordinates", in order to verify if the user has been allowed before to access the cloud from the same location and its allowed perimeter. If the user is trying to access the cloud from an unknown location a security flag is raised until a decision of whether that location should, or should not, be included in the list of trusted locations is reached. Clearly, the Location Agent should invoke mechanisms against IP spoofing.

### C. Behavior

In all types of systems (cloud and conventional), a user follows a similar pattern of actions (behavior). In other words, the behavior of a user is expected to be similar within different sessions [1] [10].

A trust security policy should take into account the behavior characteristics of its users. More specifically it is necessary to monitor the data that a user is typically accessing and to consider cases of abnormal behavior. The typical user behavior, in terms of the data that he is accessing and the actions that he is performing, will be referred as "Trusted Behavior". In order to monitor the behavior of a user the cloud provider should monitor the following information.

a) *User ID: Uniquely identifies every user in the cloud.*

b) *Application Unit: During the initialization of the proposed model, the cloud resources are logically separated in isolated application units.*

c) *Authorization granted: Boolean value of whether the user has the appropriate rights to access the specific application unit.*

d) *Type of action: Monitors the user actions; i.e. the user tried to view, write, update or delete information.*

e) *Last Action: Information about the date and the time that a user performed a specific action.*

The audit trail for data access, maintained in the "Trust Behavior Table", will be aggregated by the Trust Behavior Agent. Indicative overall aggregated values follow:

a) *The average number of accesses to each data category.*

b) *The average user throughput (bandwidth for upload and download).*

c) *Volume of data transfers from CSP to the user.*

d) *Volume of data transfers from the user to CSP.*

e) *Average duration of user access.*

f) *Unauthorized modification or view access endeavors.*

The thresholds related to data access should be clearly defined. As a minimum, one threshold for every aggregated value is needed. The Trust Behavior Agent will monitor all users' data accesses and if any of the aforementioned thresholds has been violated a security warning will be raised from the agent. A relevant algorithm will process the information and will decide if the specific user should be excluded from the trusted data access behavior or not.

### D. Resources

A cloud user typically consumes specific resources while using the cloud. By Resources we refer to network and hardware components that the user consumes while connected to cloud. The various resources utilized by a user during a specific session will be monitored and will be referred as "Trusted Resources".

The trust security policy of the proposed model will take into account the resources consumed by a user and in case of excessive use a security warning will be issued. In order to maintain a "Trusted Resources" table, the following information will be traced:

a) *User ID: Uniquely identifies every user in the cloud.*

b) *Unique Device ID: Uniquely identifies each device that a client is utilizing. Maintained in the Trusted Access Point table.*

c) *Session Length: The total session time.*

d) *Bandwidth: Bandwidth of cloud network used.*

e) *Device Memory: Device memory used; depicted as percentage of the total device memory.*

f) *Cloud Memory: Cloud memory used; depicted as percentage of the total cloud memory.*

g) *CPU Threads: CPU usage on user's device.*

h) *Network Ports: List of ports that the user it utilizing on the cloud.*

i) *Volume of data sent: Number of bytes sent by the user during the current session.*

j) *Volume of data received: Number of bytes received by the user during the current session.*

The above information will be maintained by a Trust Resource Agent. Thresholds, regarding the resource limits, are necessary. During each session the Trust Resource Agent will monitor the consumption of cloud resources and in case that the thresholds are violated a security warning will be issued.

### E. Authentication

Another major parameter of the proposed trust model is the authentication behavior of the cloud user. To this end, the following information will be monitored:

a) *User ID : Uniquely identifies every user in the cloud.*

b) *Unsuccessful Logins: Number of times that the user tried to access the cloud services without success.*

c) *Token Used: Metric regarding the security of the tokens used*

d) *Wrong authentication method: In cloud environments that support multiple authentication methods the endeavor to use the wrong method should be monitored.*

The above information will be processed by a "Trust Authentication Agent". A trust authentication value per user will be calculated/updated, based on pre-defined values, during every authentication process. When the value for a user falls below a specific threshold, he will not be considered a trusted user any more. Log in will be banned and further procedures will be required in order to reestablish trust.

### F. Feedbacks

In cases of outsourcing, feedback on consumers who had transactions with other service providers is required. Specifying a common feedback trust metric, regarding trustfulness, between providers, will facilitate the consideration of this information. To this end a "Feedback Trust Table", should be maintained in a central repository within the perimeter of the cloud provider:

a) *User ID : Uniquely identifies every user in the cloud.*

b) *Unsuccessful Logins: Number of times that the user tried to access the cloud services without success.*

c) *Token Used: Metric regarding the security of the tokens used*

d) *Wrong authentication method: In cloud environments that support multiple authentication method the endeavor to use wrong method should be monitored.*

The above information will be processed by a "Provider's Feedback Agent". Every time a user endeavors to access the cloud, the agent will search the relevant table for feedbacks. If the overall feedback value is below a threshold, the user will not be considered trusted and relevant actions should be taken.

### *G. Access Point Security*

Since trust management is part of the security policy, it is evident that the security of the access point – user's computer, phone tablet, etc. – should be taken into account as an important parameter in the trust metric. To this respect, a Security Evidence collector should be available on the provider's side and assuming that the user gives his consent, the agent will collect information regarding the user's device security. The most important items that should be checked are the following:

*a) Use of antivirus*

*b) Use of firewall*

*c) Operating System's Updates and Patches are installed*

*d) List of Software installed*

Based on the collected data, an access point security value will be assigned to every user's device. If the security value for a user device is below some threshold, it will not be allowed to enter the cloud.

## III. TRUST METRIC

The definition of a Trust Metric facilitates the quantification of the degree to which a cloud user can be trusted by a cloud provider and it is necessary to establish trust between the two entities. A simple way to implement this trust metric could be the use of a binary discrete model where the trust values are set 'high', for a highly trusted entity, or 'low' for an untrusted entity.

In order to measure trust with the proposed model, a metric that will quantify, in a general manner, the trustfulness of each user is necessary. The range of trust values (TV) is set to be between 0 to 10; 0 being the minimum trust value and 10 the maximum. Furthermore, the proposed trust metric will employ a weighting factor for every of the aforementioned trust parameters. The weighting factors will represent the importance of each trust parameter and are:

- WAP : Weighting of Trusted Access Point
- WL : Weighting of Geo-location characteristics
- WDA : Weighting of Data Access
- WR : Weighting of Resources
- WA : Weighting of Authentication
- WF : Weighting of Feedback
- WAS: Weighting of Access Point Security
- WFP1…N : Weighting of future parameters

Weights will take values between 0 to 1. The proposed Trust Metric will be:

$$T_{AP}*W_{AP}+T_L*W_L+T_{DA}*W_{DA}+T_R*W_R+T_A*W_A+T_F*W_F+T_{AS}*W_{AS}+T_{FP1}*W_{FP1}+T_{FP2}*W_{FP2}+\ldots\ldots+T_{FPn}*W_{FPn}$$

## IV. CONCLUSIONS & FUTURE WORK

Cloud Computing is a widely accepted technology but it raises a lot of security issues. The goal of our work is to improve the current status by applying proper trust management methods and surpass security risks. In this paper the trust parameters that a cloud trust model should take into account are presented together with an analysis of how these parameters can be monitored. Furthermore, the need for a trust metric, that will quantify the trust of the cloud provider to the user, has been highlighted.

For the future, we aim to provide an overall simulation of the proposed trust model, presenting experimental results from measurements of the trust parameters and the way they are used to calculate the trust metric.

## ACKNOWLEDGMENT

This work has been partially supported by the Research Center of the University of Piraeus.

## REFERENCES

[1] L. Wenjuan, P. Lingdi, and P. Xuezeng, "Use trust management module to achieve effective security mechanisms in cloud environment," in International Conference on Electronics and Information Engineering (ICEIE), vol. 1, Kyoto, Japan, 2010, pp. 14-19.

[2] Z. Georgiopoulou, C. Lambrinoudakis,"Literature Review of Trust Models for Cloud Computing", International Conference On Cloud Computing And Big Data (CloudCom-Asia), Hong Kong, 2016.

[3] P. D. Manuel, T. Selve, and M. I. Abd-EI Barr, "Trust management system for grid and cloud resources" in First International Conference on Advanced Computing (ICAC 2009), Chennai, India, 2009, pp. 176-181.

[4] Y. Zhimin, Q. Lixiang, L. Chang, Y. Chi, and W. Guangming, "A Collaborative Trust Model of Firewall-through based on Computing" in 14th International Conference on Computer Supported Cooperative Work in Design (CSCWD), Shanghai, China, 2010, pp. 329 - 334.

[5] Geolocation: Risk, Issues and Strategies, ISACA, Geolocation: Risk, Issues and Strategies

[6] B. Tang , R. Sandhu, "Cross-Tenant Trust Models in Cloud Computing", Information Reuse and Integration (IRI), 2013 IEEE 14th International Conference on 14-16 Aug. 2013.

[7] B. Eriksson, P. Barford, J. Sommersy, and Robert Nowak, "A Learning-based Approach for IP Geolocation NIST Interagency Report 7904, December 2012

[8] E. K. Banks, M. Bartock, K. Fiftal, D. Lemon, K, Scarfone, U. Shetty et al., "Trusted Geolocation in the Cloud: Proof of Concept Implementation", International Journal of Computer Science and Information Technologies, Vol. 3 (2) , 2012, 3328 – 3333.

[9] B. K. Dewangan1, P. Shende2, "The Sliding Window Method: An Environment To Evaluate User Behavior Trust In Cloud Technology", International Journal of Advanced Research in Computer and Communication Engineering, Vol. 2, Issue 2, February 2013.

[10] T. Li-qin, L. Chuang "Evaluation of User Behavior Trust in Cloud Computing" 2010 International Conference on Computer Application and System Modeling (ICCASM ,2010)

# The Greater The Power, The More Dangerous The Abuse: Facing Malicious Insiders in The Cloud

Nikolaos Pitropakis
School of Electrical and Computer Engineering
Georgia Institute of Technology
Atlanta, United States of America
e-mail: pitropakis@gatech.edu

Christos Lyvas, Costas Lambrinoudakis
Department of Digital Systems
University of Piraeus
Piraeus, Greece
e-mail: {clyvas,clam}@unipi.gr

***Abstract*—The financial crisis made companies around the world search for cheaper and more efficient solutions to cover their needs in terms of computational power and storage. Their quest came to end with the birth of Cloud Computing infrastructures. However, along with the new promising technology, new attack vectors were born, and one old and known threat, that of Malicious Insiders reappeared. Insiders can use their privileged position inside the Cloud infrastructure to accomplish or help in attacks against a Cloud infrastructure. In this paper, we propose a practical and efficient intrusion detection system solution for Cloud infrastructures based on Graphical Processing Unit (GPU) acceleration. Our solution monitors the deployed virtual machines operations and especially those of the host Operating System's, known as Dom0, correlating the collected information to detect uncommon behavior based on the Smith-Waterman algorithm. Our proposal makes possible the cooperation of a variety of known hypervisors along with every known GPU acceleration unit used, thus offering the maximum of security mechanics while at the same time minimizing the imposed overhead in terms of Central Processing Unit (CPU) usage.**

***Keywords-Cloud Computing; Security; Malicious Insider; IDS; GPU Acceleration.***

## I. INTRODUCTION

While economic growth is considered low in the vast majority of the global market, Cloud Computing infrastructures have grown beyond imagination. Their revenues jumped by 25% for 2016 with strong estimated growth ahead. Leading Amazon Web Services (AWS) and Microsoft Azure grew 53% in 2016 [9]. AWS, which introduced the concept of Cloud Computing managed to generate revenue of 13 billion dollars in 2016. As migration services become more convenient and at the same time more appealing, more companies will choose the pay-per-use model that Cloud Computing offers.

Cloud Computing by design cannot offer physical isolation among Virtual Machines (VMs), since all resources are shared. Various attack vectors have been developed [24] and continue to be updated following the lead of security experts, trying to identify shared resources and gain unauthorized access to them. Hypercall attack injection [18], co-residency detection, shared memory vulnerabilities [26] and privilege escalation [7], are only a few examples of the attack vectors that could harm the confidentiality, integrity and availability of Cloud systems and data. It is a fact that Cloud infrastructure's attack surface is an expanded version of older Information Technology (IT) infrastructures, because a potential adversary can make use of additional attacking points to explore a vulnerability (e.g., a VM, a management platform or other components). Malicious Insider threat has reappeared and has become the main reason for data leakage as 1 out of 3 organizations have experienced an insider attack in the year 2016 [10].

Several approaches have been proposed to augment security in Cloud infrastructures. Most of them inherit their operational methodologies from conventional IT systems. The most popular approaches among the community try either to scatter the information among the whole infrastructure (in terms of data storage) [13] or implement multiple Intrusion Detection Systems (IDS) [17] and audit mechanisms [15]. Several of them monitor system calls to detect malicious activities [2][25][29]. The recent trend is to migrate the entire VM to another part of the infrastructure, thus forcing the potential attacker to be one step behind [43]. Most of them are unable to detect attacks against the Cloud from privileged users and especially attacks, which are orchestrated by multiple VMs.

Thus, we introduce Modified And Deterring Realtime Observation Wards (MAD CROW) for detecting malicious activities against the VM and against the Cloud infrastructure itself. The principle of our approach is to monitor the hypercalls of the VMs independently and the system calls of the privileged domain (Dom0 in XEN [41], Virtual Machine Manager (VMM) in Kernel-based Virtual Machine (KVM) [14]), in a way similar to a host based IDS, combining all gathered information to protect each VM and the whole Cloud infrastructure at the end of the day.

To be more specific, we make use of mechanisms that trace hypercalls (Xentrace in the case XEN [42], Perfm KVM in the case of KVM [20]) and systemcalls (strace command [34]) and process them in order to generate attack patterns and process abnormal behaviors. In contrast to other cloud IDSs [5] that use machine learning classifiers as black-box, the proposed system generates attack patterns using the Smith-Waterman algorithm [30] and performs similarity tests between the attack patterns and the data (hypercalls and system calls) collected to decide whether the cloud infrastructure is under attack or not, with a certain level of confidence. Since our approach operates on the Cloud infrastructure as a service layer, in a transparent manner, no modifications to the underlying layers are required.

Overall, the contributions of the paper could be summarized as follows:

- We introduce a hybrid solution, which depends on hypercalls and system calls to detect abnormal behavior in Cloud infrastructures.
- We enhance the performance of this solution using GPU acceleration instead of CPU computational resources
- Our solution is adaptable depending on the resources (GPU) and the Cloud infrastructure (hypervisor used)

The rest of the paper is organized as follows: Section II offers some background information while Section III provides a related literature review. Section IV introduces the malicious insider threat model. Section V presents our approach to detect malicious activities in Cloud infrastructure. Finally, Section VI draws the conclusions giving some pointers for future work as well.

## II. BACKGROUND

### A. Hypervisors

A hypervisor is in most cases a software, which acts as a layer between the hardware and the VMs. Basically, it is a level of abstraction that isolates either operating systems or applications from the underlying computer hardware. This abstraction allows the underlying host machine hardware to independently operate one or more virtual machines as guests, allowing multiple guest VMs to effectively share the system's computational resources, such as processor, memory, storage, network bandwidth, etc. There are two implementations of the hypervisor concept worth mentioning, one is XEN and the other is KVM.

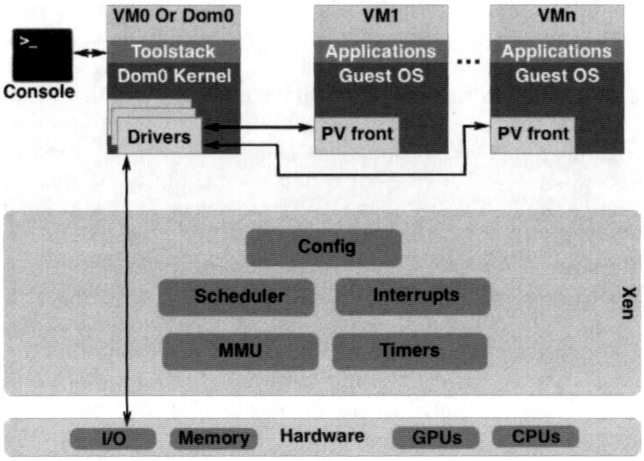


Figure 1. XEN Architecture.

In the case of XEN in Figure 1. , its designers developed a microkernel, placed over the computer's hardware, making possible to run many instances of the operating system. Domain 0 is the privileged VM, containing all the drivers for the hardware and the control platform for the rest of the VMs. As demonstrated in Figure 2. KVM is also a mini kernel, this time completely attached to the Linux kernel, meaning that every distribution after 2.6.20 contains the KVM hypervisor by default. The difference is that instead of using a middleware with drivers, as XEN does, KVM has excellent hardware support.

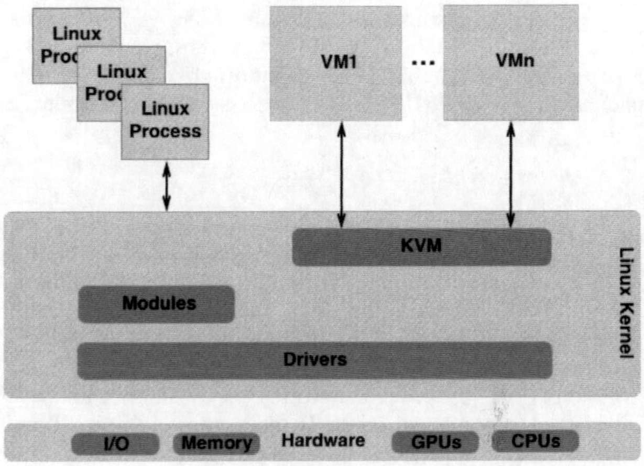


Figure 2. KVM Architecture.

### B. Hypercalls

In either case, as the hypervisor is responsible for monitoring all privileged actions, VMs have to transfer control into the hypervisor to execute sensitive instructions. This procedure is materialized by hypercalls. The latter are very similar to system calls in conventional operating systems. A software interrupt transfers control from the VM into the hypervisor, where every operation is validated and then executed. After the operation is completed, the control returns to the VM that made the call initially. Hypercalls, as system calls, differ depending if the architecture is x86 or x64. Their structure is similar to system calls, including parameter passing (for example a XEN hypercall definition: HYPERVISOR_mmu_update(const struct mmu_update reqs[], unsigned count, unsigned *done_out, unsigned foreigndom)).

### C. Graphical Processing Unit Acceleration

The creation and usage of more computational resources demanding algorithms, along with the birth of big data, pushed the worldwide community towards parallel computing. As CPUs can be too expensive, the scientific community turned to GPUs. Modern GPUs have an architecture that enables them to make fast simple mathematical and logical calculations, using multiple cores, which were commonly used for graphics representation. When a medium ranged GPU can offer more than 1000 cores, it is more energy and cost efficient than any other CPU antagonist. There are two technologies commonly used, NVIDIA's Compute Unified Device Architecture (CUDA) [19] and AMD's High Performance Computing [4], which relies on OpenCL™ cross-platform programming language [45].

It is feasible to access GPUs at high performance, within all the major hypervisors, thus taking advantage of all the benefits that Cloud Computing platforms can offer, along with the accessibility of on-demand accelerator hardware. This procedure is called GPU passthrough technology and permits any virtual machine to access one or more GPUs. It is accomplished using two strategies, either API remoting with device emulation or PCI passthrough. Recently, researchers proved that GPU passthrough technology can take advantage of 96-100% of the base systems performance [39].

## III. Related Work

Several attempts to track, disable or counter the malicious insider threat have been recorded. However, the majority of these solutions achieve their goal by focusing on a very specific aspect of the cloud, such as the employees or the network, while only a minority of them aim to provide a general purpose solution [3][11][15][28][32][33][35][36]. Solutions that propose monitoring of system calls and invocation of statistical methods for identifying normal and malicious acts are [2][8][12][21][23][25][29].

Coull's work [6] has inspired the initial CROW method. They used the system calls as a series of genes and made use of the Smith Waterman algorithm. However, they did not use entire patterns, something that has resulted in many false positives and false negatives. Compute Unified Device Architecture (CUDA) involvement was proposed by Ioannidis et al. [37] for executing Snort [31]. In [1] Haddad et al. propose a scheme aiming to detect network attacks, consisting of Snort for signature based detection and Support Vector Machine (SVM) for anomaly detection. Furthermore, Vasiliadis et al. [38] proved that GPU acceleration is so efficient that can be used by malicious parties in order to increase the robustness of malware against analysis and detection.

Milenkoski et al. [18] created "HInjector", which is a customizable framework, able to inject hypercall attacks during regular operation. This is the reason why Wang et al. [40], created a mechanism that aims to protect the hypercall interface by preventing untrusted hypercalls from running, using randomization techniques.

## IV. Threat Model

According to Maybury et al. [16] the term "insider", for an organization system, applies to anyone with approved access, privilege, or knowledge of the information system and its services and missions. "Malicious insider" is defined as someone motivated to adversely impact an organization's mission through a range of actions that compromise information confidentiality, integrity, and/or availability taking advantage of his/her privileges. This terminology covers mostly traditional IT systems. A modern update would be that a malicious insider is someone who acts either actively or passively. In the first case, an active malicious insider is motivated by himself to harm an organization. A passive malicious insider, is a victim of phishing or other social attack (social engineering, phishing, etc.), whose actions are orchestrated by an external attacker. Consequently, he uses his privileges to harm an organization, without his will.

In the case of Cloud Computing, we define as insider an entity who: (a) Works for the cloud host, (b) Has privileged access to the cloud resources and (c) Uses the cloud services. All cloud insiders are mostly privileged users, who either at will or not, compromise a Cloud infrastructure's security. Depending on their privileges, the impacts from their actions vary from a temporary break of network or a service, to users' privacy violation or loss/exposure of data. There is infrastructure related information, such as the network topology that can be extracted only by privileged users. For example, a malicious user will try to make a map of all available VMs, in order to choose his next target, which will give him more information and will help him to violate the security of a Cloud infrastructure or a user's privacy.

As hypercalls are like system calls, this gives the ability to the potential attackers to perform or inject hypercall attacks, which can take any form known from system calls, such as argument highjacking or mimicry [44]. Another tactic commonly used, is to fake a series of hypercalls with ultimate purpose to sniff the information from other VMs. In addition to that, Cloud infrastructures lack physical isolation by default because of their architecture, something that offers the opportunity to several VMs to get information from shared sources of the Cloud ecosystem such as memory (cache or main memory) retrieving personal information for the co-residents. Ristenpart et al. [26] first proved this concept by performing cross VM side channel attacks on Amazon EC2, measuring in that way the activity of other users. Similarly, Rochsa and Correia [27] proved that, by using the memory of a VM, sensitive information about its users can be acquired, such as social security number, credentials and other personal information.

There are other cases, where attackers combine utilities and tools, whose functionalities are commonly perceived as benign, in order to perform an attack. An example of such a case are the commands "nslookup", "ping" and the nmap tool, which can access publicly available information regarding network topologies and OS, for a specific ecosystem of VMs. The results from those commands orchestrate a "co-residence" or "co-tenacy" attack [26]. Furthermore, following the way of thinking of commonly employed Advanced Persistent Threats, this kind of information may prove useful in the future as it leads to exploits of vulnerabilities relevant to OS version and the other characteristics of a VM. Another kind of attack that can be performed inside a virtual network, is a network stress attack named "smurf" where the attacker launches numerous ping requests, thus congesting the corresponding public and private interfaces and eventually causing Denial Of Service. Modified And Deterring Cloud Realtime Observation Wards

### A. Overview

The proposed scheme, namely MAD CROW is a modified and improved version of another proposed solution [22]. Its goal is to facilitate detection of malicious privileged users in the cloud, regardless of if they use the non-privileged VM, or the privileged VM Domain0 or Dom0 or VM0. It also provides functionality of traditional IDS implementations by individually monitoring the health of each employed VM. Its unique feature is the use of both hypercalls for the non-privileged VMs and system calls for Dom0. To the best of our knowledge, it is the first of this kind. It's high level architecture is depicted in Figure 3.

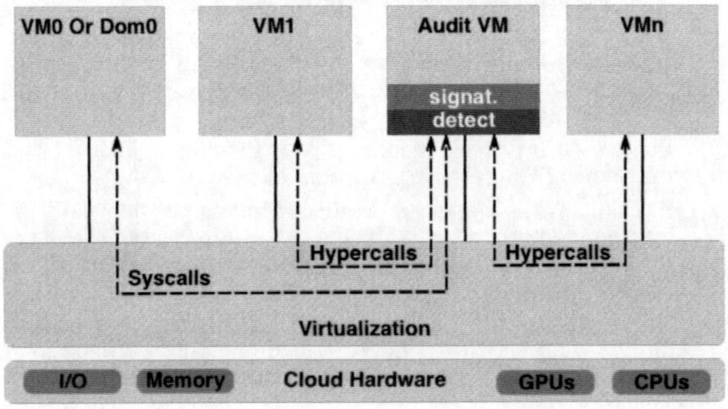


Figure 3. The MAD CROW Architecture.

As highjacking techniques exist and can fool the system call tracing inside a VM, the proposed scheme makes use of a filtering system for hypercalls. Each time a hypercall is initiated, it is recorded in the hypercall sequence of the specific VM that made the call into the audit VM. So, we propose a unified mechanism, which has signatures in terms of hypercall sequences relevant to the operations of each VM. This mechanism constantly detects the hyper calls through the hypervisor, using GPU acceleration instead of CPU usage. Whenever an attack signature is detected by the audit VM, a security alert is generated for the security officers to act. In the case of Dom0 as it is the privileged VM and the highest in the hierarchy, being able to damage the entire cloud infrastructure, the system calls detection is mandatory. To be specific, a mechanism is installed inside the privileged VM and detects its system calls through the kernel. Whenever something abnormal is detected, an alert reaches the audit VM. In both cases, the detection is achieved using GPU acceleration and passthrough technology, in both the Audit VM and privileged VM tracking mechanism.

The sub-system, which implements the audit mechanism, is responsible to monitor the health of each of the VMs either through hypercalls (non-privileged) or through system calls (privileged). Additionally, it generates new attack signatures, based on the hypercall and system call patterns of the attacks. The proposed scheme makes also use of a detection module, which monitors each VM and utilizes the attack signatures for computing their similarity with the sequences of hypercalls generated by the non-privileged VMs. In the case of the privileged VM, the same monitoring is achieved using system calls attack signatures. Calculating the similarity score is a very intense procedure, in computational terms, especially in terms of CPU and RAM.

With respect to GPU passthrough technology, our approach focuses on transferring the majority of the introduced overhead to the GPUs. Consequently, the rest of the computational resources of the infrastructure remain almost idle in terms of usage so as to serve the needs of the other users. This procedure has become possible through the architectures of NVIDIA's Compute Unified Device Architecture (CUDA) and AMD's High Performance Computing, which uses OpenCL™ cross-platform programming language [45]. Both are parallel computing platforms that provide access to the virtual instruction set and memory of GPUs.

### B. *Attack Signature Generation*

The attack signature generation process is very similar to the CROW methodology [22], but with one major difference. This time we track system calls, for the privileged VM, and hyper calls for all other VMs. The methodology is very simple and intuitive. A significant number of hypercalls and system call patterns is collected, following multiple executions of the same attack. Then, we make use of the Smith Waterman algorithm [30], to process our data. Each hypercall and system call consists of symbols, drawn from a finite discrete alphabet. So, our goal is to find the longest common subsequence to all sequences in a set of sequences, making the Smith Waterman algorithm an excellent choice for our purpose.

The signature extraction is very similar to malware analysis, since the attack is known a priory. Thus, the malware is executed several times in order to get the corresponding signatures. More specifically, the algorithm runs in pairs of sequences of the hypercalls or system calls for the same attack. Then, the number of sequences is reduced to half, using the best similarity match either for hyper calls or for system calls. After all results have been processed, the attack signature is generated. It must be stressed that the privileged VM is able to execute a significant number of attacks on its own, while all the others can both act alone or even cooperate in order to achieve a successful attack. Consequently, according to Figure 4. the proposed methodology can retrieve the appropriate information and when all the segments of an attack are collected to signal an alarm, even though other benign executions interfere and create noise in the sequences of either hypercalls or system calls. We should not forget that simple commands, such as "nslookup" are harmless on their own, but when combined with others may result in mapping an entire network ecosystem [26].

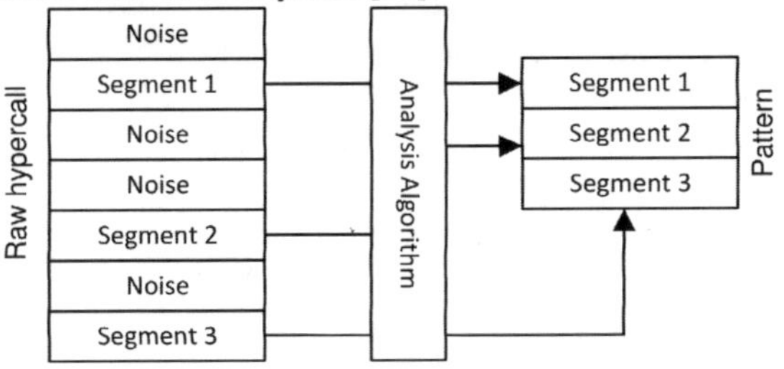


Figure 4. The segments of the attack pattern are found through the hypercall sequence using as analysis the Smith-Waterman algorithm

### C. Detection

The attack signatures created from the former procedure, either as sequences of hypercalls or as sequences of system calls, are used for the detection of potential malicious acts. Specifically, the audit VM, keeps signatures in a database. To achieve the detection of an attack against the VM or the cloud infrastructure itself, the hypercalls of the VMs and the system calls of the privileged VM are monitored and forwarded to the detection module.

Its task is to identify the attack segments into the entire sequence of hypercalls or system calls, avoiding the possible noise that has been created by various other irrelevant system procedures and thus making the same steps as the attack signature generation. In the case where all the segments of an attack are identified, then an alert in the audit VM is triggered. This alert motivates the operators of the audit station to take immediate action and enforce the employed policy.

It must be noted that even in cases where the attack segments are executed in different VMs, which is a typical choice of attackers in order to avoid detection, the proposed scheme will again detect the attack. Additionally, a handshake, between the audit station and each of the VMs, is initiated every two seconds in order to update the audit station about VM communication and thus protect the system from potential actions that aim to hide an attack.

## V. CONCLUSIONS AND FUTURE WORK

Considering modern IDS systems do not focus on cloud insider attacks, the MAD CROW detection method has been proposed. It utilizes both hypercalls and system calls to detect privileged user attacks. The detection mechanism is based on Smith Waterman algorithm, adapted in a parallel implementation, usable by any GPU architecture and passthrough technology.

Currently, we are experimenting with different implementations and GPU setups, willing to achieve maximum stability, efficiency and productivity. Our experimentation includes different machine learning techniques and feature extraction that would allow us to improve the signature generation mechanism and consequently the accuracy of our detector.

## ACKNOWLEDGMENT

This work has been partially supported by the Research Center of the University of Piraeus.

## REFERENCES

[1] A. Haddad, Zayed, M. Hanoune, and A. Mamouni, "A Collaborative Network Intrusion Detection System (C-NIDS) in Cloud Computing." International Journal of Communication Networks and Information Security 8, no. 3, p. 130, December 2016.

[2] A. Suaad S., and S. D. Wolthusen, "Detecting anomalies in IaaS environments through virtual machine host system call analysis." Internet Technology And Secured Transactions, 2012 International Conferece For. IEEE, pp. 211-218, December 2012.

[3] M. A. AlZain, E. Pardede, B. Soh, and J. A. Thom, "Cloud computing security: from single to multi-clouds." System Science (HICSS), 2012 45th Hawaii International Conference on. IEEE, pp. 5490-5499, January 2012.

[4] AMD High Performance Computing. [Online]. Available from: http://www.amd.com/en-us/products/graphics/workstation/firepro-remote-graphics/gpu-compute# .12 January 2017

[5] A. Bakshi, and B. Yogesh, "Securing cloud from ddos attacks using intrusion detection system in virtual machine." Second International Conference on Communication Software and Networks, (ICCSN'10), IEEE, pp. 260-264, 2010

[6] S. Coull, J. Branch, B. Szymanski, and E. Breimer, "Intrusion detection: A bioinformatics approach." Computer Security Applications Conference, 2003. Proceedings. 19th Annual, IEEE, pp. 24-33, December 2003

[7] Enisa, "Cloud Computing – Benefits, Risks and Recommendations for Information Security" , 2009

[8] E. Eskin, W. Lee, and S. J. Stolfo, "Modeling system calls for intrusion detection with dynamic window sizes." DARPA Information Survivability Conference & Exposition II (DISCEX'01), Proceedings. Vol. 1. IEEE, PP/ 165-175, 2001.

[9] Geekwire. [Online]. Available from: http://www.geekwire.com/2017/cloud-computing-revenues-jumped-25-2016-strong-growth-ahead-researcher-says/. 12 January 2017

[10] Helpnetsecurity. . [Online]. Available from: https://www.helpnetsecurity.com/2016/09/30/insider-attack/. 12 January 2017

[11] C. H. H. Le, "Protecting Xen hypercalls", Doctoral dissertation, University of British Columbia, July 2009

[12] S. A. Hofmeyr, S. Forrest, and A. Somayaji, "Intrusion detection using sequences of system calls." Journal of computer security 6, no. 3, pp. 151-180, 1998.

[13] R. L. Krutz, R. D. Vines, "Cloud Security: A Comprehensive Guide to Secure Cloud Computing." Wiley Publishing, Indianapolis, August 2010.

[14] KVM Hypervisor. [Online]. Available from: http://www.linux-kvm.org/. 12 January 2017

[15] G. Magklaras, S. Furnell, and M. Papadaki, "LUARM-An audit engine for insider misuse detection." WDFIA, pp. 133-148, 2011.

[16] M. Maybury, P. Chase, B. Cheikes, D. Brackney, S. Matzner, T. Hetherington, B. Wood, C. Sibley, J. Marin, and T. Longstaff, "Analysis and detection of malicious insiders." MITRE CORP BEDFORD MA, 2005.

[17] C. Mazzariello, R. Bifulco, and R. Canonico, "Integrating a network IDS into an open source cloud computing environment." Sixth International Conference on Information Assurance and Security, IEEE, pp. 265-270, 2010

[18] A. Milenkoski, B. D. Payne, N. Antunes, M. Vieira, and S. Kounev, "HInjector: injecting hypercall attacks for evaluating VMI-based intrusion detection systems." Poster Reception at the 2013 Annual Computer Security Applications Conference (ACSAC 2013), 2013.

[19] NVIDIA CUDA. [Online]. Available from: http://www.nvidia.com/object/cuda_home_new.html. 12 January 2017

[20] Perf KVM. . [Online]. Available from: http://www.linux-kvm.org/page/Perf_events. 12 January 2017

[21] N. Pitropakis, A. Pikrakis, and C. Lambrinoudakis. "Behaviour reflects personality: detecting co-residence attacks on Xen-based cloud environments." International Journal of Information Security 14, no. 4, pp.299-305, 2015.

[22] N. Pitropakis, D. Geneiatakis, and C. Lambrinoudakis, "Till All Are One: Towards a Unified Cloud IDS." International Conference on Trust and Privacy in Digital Business. Springer International Publishing, pp. 136-149, 2015.

[23] N. Pitropakis, D. Anastasopoulou, A. Pikrakis, and C. Lambrinoudakis, "If you want to know about a hunter, study his prey: detection of network based attacks on KVM based cloud environments." Journal of Cloud Computing 3, no. 1 p 20, 2014.

[24] N. Pitropakis, E. Darra, N. Vrakas, and C. Lambrinoudakis, "It's All in the Cloud: Reviewing Cloud Security." Ubiquitous Intelligence and Computing, 2013 IEEE 10th International Conference on and 10th International Conference on Autonomic and Trusted Computing (UIC/ATC). IEEE, pp. 355-362, 2013.

[25] S. Rawat, V. P. Gulati, A. K. Pujari, and V. R. Vemuri, "Intrusion detection using text processing techniques with a binary-weighted cosine metric", Journal of Information Assurance and Security 1, no. 1, pp. 43-50, 2006.

[26] T. Ristenpart, E. Tromer, H. Shacham, and S. Savage, "Hey, you, get off of my cloud: exploring information leakage in third-party compute clouds." Proceedings of the 16th ACM conference on Computer and communications security (CCS), ACM, pp. 199-212, 2009.

[27] F. Rocha, and M. Correia, "Lucy in the sky without diamonds: Stealing confidential data in the cloud." Dependable Systems and Networks Workshops (DSN-W), 2011 IEEE/IFIP 41st International Conference. IEEE, pp. 129-134, 2011.

[28] R. Sandhu, R. Boppana, R. Krishnan, J. Reich, T. Wolff, and J. Zachry, "Towards a discipline of mission-aware cloud computing." Proceedings of the 2010 ACM workshop on Cloud computing security workshop, ACM, pp. 13-18, 2010.

[29] A. Sharma, A. K. Pujari, and K. K. Paliwal, "Intrusion detection using text processing techniques with a kernel based similarity measure." computers & security 26, no. 7, pp. 488–495, 2007.

[30] T. F. Smith, and M. S. Waterman, "Identification of common molecular subsequences." Journal of molecular biology 147, no. 1,pp. 195–197, 1981.

[31] Snort IDS. [Online]. Available from: https://www.snort.org/ . 12 January 2017

[32] J. Spring, "Monitoring cloud computing by layer, part 1.", IEEE Security & Privacy 9,no. 2, IEEE, pp. 66-68, 2011.

[33] S. J. Stolfo, M. B. Salem, and A. D. Keromytis, "Fog computing: Mitigating insider data theft attacks in the cloud." Security and Privacy Workshops (SPW), 2012 IEEE Symposium. IEEE, pp. 125-128, 2012.

[34] Strace command. [Online]. Available from: https://linux.die.net/man/1/strace. 12 January 2017

[35] S. Sundararajan, H. Narayanan, V. Pavithran, K. Vorungati, and K. Achuthan, "Preventing Insider attacks in the Cloud." Advances in Computing and Communications, Springer Berlin Heidelberg, pp. 488-500, 2011.

[36] A. Tripathi, and A. Mishra, "Cloud computing security considerations." Signal Processing, Communications and Computing (ICSPCC), 2011 IEEE International Conference, IEEE, pp. 1-5, 2011.

[37] G. Vasiliadis, S. Antonatos, M. Polychronakis, E. P. Markatos, and S. Ioannidis, "Gnort: High performance network intrusion detection using graphics processors International Workshop on Recent Advances in Intrusion Detection 2008, Springer Berlin Heidelberg , pp. 116-134, 2008.

[38] G. Vasiliadis, M. Polychronakis, and S. Ioannidis, "GPU-assisted malware." International Journal of Information Security 14, no. 3, pp. 289-297 , 2015.

[39] J. P. Walters, A. J. Younge, D. I. Kang, K. T. Yao, M. Kang, S. P. Crago, and G. C. Fox, "GPU passthrough performance: A comparison of KVM, Xen, VMWare ESXi, and LXC for CUDA and OpenCL applications.", IEEE 7th International Conference on Cloud Computing, IEEE, pp. 636-643, 2014.

[40] F. Wang, P. Chen, B. Mao, and L. Xie, "Randhyp: preventing attacks via xen hypercall interface." IFIP International Information Security Conference, Springer Berlin Heidelberg, pp. 138-149, 2012.

[41] XEN Hypervisor. . [Online]. Available from: http://www.xenproject.org/developers/teams/hypervisor.html. 12 January 2017

[42] Xentrace. [Online]. Available from: https://blog.xenproject.org/2012/09/27/tracing-with-xentrace-and-xenalyze/ 12 January 2017

[43] Y. Zhang, M. Li, K. Bai, M. Yu, and W. Zang, "Incentive compatible moving target defense against vm-colocation attacks in clouds.", IFIP International Information Security Conference, Springer Berlin Heidelberg, pp. 388-399, 2012.

[44] Z. Wang, X. Jiang, W. Cui, and P. Ning, "Countering Kernel Rootkits with Lightweight Hook Protection.", 16th ACM Conference on Computer and Communications Security, ACM, pp. 545–554, 2009.

[45] OpenCL™. [Online]. Available from: https://www.khronos.org/opencl/ 12 January 2017